The Metaphysics of
Self-realisation and Freedom

The Metaphysics of Self-realisation and Freedom

Part 1 of The Liberal Socialism of Thomas Hill Green

Colin Tyler

imprint-academic.com

Published in the UK by
Imprint Academic, PO Box 200, Exeter EX5 5YX, UK

Published in the USA by Imprint Academic
Philosophy Documentation Center
PO Box 7147, Charlottesville, VA 22906-7147, USA

ISBN 978 184540 119 1

A CIP catalogue record for this book is available from the
British Library and US Library of Congress

imprint-academic.com/idealists

'Apropos of someone feeling an acute morbid sense of being wicked. Poor fellow, said Green, the sense of Sin is very much an illusion. People are not as bad as they fancy themselves.'
John Addington Symonds to Charlotte Byron Green, 7 October 1882

'the feeling of oppression, which always goes along with the consciousness of unfulfilled possibilities, will always give meaning to the representation of the effort after any kind of self-improvement as a demand for "freedom."'
T.H. Green, 'On the Different Senses of "Freedom" as Applied to Will and to the Moral Progress of Man', §18

'social life is to personality what language is to thought.'
T.H. Green, Prolegomena to Ethics, §183

'we only find unity in the world because we have an idea that it is there, an idea which we direct our powers to realise'
T.H. Green, Prolegomena to Ethics, §149

Contents

Preface

I was introduced to Green's political thought by Peter Nicholson, while a Master's student at the University of York between 1991 and 1992. I had been looking for a philosophical theory that combined coherently John Stuart Mill's liberalism with Hegel's conception of the state as an ethical community. I found in Green an approach that achieved this, although I now see as do many others, it is more helpfully conceived as combining Aristotle's eudaimonism with Fichtean form of Kantian ethics. The greater complexities of Green's intellectual debts are explored below (§§2.II–III). There was very little mainstream academic interest in Thomas Hill Green when I began my Master's dissertation. In part, this was due to his poor reputation in the philosophical mainstream, usually among people who had read little if anything of his actual writings. This low estimate was also due in part to the systematic nature of Green's philosophy, something that means that one can only really begin to make sense of any particular aspect of his philosophy once one understands something of that complex, internally-differentiated system. In this sense, the systematic nature of his philosophy makes it more difficult to consider particular discrete issues and problems. Unfortunately, problem-solving is the preferred subject-matter of most contemporary philosophers, at least in the Anglo-American world. Another serious hindrance to a wider acceptance of Green's philosophy is the need to begin with a careful, time-consuming, scholarly interpretation of his texts, a requirement viewed apparently with suspicion by many Anglo-American philosophers.[1] Finally and also very importantly, Green's arguments are inherently difficult, something that is compounded by his frequently prolix philosophical writing style.

Against all these odds, Green's standing among philosophers has improved slowly since the late 1990s, due not least to the inauguration in 2003 of the Imprint Academic series on Green of which the present book is a part. Unfortunately, the revival of interest in Green's philosophy was only just beginning when I completed my doctorate (supervised by Peter Nicholson) at the end of 1995, and it was gaining momentum only slowly when my thesis was published in a largely unaltered form towards the end of 1997.[2] I have continued to work on the British idealists since that time, and in spite of what I am very pleased to say were uniformly positive reviews, I have always had a nagging awareness that the book was unfinished business. I am, therefore, very grateful to Keith Sutherland and Imprint Academic

---

[1]   See David Weinstein's very apposite remarks on this subject in his *Utilitarianism and the New Liberalism* (Cambridge: Cambridge University Press, 2007), pp. 1–4.

[2]   Colin Tyler, *Thomas Hill Green (1836–1882) and the Philosophical Foundations of Politics: An internal critique* (Lampeter and Lewiston, N.Y.: Edwin Mellen, 1997).

not only for agreeing to publish this very extensively revised version of the work, but also for agreeing to divide what has become a very long manuscript into two discrete books, as parts of a critical analysis of what I see now as Green's liberal socialism.

The present book, *The Metaphysics of Self-realisation and Freedom*, is based on the introduction and first two chapters of the original thesis/book. Yet, I have treated the original purely as a draft, and have not felt bound to retain any of it. Simply in terms of quantity however, it is now more than three times the length (in terms of words) of the original. The new material that has been introduced is of three broad types. First, I have attempted to deepen my critical analysis, and to correct errors of interpretation, logic, grammar and style. Second, I have attempted to consider all of the major scholarship that has appeared since 1997. Third, I have made use of the previously unpublished manuscripts that several of us have made available in the past thirteen years. As a result of these great many additions, much of the text is completely new, including almost all of the first two chapters, as well as chapters seven, eight and nine. Chapters three and four have also been largely rewritten and restructured, while chapters five and six have been heavily revised and greatly extended. In fact, the resulting book differs so significantly in length, argument and depth from the material in the original version that it constitutes a new work.[3]

I have incurred a great many intellectual debts during the preparation of this book. As well as supervising my doctorate from 1992 to 1995, Peter Nicholson has continued to provide his usual invaluable expertise, insight and support, both as editor of this Imprint Academic series, and through his own writings on Green and the idealists. The same is true of Bill Mander and Maria Dimova-Cookson. Indeed, Bill and Peter offered many comments on earlier drafts of this book, as have Owen Fellows and Sean Magee, two of my doctoral students. I am particularly grateful to each of these scholars for this time-consuming input. While Bill, Maria, Peter and I disagree on many issues regarding Green, some of them fundamental, it is one of the great strengths of the community of scholars working on the British idealists and New Liberals at the present time that we can debate our differences fully and frankly, while still listening carefully to each other. My criticisms of the existing scholarship in this book are offered in that spirit. I am also grateful to Jim Connelly and Noël O'Sullivan, my colleagues in the Centre for the Study of British Idealism at the University of Hull. My sincere thanks go also to others at Hull and beyond, some of whom have commented on earlier drafts of this material and especially James Allard, David Boucher, Thom Brooks, Glenn Burgess, Alberto de Sanctis, Claire Hairsine, Denys Leighton, Justin Morris, Avital Simhony, Pip Tyler, Will Tyler, Andrew Vincent, Dave Weinstein and Richard Woodward. I also wish to reaffirm my gratitude to the following people, whom I thanked in the original thesis: Diane Adams, Richard Bellamy, Steve Benson, Jenny Bradford, Dave Brittan, Frank Brogan, Alex Callinicos, Matt Carter, Steve Cinderby, Richard Cookson, John Horton, Natalie Humphreys, Linda Lofthouse, Andy McLellan, Sue Mendus,

[3]   Hopefully, it will differ from the original in one other crucial respect: the book distributor's warehouse burnt down the day after it received the first printing of the original book!

Andrea Micocci, Caroline Moore, Jeremy Nolan, Massimo Paradiso, Gill Pulpher, Rod Rhodes, Giuseppe Tassone, Andrew Tesseyman, and Angie Wilson.

I have carried out a significant amount of archival work for this new book, and in this regard I am pleased to thank the Master and Fellows of Balliol College, Oxford for their permission to consult and quote from their holdings of Green's papers. I also wish to thank the Principal and Fellows of St. John's College, Oxford, for their hospitality during my time as a Visiting Scholar with them in the summer of 2007.

As always however, by far my greatest and yet least tangible debts are owed to Pip, my wife, and of course to Lucy, our cat, for their continuing love, support and patience. This book is dedicated to my mother Edna and my brother Will, as well as to the memory of my father, Bill.

Of course, I alone am responsible for the use made of this assistance.

Colin Tyler
University of Hull
9 March 2010

Abbreviations

References within this book are given in the following format: §[chapter].[section]

Items referenced by section number are listed below followed by an asterisk. All other references are to page numbers. The following abbreviations are also used below:

'Harris' = Paul Harris and John Morrow, eds., *T H Green: Lectures on the Principles of Political Obligation and Other Writings* (Cambridge: Cambridge University, 1986).
'*Works*' = R.L. Nettleship and Peter P. Nicholson, eds., *Works of Thomas Hill Green*, 5 vols. (Bristol: Thoemmes, 1997)

Writings of Thomas Hill Green

'Aristotle': 'Philosophy of Aristotle', *Works* III, pp. 46–91.
'Christian Dogma': 'Essay on Christian Dogma', *Works* III, pp. 161–85.
'Conversion of Paul': 'Conversion of Paul (Extract from lectures on the epistle to the Galatians)', *Works* III, pp. 186–9.
DSF: 'On the Different Senses *of "Freedom"* as Applied to Will and the Moral Progress of Man', *Harris,* pp. 228–49.*
'Elementary': 'Two Lectures on "The Elementary School System of England"' [1878], *Works* III, pp. 413–55.
Ellerton 1: '1860 Ellerton Essay: Life and Immortality brought to light by the Gospel', *Works* V, pp. 57–81.
Ellerton 2: '1861 Ellerton Essay: The State of Religious Belief among the Jews at the Time of the Coming of Christ', *Works* V, pp. 83–104.
'English Revolution': 'Four Lectures on the English Commonwealth', *Works* III, pp. 277–364.
'Faith': 'Faith: Address on 2 Corinthians v. 7', *Works* III, pp. 253–76.
FC: 'Force of Circumstances', *Works* III, pp. 3–10.
'Grading': 'Lecture on the Grading of Secondary Schools', *Works* III, pp. 387–412.
'Hedonism': 'Hedonism and the Ultimate Good', *Mind*, vol. 2, no. 6 o.s. (April 1877), 266–69.
'Hodgson': 'An Answer to Mr. Hodgson', *Works* I, pp. 521–41.
'Hume I': 'Introductions to Hume's "Treatise of Human Nature": I. General Introduction', *Works* I, pp. 1–299.*
'Hume II': 'Introduction to the Moral Part of Hume's "Treatise"', *Works* I, pp. 301–71.*
ICG: 'The Influence of Civilisation on Genius', *Works* III, pp. 11–9.

'Immortality': 'Fragment on Immortality', *Works* III, pp. 159–60.

'Incarnation': 'Incarnation (Extract from lectures on the Fourth Gospel)', *Works* III, pp. 207–20.

IPR: 'Review of J. Caird, "Introduction to the Philosophy of Religion"', *Works* III, pp. 138–46.

'Kant': 'Lectures on the Philosophy of Kant', *Works* II, pp. 2–155.*

'Legislative interference': 'Legislative interference in moral matters', Harris, pp. 306–9.

'Lewes I': 'Mr. Lewes' Account of Experience', *Works* I, pp. 442–70.*

'Lewes II': 'Mr. Lewes' Account of the Social Medium', *Works* I, pp. 471–520.*

LLFC: 'Lecture on "Liberal Legislation and Freedom of Contract"', Harris, pp. 194–212.

'Logic': 'Lectures on Logic', *Works* II, pp. 157–366.*

'Loyalty': 'Loyalty', Harris, pp. 304–6.

'Moral Philosophy': 'Notes on Moral Philosophy', Harris, pp. 310–3.*

'Oxford High School': 'Lecture on "The Work to be Done by the New Oxford High School for Boys"', *Works* III, pp. 456–76.

PE: *Prolegomena to Ethics*, A.C. Bradley, ed., *Works* IV.*

'Pleasure': '*Pleasure* as the Chief Good', in Colin Tyler, ed., *Unpublished Manuscripts in British Idealism: Political philosophy, theology and social thought*, 2 vols. (London and New York: Thoemmes Continuum, 2005; Exeter and Charlottesville, VA: Imprint Academic, 2008), vol. 1, pp. 82–87.

'Pol. Econ.': 'Notes on ancient and modern political economy', Harris, pp. 313–17.*

'Popular Philosophy': 'Popular Philosophy in its Relation to Life', *Works* III, pp. 92–125.

PPO: 'Lectures on the Principles of Political Obligation', Harris, pp. 13–193.*

'Rev. Caird's Kant': "Review of E. Caird, 'Philosophy of Kant'", *Works* III, pp. 126–37.

'Sittlichkeit': 'Metaphysic of Ethics, Moral Psychology, Sociology or the Science of Sittlichkeit', in Colin Tyler, ed., *Unpublished Manuscripts in British Idealism: Political philosophy, theology and social thought*, 2 vols. (London and New York: Thoemmes Continuum, 2005; Exeter and Charlottesville, VA: Imprint Academic, 2008), vol. 1, pp. 14–71.

'Spencer I': 'Mr. Spencer on the Relation of Subject and Object', *Works* I, pp. 373–409.*

'Spencer II': 'Mr. Spencer on the Independence of Matter', *Works* I, pp. 410–41.*

'Watson': 'Review of J Watson, "Kant and his English Critics"' [1881], *Works* III, pp. 147–58.

WG: ' "Witness of God" ': Address on 1 Corinthians v. 7, 8', *Works* III, pp. 230–52.

WNT: 'Fragment of An Address on Romans x. 8, "The Word is Nigh Thee"', *Works* III, pp. 221–29.

'Works of Finction': 'The Value and Influence of Works of Fiction in Modern Times', *Works* III, pp. 20–45.

Introduction to The Liberal Socialism of Thomas Hill Green

I

Aim and Scope of *The Liberal Socialism of Thomas Hill Green*

The past decade or so has seen something of a renaissance of scholarly interest in the life and thought of Thomas Hill Green (1836–1882). Historians have done much to overcome the previous dominance in British idealist historiography of Melvin Richter's *Politics of Conscience,* a book which no matter how important and impressive it remains as a scholarly achievement, reflected strongly its own cultural prejudices and especially the prejudices that caricatured the Victorians in various ways.[1] Philosophers with particular interest in British idealism and New Liberalism have subjected Green's philosophical arguments themselves to rigorous assessment.[2] Philosophers such as David Brink, Gerald Gaus, T.H. Irwin and John Skorupski who have different primary research interests have also produced very interesting work on various aspects of Green's system.[3] Both the historians and the philosophers have been helped by the significant amount of previously

---

[1]   See, for example, Melvin Richter, *Politics of Conscience: T.H. Green and his age* (London: Weidenfeld & Nicolson, 1964). Colin Tyler, Review of M. Richter, *Politics of Conscience, Bradley Studies,* 3:2 (Autumn 1997), 192-98. Matt Carter, *T.H. Green and the Ethical Socialist Tradition* (Exeter: Imprint Academic, 2003); Denys Philip Leighton, *Greenian Moment: T.H. Green, Religion and Political Argument in Victorian Britain* (Exeter: Imprint Academic, 2004). Alberto de Sanctis, *'Puritan' Democracy of T.H. Green, with some unpublished writings* (Exeter: Imprint Academic, 2005). Duncan Kelly, 'Idealism and Revolution: T.H. Green's *Four Lectures on the English Commonwealth* [sic]', *History of Political Thought,* 27:3 (2006), 505–42. Denys P. Leighton, 'T.H. Green and the Dissidence of Dissent: On religion and national character in nineteenth-century England', *Parliamentary History* 27:1 (February 2008), 43–56.

[2]   For example, Maria Dimova-Cookson, *T.H. Green's Moral and Political Philosophy: A pheonemological perspective* (Houndsmill: Palgrave, 2001); see also various chapters in Maria Dimova-Cookson and W.J. Mander, eds., *T.H. Green: Ethics, metaphysics, and political philosophy* (Oxford: Clarendon, 2006); Colin Tyler, *Idealist Political Philosophy: Pluralism and conflict in the absolute idealist tradition* (London and New York: Continuum, 2006), David Weinstein, *Utilitarianism and the New Liberalism* (Cambridge: Cambridge University Press, 2007), chapters 2 and 4; David Boucher, *Limits of Ethics in International Relations: Natural law, natural rights and human rights in transition* (Oxford: Oxford University Press, 2009), chapter 8 *passim.*

[3]   For example, David O. Brink, *Perfectionism and the Common Good: Themes in the philosophy of T.H. Green* (Oxford: Clarendon, 2003). Brink, Irwin, Skorupski and Gaus have chapters in Dimova-Cookson *et al.,* eds., *T.H. Green.* This is not to imply that they have not all written very interestingly on Green and the idealists before, of course.

unpublished material that has appeared in the past few years.[4] The new scholarly consensus is that his thought is much more resilient and interesting than was previously alleged.

This book presents a philosophical analysis and critique of the first stages of Green's mature thought, with a special emphasis on what can be characterised as the theory of the individual in his liberal socialism. As such it makes only passing reference to the new historical scholarship. It argues that Green produced a largely coherent and detailed analysis of the metaphysical structure of human consciousness, and that, on the basis of this analysis, he developed powerful ethical and political philosophies with radical implications for the existing structure of society and politics. It defends these claims through a close analysis of Green's published and unpublished writings. It begins with a critical analysis of his influences and his conception of philosophical system-building (chapter two), and of his 'metaphysics of experience or knowledge' (chapters three and four), before moving to his theory of the will (chapters five and six), and his theory of the true good (chapters seven and eight). Chapter nine offers a provisional summary of Green's metaphysics of self-realisation and freedom, before responding to John Skorupski's reading of Green's theory of personal good as a prelude to a rebuttal of G.E. Moore's critique of Green's allegedly metaphysical ethics and the world-view that underlies it. This response lays the foundations for the discussion of his writings on civil society, capitalism and the state, in the second part of *The Liberal Socialism of T.H. Green*.[5]

The present chapter introduces this discussion by sketching the various leading scholarly assessments of Green's socialist credentials (§1.II), before examining in some detail his own stated attitude to socialism. Finally (§1.III), an indication is given of the reasons for understanding his philosophical system as justifying a form of 'liberal socialism'.

II
Green and the Socialist Tradition

Ultimately, Green constructed what R.L. Nettleship called 'a working theory of life.'[6] (See §7.IV.) The general character of this theory has been a matter of intense debate. Liberal scholars have tended to characterise Green as an aspirant but inadequate liberal. The following analysis suggests that there is another more illuminating way to categorise his thought: namely, as a form of 'liberal socialism'.

---

[4]   A great deal of material appears in Peter P. Nicholson, ed., *Collected Works of T.H. Green. Vol. 5 Additional Writings* (Bristol: Thoemmes, 1997), but see also Colin Tyler, ed., *Unpublished Manuscripts in British Idealism: Political philosophy, theology and social thought*, 2 vols. (Bristol: Thoemmes Continuum, 2005; Exeter: Imprint Academic, 2008), pp. 1–188, and de Sanctis, *'Puritan' Democracy of T.H. Green*, pp. 174–96. See also Colin Tyler, ed., 'Recollections Regarding T.H. Green', *Collingwood and British Idealism Studies*, 14:2 (2008), 5–78.

[5]   This critical analysis continues in my *Civil Society, Capitalism and the State: Part 2 of The Liberal Socialism of Thomas Hill Green* (Exeter: Imprint Academic, forthcoming in 2011), focusing on Green's theory of the common good, citizenship and public service, conscience and social criticism, civilisation and progress, rights, the state, capitalism and international relations.

[6]   R.L. Nettleship, 'Professor T.H. Green: In memoriam', *Contemporary Review*, 61 (January–June 1882), 862; see also Tyler, *Idealist Political Philosophy*, chapter 2.

In itself, this is controversial. Some have argued that, in Vincent Knapp's words, 'Green's doctrine of the exorability of [private] property did run counter to accepted laissez-faire dogmas, but it was in no way socialistic'.[7] In opposition to this view, James Kloppenberg and others have claimed that Green 'self-consciously and painstakingly drew connections between knowledge, responsibility, and reform, and [his] political writings represent an important, intermediate step in the convergence of socialism and liberalism towards social democracy and progressivism.'[8] Neither Knapp nor Kloppenberg were the first nor the last to come to their respective contradictory conclusions.[9] In 1880, the English translator of Marx's *Capital* Edward Aveling, argued that advanced radicals, especially those like Green of a republican cast, were ripe for conversion to socialism, by which he meant his own form of Marxism.[10] Most recently, scholars have tended to stress the kinship between Green's position and 'ethical socialism' or 'social democracy', with the former Deputy Leader of the UK Labour Party Roy Hattersley referring to him as 'the only genuine philosopher English social democracy ever possessed', a position echoed by at least one other Labour MP.[11]

The dispute over Green's radical credentials arises in part from the contested nature of the generic concept of 'socialism' itself. It is understandable therefore that the most successful discussions have sought to locate theories within a defining although unstructured field of tendencies or commitments rather than insisting on a single definition.[12] The problem is however that even if such conceptual markers

[7] Vincent J. Knapp, 'T.H. Green on the Exorability of Property', *Agora*, 1 (1969), 63.

[8] James T. Kloppenberg, *Uncertain Victory: Social democracy and progressivism in European and American thought* (New York and Oxford: Oxford University Press, 1986), p. 147.

[9] Not socialist: Francis Coker, *Recent Political Thought* (New York: Appleton-Century-Crofts, 1934), p. 426 and Alan J.M. Milne, *Social Philosophy of English Idealism* (London: Allen and Unwin, 1962), p. 156; socialist roots: George H. Sabine, *History of Political Thought*, revised by T.L. Thorton (Hindsale: Dryden, 1973), pp. 667–68; Vrajendra R. Mehta, 'T.H. Green and the Revision of English Liberal Theory', *Indian Journal of Political Science*, 35 (1974), 48–49; Andrew Reeve, Property (London: MacMillan, 1986), pp. 184–85.

[10] Edward Aveling, *Socialism and Radicalism* (London: Twentieth Century, n.d. [1880]), especially pp. 1–3. Aveling does not mention Green. On Green's advanced radicalism and republicanism, see Tyler, *Idealist Political Philosophy*, chapter 2.

[11] Roy Hattersley, *Edwardians* (London: Abacus, 2004), p. 383. Hattersley's is a long-standing admiration for Green, see for example his *Choose Freedom: The future for democratic socialism* (London: Michael Joseph, 1987), pp. 76–80 passim. Jon Cruddas [Labour MP for Dagenham], 'Labour is in the middle of its gravest crisis in 30 years. It needs to rediscover the radicalism that animated its founders', *New Statesman*, 7 September 2009, 24.

[12] This obtains no matter how interesting the attempt. See for example, Michael Freeden, *Ideologies and Political Theory: A conceptual approach* (Oxford: Clarendon, 1996), parts 1 and 4. R.N. Berki identified 'four basic tendencies' within the socialist tradition, which he noted often pulled in different directions, even while often being held by the same socialist or group of socialists at the same time (R.N. Berki, *Socialism* (London: J.M. Dent, 1974), pp. 24-29): 'Egalitarianism', (allegedly) leading to 'a conception of "community" which is considered to be higher than its individual members taken in isolation'; 'Moralism', whose 'chief values ... are social justice, peace, co-operation, brotherhood', and which 'holds human life sacred, but at the same time recognizes human nature as being imperfect, gullible, and in need of constant care and attention'; 'Rationalism', 'the chief values [of which] are individual happiness, reason, knowledge, efficiency in production, the rational purposeful organization of human society in the interest of progress'; and finally, 'Libertarianism', which 'is the demand for freedom in the sense of the total absence of restraint, external and internal. Its chief values are nature, human nature, sincerity, authenticity, individuality, variety, diversity, and happiness in the sense of the

can help map particular ideological movements at particular times and places, they are usually so general that they offer few insights into particular thinkers.[13] A more fruitful starting-point (although it can be only a starting-point) is to reconstruct the respective positions of individuals who either identified themselves as socialists, or who were identified as such by others, so as to indicate the senses in which the individual could be called a socialist.[14]

The particularity of the reading defended in this book can be brought out by contrasting it briefly here (and at various points in the rest of the book) with that set out by the most recent and most sustained defender of the 'ethical socialist' reading. Matt Carter, himself the General Secretary of the Labour Party from December 2003 to November 2005, has argued that Green was an 'ethical socialist'. Carter associates this doctrine with two main claims: it 'places individual moral development and character above simple state reforms'; and it 'holds that individuals are bound together through organic social relations that mean individuals can reach their potential only through the help of others.'[15] For Carter, ethical socialism is a doctrine that links liberalism and socialism through the presence in certain strands of these respective doctrines of a 'group of influential shared concepts: such as, the common good, positive freedom and equality of opportunity.'[16] More precisely, Carter bases his case on the following claims.

> The essential features of this new idealist-inspired ideology were: a belief in a common good, which could unite the interests of different individuals; the support for equality of opportunity, to help create a less class-ridden society; a positive view of liberty, meaning more than simply freedom from interference; and the belief in the role of the state as more than a "policeman", but as the representative of the whole community and able to help shape social conditions for the better. It is these features which distinguished the idealists' work from traditional liberalism, and these elements which they turned into a justification for socialism.'[17]

Carter's summary of Green's position is accurate as far as it goes.[18] Yet, it fails to place due weight on the fact that Green saw individual conscientious self-determination and personal responsibility as the central, necessary features of a virtuous, 'free life'. In this sense, Carter's account understates significantly Green's acute consciousness of the danger that inappropriate state action would create what is now termed a 'culture of dependency'. The liberal elements of Green's position spring in large part from this deep concern. The phrase 'liberal socialism'

---

completely unfettered enjoyment of human instinctual energies.' Berki argues that while most socialists can accept these propositions in some form, their respective understandings of those propositions vary widely and can be given very different relative weights.

[13] On related matters, see Colin Tyler, 'Performativity and the Intellectual Historian's Re-enactment of Written Works', *Journal of the Philosophy of History*, 3:2 (2009), 146–66.

[14] For one example of this alternative approach, see Mark Francis and John Morrow, *History of English Political Thought in the Nineteenth Century* (London: Duckworth, 1994), chapter 14.

[15] Carter, *Ethical Socialism*, pp. 7–8.

[16] Carter, *Ethical Socialism*, p. 9.

[17] Carter, *Ethical Socialism*, p. 3.

[18] See further Colin Tyler, 'Review Article: Elitism and anti-elitism in nineteenth century democratic thought', *History of European Ideas*, 32 (2006), 345–55.

is adopted here in relation to Green in order to minimize the danger that if he is styled as an ethical socialist, he is more likely to be read as holding that the state can make its citizens moral and that it must actively educate them to act well, and subsequently 'monitor' their performance.[19] The point at issue is the lack of trust implied in that vision, something that stands in opposition to the presumption of competence on which Green builds his political theory, not least as that was reflected in his advocacy of franchise reform at the time of the Second Reform Act (1867).[20]

The difference may seem to be merely one of emphasis, but in reality it is very important, not least because it implies very different presumptions regarding the appropriate way to determine the area of legitimate state action. Green's principled socialist pragmatism includes not a merely contingent attachment to liberal freedoms, but an essential one. 'Liberal' is the necessary qualifier of 'socialism'. At the heart of his theory stands the value of individual self-development, and a sophisticated relational ontology of the individual self, combined with a commitment to moral individualism which anticipates contemporary liberal philosophy, for example as espoused by Joseph Raz and his followers.[21] These philosophical commitments produce practical tendencies. Hence, for Green, the state should concern itself primarily with the removal of hindrances to the individual's own efforts to develop themselves according to their respective understandings of what their development would consist in. He resists attempts to intervene positively to push individuals to make particular choices regarding which actions to perform and which plans to pursue. The state can address external impediments to individual self-realisation then, such as arise out of abusive terms and conditions at work, while leaving individuals to act on their own internal conscientious assessments of their best interests as beings with higher capacities. It is for this reason that I believe in spite of the undeniably strong and essential moral facets of Green's position, the term 'liberal socialism' is more apposite than Carter's 'ethical socialism'.

These liberal elements informed Green's expressed attitude to the socialism of his day. While 'socialism' was hotly debated and positions were staked out with some clarity in Britain in the late 1880s and the early 1890s, aside from the Marxists and the French traditions of Fourier and Saint-Simon the term's meanings had been rather less clear in the immediately preceding years.[22] This is especially true of Green's own understanding of 'socialism'. That may go some way to

---

[19] Scholars disagree over the most appropriate meanings to give to both 'ethical socialism' and 'liberal socialism' in other contexts as well. For the view that they are fairly distinct forms of socialism (with the latter being 'more nuanced' than the 'anti-market' tendencies of the former), see Jim Tomlinson, 'Limits of Tawney's Ethical Socialism: A historical perspective on the Labour Party and the market', *Contemporary British History*, 16:4 (2002), 1–16.

[20] Tyler, *Idealist Political Philosophy*, chapter 2 passim.

[21] See, for example, Joseph Raz, 'Practice of Value' and 'More on Explaining Value: Replies and comparisons', in R. Jay Wallace, ed., *The Practice of Value* (Oxford: Clarendon, 2003), pp. 15–59, 121–56.

[22] Michael Freeden, *The New Liberalism: An ideology of social reform* (Oxford: Clarendon, 1986 [1978]); Peter Clarke, *Liberals and Social Democrats* (Cambridge: Cambridge University Press, 1978). For a contemporaneous account of socialism in the 1860s and early 1880s, see John Rae, *Contemporary Socialism* (London: William Isbister, 1884).

explaining why he uses the word very rarely. It does not appear in any of the writings published before or shortly after his death. In the 'Notes on Ancient and Modern Political Economy' (which Nicholson dates to sometime between 1866 and 1875, when Green was a Greats tutor), Green describes *'practical* socialism in modern times' in minimal terms, as the 'doctrine (a) that wages should be regulated otherwise than by competition ([i.e] competition of labourers for employment and of masters to get work done most cheaply and quickly), and (b) that accumulation of capital should be limited.'[23] In commenting on this passage, Green stresses the importance of what would now be called structural adjustment problems, focusing particularly on the effects of the fluidity of capital relative to that of labour, and especially on the resulting unemployment, poverty and resentment felt toward the capitalists by the labourers. Hence he criticises the 'folly of Louis Napoleon in trying to keep socialists quiet by attracting rich people to Paris', a policy pursued between 1853 and 1870.[24]

During a trip to Dresden in 1862, Green praised the German people, writing in a letter, that 'The social equality, and the apparent absence of vice and distress, relieve one's soul from many burdens, and personally I don't much mind about the stagnation.'[25] This view underpinned his remarks in a letter he sent during a similar visit in 1863. Nettleship reported the following, quoting a now-lost letter from Green.

> In the following year he was at Heidelberg, very apprehensive about the prospects of Germany, where Bismarck's ordinance against the press had "shorn the liberal papers of leading articles." Yet he had "confidence in the future of Prussia, for the soldiers can all read, and the artisans (who are strong at Berlin, though I fear not elsewhere) seem to be free from the worse forms of socialism, and under the guidance of Schulze-Delitsch to be developing schemes of co-operation and self-help."[26]

In part, Green may have been cautious about the socialists of the day because many were atheists, especially on the Continent. One might think here of positivists, not least Comtists, who characterised their social theory and politics in mechanical rather than the spiritual terms that one finds in the Italian republican Guiseppe Mazzini, one of the great influences on Green.[27] In 1881, he expressed his hostility to the French radical minister Paul Bert for being a 'medical Atheist', and, in England, he would have no doubt been aware of the likes of Henry Myers Hyndman.[28] One

[23] Green, 'Notes on Ancient and Modern Political Economy', Harris, p. 316; also printed with slight differences in Green's *Works* V, p. 186.

[24] Paul Harris and John Morrow, 'Notes', in T.H. Green, *Lectures on the Principles of Political Obligation, and other writings*, eds. Paul Harris and John Morrow (Cambridge: Cambridge University Press, 1986), p. 366n14.

[25] Nettleship, *'Memoir'*, p. xliii. He went on to: 'Some people might be annoyed by the unquestionable and universal ugliness of the women, but to make up for this they seem much more sensible, and more companionable for the men.'

[26] Nettleship, *'Memoir'*, p. xlii.

[27] Guiseppe Mazzini, 'Duties of Man', in his *Life and Writings*, 6 vols. (London: Smith, Elder, 1891), vol. 4, chapter IV.

[28] John St Loe Strachey, 'Recollection', in Tyler, ed., 'Recollections', 64–65. The socialist atheists Edward Bibbens Aveling and George Bernard Shaw were not sufficiently famous even when

must be careful however, as while atheists tended to be political radicals, not all atheists were socialists.[29] Moreover, Green had been influenced as a young man by Christian Socialists such as F.D. Maurice and Charles Kingsley (see §2.III).

In spite of Green's apparent reservations regarding socialism, the poet J.A. Symonds, one of Green's closest friends for the whole of his adult life and latterly his brother-in-law, was unequivocal regarding Green's socialist credentials. The root of Green's radicalism Symonds found in what he called on one occasion, 'his religious instincts & sympathy with the people, refined & fortified by reflection'.[30] He wrote to his sister, Green's widow, on this subject in November 1886.

> Green's practical grasp on political conditions & his sympathy with the vast masses of a nation, the producers & bread-makers, the taxpayers & inadequately represented, strike all alike. Personally I may say that he inducted me into the philosophy of democracy & socialism – not in any sentimental or visionary or reactionary way – but on the grounds on wh[ich] both democracy & socialism are active factors in modern politics. I should say that in this respect he showed a singular statesmanlike faculty – the faculty of feeling by a kind of penetrative insight that modern society had ripened to a point at wh[ich] the principles of democracy & socialism had to be accepted as actualities.[31]

Even though both Symonds and Green were concerned by 'crude socialistic revolutionary movements', they sought the lessening of class-distinctions ('the blending of Social Strata') so as to bring about what Symonds called the 'right sort of Socialism'.[32] In this regard, Green conceptualises the good individual as the respectable citizen or yeoman, or what Symonds refers to as Green's 'own

---

Green died in March 1882 for it to be likely that he had heard of them.

[29] The atheist George Jacob Holyoake advocated co-operatives very much as Green did. In a speech shortly before his death, Green referred to opinions of the radical republican and atheist MP Charles Bradlaugh on religion and birth control to be 'as repugnant to him as they could be', having noted already, in his 1867 'Lectures on Moral and Political Philosophy', that Bradlaugh was 'despised' (Green, 'Liberalism in Oxford and the Country', 7 March 1882, in *Works* V, p. 396, and his 'Lectures on Moral and Political Philosophy [1867]', in *Works* V, pp. 119–20). Bradlaugh publicly opposed 'socialism' in the mid-1880s (hence immediately following Green's death), although he meant 'communism' specifically: 'I understand and define Socialism as denying all individual property, and as affirming that society, organised as the State, should own all wealth, direct all labor, and compel the equal distribution of all produce. I understand a Socialistic State to be that State in which everything would be common as to its user, and in which all labor would be controlled by the State, which, from the common stock, would maintain the labourer and would take all the produce of the labor. That is, I identify Socialism with Communism.' Charles Bradlaugh, *Socialism: Its fallacies and dangers* (London: Freethought, 1887), p. 3. For the transcript of his famous debate with H.D. Hyndman, see H.M. Hyndman and Charles Bradlaugh, *Will Socialism Benefit the People? Debate between Mr. H.M. Hyndman and Mr. Charles Bradlaugh at St. James's Hall on Thursday, April 17th, 1884* (London: Freethought, 1884).

[30] See letter from John Addington Symonds to Charlotte Byron Green, 7 October 1882, in John Addington Symonds, *Letters*, 3 vols., eds. Herbert M. Schueller and Robert L. Peters (Detroit: Wayne State Press, 1968-69), vol. 2, p. 776. Immediately prior to this Symonds refers to Green's 'philosophical Christianity & philosophical Democracy'.

[31] Letter from Symonds to Charlotte Byron Green, 3 November 1886, in Symonds, *Letters*, vol. 3, p. 176.

[32] Letter from Symonds to Albert O. Rutson, 3 October 1885, in Symonds, *Letters*, vol. 3, pp. 84–85; letter from Symonds to Edward Carpenter, 21 January 1893, in Symonds, *Letters*, vol. 3, p. 808.

conception of manly sober citizenship'.[33] This core value has affinities to both republicanism and some forms of socialism, such as those supported by Christian socialists.[34] It underpins his aspiration that the English education system should be restructured so that

> every ... citizen will have open to him at least the precious companionship of the best books in his own language, and the knowledge necessary to make him really independent; when all who have a special taste for learning will have open to them what has hitherto been unpleasantly called the "education of gentlemen." I confess to hoping for a time when that phrase will have lost its meaning, because the sort of education which alone makes the gentleman in any true sense will be within the reach of all. As it was the aspiration of Moses that all the Lord's people should be prophets, so with all seriousness and reverence we may hope and pray for a condition of English society in which all honest citizens will recognise themselves and be recognised by each other as gentlemen.[35]

This section has indicated that Green's failure to align himself explicitly with 'socialism' may have a number of causes. Not least, it must be remembered that in the 1870s and 1880s, the term tended to refer to political systems based on social engineering and control by 'industriels', 'phalanxes' or the state, as advocated by followers of the positivists Charles Fourier, Claude-Henri de Saint-Simon and Auguste Comte.[36] Green feared that this type of socialism would destroy the possibility of a positively free life by crushing the subjective freedom of the individual, including their collective action in and through voluntary associations and decentralised political action.[37] In fact, Green's reservations regarding socialism echo strongly Guiseppe Mazzini's vigorous defence of cooperative republicanism over socialism's allegedly elitist and centralising tendencies.[38] Indeed, one finds Mazzini himself raising much the same objections against 'socialism' on precisely the grounds that it denies the 'essential elements of human life – such as Religion, Association, Liberty' and private property.[39] Yet, one can still be a socialist without

---

[33] Letter from Symonds to Charlotte Byron Green and others, 7 October 1882, in Symonds, *Letters*, vol. 2, p. 777. See also Tyler, *Idealist Political Philosophy*, chapter 2, and Tyler, *Civil Society, Capitalism and the State*.

[34] See further Colin Tyler, 'Contesting the Common Good: T.H. Green and contemporary republicanism', in M. Dimova-Cookson *et al.*, eds., *T.H. Green*, pp. 262–91.

[35] 'Oxford High School' 475–76. Even though Green restricts his concerns to 'Oxford citizens' in this passage, its context makes clear that it applies for the whole of England, and indeed all civilised countries. It applies also to women as well as men.

[36] See, for example, Edward Caird, *Social Philosophy of Religion of Comte* (Glasgow: James Maclehose, 1885), a collection of articles first published in the *Contemporary Review* between May and September 1879.

[37] For example, in the *Principles of Political Obligation*, Green objects that state control of inheritance and bequest 'would imply a complete regulation of life' by society (PPO 223; see PPO 222–24). See further Peter P. Nicholson, 'T.H. Green and State Action: Liquor Legislation', *History of Political Thought*, 6 (1985), 517–50.

[38] Determining the extent of Mazzini's influence on Green is made more difficult by the fact that the same views are found in John Stuart Mill's *Principles of Political Economy* (which we know Green read) and his *Auguste Comte and Positivism* (which he seems likely to have read).

[39] Mazzini, 'On the Duties of Man', p. 346; for Mazzini's attack on 'socialism', see *ibid.*, pp. 344–65.

being a positivist of any of the types that concern Mazzini, as Green's liberal socialism proves.

III
Green's 'Liberal Socialism'

In recent times, several prominent politicians and political philosophers have referred to themselves as 'liberal socialists'.[40] Noberto Bobbio adopts the phrase from an Italian tradition that can be traced back to the idealist Benedetto Croce and the inter-war liberal socialists Piero Gobetti, Guido Calogero and Carlo Rosselli.[41] Bobbio uses the label to denote a form of politics characterised by an endorsement of liberal democratic forms of, in Bellamy's formulation, 'constitutionalism, parliamentarism, and a competitive multi-party system' combined with a greater democratisation and decentralisation of political and economic institutions and, thereby, claims Bobbio, a greater democratisation and decentralisation of collective power more generally.[42]

While endorsing key aspects of Bobbio's position, the agonal theorist Chantal Mouffe has criticised what she sees as Bobbio's atomistic assumptions: 'It is necessary to theorize the individual, not as a monad, an "unencumbered" self that exists prior to and independently of society'.[43] Her own alternative 'liberal socialism' attempts to ground a pluralistic model of the self on a postmodern ontology, such that the individual is conceived 'as a site constituted by an ensemble of "subject positions", inscribed in a multiplicity of social relations, the member of many communities and participant in a plurality of collective forms of identification.' Yet, this alternative ontology has itself attracted significant criticism, not least from those concerned by the individual's apparent passivity in the determination of their own concrete identities, which is implied by the notion of the individual being 'a site constituted' by social forces, and by the apparently attendant conception of the pre-social self as an empty husk lacking inherent expressible human needs. One very significant concern is that Mouffe's rejection of anything approaching what she understands to be 'essentialism' means that she is unable to conceptualise adequately individual alienation, itself one of the key facets of any adequate theory of oppression and, by extension, of any adequate theory of an enriching and just social order.

Consequently, while Mouffe is correct to reject ontological atomism, many of her critics worry that her alternative to this implied determinate essentialism seems to collapse into a largely vacuous conception of the self in which the individual's

---

[40] In addition to the British and Italian traditions discussed in this chapter, see the analysis of the Belgian tradition of 'liberal socialism' presented in John Cunliffe and Guido Erreygers, 'Moral philosophy and economics: The formation of François Huet's doctrine of property rights', *European Journal of the History of Economic Thought*, 6:4 (Winter 1999), 581–605.

[41] Richard Bellamy, 'Introduction', in Norbetto Bobbio, *Future of Democracy: A defence of the rules of the game*, trans. R. Griffin, ed. Richard Bellamy (Cambridge: Polity, 1987), pp. 2–3. See further James Martin, 'Italian liberal socialism: Anti-fascism and the third way', *Journal of Political Ideologies*, 7:3 (2002), 333–50.

[42] Bellamy, 'Introduction', p. 3.

[43] Chantal Mouffe, 'Towards a Liberal Socialism', in her *Return of the Political* (London and New York: Verso, 1993), p. 97.

multiple identities are imposed by the social relations in which one finds oneself. Hence, the self becomes a potentially chaotic amalgam of 'subject positions'. What is needed is a conception of the self that has an essential core of abstractly-specified universal needs and rationalising tendencies, which still leaves sufficient space to conceptualise the influence that the individual's various social activities exert in the construction of their determinate personalities.

Another possible route when seeking a viable form of liberal socialism would be to return to earlier philosophers, such as John Stuart Mill and Leonard T. Hobhouse.[44] Recently, Bruce Baum has argued for Mill's credentials as a liberal socialist, on the grounds that towards the end of his life at least he 'advanced a form of cooperative liberal democratic market socialism'.[45] Baum argues that Mill believed such a position would accord due respect simultaneously to 'individual freedom, decentralized power, and industrial democracy within a market economy'.[46] Mill's acceptance of the legitimacy of private property was tempered by an awareness of the need to redistribute income and wealth on grounds of social justice in some instances, as well as to control the accumulation of power in the hands of the wealthy through the regulation of ownership of the means of production. The implications of Mill's acceptance of the need for competition were transformed, Baum argues, by his forceful advocacy of the organisation of production through workers cooperatives.

Baum goes on to criticise Mill's liberal socialism however, for allegedly failing to anticipate the internationalisation of capitalist production, and, less anachronistically, for underestimating the anti-cooperativist power of large-scale capitalist firms.[47] Baum criticises Mill also for failing to take due account of the injustice of rewarding individuals who happen to be born as or socialised into being 'unusually talented and who form highly productive co-operatives'.[48] Baum argues that Mill 'also fails to address directly broader socialist commitments to social solidarity and community entitlements.'[49] One might also question Mill's elitism, not least as reflected in his adoption of a position on the 1867 Reform Act that was rather less radical than that of Green (except on the question of votes for women) and the educative role that he assigned to the middle-classes in local and municipal government, as well as the philosophical inadequacies of his associationist epistemology, which Green attacked at length.[50]

Besides Mill, another near-contemporary of Green is the New Liberal Leonard T. Hobhouse, who characterised himself explicitly as a 'liberal socialist' in his

[44] J.A. Hobson could be added to this list, although he is not discussed below. See Weinstein, *Utilitarianism*, chapter six.
[45] Bruce Baum, 'J.S. Mill and Liberal Socialism', in Nadia Urbinati and Alex Zakaras, eds., *J.S. Mill's Political Thought: A bicentennial reassessment* (Cambridge: Cambridge University Press, 2007), p. 104.
[46] Baum, 'J.S. Mill and Liberal Socialism', p. 101.
[47] Baum, 'J.S. Mill and Liberal Socialism', pp. 120–21.
[48] Baum, 'J.S. Mill and Liberal Socialism', p. 119, quoting G.A. Cohen, 'Future of a Disillusion', *Queen's Quarterly*, vol. 99, no. 2 (Summer 1992), 290.
[49] Baum, 'J.S. Mill and Liberal Socialism', p. 122.
[50] Tyler, *Idealist Political Philosophy*, pp. 64–84 *passim*; Tyler, 'Elitism and Anti-elitism', 345–53; and 'Logic' 34–144.

profoundly influential 1911 book *Liberalism*. 'If … there be such a thing as a Liberal Socialism', he wrote,

> … it must clearly fulfil two conditions. In the first place, it must be democratic. It must come from below, not from above. Or rather, it must emerge from the efforts of society as a whole to secure a fuller measure of justice, and a better organization of mutual aid. It must engage the efforts and respond to the genuine desires not of a handful of superior beings, but of great masses of men. And, secondly, and for that very reason, it must make its account with the human individual. It must give the average man free play in the personal life for which he really cares. It must be founded on liberty, and must make not for the suppression but for the development of personality.[51]

If liberal socialism is understood in this way, and even though Hobhouse drew rather different, more centrist policy implications from this conception than did either Green or Mill, Green was also a liberal socialist.[52] Moreover, arguably like Mill, although offering another possible form of liberal socialism Hobhouse failed to develop a conception of the individual that is as coherent and as compelling as that developed by Green.

Green's fundamental public value is the 'free life' of the individual.[53] A free life is a life self-consciously directed towards the realisation and enjoyment of the best that the individual has in him or herself to be. It is concerned with one's life as a whole made of parts of particular beliefs, commitments, values and plans. As a value in the public realm, 'free life' is characterised primarily by its procedural features rather than the concrete ends sought, in the sense that one's fellow citizens should be concerned in all but the most extreme cases with ensuring that one can exercise one's capacity to reason, and not with what one decides after reasoning. Hence, Green holds freedom from external interference to be valuable because – and, hence, to the extent that – it enables the individual to make informed choices about how they wish to act and how they wish to develop. The determination of what will allow the individual to develop should be left to the individual themselves, except in cases where it can be demonstrated that they lack the capacity to make informed choices.

Given the fact that, ontologically, individuals are what they are in part because of the society in which they have been raised and live, Green conceives legitimate politics to be a collective endeavour, geared up to the service of the good of the whole society, with each citizen bearing their part in that endeavour. Yet, this collective endeavour can only live up to its ideal where every not-obviously-incompetent person is free to choose to bear the burdens of citizenship. (The rather inelegant phrase 'not-obviously-incompetent person' is vital here, as it highlights

---

[51] Leonard T. Hobhouse, *Liberalism* (London: Williams and Norgate, n.d. [1911]), pp. 172–73. For the contrast between Green's liberal socialism and John Stuart Mill's elitist model, see Tyler, 'Elitism and Anti-elitism', 345–55, especially 345–51.

[52] That one can say much the same of Fichte is interesting when one appreciates his likely influence on Green (see §2.III below). See also Nedim Nomer, 'Fichte and the Idea of Liberal Socialism', *Journal of Political Philosophy*, 13:1 (2005), 53–73.

[53] On the nature of a 'free life', see further PE 151–56, 166, 176, 207–08, 211, 215–16, 230, 233, 248.

Green's belief that every adult should be presumed to be capable of living virtuously, unless and until they have proven that they are not.)[54] Consequently, he holds that large areas of public action that are currently undertaken by the state should be undertaken by individuals as free and equal members of decentralised associations. Throughout, he stresses the vital importance of defending certain key liberal freedoms, especially freedom of expression and association, liberal democratic constitutional forms, open government and the rule of law. Yet, the vagaries of birth, fortune and natural endowment mean that if every person is to be treated as a free and equal member of their society, then the state must step in to protect individuals from abuse by other individuals, groups and less personal social forms of power, for example by prohibiting certain terms and conditions of employment. Such protection must always be balanced against the dangers of crushing individual initiative and virtue. The underlying goal remains the same throughout however: enabling every member of society equally to exercise the capacity to live a free life, in his or her own particular contingently-constituted circumstances. Green's contention that this is the route to a 'free life' and so to the free development of the human spirit anticipates the social democratic tradition, which can also be characterised as liberal socialism.

Notice finally, that liberal socialism is not concerned with economic matters alone. The conditions of individual virtue and self-realisation (rather than monetary wealth) are also stressed (the good citizen should be a respectable 'yeoman', in Green's terms), social life in all its forms should be founded on mutual respect between citizens as active participants of equal worth and having equal claims as persons, irrespective of social rank (whether based on wealth, gender or any other factor), and the just society should protect all members especially the vulnerable and help to provide the contexts for free action by all members. There are important consequences, not least the fact that income redistribution should be treated as a matter of justice rather than charity. In this way, the respectable poor can make claims on the basis of what is owed to them rather than on their knees. Similarly, Green wanted education to be available free-of-charge to everyone who could not afford it, ideally with children of all classes attending the same schools. The dependence of women on their husbands should be addressed through a radical reform of the divorce laws, and, most famously, the state had a duty to protect the individual from being forced by their employers into accepting abusive terms and conditions. The latter accorded with Green's support for trade union action in pursuit of the reasonable claims of the peasants and proletariat. Politically, he sought the radical extension of the franchise, and held that part of being an intelligent active citizen is being willing to recognise not simply a right to engage in civil disobedience under certain circumstances, but indeed a duty to do so. Violent resistance is a duty under extreme circumstances, such as faced slaves

---

[54] That Green was far more positive about the capabilities and worth of real people than has been alleged by those who wish to see him as a dour moralist, is indicated by the following story from Symonds: 'Apropos of some one feeling an acute morbid sense of being wicked. Poor fellow, said Green, the sense of Sin is very much an illusion. People are not as bad as they fancy themselves.' Letter from Symonds to Charlotte Byron Green and others, 7 October 1882, in Symonds, *Letters*, vol. 2, p. 777.

and their white Northern supporters during the American Civil War, and Italian republicans during the Risorgimento.[55]

Throughout, the guiding liberal socialist concern is to foster the conditions (both personal and environmental) for the individual to have and be justified in having a sense of personal dignity, and, in Kantian terms, with the honouring of the categorical imperative to respect humanity wherever it is found and to live as an active member of a 'kingdom of ends' which draws its determinacy from its historical traditions and circumstances.[56] Yet, throughout the individual must be an intelligent and critical citizen, for it is only by seeking out and striving to correct injustices and imperfections in one's traditions, conventions, norms and institutions, as well as the associated systems of conventionally recognised rights, obligations and duties that 'Faculties which social repression and separation prevent from development' can be liberated.[57] Only then can individuals work to make themselves and their fellows the best that they can become in their own free judgements.

IV
Conclusion

W.L. Newman, one of Green's Balliol colleagues, recorded Green's admiration for the opening of the seventh book of the *Politics*, where Aristotle argues that in order to understand 'the best constitution appropriately, we must first decide what is the most desirable life' for the individual.[58] One can judge which social order (broadly conceived) is best, then, only if one first understands human nature. Similarly, it is argued in this book that one can only properly understand Green's liberal socialism if one appreciates that it presupposes a systematic philosophical justification, which accords the highest respect to human nature as that is expressed in all fields of human life, including but not restricted to philosophy, religion, literature, daily conventions and actions, social institutions, norms and practices, as well as formally-expressed and enforced rules and laws. It is shown however, that Green argues human nature has always been expressed imperfectly, partly due to the ignorance of those who live in and sustain society, and partly due to deliberate manipulation by the powerful members. For this and other reasons, Green argues that the individual must be an active and yet critical citizen, who tests all prejudices with his or her own reason, and who works assiduously to remove injustices and all other hindrances to a free life for the individual and his or her fellows. In this way, this book begins with a critical reconstruction of Green's theory of the individual will (including mind as related to will), rather than with the political and economic structures of modern capitalist societies, as scholars

---

[55] See Nicholson, 'T.H. Green and State Action'; Olive Anderson, 'The Feminism of T.H. Green: A late Victorian success story?', *History of Political Thought*, 12:4 (1991), 671–93; and Tyler, *Idealist Political Philosophy*, chapter 2.

[56] Compare 'Kant' 103–08 *et sub*, 124; PE 186, 198, 205, 214, 284–85.

[57] PE 208.

[58] Aristotle, *Politics*, Book VII, chapter 1; W.L. Newman, 'Recollection', in Tyler, ed., 'Recollections', 27.

such as Carter have done, or with God conceived as the eternal consciousness, as many critics have done. Before this however, a number of preliminary matters must be explored in the next chapter.

2

Green as a Systematic Philosopher

Philosophy does but interpret, with full consciousness and in system, the powers already working in the spiritual life of mankind, and as these powers at every stage gather a strength which they never finally lose, so the philosophical expression which they have found in one age, is not lost, however it may be qualified, in the ages that follow.[1]

I
Introduction

Green's practical commitment to reform was introduced in the preceding chapter, and his practical activities justify the further comment they have received elsewhere.[2] Yet, in the present context Green is of interest primarily because of the philosophical justification that he gave to the radical agenda. Indeed, Roy Hattersley exaggerated only slightly when he referred to Green as 'the only genuine philosopher English social democracy has ever possessed'.[3] The purpose of the present work is to examine the metaphysical foundations of his theory of self-realisation and freedom, with his related theories of society, economics and politics being examined in detail in a subsequent book.[4] Together these works constitute a critical analysis of his liberal socialism as a whole.

In order to understand Green's philosophical position properly (that is, on its own terms), something must be said now regarding his methodology and the origins of his thought. In particular, it is important to ask in what sense he was a systematic philosopher, and in what sense it is misleading to think of him as the Hegelian that he is often portrayed. Nevertheless, while these are profoundly important questions for scholars of British idealism, probably they are of less interest for anyone new to Green's thought. For this reason, the latter may wish to omit this chapter, and move straight to the analysis of Green's 'metaphysics of experience and knowledge', which begins in chapter three. For those of you who have not just skipped forward, the current chapter is structured as follows. It is

---

[1] 'Popular Philosophy' 93.
[2] For example, Peter Nicholson, 'T.H. Green and State Action: Liquor legislation', *History of Political Thought*, vol. 6, no. 3 (1985), 517–550; Olive Anderson, 'The Feminism of T.H. Green: A late Victorian success story?', *History of Political Thought*, vol. 12, no. 4 (1991), 671–93; Denys P. Leighton, *Greenian Moment: T.H. Green, Religion and Political Argument in Victorian Britain* (Exeter: Imprint Academic, 2004); Colin Tyler, *Idealist Political Philosophy: Pluralism and conflict in the absolute idealist tradition* (London and New York: Continuum, 2006), chapter 2.
[3] Roy Hattersley, *Edwardians* (London: Little Brown, 2004), p. 383.
[4] Colin Tyler, *Civil Society, Capitalism and the State: Part 2 of* Liberal Socialism of Thomas Hill Green (Exeter: Imprint Academic, forthcoming).

argued in §2.II that while Green's reputation among philosophers is now better than in the past, there remains a danger that his attitude toward religion will prove fatal to his thought. To head-off such a concern, it is shown below that his belief that philosophy is the master mode, which assimilates the insights expressed in all others, means that no peculiarly-religious propositions play a necessary role in his philosophy. This contention is developed further in §2.III, which examines the wider intellectual influences on Green. It is argued that the plurality of sources on which he drew make it misleading to characterise him as a Hegelian as many scholars have done. Green's previously underappreciated debts to Fichte and Mazzini are also discussed, and a note of caution is entered against those who claim that Green drew heavily on J.S. Mill and Hermann Lotze. §2.IV critically assesses Green's much-neglected conception of philosophical system-building, as a prelude to the examination of the first stage of what he refers to as his 'metaphysics of experience and knowledge' in chapter three.

II
Conventional Prejudices, 'Popular Philosophy' and Religion

The claim that Green's philosophical system is largely coherent and his political thought is compelling is not the received view in the secondary literature. At the most fundamental level, scholars have raised serious doubts regarding the reasonableness of Green's presuppositions. For example, Melvin Richter concluded his classic 1964 study, *The Politics of Conscience: T. H. Green and his age*, with the claim that by the 1920s and 1930s, the ideal of self-realisation championed by Green and his followers which had been 'accepted by the fathers as bold and progressive ... appeared to their sons as a set of priggish *clichés*.... The Liberal epoch had come to an end, and with it the tenure of Green's influence.'[5] Similarly, Andrew Vincent and Raymond Plant have endorsed Stefan Collini's claim that the British idealists' 'mode of thought' 'was embedded in a set of assumptions which no longer demands our allegiance', even if they did not support Collini's further claim that it was 'addressed to a range of problems which no longer command our attention'.[6] Stuart Hampshire took this characterisation to its extreme when he wrote: 'T.H. Green, who died in 1882, is a minor figure in the history of philosophy. He left no legacy of convincing argument or insight. He was an earnest, slow, rather muddled thinker, without technical brilliance or any exceptional powers of expression.'[7] Finally, Richard Bellamy has argued that 'a return to Victorian values in modern circumstances would be seriously misguided. For much of liberalism has been shaped by aspirations and beliefs which have ceased to command our allegiance and addressed social and political conditions which no longer exist.'[8]

[5]   Melvin Richter, *Politics of Conscience: T.H. Green and his age* (London: Weidenfeld and Nicolson, 1964), p. 376.

[6]   Andrew Vincent and Raymond Plant, *Philosophy, Politics and Citizenship: The life and thought of the British idealists* (Aldershot: Gower, 1984), p. 183, quoting Stefan Collini, *Liberalism and Sociology: L.T. Hobhouse and political argument in England 1880–1914* (Cambridge: Cambridge University Press, 1979), p. 253.

[7]   Stuart Hampshire, 'Oxford Virtue', *New Statesman*, 7 August 1964, p. 184.

[8]   Richard Bellamy, 'Introduction', in Richard Bellamy, ed., *Victorian Liberalism: Nineteenth century*

As a prelude to the strictly philosophical response to allegations of excessive moralism in Green, it is important to unsettle the received picture of the Victorian era in general and of Green in particular, which in Matthew Sweet's striking phrase we either 'hate' or 'patronise ... with our contemptuous sentiment'.[9] Specifically, one should address the popular misconception that Green was a uniformly dour man who parroted a narrow range of sources in such a way that it is appropriate to write him off as an unoriginal cipher for other, more interesting people's ideas. Some of Green's colleagues and disciples did little to dispel this image of him. Nettleship described the school-boy Green as 'impatient of research and averse to diffuse reading'.[10] W.L. Newman claimed that, as an adult, 'His habitual dress of black and grey suited him well and was true to his character. He was drawn ... to all that is sober suited and steady-going.'[11] When they came into their own ascendency a generation later, this image was propagated mercilessly by a certain section of the new intellectual elite, not least through Lytton Strachey's *Eminent Victorians*, Virginia Woolf's *The Hours* and in a rather more veiled form G.E. Moore's *Principia Ethica*.

It is easy then for many contemporary writers to labour still under the convenient cant initiated by this elite, in spite of their frequently claimed replacement of conventional prejudices with dispassionate scholarly insight. Certainly there is an element of truth in the picture but mainly in relation to Green's youth. John Addington Symonds's letters are crucial sources here, containing as they do a wealth of incident and information regarding Green's character as well as the events of his life. Symonds describes Green between 1859 and 1864 'with all his kindness & humour, as a man somewhat excessively austere, exacting from others no less than from himself an ascetic rule of life, & speaking with decided scorn of what was alien to his own conception of manly sober citizenship. Impregnated with Carlyle, he had a good deal of Carlyle's contemptuousness.'[12] Yet, the image of Green as an

---

political thought and practice (London: Routledge, 1990), p. 12; compare Richard Bellamy, 'A Green Revolution? Idealism, Liberalism and the Welfare State', *Bulletin of the Hegel Society of Great Britain*, 10 (1984), 34–39 *passim*; Richard Bellamy, 'T.H. Green and the Morality of Victorian Liberalism', in Bellamy, ed., *Victorian Liberalism*, pp. 147–8; Richard Bellamy, *Liberalism and Modern Society: An historical argument* (Oxford: Polity, 1992), p. 40.

[9] Matthew Sweet, *Inventing the Victorians* (London: Faber and Faber, 2001), p. 232. The whole book is engrossing. More general reflections are found in its Introduction and Conclusion.

[10] ' "He' is slow and easily "puzzled"; 'there is a certain inertness about him; he has not much "ambition"; "I" fear that he is constitutionally "indolent"; such are the judgements of his masters in 1850, 1851, and 1853. He wrote slowly in examinations, was constantly behindhand with his exercises, and had great difficulty in getting up in the morning. But a stronger reason for his apparent want of success was the fact that his heart was not in the subjects in which distinction at school is chiefly won. He had not the interest either in language or in learning which makes a great scholar. He had indeed a genuine literary sense, and his own power of expression was far above the average; but he needed the presence of something great to make him put out his strength. ... While he was thus indifferent to the study of literary form, except as a vehicle for his own best thought, he was also impatient of research and averse to diffuse reading.' Nettleship, 'Memoir', p. xii. Compare with Henry Sidgwick's praise for Green's prose style in Sidgwick, 'Recollection', in Colin Tyler, ed., 'Recollections Regarding T.H. Green', *Collingwood and British Idealism Studies*, vol. 14, no. 2 (2008), 11–12.

[11] W.L. Newman, 'Recollection', in Tyler, ed., 'Recollections Regarding T.H. Green', 26; see also Nettleship, 'Memoir', p. lxii.

[12] Letter from John Addington Symonds to Charlotte Byron Green et al, 7 October 1882, in John

'earnest', humourless individual flies in the face of numerous stories told about him by his friends. This is confirmed immediately by Symonds himself: 'All this softened, as years went by; & without losing the strength of his own character, the elevation of aims, he lost what had previously been rugged, what looked like censoriousness in his attitude.' Similarly, in his biography of Algernon Swinburne, Edmund Gosse wrote:

> T.H. Green was accustomed to chuckle as he described a meeting of the Old Mortality, where he read an essay on the development of Christian Dogma. He happened to look up once from his paper, and nearly burst out laughing at the sight of Swinburne, whose face wore an expression compounded of unutterable ennui and naïf astonishment that men whom he respected could take interest in such a subject.[13]

On a personal level, Green excited great loyalty from his friends and family, as well as being popular with their children.[14] John St Loe Strachey, nephew to both Lytton Strachey and by marriage to Green, portrays the Green of the 1870s at least in a way that is at radical variance to the comfortably dismissive caricature of a repressed and repressing man.

> I think that had I been asked to describe my Uncle when I was fifteen or sixteen, I should have said of him that he was the most amusing person I knew. In this good nature he never seemed tired of telling good stories, making happy references to characters in books, or remembering droll experiences of his own, especially in country rambles; for I think the humour of country people was more natural to him than that of the town.[15]

The picture could be filled out in a number of other ways, for example with his critical remarks on moral narcissists and those who trumpet their patriotism.[16] For the moment it seems sufficient to note that scholars usually ignore the fact that the 'dour', 'moralistic' Green even denied the existence of sin: 'Apropos of some one feeling an acute morbid sense of being wicked. Poor fellow, said Green, the sense of Sin is very much an illusion. People are not as bad as they fancy themselves.'[17]

Addington Symonds, *Letters*, 3 vols., eds. Herbert M. Schueller and Robert L. Peters (Detroit: Wayne State Press, 1968–69), vol. 2, p. 777. Henry Sidgwick saw this in Green too (Sidgwick, 'Recollections', 9–17).

[13] Edmund Gosse, *Life of Algernon Charles Swinburne* (London: MacMillan, 1917), p. 40. Gosse recounts this incident, from the meeting where Green gave his 'Essay on Christian Dogma', when discussing Swinburne's life in 1857, however Henry Nettleship recalled hearing Green give 'Christian Dogma' to the Old Mortality in 1863 or 1864 (Henry Nettleship, 'Recollection', in Tyler, ed., 'Recollections Regarding T.H. Green', 42). Green joined the Old Mortality in 1858. Green and Swinburne fell out eventually (Richter, *Politics of Conscience*, p. 83).

[14] 'He attracted children to him. Two of my girls who lived some months in his house after his marriage, retain the most vivid & affectionate memory of him. One of them was quite a baby; but when she left Oxford for Davos, she used often to ask me: "Is Uncle Tom coming today?" "How is Uncle Tom?".' Letter from Symonds to Charlotte Green et al, 7 October 1882, in Symonds, *Letters*, vol. 2, p. 779.

[15] John St Loe Strachey, 'Recollection', in Tyler, ed., 'Recollections Regarding T.H. Green', 61.

[16] For example, PE 297; and his notes for a speech on 'National Loss and Gain under a Conservative Government', 5 December 1879, in *Works* 5, p. 352.

[17] Letter from Symonds to Charlotte Green et al, 7 October 1882, in Symonds, *Letters*, vol. 2, p. 777.

(See §8.V for a philosophical consideration of the moralistic reading of Green.)

In spite of the fact that they misrepresent Green, our contemporary 'Edwardian' attacks indicate Green's transformation from a figure of philosophical interest into little more than an insignificant character in the history of philosophy. Certainly, there were some scholarly philosophical defences of various aspects of Green's system during the extended period that Hampshire, Richter, Vincent, Plant and Bellamy made the particular claims noted above.[18] Yet, they were in the minority. I hope to indicate that this situation was not justified. Indeed, some of the criticisms are obviously very weak. In many cases, for example, the claim that 'our' time no longer finds a particular argument plausible (that 'we' cannot accept *that* anymore) implies a remarkably simplistic view of the ideational structures from which communities are constructed. Most commonly, this view relies on either a naive homogenisation of social complexities, or an unfounded intellectual elitism, or some mixture of the two. Often in fact, the 'we' refers to a rather restricted group of people who are portrayed as nearly the only reasonable people in the world on this matter, by virtue of operating upon 'our' assumptions. Frequently in reality, there are just as many people who do accept the 'rejected' assumptions, and who do so on equally valid grounds. Rather than making the polemical appeal to what 'we' believe, a much more profitable and coherent approach when assessing a philosophy's force is to test its internal consistency. This is just what the present book will do in relation to Green's system.

Green saw this himself: 'about every … philosopher, the essential questions are, What are his problems, and what was his method?'[19] Or, as he put it towards the end of his life: 'When we understand what the questions exactly were that a philosopher put to himself, and how he came to put them as he did, we are more than half-way to understanding the answer'.[20] It is a commonplace that Green wrote in response to the spiritual crisis of the mid to late Victorian era. Natural science was displacing orthodox Christianity as the basis of most Western societies. The need to avert the dangers of this situation comes out clearly in the majority

---

[18] For example, Ann R. Cacoullos, *Thomas Hill Green: Philosopher of rights* (New York: Twayne, 1974); John Morrow, 'Property and Personal Development: An interpretation of T.H. Green's political philosophy', *Politics: Journal of the Australasian Political Science Association* (1981), 84–92; John Morrow, 'Liberalism and British Idealist Political Philosophy: A reassessment', *History of Political Thought*, 10:1 (1984), 91–108; Paul Harris, 'Green's Theory of Political Obligation and Obedience', in Andrew Vincent, ed., *Philosophy of T.H. Green* (Aldershot: Gower, 1986), pp. 127–42, and his 'Moral Progress and Politics: The theory of T.H. Green', *Polity*, 21 (1988–89), 538–62; Geoffrey Thomas, *Moral Philosophy of T.H. Green* (Oxford: Clarendon 1987); Peter P. Nicholson, *Political Philosophy of the British Idealists: Selected studies* (Cambridge: Cambridge University Press, 1990); Avital Simhony, 'T.H. Green's Theory of the Morally Justified Society', *History of Political Thought*, 10:3 (1989), 481–98; Avital Simhony, 'On Forcing Individuals to be Free: T.H. Green's liberal theory of positive freedom', *Political Studies*, 49 (1991), 303–20; Avital Simhony, 'Idealist Organicism: Beyond holism and individualism', *History of Political Thought*, 12:3 (1991), 515–35; Avital Simhony, 'Beyond Negative and Positive Freedom: T.H. Green's view of freedom', *Political Theory*, 21:1 (1993), 28–544; Avital Simhony, 'T.H. Green: The common good society', *History of Political Thought*, 14:2 (1993), 225–47.

[19] 'Hume I' 6.

[20] 'Rev. Caird's Kant' 134–35.

of Green's writings.[21] In his well-known early essay 'Popular Philosophy in its Relation to Life', Green characterises his society as one 'that mistakes sophistication for thought'.[22] In philosophical terms, the enemy is essentially the one faced by Immanuel Kant.[23] It is a metaphysic based on realism, particularly as expressed in the philosophical underpinnings of natural science and the writings of John Locke, David Hume and Herbert Spencer.[24] For Green, their types of empiricism (the 'popular philosophy') do not attempt to analyse experience with sufficient depth and consistency to provide a coherent conception of the principles underlying the natural and human worlds as we experience them, which is after all the only way in which they exist 'for us'. Instead, in effect they attempt to hide the gaps and incoherencies within the common-place, pre-reflective view of those worlds.

> [Popular philosophy] is the uncritical expression of the claim to be free, to enjoy, and to understand. It is an abstract or result of the various methods, poetic, religious, metaphysical, by which man has sought to account to himself for the world of his experience, as they apply directly to human life. Inconsistent with all the inconsistencies of these methods, which it takes not as criticism would reconstruct but as rhetoric has overlaid them, it brings its contradictions home to the average man at the most vital points, and is the natural parent of the modern "unsettlement".[25]

The poverty of this metaphysic expresses itself most significantly in its inability to give a consistent and convincing account of the processes involved in human moral agency.[26] In particular, it cannot give an adequate account of the self-consciousness inherent in human agency and cannot give an adequate account of the active nature of human consciousness.[27] By inhibiting the individual's rational understanding and assessment of their own agency in this way, popular philosophy, then, impairs the individual's capacity to act well: 'man, above all modern man, must theorise his practice, and the failure adequately to do so, must cripple the practice itself.'[28] The failure of realist empiricism to satisfy the innate human desire for a coherent understanding of the world is dangerous, in other words, to the extent that it encourages a particularly popular misconception of human experience and moral life.[29] In his unpublished papers, Green argues that 'the claim of the modern spirit to understand its own life (and enjoy it), results in the conviction "I always do what pleases me, and it is unprofitable I should do otherwise". Unfortunately this result is[30] incompatible with its other claim to be free.'[31] If phenomena are conceived as being purely the result of essentially arbitrary encounters of a passive

---

[21]   For example, PE especially 1–8; DSF *passim*; it recurs throughout the first and third volumes of his *Works* as well.
[22]   'Popular Philosophy' 120.
[23]   'Popular Philosophy' 97.
[24]   'Hume II' 64; PE 1–8.
[25]   'Popular Philosophy' 97.
[26]   'Popular Philosophy' 96–7.
[27]   'Popular Philosophy' 95.
[28]   'Popular Philosophy' 124.
[29]   'Popular Philosophy' 121.
[30]   Green's alternative in the manuscript reads: 'turns out [to be]'.
[31]   MS 15, T.H. Green Papers, Balliol College, Oxford.

consciousness with an otherwise mind-independent world, then the individual's place in the world is reduced to that of a mere 'creation' rather than a 'creator'. Consequently, the authority of one's moral views becomes highly questionable to the agent in that it makes them impositions rather than anything connected to what it is to be truly 'human'. The necessary incoherence of the prevalent groundwork of contemporary thought is not a purely theoretical problem for Green, then. It is not even of the first importance for Green that it is a theoretical problem. Popular philosophy must be changed primarily because it harms the daily lives of real people.

As with any coherent critique, Green's alternative to popular philosophy is implicit within his attack. Green is a philosophical idealist: in an important sense, he believes that the worlds in which we live (our worlds of meanings, values, circumstances and plans) exist only in our minds, and that, consequently, the philosopher should analyse these minds as they are expressed in the world of institutions and self-conscious action.

> For the ascertainment, in short, of what human thought and feelings are we have nothing to resort to but the analysis of what we ourselves are doing and have done. There are such things as knowledge, art, and morality, which somehow are our work. By considering what we must have done in order to their existence, and in no other way, can we learn the ultimate nature of the thought and feeling realised in them. We have to ask, for instance, what our consciousness must have done, and been in order to do, that there should be for it what we call facts, and these connected in a single world.[32]

More succinctly, he states that philosophy, particularly metaphysics, proceeds by the 'disentanglement of that which is implicit in the language, knowledge, and acts of men'.[33] As will be shown below (§§2.III–IV, 3.II), Green holds that metaphysics is concerned to uncover the presuppositions of established beliefs about facts and values (both broadly conceived), to articulate the ambiguities and inconsistencies both within and between those presuppositions, to reformulate the latter so as to remove their imperfections, before articulating the resulting collection of revised presuppositions as a systematic whole. This is what will be called below 'critical metaphysics', following D.G. Ritchie and Peter Nicholson. More than this however, it will be shown below that for Green metaphysics is concerned also to critically-assess and where necessary revise conventional beliefs in light of these systemised revised presuppositions. Again following Ritchie and Nicholson, this second task will be called here 'speculative metaphysics'. It will be shown that Green believes, to varying degrees, these interrelated processes of metaphysical enquiry find veiled expression in all branches of human intellectual achievement, including philosophy, art, religion and science, as well as the particular practical activities of daily life embodied in 'a complex organisation of life, with laws and institutions, with relationships, courtesies, and charities, with arts and graces'.[34]

---

[32]   'Lewes II' 96.
[33]   'Aristotle' 64.
[34]   DSF 23.

Ultimately, Green seeks to articulate a philosophy which emphasizes man's place at the centre of his own world.[35] Such a philosophy should set out the necessary interconnection of the outward world and the inward being of individuals. Only such a view can satisfy the individual's need for inner harmony because only such a view approaches a successful reconciliation of the different and presently disjointed aspects of human self-understanding. More than this however, Green holds that only such a view captures the religious impulses which he takes all truly self-comprehending people to recognise within themselves. For example, he asks 'how does the individual interpret himself? As a succession of pains and pleasures gathered into a unity, or as the dwelling-place of a spirit that filleth and searcheth all things?'[36] He sides with the latter and argues that 'the moral man ... [is] the many-sided development of a single spiritual principle' with this 'single spiritual principle' being called alternatively the 'eternal consciousness' or 'God'.[37] Hence, Andrew Vincent and Raymond Plant have argued that:

> The importance of Green's theological and philosophical thought on religion cannot be overstated. ... This philosophical interpretation of ordinary religious consciousness enabled Green ... to claim that ... [his] philosophy, though metaphysical, was a reconstruction of ordinary consciousness. As such philosophy itself was part of the divine service.[38]

Focussing on the religious aspects of Green's philosophy is likely to discourage many contemporary philosophers from taking Green seriously. For this reason among many others, it is necessary to stress that, even though Green wishes to establish that true religious beliefs fully harmonise with each other, he achieves this by translating these beliefs into the constituents of a strictly philosophical system. This comes out clearly in Green's *Essay on Christian Dogma*.

> Christian dogma, then, must be retained in its completeness, but it must be transformed into a philosophy. Its first characteristic, as an intuition become abstract, must vanish, that it may be assimilated by the reason as an idea. The progress of thought in general consists in its struggle to work itself free from the mere individuality and outwardness of the object of intuition. The thing as sensible, *i.e.* as presented in an individual moment in time and space, must become the thing as known, *i.e.* as constituted by general attributes. Again, from being supposed to be known only so far as it exists, it must be understood also to exist only so far as it is known. ... To the modern philosopher ... Christ is the necessary determination of the eternal subject, the objectification by this subject of himself in the world of nature and humanity. ... If the idea of the philosopher is the truth, it may be said the intuition of the philosopher must be delusion. On examination,

[35] 'Popular Philosophy' 117–18.
[36] 'Popular Philosophy' 122.
[37] 'Popular Philosophy' 100.
[38] Vincent *et al.*, *Philosophy, Politics and Citizenship*, pp. 16–17. On Green's religious thought, see Colin Tyler, 'Thomas Hill Green', in Edward N. Zalta, ed., *Stanford Encyclopaedia of Philosophy*, section 2: URL http://plato.stanford.edu/archives/sum2006/entries/green/#2

however, it will be found that there is a sense in which the idea is at once the complement of the intuition and its justification.[39]

The resulting philosophical system must stand on its own merits; that is, apart from religious faith. It cannot rely upon biblical evidence or any other transcendent 'grounding'. Moreover, it must be articulate, in a way that is less important in the case of religion. Obviously, it must rest upon certain assumptions, as must every proposition and wider endeavour even the least 'metaphysical'. Yet, each presupposition must avoid being an 'intuition become abstract' and instead must 'be assimilated by reason as an idea'. As a core part of this assimilation process, philosophers should attempt to articulate this universe in its completeness as one system with conceptual clarity, rather than in the figurative and hence (in comparison to philosophy) inadequate terms of religion, poetry and pre-reflective experience.

Philosophically, Green's analysis proceeds on the assumption that the fundamental structural principles of a rational world would form a harmonious system, meaning that when understood correctly, phenomena could be explained fully by making reference to these underlying categories (including principles of relation).[40] Consequently, the metaphysician should attempt to discover what is logically required if the known world is to exist in accordance with a coherent system of categories. In this way, one can begin to distinguish intelligently between the truly valuable elements of the world and the latter's ambiguities and imperfections. This explains the philosophical significance of the search for knowledge, and hence of what Green calls the 'metaphysics of experience or knowledge'. As has been noted already, it will be established in chapters three and four he argues that, when properly conducted, philosophical enquiry establishes the harmonising power of human consciousness, a power which he labels the 'eternal subject or consciousness' and which he equates to God. Yet, Green holds also that the force of the arguments that lead to this conclusion is independent of the individual's knowledge of the reason for the existence of the eternal consciousness.

> 'It is in a sense mysterious that there should be such a thing as a world at all. The old question, why God made the world, has never been answered, nor will be. We know not why the world should be; we only know that there it is. In like manner we know not why the eternal subject of that world should reproduce itself, through certain processes of the world, as the spirit of mankind, or as the particular self of this or that man in whom the spirit of mankind operates. We can only say that, upon the best analysis we can make of our experience, it seems that so it does.'[41]

Notice that Green does not claim to have definitely found 'the Truth' (for example, in the sense of some postmodern 'logocentric' caricature). Instead, he is attempting simply to produce the 'best analysis' of the facts which constitute

---

[39] 'Christian Dogma' 182–83.
[40] 'Popular Philosophy' 93.
[41] PE 100. Chapters three and four of the present book explore many aspects of such passages.

the world. Throughout, he remains modest about the proper ambitions of the philosopher, as J.A. Symonds noted:

> He used to repeat that Philosophy is not a Mystery, that the philosopher cannot be expected to know more for certain than the rest of men about such things as Immortality, that his Superiority consists in knowing his own thoughts & what man must think, that the old religious language receives through exact thinking a new vitality, that it is our prime business to take account of what & how we think – & so forth.[42]

One must appreciate this fact if one is to understand Green correctly: his philosophy prioritises personal judgement, not dogma and rote-learning. Judgement is critical, on-going, and is careful to show fidelity to the evidence that one discerns to be well-founded after testing it through the exercise of one's own personal reason. It also accepts the fallibility of that reason, hence it is willing to give serious thought to possible objections. Green is an objectivist in that he believes one can be correct or incorrect in one's beliefs; he is a humanist in that he valorises careful personal judgement on spiritual matters.

Geoffrey Thomas has claimed that 'There was a religious motivation to Green's thought, although only a slight religious content to his philosophy.'[43] The preceding discussion indicates that, in truth, it is more accurate to write 'although only a slight *uniquely and exclusively* religious content to his philosophy'. The only prominent and exclusively religious aspect is found in his characterisation of the 'eternal consciousness' as a personalised interventionist God.[44] It will be argued in chapters three and four that, as this is far more a matter of presentation than substance, Green's philosophical method and substantive claims are available to atheists. In part this reflects the fact that, in addition to Scripture, the Christian tradition and daily Christian insight, Green drew extensively on non-religious sources. Consequently, even though Green's intellectual provenance is not the central focus of this book, something still should be said about the sources of the constitutive elements of Green's own philosophy.[45]

III
The Wider Intellectual Influences on Green

Philosophically, the main reason that one might have for seeing Green as a man of limited interests and insight are his allegedly immense debts to Kant and especially Hegel. It is undeniable that Green became infatuated with Hegel at least for a time after coming under Benjamin Jowett's influence on going up to Balliol in 1855. John Conington, one of Green's private tutors to whom he was especially close as an undergraduate, is reported to have 'said of him [as a young man]

---

[42] Letter from Symonds to Charlotte Green *et al.*, 7 October 1882, in Symonds, *Letters*, vol. 2, p. 778.

[43] Thomas, *Moral Philosophy of T.H. Green*, p. 12.

[44] PE 187; DSF 21.

[45] The writings of philosophers such as Aristotle, Rousseau, Kant, Fichte and Hegel are mentioned where this is helpful to developing the critique of Green's system, but other particular debts are not examined to any significant extent.

that he was "radical in politics and a spiritualist in philosophy"; that his reading oscillated "between Hegel and the Morning Star"; that his main idea was "to bring the young dissenting preachers to Oxford and turn them into Hegelians".'[46] It was in August 1862 or very shortly afterwards that Green began to study Hegelian Tübingen Biblical Criticism, from which he seems to have adopted the Christology and a belief in the historical contingency of the doctrines and authority of the various Christian churches (Roman Catholicism, Anglicanism, and so on). In the same vein, the rudiments of the two articles that Green published in 1866 and 1868 respectively, on 'The Philosophy of Aristotle' and 'Popular Philosophy in its Relation to Life', portray Hegel as the culmination of a powerful intellectual tradition. Hegel, he wrote, 'articulated the message which had been forming itself for utterance in the mouths of Kant, Fichte and Schelling'.[47] Hegel also figures positively and at length in Green's 'Lectures on Moral and Political Philosophy', apparently given in 1867, about a year after referring to 'my Hegelian philosophy' in a letter to James Bryce.[48] J.A. Symonds recorded that 'The rhetorical passages in Hegel were often dwelt on by him,'[49] and, more substantially, 'The powerful hold wh[ich] Hegel took upon him, was the hold wh[ich] a mystagogue might take upon a neophyte. He was dazzled by the revelation, rapt with delight at the panorama of the world unfolded to him.'[50] Indeed, what Green himself described towards the end of his life as the permanently valuable aspects of Hegel's writings encapsulated the core of Green's own philosophical system.

> That there is one spiritual self-conscious being, of which all that is real is the activity or expression; that we are related to this spiritual being, not merely as parts of the world which is its expression, but as partakers in some inchoate measure of the self-consciousness through which it at once constitutes and distinguishes itself from the world; that this participation is the source of morality and religion; this we take to be the vital truth which Hegel had to teach.[51]

Yet, it is evident that Green became highly circumspect about the success of Hegel's system, cautioning his readers that while one 'cannot drink too deep of Hegel, [one] should sit rather looser to the "dialectical" method than Dr. [John] Caird has [in his *Introduction to the Philosophy of Religion*]'.[52] F.H. Bradley went so far as to write 'Green was in my opinion no Hegelian, & in some respects was

---

[46] Henry Nettleship, 'Professor Henry Nettleship's Recollections', in Tyler, ed., 'Recollections Regarding T.H. Green', 43; see also *ibid.*, 32, 36, 40–41, 42.

[47] 'Rudiments' 7.

[48] Green, 'Lectures on Moral and Political Philosophy', *passim* but especially pp. 173–82; letter from Green to James Bryce, 23 March 1866, *Works*, 5, p. 420.

[49] See letter from Symonds to Charlotte Green *et al.*, 7 October 1882, in Symonds, *Letters*, vol. 2, p. 775.

[50] Letter from Symonds to Charlotte Green *et al.*, 7 October 1882, in Symonds, *Letters*, vol. 2, p. 778, my additions in square brackets.

[51] Green's review of John Caird's IPR 146; see also James W. Allard, *Logical Foundations of Bradley's Metaphysics: Judgement, inference, and truth* (Cambridge: Cambridge University Press, 2005), p. 17.

[52] IPR 146. See further Ben Wempe, *T.H. Green's Theory of Positive Freedom: From metaphysics to positive freedom* (Exeter: Imprint Academic, 2004), chapter 1.

anti-Hegelian.'[53] In fact, one might even question T.M. Lindsay's inclusion in 1877 of Green among the membership of a 'small but energetic Hegelian school' that he believed 'has found refuge in England and America'.[54] It is far safer to place the other philosophers, Edward Caird, J.H. Stirling and William Wallace, within this 'school'. Indeed, Caird was happy to describe himself as 'in the main an unregenerate Hegelian' in 1893, a description that appears to have remained accurate for the rest of his life, and much the same could have been said for Stirling and Wallace as well.[55] Green was different however. In fact, one should question the extent to which reading Hegel determined the direction of Green's mind at all, even in the 1860s. First, it is unclear at what date Green started to read Hegel in depth. Charles Parker mentions a reading-party attended by Green and himself in 1857, writing of the books that they read:

> I think they were the early Greek philosophers (what fragments we could get), Plato (Republic and passages from many minor dialogues), Aristotle (Ethics, Politics, and parts of the Metaphysics and Organon), Bacon's Novum Organum, Bishop Butler (on Conscience and such fundamental questions) and I am afraid the merest scraps of other modern philosophers, Locke and Berkeley, Hume and Reid, Kant and Hegel.[56]

For the most part, Parker is listing the required reading for the *literae humaniores* final school. Parker did observe a more unusual interest however, when he wrote that at this time (1857) Green 'seemed much taken by what little we knew of Hegel's logic, embracing in one vast syllogism the universe of thought and of existence.'[57]

Second, it is interesting that although in later life Green became weary of the Oxford requirement that he taught Aristotle each year, Parker cites the *Nicomachean Ethics* as Green's favoured starting-point for philosophical discussions in the late 1850s.[58] W.L. Newman records that Green 'once spoke to me in terms of high approval of the beginning of the Seventh Book of Aristotle's Politics (old order).'[59] This passage is especially significant in the context of Green's own philosophical position, as it highlights one of its key presuppositions of the nature of the good society and the legitimate application of collective power: 'If we wish to investigate the best constitution appropriately, we must first decide what is the most desirable life' for the individual.[60] In fact, Aristotle is the very first philosopher that we know Green to have read (in 1852).[61] Indeed, one might think that even Green's

---

[53] Letter from F.H. Bradley to William James, 14 May 1909, in F.H. Bradley, *Selected Correspondence January 1905–June 1924*, ed. Carol A. Keene (Bristol: Thoemmes, 1999), p. 92. See also his letter to G.F. Stout, 26 January 1893, in his *Selected Correspondence June 1872–December 1904*, ed. Carol A. Keene (Bristol: Thoemmes, 1999), pp. 60–63.

[54] T.M. Lindsay, 'Recent Hegelian Contributions to English Philosophy', *Mind*, 2:8 os (October 1877), 476.

[55] See Tyler, *Idealist Political Philosophy*, chapter 3.

[56] Charles Stuart Parker, 'Recollections', in Tyler, ed., 'Recollections Regarding T.H. Green', 58.

[57] Parker, 'Recollections', 59.

[58] Parker, 'Recollections', 59; on Green's later aversion to Aristotle, see Wempe, *T.H. Green's Theory of Positive Freedom*, pp. 49–55 passim.

[59] Newman, 'Recollections', 27.

[60] Aristotle, *Politics*, 1323a14.

[61] Nettleship, 'Memoir', pp. xiv–xv.

mature conception of 'ethics' accords better with Aristotle's theory of the good life as a state of being for the soul of the individual, rather than as a theory of legitimate other-regarding action and personal moral responsibility. Similarly, it can be argued that his theory of the eternal consciousness has definite overtones of Aristotle's 'prime mover', an influence that he himself gestured toward even if he did so cautiously (see §4.II).[62] More than this, Aristotle constructs his theory using other concepts and propositions which Green also takes to be pivotal: distinctively human action, the 'divine principle', self-consciousness, theoretical and practical reason, eudaimonia, virtue and the common good, in addition to the interrelation between human nature and the proper structure of the collective life.[63] There are other similarities between their respective assessments of the value of pleasure, and methodologically in their respective appeals to common judgements (as opposed to mere conventional prejudices).[64] Certainly, Aristotle and Green differ at crucial points in their respective interpretations of these various aspects (most explicitly in relation to virtue, and in the relative importance of the lives of contemplation and of citizenship), but clearly Green learnt much from Aristotle, presumably when a school pupil, a student and an academic, in addition to what he accumulated indirectly through Aristotle's numerous and frequently inchoate influences on Victorian culture.[65] Indeed, Green seems to have been much more heavily influenced by Aristotle than he was by Plato, even though Green's proposals for school reform echo strongly Plato's *Republic*.[66]

Green corrected Aristotle with the idealist tradition and not least with Kant, putting particular weight on the latter's metaphysics and ethics (especially the 'good will', 'categorical imperative' and 'kingdom of ends').[67] As Ritchie pointed out, this is in effect what Hegel did as well, although Green seems to have redone this work independently of Hegel's treatment.[68] Even if we do not know when Green first read Kant, there is some evidence that he was already an idealist when he came under Jowett's influence at Oxford in 1855.[69] He had already been heavily influenced by Thomas Carlyle, who had definite idealist sympathies.[70] As a schoolboy he also read and occasionally went to hear speak Christian Socialists, such as F.D. Maurice and Charles Kingsley, managing to make Henry Sidgwick 'believe in

---

[62] 'Aristotle' 88.
[63] These themes recur throughout Aristotle's works, but the following are some significant passages: distinctively human action, *Ethics*, book 1, chapter vii, 10.v; the 'divine principle', *Ethics* 10.vii; self-consciousness, including theoretical and practical reason, *Ethics* 6; eudaimonia, *Ethics* 1.vii–xii, *Politics* 7.i–iii; virtue, *Ethics* especially 2 to 7; the common good, *Politics* 1.i.
[64] For example, Aristotle's *Ethics*: pleasure, book 10, chapters i–v; common judgements, book 1, chapters iii–iv, viii.
[65] See, for example, PE 246–90 *passim*, 'Aristotle', and, on the wider background, Frank M. Turner, *Greek Heritage in Victorian Britain* (New Haven and London: Yale University Press, 1981).
[66] See, for example, 'Grading', 'Elementary' and 'Oxford High School'.
[67] This comes most clearly of course in Green's 'Kant'.
[68] David G. Ritchie, *Principles of State Interference: Four essays on the political philosophy of Mr. Herbert Spencer, J.S. Mill, and T.H. Green*, third edition (London: Swan Sonnenschein, 1902), p. 139.
[69] See Sidgwick's well-known Newbold Bridge story, in Sidgwick, 'Reminiscences of T.H.G.', in Tyler, ed., 'Recollections Regarding Thomas Hill Green', 12, also in Nettleship, 'Memoir', p. xv.
[70] Sidgwick, 'Reminiscences of T.H.G.', 10–11; see also Nettleship, 'Recollections', 34.

Kingsley as a social reformer'.[71] Further unsettling the received picture of Green's philosophy as 'Hegelian', there is R.L. Nettleship's observation that even as an undergraduate Green had read many other writers who articulated positions that were very similar to those he later praised in Hegel:

> The writers from whom he seems at his time to have assimilated the most were Wordsworth, Carlyle, Maurice, and probably Fichte in his lectures on the "nature" and "vocation" of "the scholar" and of "man." In them he found the congenial idea of a divine life or spirit pervading the world, making nature intelligible, giving unity to history, embodying itself in states and churches, and inspiring individual men of genius.[72]

In his recollections of Green, Henry Nettleship refers to a trip to Dresden that he took with Green and a group of other Oxford and Cambridge men in August 1862, at which time, he wrote, 'I think [Green was] beginning to study German philosophy'. Nettleship records that Green read Goethe's *Wilhelm Meister* and does not mention Hegel. Even at this age and so apparently before he had made a serious study of Hegel's own writings, Green was attracted to writers who emphasised man's place at the centre of his world, seeing a necessary union and coherence of the outward world and the inward being of the individual.[73] This endorsement comes through clearly in his admiration for certain romantic poets. For example, in 1868 he wrote that Wordworth's philosophy

> led man up to the recognition of his own greatness, as universalised by communion with nature and intercourse with his kind. It was conversant, not with the subtleties of the imagination, but with the great, the obvious, the habitual, with the common earth, the universal sky, the waters rolling evermore, the abiding social powers that lift man out of his animal self, and render him "magnanimous to correspond with heaven" …[74]

In addition to his very frequent invocations of John Milton and Wordsworth (including his generous reported description of the latter's 'Ode to Duty' as 'the high-water-mark of modern poetry'),[75] in the second of his 1874 introductions to his

---

[71] Sidgwick, "Reminiscences of T.H.G.", 12; Nettleship, "Memoir", p. xiv. 'Of Henry Sidgwick he used to say: "I can never think of him but as the chubby pot-bellied little Rugby boy." Letter from Symonds to Charlotte Green et al, 7 October 1882, in Symonds, *Letters*, vol. 2, p. 774.

[72] Nettleship, 'Memoir', p. xxv.

[73] Sibree's translation of Hegel's *Philosophy of History* appeared in early 1858, and it seems very likely that Green would have read it. He seems to have read it by the time he wrote the first Ellerton Essay, which was submitted for the competition on 11 April 1860 (Ellerton 1).

[74] 'Popular Philosophy' 120, quoting John Milton, *Paradise Lost, with variorum notes* (London: Samuel Holdsworth, 1841), book 7, l. 511. Compare 'Popular Philosophy' 117–20; also 'There wanted yet the master-work, the end / Of all yet done; a creature, who, not prone / And brute as other creatures, but endu'd / With sanctity of reason, might erect / His stature, and upright with front serene / Govern the rest, self-knowing; and from thence / Magnanimous, to correspond with heaven: / But grateful to acknowledge whence his good / Descends; thither with heart, and voice, and eyes / Directed in devotion, to adore / And worship God Supreme, who made him chief / Of all his works:' John Milton, *Paradise Lost*, book 7, ll. 505–16.

[75] Nettleship, 'Memoir', p. xviii; 'At Coniston & in rambles over the Lake Country [in 1860] I learned through him to appreciate the ruder & sterner aspects of nature & to feel Wordsworth. He was splendid face to face with storm or mist upon the crags – so full of vigour & of keen life – yet always apprehensive of danger.' Letter from Symonds to Charlotte Green *et al*, 7 October

edition of Hume Green lists 'Wesley, Wordsworth, Fichte, Mazzini, and the German theologians' as awakening the current English generation to the inadequacies of utilitarian explanations of 'large fields of human experience'.[76] There were other influences as well of course. John St Loe Strachey, Green's nephew by marriage, recorded that while staying at Green's house in the mid-1870s, in addition to Wordsworth and Carlyle (especially the latter's *Letters and Speeches of Oliver Cromwell*), Green's favourite reading matter was John Milton, Jonathan Swift and William Shakespeare, as well as William Cowper's 'Boadicea, An ode', Alexander Pope's 'Essay on Man', Arthur Young's various 'Tours', volumes of *State Trials*, the *Annual Register* and *Parliamentary Debates*.[77]

Of these influences, Green's debts to J.G. Fichte in particular are ripe for further research, not least in light of a recent suggestion that Fichte himself should be understood as a liberal socialist.[78] At present they are mentioned only occasionally in the secondary literature and are never explored in any depth.[79] The following remarks serve as suggestions of starting-points for such research. Paul Harris and John Morrow are correct when they note that 'on at least one crucial point, the centrality of personality, Green is far closer to Fichte than to Hegel.'[80] Certainly, Fichte was being discussed in Oxford at this time.[81] In 1864, Walter Pater's first essay to the Old Mortality on Fichte's notion of the ideal student caused much controversy due to Pater's denial of the immortality of the soul. The extent of Green's involvement with these discussions remains unclear, although one can presume that he would have been very well informed about Pater's paper at least, and probably actively involved in the meeting at which it was presented, given that he had been a leading member of the Society since he first joined in the Easter term 1858.[82] Green's contemporaries were divided over any direct influence. For example, even though Ritchie accepted Andrew Seth's observation that similarities existed between Green and Fichte's thought, he did not believe that Fichte had been a significant influence on Green's philosophy: 'so far as I know, Green himself was never in any special way a student of Fichte'.[83] Against this view

---

1882, in Symonds, *Letters*, vol. 2, p. 772.

[76] 'Hume II' 64.

[77] John St Loe Strachey, 'Recollections', in Tyler, ed., 'Recollections Regarding T.H. Green', 65–66.

[78] Nedim Nomer, 'Fichte and the Idea of Liberal Socialism', *Journal of Political Philosophy*, 13:1 (2005), 53–73.

[79] Paul Harris and John Morrow, 'Introduction', to T.H. Green, *Lectures on the Principles of Political Obligation, and other writings*, ed. Paul Harris and John Morrow (Cambridge: Cambridge University Press, 1986), pp. 2, 7–8; Thom Brooks, Review of Colin Tyler, *Thomas Hill Green (1836–1882)...*, *Bulletin of the Hegel Society of Great Britain*, nos. 51–52 (2005), 143.

[80] Harris *et al.*, 'Introduction', p. 7.

[81] Gerald Monsman, 'Pater, Hopkins, and Fichte's Ideal Student', *South Atlantic Quarterly*, 70 (1971), 365–76; see also William Wallace, 'Relations of Fichte and Hegel to Socialism', in his *Lectures and Essays on Natural Theology and Ethics*, ed. Edward Caird (Oxford: Clarendon, 1898), pp. 427–47.

[82] Gerald C. Monsman, 'Old Mortality at Oxford', *Studies in Philology*, 67:3 (July 1970), 360. The whole article provides interesting background (*ibid.*, 359–89). Pater's essay does not appear to have survived.

[83] David George Ritchie, Review of Andrew Seth, *Hegelianism and Personality*, *Mind*, 13 (1888), 256, citing Andrew Seth, *Hegelianism and Personality* (Edinburgh and London: William Blackwood,

stands Lewis Nettleship's remark, quoted above, that 'probably' Green read at least some pieces from Fichte's *Popular Works* as a young man, and read Fichte again towards the end of his life.[84] Moreover, contrary to Harris and Morrow's claim that the 'theological form' Green gave to his normative philosophy was unrelated to Fichte's influence, Green's re-reading of Fichte's *On the Nature of the Scholar* does seem to be reflected in his invocation at one crucial stage of the *Prolegomena* of the notion of the 'divine idea' (a notion that seems to have been at the heart of the Pater controversy).[85] Green also frequently uses the term 'vocation' in a Fichtean sense, especially when characterising the individual's telos in the *Prolegomena*.[86] He also quotes Fichte in German in the *Prolegomena*, and includes a translation of the same passage in his 'Lectures on Kant'.[87] In fact, Fichte's more pervasive influence seems to be evident also in what will be argued in the remainder of this book to be the self-generating notion of personality and, indeed, in the structure and content of Green's metaphysics more generally.

In a similar vein, James Allard has reminded scholars of Hermann Lotze's influence on British philosophy, and not least of Green's evident respect for Lotze's *System der Philosophie*.[88] There is much to be said for this link. In his preface to the English edition of Lotze's *System* initiated by Green, Bosanquet reported Green's remark that 'The time which one spent on such a book as that (the "Metaphysic") would not be wasted as regards one's own work.'[89] Allard develops Nettleship's intriguing conjecture that Green was drawn to Lotze's philosophy as a more successful alternative to Hegel's logic.[90] Clearly Green thought it was worth undertaking a significant portion of the translation of Lotze's *Metaphysic* himself and organising others to do the rest.[91] It is important however to exercise some caution here. There is no direct evidence for this conjecture (which is not to say that Nettleship and Allard are incorrect). Moreover, Green's reported comment to Bosanquet that 'The time which one spent on … (the "Metaphysic") would not

---

1887), p. 39.

[84]   Nettleship, 'Memoir', pp. xxv, cxxv.

[85]   Harris *et al.*, 'Introduction', p. 8. Green uses the phrase 'divine idea' at PE 183–84, 190, 247. Compare to Fichte, 'On the Nature of the Scholar', in Johann G. Fichte, *Popular Works*, trans. William Smith, fourth edition, 2 vols. (London: Trubner, 1889), vol. 1, especially lectures I and II. Moreover, his 'Fragment on Immortality' echoes at least one reading of Fichte's conception of immortality, the one apparently presented by Pater in his 1864 essay (see Monsman, 'Pater, Hopkins, and Fichte's Ideal Student', 370–74).

[86]   Green uses the phrase 'vocation of man' at PE 173, and refers to man's telos as his 'vocation' in essentially the same manner at PE 164, 176, 197, 237, 240, 250, 285, 353.

[87]   PE 193; also 'As Fichte says, "As surely as man is man, so surely is he aware of a necessity laid upon him to do something, quite irrespectively of ulterior objects, simply that it may be done, and to abstain from doing something else simply that it may not be done." ' ('Kant' 94) Green does not say where this passage occurs in Fichte's writings.

[88]   Allard, *Bradley's Metaphysics*, pp. 21–22.

[89   Bernard Bosanquet, 'Editor's Preface', in Rudolf Hermann Lotze, *Logic in three books of thought, of investigation, and of knowledge*, English translation ed. Bernard Bosanquet (Oxford: Clarendon, 1884), p. v.

[90]   Nettleship, 'Memoir', p. cxxv.

[91]   The published English edition includes Green's own translations of Book 1 and Book 3, chapter 3, in Rudolf Herman Lotze, *Metaphysic in Three Books: Ontology, Cosmology, and Psychology*, ed. Bernard Bosanquet, 2 vols. (Oxford: Clarendon, 1884), vol. 1, pp.1–229, 315–56.

be wasted as regards one's own work'[92] becomes less remarkable when contrasted with his even more laudatory comment which A.D. Liddell reported to Charlotte Green that 'reading [Goethe's] Faust was an "epoch in a man's life"'.[93]

It is very likely that Green organised and contributed to the translation of works that he thought were wrongly neglected by English readers. One can only really find solid evidence that Green knew of Lotze for the period after his appointment as Whyte's Professor, when he initiated the project to translate Lotze's *System der Philosophie*.[94] In fact, the work on Lotze was unusual predominantly in the sense that it was actually completed. It is worth remembering that the English edition that eventually appeared formed part of what might be called the 'Green memorial writings', that is writings that were produced in the 1880s to continue the work of the dead hero and to spread his influence. The most obvious examples of other such writings are Green's own posthumous *Works*, Lewis Nettleship's *Memoir*, the collection *Essays in Philosophical Criticism* edited by Andrew Seth and R.B. Haldane, and Mrs Humphry Ward's *Robert Elsmere*.[95] In this sense, Green's translation of Lotze benefited from Green's death in a way that other of his projected translations did not. For example, the new translation of Aristotle's *Ethics* which he planned with Edward Caird was shelved.[96] Similarly, his planned and partially executed translation of F.C. Baur's *Church History of the First Three Centuries* progressed slowly from 1863 until 1878 when the Rev. Allan Menzie's English translation was published.[97] Other partial translations also survive among Green's Balliol papers, although of varying extent and in varying degrees polish. These works, most of which Nettleship catalogued rather disingenuously for modern eyes as 'analyses', include important and often extensive sections of Plato's *Republic*, Aristotle's *De Anima* and the *Politics*, Kant's *Groundwork of the Metaphysics of Morals* and his *Critique of Practical Reason*, as well as Hegel's *Philosophical Propaedeutic*, and the section on 'Das Natturecht' from *Gott und der Mensch* (1866–73, second edition 1874) a book written by Hermann Ulrici, himself an associate of Johann Gottlieb Fichte's son Immanuel Hermann Fichte.[98]

---

[92] Bernard Bosanquet, 'Editor's Preface', in Lotze, *Logic*, p. v.

[93] Letter from A.D. Liddell to Charlotte Byron Green, 6 July 1882 (1.b.7 (new cataloguing system), Green's Papers, Balliol College, Oxford). Liddell does not specify that it meant Goethe's *Faust*, but it seems the most likely option. The most likely alternative would be Christopher Marlowe's 1604 play *The Tragical History of Dr Faustus*. Similarly: 'He showed me many fine things in Goethe's poems – espy the Proemium to Gott und Welt.' Letter from Symonds to Charlotte Green, 7 October 1887, in Symonds, *Letters*, vol. II, p. 774.

[94] Nettleship, 'Memoir', p. cxxv.

[95] Green, *Works*; Nettleship, 'Memoir'; Seth, Andrew and Richard B. Haldane, eds., *Essays in Philosophical Criticism* (London: Longmans, Green 1883) and Mary A. Ward, *Robert Elsmere*, 2 vols. (London: Macmillan, 1888). One might also add Ritchie, *Principles of State Interference* and W.H. Fairbrother, *Philosophy of Thomas Hill Green* (London: Methuen, 1896). J.H. Muirhead, *Service of the State: Four lectures on the political teaching of T.H. Green* (London: John Murray, 1908) seems a little too late to be part of what I refer to as the 'Green memorial writings'.

[96] Green's 'Philosophy of Aristotle' is styled as a review of the second revised version of Sir Alexander Grant's edition of Aristotle's *Ethics* (first edition published in 1857, second edition 1866, third edition 1874).

[97] Letter from Green to Mrs Blanche Clough, 12 December 1869, in *Works* 5, pp. 431–33, and especially the associated editorial note (p. 432n50).

[98] For the references to these various 'analyses', see Thomas, *Moral Philosophy of T.H. Green*, pp.

The question even remains open as to whether Green favoured Lotze's *System* over works that he did not begin to translate for his students. This applies not least in regard to those works that Green had no need to translate. For example, there were various English editions of Kant, an English edition of Fichte's *Popular Works* which had appeared in 1848 and 1849 (with revised editions appearing in 1859 and 1873, and many of the component discourses appearing separately slightly earlier in the 1840s), John Sibree's 1857 English translation of the *Philosophy of History*, selections from Hegel's 'greater' *Logic* in J.H. Stirling's 1865 *Secret of Hegel* and William Wallace's 1874 translation of the smaller *Logic*.[99]

One must be careful, then, about attributing too great an influence to Lotze. One must be just as careful when assessing J.S. Mill's influence on Green. Certainly, a significant community of interest exists between them, not least in that both place a theory of self-realisation at the hearts of their respective normative positions. Yet, none of Green's contemporaries claimed that Green derived his theory of self-realisation from Mill. Moreover, although Green admired Mill on a personal level, he was highly critical of Mill's logic, and he seemed more willing to countenance 'a great social resolution which would be called the tyranny of the majority' against the brewing interest.[100] Mill's influence on Green's discussion of economics seems to have been overstated also. Rather than citing the former's *Principles of Political Economy* as Green's primary source for the latter part of the 'Notes on ancient and modern political economy' as do Paul Harris and John Morrow, one might turn instead to Guiseppe Mazzini.

Green's discussion of the right to property in the *Principles of Political Obligation* draws on Mazzini's chapter on 'The Economical Question' in the latter's *Duties of Man*.[101] His claim that 'Landless countrymen, whose ancestors were serfs, are

381, 383–84 *passim*.

[99] James Hutchison Stirling, *Secret of Hegel: Being the Hegelian System in Origin, Principle, Form, and Matter*, 2 vols. (Edinburgh: Oliver and Boyd, 1865), the second edition appeared in 1898. Johann G. Fichte: *On the Nature of the Scholar and its Manifestations* (London: John Chapman, 1845), *The Destination of Man*, trans. P. Sinnett (London: Chapman, 1846), *Vocation of the Scholar*, trans. W. Smith (London: John Chapman, 1847), *Vocation of Man* (London: John Chapman, 1848). See Daniel Breazeale, 'Introduction', in Fichte, *Popular Works*, vol. 1, pp. xxii–xxvi.

[100] 'One of the last books that he read was the *Journals and letters of Caroline Fox*, and it drew from him the remark that he would rather have been Mill than Carlyle, "he seemed to have been such an extraordinarily good man." Nettleship, 'Memoir', p. cxliv. 'Logic' 34–144; 'They should remove that which made morality impossible. They had been told by some that they ought to trust to education, moral suasion, and the improvement of the dwellings of the poor for altering the present state of things [in relation to alcoholism and the power of the brewing interest], but he did not find that people who told them this were most active in promoting them. However useful the various agencies employed for elevating working men were, none of them would be effective until they had broken the back of the drink traffic by a great social resolution which would be called the tyranny of the majority.' Green, *Works*, 5, p. 245 (speech under the auspices of the Oxford Auxiliary of the United Kingdom Alliance, 24 November 1874). See also Carter, Matt, *T.H. Green and the Ethical Socialist Tradition* (Exeter: Imprint Academic, 2003), pp. 10–11, especially references in p. 10n27.

[101] Harris *et al.*, 'Notes', in Harris et al, eds., *T.H. Green*, pp. 365–66 *passim*; Joseph Mazzini, *Life and Writings*, 6 vols., new edition (London: Smith, Elder, 1891), vol. 4, pp. 335–65. On Green's admiration for Mazzini, whose *Duties of Man* was published in 1862, see Nettleship, 'Memoir', pp. xlii–xliv; letter from Green to Henry Scott Holland, 6 October 1872, *Works* 5, p. 442; see also A.V. Dicey, 'Recollection', in Tyler, ed., 'Recollections regarding T.H. Green', 21–22.

the parents of the proletariate of great towns' seems to echo Mazzini's statement that 'You were first *slaves*, then *serfs*. Now you are *hirelings*.'[102] Mazzini invokes Proudhon's claim that the poor's title to their property is so unenforced legally as to not really warrant being understood as a meaningful right at all, a claim that one finds in Green as well.[103] For Mazzini as for Green, custom and legislation, rather than the unfettered workings of the free market, are the most significant sources of the injustices of the current distribution of property.[104] Green's emphasis on associational life over state centralism, and even the derivation of rights and duties from the demands of the common good, also find their precursors in Mazzini even if in terms that are underdeveloped philosophically.[105] These and other debts to Mazzini help to give substance to A.V. Dicey's observation that as undergraduates he, Green and the other members of the Old Mortality were 'advanced radicals, not to say Republicans'.[106] This was an affiliation that Green at least retained for the rest of his life. Nevertheless, Green was a critical reader of Mazzini as he was of all his sources. Witness, for example, his rejection of Mazzini's claim that Humanity as a single entity can 'progress'.[107] Moreover, if Mazzini was a significant source for Green, Green had to develop his own philosophical underpinnings for his thought as they are not provided by Mazzini himself.

Given the range of influences discussed in this section, it is interesting to reflect on David Ritchie's observation from 1891 that

> It is rather common to hear [Green] classed as one of "the English school of Hegelians." He would certainly not have acknowledged the title himself, and it is really inaccurate – unless it be very carefully qualified. If we are to connect him with any particular names of philosophers, it would be least misleading to say that he corrected Kant by Aristotle and Aristotle by Kant.[108]

There is a great deal of truth in this (see also §§7.II, 8.VI). In addition to the debts to Aristotle noted above, Green lectured extensively on Kant for many years, and his own positive writings on the 'metaphysics of experience or knowledge' and ethics, invoke Kant frequently and explicitly.[109] Nevertheless, hopefully the preceding discussion of Green's influences has indicated also that the real picture is far more complex. For all of the depths of his appreciation of Kant's momentous achievements, Green remained a critical reader throughout his

---

[102] Mazzini, *Duties of Man*, p. 343; PPO 229.

[103] PPO 221. Mazzini, *Duties of Man*, pp. 338–49 *passim*.

[104] Mazzini, *Duties of Man*, pp. 346–49.

[105] Mazzini, *Duties of Man*, associational life, chapter 10; common good, pp. 221–22.

[106] A.V. Dicey, quoted in William Knight, *Memoir of John Nichol* (Glasgow: MacLehose, 1896), p. 140; see Tyler, *Idealist Political Philosophy*, especially chapter 2, and Colin Tyler, 'Contesting the Common Good: T.H. Green and contemporary republicanism', in Maria Dimova-Cookson and W.J. Mander, eds., *T.H. Green: Ethics, metaphysics and political philosophy* (Oxford: Clarendon, 2006), pp. 262–91 *passim*.

[107] PE 181, 184–85.

[108] Ritchie, *Principles of State Interference*, p. 139.

[109] Virtually any of Green's writings on epistemology and ethics could be cited in evidence of Kant's influence on Green, but the most obvious and philosophically important ones are 'Kant' and PE *passim*.

adult life. Moreover, in addition to Plato, Aristotle, Scripture especially St. Paul, Milton, Swift, Kant, Goethe, Burke, Fichte, Hegel, the Tübingen school especially Baur,[110] Wordsworth, Carlyle, Maurice, Kingsley, Mazzini and Lotze, one can find many other important influences: Locke on Green's theories of relations and civil disobedience, say, or Rousseau's theory of the general will on his theory of community. In this sense, Green is not unusual, as almost every thinker worth studying is informed by a plethora of influences, even if, as he is, they tend to be drawn from one loose intellectual tradition. One thing can be said however is that the particular combination of influences drawn on by Green should make one deeply sceptical about the recent attempt to ally him with Christian moralism understood as 'the ideal of conscience and service' to the exclusion of the romantic Goethean 'ideal of individuality'.[111] The contrast between Christian moralism and Goethean romanticism is too crude to capture the nuances of Green's position, as will become clearer below and as will be made clear provisionally at least, towards the end of this book (§8.IV). As a consequence, Green's thought marks far less of a break from that of J.S. Mill (the conclusion drawn from the recent use of the contrast), and his thought is far less institutionalised, moralistic and dower than the next generation liked to portray him. Fortunately, the new scholarship on Green is helping to expose the 'Edwardianism' of the stream of hostile critics that held sway almost until the present day.

Unfortunately, even Green's now-apparent intellectual pluralism may not allay totally the fears of contemporary philosophers that are created by his stated aspiration to produce a coherent philosophical system. It might seem to anyone who is not sensitive to his fallibilism that he has escaped the irrationality of religion only to be caught in the excessive intellectualism of a dogmatic philosophy. To establish that this is not the case, it is important to analyse what Green meant by 'system' and the way in which he sought to formulate it. This is the subject of the next section of this chapter.

IV
Green's Philosophical System

Green drew on a great variety of influences from a range of modes of human discourse when constructing his philosophical system: philosophical and theological texts, poetry and novels, as well as social norms, conventions and established institutions. Yet, 'popular philosophy' is also an amalgam of these sources: 'It is an abstract or result of the various methods, poetic, religious, metaphysical, by which man has sought to account to himself for the world of his experience, as they apply directly to human life.'[112] For Green, popular philosophy is deficient most fundamentally, however, because it is unsystematic. Given the weight accorded to this difference, it becomes especially important to ask how one does actually square

---

[110] On Green's admiration for Edmund Burke and F.C. Baur, see letter from Symonds to Charlotte Symonds *et al.*, 7 October 1882, in Symonds, *Letters*, vol. 2, pp. 774, 775.

[111] John Skorupski, 'Green and the Idealist Conception of a Person's Good', in Dimova-Cookson *et al.*, eds., *T.H. Green*, p. 72; see further pp. 72–75.

[112] 'Popular Philosophy' 97.

Green's own intellectual pluralism with his claim that one should understand his philosophy as a 'logical system of beliefs'?[113] Thom Brooks has argued against such a reading: 'I remain unconvinced', he writes, 'that this systematic approach to studying Green's thought adds something new to our understanding of how we should read his work.'[114] He continues a little later:

> I take it that an internal critique of Green's system may find certain inconsistencies in his system. The question then becomes: "what counts as part of the system"? Only those parts that are internally consistent with the rest of the system? Or, if we find inconsistencies, does this mean that the system is itself problematic?[115]

In Henry Sidgwick's words, how does one 'distinguish the contradictions which' one takes 'to be evidence of error from those which' one regards 'as intimations of higher truth'?[116] The first point to make in response seems uncontroversial: any system – and indeed any argument – is problematic when inconsistencies (or omissions or indeterminacies) are present, and the seriousness of those problems depends in part on the significance for the wider system or argument of the points at which they occur. This issue does not seem specific to Green or even to systematic thinking as such: how damaging is the mere possibility of these deficiencies in, say, Rawls's theory of justice or Nietzsche's critique of Christian morality? It is simply a difficulty to be faced by every philosophical argument and not merely philosophical systems per se.

The second point to make in response to Brooks is one of scope. As was noted above (and in the first edition), the following book is concerned with what I claim to be Green's mature system: the one he set out primarily in his writings after 1878, when he became Whyte's Professor of Moral Philosophy.[117] My focus is on this period in Green's intellectual life because I take seriously Nettleship's claim that it was only after this time that Green 'was able to develop his principles more systematically than the position of a college tutor and the requirements of the examinations had hitherto allowed'.[118] I take this claim seriously because it is clear that Green aspired to articulate a philosophy that was true, and, as is established at length in chapters three and four, he held truth to be a quality of a coherent system of thought. Indeed, even in 'Popular Philosophy in its Relation to Life', Green highlighted the systematic nature of true philosophy: 'Philosophy does but interpret, *with full consciousness and system*, the powers already working in the spiritual life of mankind'.[119] Moreover, Green structures the *Prolegomena* so as to make it form a systematic whole, although with some digressions to applications of it as a critical tool for assessing and correcting divergent doctrines, especially

---

[113] PE 1.

[114] Brooks, Review of Tyler, *Thomas Hill Green*, 141.

[115] Brooks, Review of Tyler, *Thomas Hill Green*, 143.

[116] Henry Sidgwick, reported by F.C.S. Schiller, in A. Sidgwick and E.M. Sidgwick, *Henry Sidgwick: A memoir* (London: MacMillan, 1906), p. 586n1.

[117] Alberto de Sanctis for one focuses on an earlier period, in his *'Puritan' Democracy of T.H. Green, with some unpublished writings* (Exeter: Imprint Academic, 2005).

[118] Nettleship, 'Memoir', p. cxxv.

[119] 'Popular Philosophy' 93, emphasis added.

in relation to ancient Greek ethics and utilitarianism.[120] Moreover, the material that makes up the *Prolegomena* forms the foundations of Green's *Lectures on the Principles of Political Obligation* and was presented in that order to his students.[121] Green refined his earlier thoughts to arrive at this system, meaning that one can also make careful use of texts written prior to 1878.[122] Indeed, this may go some way to explaining Green's initial caution about publishing parts of the *Prolegomena* in the journal *Mind*.

Nevertheless, Brooks is quite correct to raise the question of the nature of Green's system or, in the phrase the latter uses in a slightly different context, a 'logical system of beliefs'.[123] Green does not give a clear statement of what he takes the structure of a philosophical system to consist in. There are clues however. Most fundamentally and as will be established in chapter three, Green holds that the primary datum from which knowledge can be gleaned is experience. To become elements of an intellectual system, particular ideas must be intelligible, and related to other elements that are part of what Oakeshott would call the same 'mode'.[124] The central philosophical activities are to seek 'to reject what is temporary and accidental in [one's intellectual and wider cultural context], while retaining what is essential', for only in this way is it possible to 'disentangle the operative ideas from their necessarily imperfect expression'.[125] Philosophically, the latter requires that ideas are gleaned from experience via processes of analysis and inference, before being rationally and fully articulated (rather than being apprehended in mere 'feeling' as with poetry, or divine revelation and imagination as with religion). In this sense, philosophy is the master mode which seeks to draw out permanent but partial truths that are struggling to find expression in other modes of intellectual life, before attempting to organise them into a complete and internally-consistent system of true propositions.[126] (The earlier discussion of Green's religious thought provides one example of this process (§2.II).)

What does Green mean when he styles the connections between these elements as 'logical'?[127] A more complete answer is given below in chapter three and, for the moment, I simply suggest the following as a reading. First, it is important to appreciate that Green is one of those 'who identify logic and metaphysic; who hold that the question of logic, What is the method by which knowledge is attained? is inseparable from the question of metaphysic, What are the necessary forms (the primary relations) of the objects of knowledge or the objective world?'[128] More specifically, he grounds his metaphysics on his logic understood as the processes

---

[120] See Green's letter to G. Croom Roberts, 16 June 1881, in *Works* 5, pp. 483–84.

[121] Nettleship, 'Memoir', p. cxxv.

[122] Green's recently published early philosophy lectures anticipate the *Prolegomena* in many ways, for example ('Sittlichkeit').

[123] PE 1. On the systematic nature of Green's philosophy, see also Andrew Vincent, 'Metaphysics and Ethics in the Philosophy of T.H. Green', in Dimova-Cookson *et al.*, eds., *T.H. Green*, especially p. 90.

[124] Michael Oakeshott, *Experience and its Modes* (Cambridge: Cambridge University Press, 1933).

[125] PE 279, 319.

[126] See, for example, PE 1–8 *passim*.

[127] PE 1.

[128] 'Logic' 1.

of analysis (the task of the philosopher in her role as what will be called below a 'critical metaphysician') and inference (or 'synthesis') (in her role as a 'speculative metaphysician'). Green saw these as complementary processes that issued in the growth of knowledge. It is through them that one is able 'to disentangle the operative ideas from their necessarily imperfect expression'.[129] This growth is achieved through the exercise of 'thought', itself conceived as 'a process from the more abstract to the more concrete'.[130]

> Thus "concrete" objects are gradually constituted by a process which is conjointly one of synthesis and analysis. It is not that there is first analysis and then synthesis, or *vice versa*, but that in and with the putting together of experiences, the world before us, which is *for us* to begin with confusedly everything and definitely nothing, is resolved into distinctness; or, conversely, that as resolved into distinctness, it assumes definite features which can be combined. Every sensation attended to implies a detachment of it from the flux of successive feelings, and so far an analysis by which it and they are alike to a certain extent determined, and also a synthesis of it with them.[131]

The growth of knowledge is the move to a more determinate consciousness of a concrete whole of objective facts, underpinned by what Green calls on a number of occasions a 'world of experience'.[132] Knowledge is, then, the consciousness of the interrelation of those facts each of which presupposes a perfectly coherent (sc. internally consistent and complete) network of categories and laws of relation. Hence, I suggest that, for Green, one's 'system of beliefs' is 'logical' to the extent that the ways in which one conceives and relates one's beliefs presuppose this perfectly coherent network. In line with this position, Green holds all relations to be internal relations, and internal coherence to be the test of truth.[133] In practice however, human beings, taken individually and in communities, are imperfect beings. Consequently, the beliefs which they hold and the categories and relations presupposed by those beliefs, appear to be of two types: necessary and contingent. That this perceived division is a mark of human imperfection is made clear in the (shared) 'Rudiments' to Green's 1866 article on 'The Philosophy of Aristotle' and his 1868 article on 'Popular Philosophy':

> The universe involves a relation of two elements – necessary and contingent. That the contingent is not merely contingency is implied in the fact of its being in relation to the necessary. It is, in truth, that which is evermore being systematized and so becoming necessary. We may, however, abstract the necessary element from the contingent, and treat it as a system not yet applied to that which it systematizes, remembering at the same time that in its truth it implies such an application, i.e. that when thought *out* it is found to necessitate it.[134]

---

[129] PE 319. PE 319 refers to customs and the like, but his point applies for all conventional thoughts.
[130] 'Logic' 1, 32.
[131] 'Logic' 32.
[132] For example, PE 8, 10, 38–43, 50, 86; compare with 'Kant' 49–54, especially 54.
[133] PE 69. See also Harold H. Joachim, *Nature of Truth* (Oxford: Clarendon, 1906), chapter III.
[134] 'Rudiments' 3.

Finally, it should be noted that if they are to be true then these elements (beliefs) must be related to each other on the basis of a coherent common *a priori* organising principle: Presented in the rapt unreasoned form of poetic utterance, not professing to do more than represent a mood of the individual poet, it is welcomed by reflecting men as expressing deep convictions of their own. Such men seem little disturbed by the admission of a joint lodgement in their minds of inferences from popularised science, which do not admit of being reconciled with these deeper convictions in any logical system of beliefs.[135] It will be established in the fourth chapter that the agent arrives at a conception of this principle via a process akin to what Stendhal called later and in a different context 'crystallisation': 'a mental process which draws from everything that happens new proofs of the perfection of the loved one.'[136] In the present context, crystallisation drives the individual's continual effort to attain an ideal of perfect knowledge. In non-figurative terms, the organising principle offers hope that ultimately one could understand the world as reflecting a coherent system of fundamental concepts, an aspiration that acts as a spur to continued effort to formulate it, in spite of the irrationality and distortions of actual human beliefs and existence. In that it problematises these irrationalities and distortions, the principle also functions as a critical standard. One sketches as coherent a theory as one can using the fragments of which one is currently aware, before trying to identify ambiguities and lacunae. Crystallisation offers the hope that these ambiguities and lacunae could be removed at least in an ideal world, and that perfectly rational knowledge would then be achieved.

Green seeks, then, to draw out the meanings that are 'pregnant' within texts, institutions and practices, although, as with all internally complex experiences, they need to be handled with particular care.[137] The manner in which one should handle these elements must depend to some degree on the respective statuses that Green accords to them as building-blocks of that system.[138] He treats some elements of experience as given, or, more properly, critically endorsed, as they are fully accepted without alteration once the individual has critically assessed their initial authoritative status (initially this status was at best apparently self-evident). In this way, the individual takes 'epistemic responsibility' for these critically endorsed elements.[139] They form stable, inviolable if partially inchoate facts. They include the fact that individuals know things, and that the only objects of intrinsic value are individual persons as beings with higher capacities. Other examples include personal freedom and 'the mystery of our moral nature', which are brought together in 'the consciousness of a moral ideal and the determination of human action thereby'.[140] Moreover, the philosopher should attempt to articulate the practical

---

[135] PE 1.

[136] Stendhal, *Love*, trans. G. Sale and S. Sale (Harmondsworth: Penguin, 1975), p. 45.

[137] 'Watson' 148.

[138] This method is explored in greater depth in §§3.II, IV in the context of his 'metaphysics of experience or knowledge', and in the chapter regarding his theory of conscientious citizenship in my *Civil Society, Capitalism and the State*.

[139] David O. Brink, *Perfectionism and the Common Good: Themes in the philosophy of T.H. Green* (Oxford: Clarendon, 2003), pp. 20–21; see further §3.11 below.

[140] PE 8.

manifestations of the individual's moral nature in what is called 'according to the terminology in vogue', 'the phenomena of a moral life – to have a conscience, to feel remorse, to pursue ideals, to be capable of education through appeals to the sense of honour and of shame, to be conscious of antagonism between the common and private good, and even sometimes to prefer the former.'[141] Each of these is a facet of what Green describes in the last sentence of the *Prolegomena* as 'the theory of the ultimate good as a perfection of the human spirit resting on the will to be perfect (which may be called in short the theory of virtue as an end in itself)'.[142]

Other elements are to be treated as dissolvable appearances, while yet further elements are retained although in a reconceived form. The final elements are necessary presuppositions and necessary implications of the stable parts within the philosophical system. These parts interrelate in various ways. For example, and this is a profoundly important example as chapter four makes clear, Green holds it to be a solid fact that individual persons are the only entities that can have experiences, whereas God should be reconceived as the idea of a spiritual principle or eternal consciousness that is projected as an ideal that is necessary to make sense of the belief that individual persons know objectively true facts about the empirical and normative worlds. He argues that individual consciousnesses cannot be conceived coherently as epiphenomena (as mere adjuncts of a corporate consciousness), because it is only on the basis of accepting the existence of discrete individual consciousnesses that one has reason to believe in the existence of an eternal consciousness. Such a denial of the separateness of persons 'would be in contradiction of the very ground upon which we believe that a divine principle does so realise itself in [the individual] man'.[143] The philosopher must articulate, then, the sense in which the self of every person is both 'individual and universal'.[144]

The critically endorsed parts of one's experiences can find their appropriate places at any conceptual level of the philosophical system: as principles of metaphysics, ethics, social theory, political philosophy, or any other facet. The philosopher's analytic function consists in identifying, testing and critically endorsing these parts as well as reconceiving them where appropriate. Her synthetic function consists in explicating and systematising those stable parts so as to form a 'world'. There is an inherently reciprocal relationship between analysis and synthesis however, in that frequently the synthetic process exposes a need for certain parts to be reconceived (even reconceived once more). Constructing a coherent system is a never-ending project then.

One can get a further idea of what Green seems to have in mind from Brooks's own very brief statement of the sense in which Hegel had a system: 'With Hegel, each step of his dialectic follows necessarily from each preceding step.'[145] The problem is that it is notoriously unclear what Hegel means when he claims that a step is 'necessary'. Indeed, this vagueness is captured well (intentionally) in

---

[141] PE 7.
[142] PE 382.
[143] 'Popular Philosophy' 96; PE 182; compare PE 80–85, 99–102, 182.
[144] 'Popular Philosophy' 99–100.
[145] Brooks, Review of Tyler, *Thomas Hill Green*, 143.

Brooks's statement that 'there is allegedly some kind of logical link between the various claims. It is more than simply stating more than once a given view or position.'[146] Michael Inwood begins his analysis of the notion of 'system' in Kant, Hegel and Fichte with the fact that '*Systéma*', the Greek root of 'system', means simply 'an articulated whole composed of several parts'.[147] He goes on to note Kant's more precise definition: 'the unity of manifold cognitions under an idea. The idea is the rational concept of the form of a whole, in so far as the concept determines *a priori* both the scope of the whole and the place of the parts in relation to each other'.[148] The question remains for those who accept even Kant's more precise definition, whether there is only one objective system (one system that is complete and perfectly internally-consistent), or whether there can be a plurality of equally-valid systems. Inwood ascribes the former view to Hegel, and the latter to Fichte, whom he quotes from the First Introduction to the *Science of Knowledge*: 'What sort of philosophy one chooses depends on what sort of man one is; for a philosophical system is not a dead piece of furniture that we can accept or reject as we wish; it is animated by the soul of the person who holds it.'[149]

Accepting Inwood's characterisation for the sake of argument, does Green stand with Hegel's objectivism or Fichte's 'personal idiosyncrasy'? To the rather casual reader, it might seem that Green's writings contain elements of both. For example, at the same time that he holds that for the world to exist 'objectively', a certain single system of fundamental categories must be presupposed, he also asserts that 'we only find unity in the world because we have an idea that it is there, an idea which we direct our powers to realise', a claim that may imply some form of subjectivism.[150] This paradox can be resolved at least partially by distinguishing the presuppositions of one's beliefs from the implications of those presuppositions. We have seen already (and it will be argued at length in chapter three) that Green believes the philosopher should undertake analysis to discover presuppositions and inference to trace out implications, thereby fulfilling the twin functions of being respectively both a critical metaphysician and a speculative metaphysician. These processes are also defended in the 'Rudiments' to Green's articles on the 'Philosophy of Aristotle' and 'Popular Philosophy in its Relation to Life'. In these 'Rudiments', Green argues that:

> The metaphysician['s] … concern is with the analysis of that which is already known, and with the new synthesis which results therefrom. Penetrating the intelligible world, he seeks to disentangle its elements, and to "put them together" again no longer as a material presented from without, but as the complex realization, the organized body, of the spirit which contemplates them. … The ridicule which the assertion of such an office excites is a witness to its difficulty and remoteness from ordinary interests.[151]

---

[146] Brooks, Review of Tyler, *Thomas Hill Green*, 143–44.

[147] Michael Inwood, *Hegel Dictionary* (Oxford: Blackwell, 1992), p. 265.

[148] Kant, *Critique of Pure Reason*, A832, B860, as quoted in Inwood, *Hegel Dictionary*, p. 265.

[149] Fichte, *Science of Knowledge*, as quoted in Inwood, *Hegel Dictionary*, p. 266. One finds this claim also in F.C.S. Schiller, 'Axioms as Postulates', in Henry Sturt, ed., *Personal Idealism: Philosophical essays by eight members of the University of Oxford* (London: MacMillan, 1902), pp. 50–51.

[150] PE 149.

[151] 'Rudiments' 2. Problematically for those who wish to see a fundamental discontinuity between

As will be argued in chapter three, Green held that only the individual can carry out the requisite analysis and inference, and that the datum of analysis is experience, with the object being the full articulation of the unseen structures that determine reality.[152] For this reason, there will be as many different, imperfect networks (proto-systems, if you like) as there are individuals (a claim that forms the basis of Green's theory of conscientious agency, among other things). This plurality is manifested in all aspects of the individual's life: for example, the object that realises the true good 'will vary in different ages and with different persons, according to circumstances and idiosyncrasy.'[153] Each of these networks of categories is a particular, imperfect manifestation of the same perfectly coherent (sc. internally-consistent and complete) system of clearly specified categories. In this final regard, Green differs from Fichte, whose 'systems' are different from one another, even though they are at least in principle equally valid, with validity being assessed solely by their own respective determinate criteria for internal coherence. Green is closer here to Hegel than to Fichte then, in the sense that his networks are imperfect when measured according to the one ultimately coherent system. The networks are at best different potential routes to the same (actually unrealisable) end.

Green's pluralistic conception of system-building has profound implications for the character of his thought. For example, his belief that there are many routes to the same ideal sheds light on his attitude towards his sources. Most significantly, acknowledging Green's 'mid-wife' method helps one to appreciate that as well as reading texts whole he could dip into them in order to gain nuggets of insight, 'essential' elements or 'operative ideas'. This comes through clearly in Nettleship's 'Memoir'.

> Though he was constantly reproaching himself with his ignorance of philosophical literature, he never overcame his native repugnance to wide reading. He liked, as he used to say, to "browse" amongst books, and it was by brooding over the great saying of philosophers rather than by traversing their systems in detail, that he seemed to get most of his intellectual nourishment. His mind was reflective, not accumulative. He always seems to be strengthening his hold upon certain fundamental truths, and this tenacity arose, not from prejudice or the force of habit, but from a growing experience of their reasonableness. Probably no amount of extraneous reading would have materially affected his ultimate convictions[154]

Green's penchant for intellectual grazing raises the possibility of great intellectual pluralism in the influences on him, at the same time as exposing the unpredictability of precisely which elements he would appropriate from any one given text and in what ways he would integrate them into his own

---

the first (concerning 'Nature') and second (concerning 'Man') books of the *Prolegomena*, Green goes on: 'This gives the distinction between Logic and Metaphysic on the one hand, and the philosophy of Nature and Man (Spirit) which is the true *applied* Logic on the other.' ('Rudiments' 3); see also *ibid*. 3–4.

[152] I owe this way of phrasing the last point to Rex Martin (personal communication).

[153] PE 239.

[154] Nettleship, 'Memoir', pp. cxxv–vi.

philosophical system. There is a significant danger of distorting Green's system by attributing a determining role to any other philosopher, as many treatments come close to doing in effect although not in intention. If he did read 'independently' and pluralistically, then this makes it less profitable to try to interpret his system as, say, 'Aristotelian', 'neo-Aristotelian', 'Kantian', 'neo-Kantian', 'Fichtean', 'neo-Fichtean', 'Hegelian' or 'neo-Hegelian'. Avoiding this tendency, one should read his texts simply for what they are: namely, expressions of aspects of the Greenian philosophical system.

Every method has inherent problems, and Green's own systematising method is no exception. His aspiration 'to reject what is temporary and accidental ... while retaining what is essential'[155] can be a very dangerous one for a philosophical interpreter, just as certainly it is for an intellectual historian. Easily, it could lead a reader to misinterpret the chosen text by selecting out those elements of it that, for whatever reason, attract one's attention. The philosophical critic might be encouraged to make a tacit appeal to the authority of an earlier philosopher as a way of bolstering their own preferred philosophical position.

The interpretation presented below seeks to resist the temptation to exclude some elements of Green's system in order to present a message that was 'pregnant' within his writings, in the sense of struggling to find expression and thereby go beyond his actual, stated position.[156] It will be kept firmly in mind that Green is developing a philosophical system, rather than a series of discrete philosophical insights, and that the meaning and import of any particular element is ultimately a function of its place within that system. The following analysis rejects Green's mid-wife method then, asking instead which arguments in Green's writings are required philosophically in order to deliver his conclusions (that is, which are necessary parts of his philosophical system) and which are from a philosophical perspective unnecessary 'add-ons'. Clearly, this is not a straightforward task. At the end of chapter four, for example, I consider Nicholson's claim that humanising the eternal consciousness in the manner that I propose there, would radically undermine the theory's appeal even to Green himself. I argue there that while Nicholson's concerns are probably highly apposite and important for the historian, they are not significant philosophically. More generally, this book seeks to distinguish those arguments made in Green's writings that are required for his system to be coherent, from those that are inessential.[157]

The critical analysis that follows aims to suggest 'repairs' for essential aspects that are philosophically weak, and to reject the philosophically deficient inessential

---

[155] PE 279, 319.

[156] 'Watson' 148. See also Colin Tyler, 'Performativity and the Intellectual Historian's Re-enactment of Written Works', *Journal of the Philosophy of History*, 3:2 (2009), 167–186.

[157] It will become clear that a large part of the interpretative problem arises from Green's infamous writing style. The following passage is interesting in light of this and of the fact that A.C. Bradley divided many of Green's very long paragraphs while editing the manuscript of the *Prolegomena*: 'He had a theory, in composing, that all superfluous words should be extirpated – the fewest & most compressed used – that, if possible, an essay should consist of one indivisible paragraph, the connected expression of a single proposition or a single syllogism.' Letter from Symonds to Charlotte Green *et al.*, 7 October 1882, in Symonds, *Letters*, vol. 2, p. 776. The passage appears in Nettleship, 'Memoir', p. xxxvii as well.

elements, such as the theistic gloss that Green gives to his theory of the eternal consciousness. In that sense, I am 'more interested in defending a picture of Green's views with some minor (and some important) improvements, a picture that is more coherent than his original rendering'.[158] As was observed above then, mine is a philosophical analysis, critique and (as it turns out, limited) reformulation, rather than an intellectual history as such. Obviously, this is not to denigrate intellectual history, it is simply to note that intellectual history is not what is attempted in this book.

On a more general level, scholars such Brooks who raise serious doubts regarding such a method offer no better suggestions as to how one should deal with this type of ubiquitous and indeed unavoidable problem. Every interpretation and every philosophical assessment of a complex text requires the selection of some propositions as core and others as peripheral or even aberrant. This is especially the case with a work which has a strong central underlying message, even if it is not always clearly expressed. This book concludes that ultimately a few difficulties with Green's system do remain, but it is sensible to ask which philosophy has no difficulties? The real question is whether or not the project (Spencer's transfigured realism, Barry's liberal universalism, Kantianism, Rawlsianism, Hegelianism, and so on) remains viable. I believe that the following detailed analysis and internal critique of Green's system makes a strong case for the believing that Green's project has much more in its favour than many others (including many that currently are more popular in philosophical circles), and so is still worth pursuing.

V
Conclusion

It has been argued here that there is much more to be said in Green's favour than has been previously recognised. Rather than being a purveyor of dusty and dead arguments, he drew on a wide range of sources when developing his philosophical system. Experience was to be searched for the stable facts contained within the flux of personal experiences, and the metaphysician was then to distinguish them from dissolvable appearances and to reconceive other elements so as to draw out what was stable and of permanent value in each. The stable elements would then be used to form parts of a philosophical system. Yet, this chapter has sought only to introduce these ideas. The next chapter begins the critical analysis of Green's substantive philosophical system, focusing on what he referred to rather ambiguously as his 'metaphysics of experience or knowledge'. Particular attention is paid to the operations associated with critical metaphysics and speculative metaphysics (analysis and inference, respectively). This leads into a critical analysis in the fourth chapter of the most controversial aspect of his whole system: his notion of the 'eternal consciousness'.

---

[158] Brooks, Review of Tyler, *Thomas Hill Green*, 143.

3

The 'Metaphysics of Experience or Knowledge'

Human freedom must be understood in some different sense from that with which our anthropologists are familiar, if it is to stand in the way of the scientific impulse to naturalise the moral man.[1]

I
Introduction

It is widely recognised that the heart of a truly free life is intentional action, and intentional action is self-conscious action based on reasons.[2] Reasons in their turn are formulated and have force for the individual because of her understanding of the nature of herself as a person and of the world in which she lives. This helps to explain why Green founds his ethical and political thought on the contention that human actions, and the meanings, values, plans and social institutions that constitute their context and condition their imperfect motivations, are manifestations of a self-realising impulse of the human mind. Those manifestations are always imperfect because they are always at least tainted, and frequently profoundly distorted, by the effects of ignorance, selfishness and power. To begin to establish this claim, Green examines the most basic form of human activity: cognition. Unfortunately, the most complete analysis that he provides, in the first book of the *Prolegomena to Ethics*, is generally regarded as one of the weakest parts of his corpus. Commentators have ridiculed it, and described it as mystical, vague, confused, and 'an assemblage of dusty old Kantian arguments about the relation between sensation and judgement, combined with intense moral earnestness'.[3] Nonetheless, in 1949 John Dewey and Arthur Bentley claimed that theories such as Green's retained some interest in spite

---

[1] PE 6.
[2] See, for example, Joseph Raz, 'Introduction', in his *Engaging Reason: On the theory of value and action* (Oxford: Oxford University Press, 1999), p. 1. The thought is fundamental to the remainder of Raz's volume.
[3] Richard Rorty, *Consequences of Pragmatism: essays 1972–1980* (Brighton: Harvester, 1982), p. 147. Ridicule, George S. Fullerton, 'The "Knower" in Psychology', *Philosophical Review*, 4:1, 9–11; W.D. Hudson, *Century of Moral Philosophy* (Guildford and London: Lutterworth, 1980), pp. 48–9. Mystical, Nettleship, 'Memoir', p. cv; G.S. Brett, 'T.H. Green', in J. Hastings, ed., *Encyclopaedia of Religion and Ethics*, 13 vols. (Edinburgh: T. and T. Clark, 1908–27), vol. 6, p. 439. Vague, Alfred W. Benn, *History of English Rationalism in the nineteenth century*, 2 vols. (New York: Russell and Russell, 1962 [1906]), pp. 407–10 *passim*; Frederick Copleston, *History of Philosophy VIII: Bentham to Russell* (London: Burns and Oates, 1966), p. 171. Confused, S.S. Laurie, 'Metaphysics of T.H. Green', *Philosophical Review*, 6:2 (1897), 113–31 *passim*; Amal K. Mukhopadhyay, *Ethics of Obedience: A study of the philosophy of T.H. Green* (Calcutta: World Private, 1967), pp. 20–31.

of the fact that they were then 'almost wholly discarded'.[4] Recent assessments of the first book by scholars such as Peter Nicholson, W.J. Mander and David Brink have been more favourable than in the past, although Leslie Armour and Maria Dimova-Cookson have argued that deeper problems arise for the remainder of Green's system due to the position he adopts at the opening of the *Prolegomena*.[5]

Against this background, the present chapter performs two main tasks. Firstly, it establishes that Green's 'metaphysics of experience or knowledge'[6] is far more coherent and plausible than has commonly been supposed. Certainly in the religiously-tainted terms in which often Green presents it in the *Prolegomena to Ethics* – particularly with its attribution of agency to the 'eternal consciousness' – it does constitute the least plausible aspect of his theory. In reality however, while the eternal consciousness plays a necessary philosophical role, Green's theistic gloss is not a necessary part of his system. Consequently, it will be established in the next two chapters that one should not reject the whole theory simply because of rejecting the religious aspects of the eternal consciousness. Instead, it will be demonstrated that the eternal consciousness can be understood as equating simply to the 'human spirit' rather than God, without doing significant violence to this facet of Green's metaphysics.

Secondly, this chapter and chapter four pave the way for a detailed examination of Green's claim that the human capacity for having experiences is a crucial facet of his argument that every individual has free will and so is a moral (as opposed to an amoral) being.[7] As the preceding chapter established, developing a powerful justification of such a position was especially important for Green, as correctly he saw the intellectual and cultural current of his time to be coming to favour a

---

[4]   John Dewey and Arthur F. Bentley, *Knowing and the Known* (Boston: Beacon, 1949), p. 139. For Dewey's reaction to Green's epistemology, see his following writings: 'Psychological Standpoint' [1886], in his *Early Works*, 5 vols. (Carbondale and Edwardsville, Ill.: Southern Illinois University, 1969–72), vol. 1, pp. 122–3; 'Psychology as Philosophic Method' [1886], in his *Early Works*, vol. 1, p. 153; 'Metaphysical Method in Ethics' [1896], *Early Works*, vol. 5, p. 25n2; James T. Kloppenberg, *Uncertain Victory: Social democracy and progressivism in European and American thought, 1870–1920* (New York and Oxford: Oxford University Press, 1986), pp. 46–55 *passim*, 76.

[5]   See Peter Nicholson, 'Green's "Eternal Consciousness"', in Maria Dimova-Cookson and William J. Mander, eds., *T.H. Green: Ethics, metaphysics and political philosophy* (Oxford: Clarendon, 2006), W.J. Mander, 'In Defence of the Eternal Consciousness', in Dimova-Cookson *et al.*, eds., *T.H. Green*, pp. 187–206; David O. Brink, *Perfectionism and the Common Good: Themes in the philosophy of T.H. Green* (Oxford: Clarendon, 2003). The more hostile literature includes: Peter Hylton, 'Metaphysics of T.H. Green', *History of Philosophy Quarterly*, 2:1 (1985), 91–110; David Crossley, 'Self-conscious Agency and the Eternal Consciousness: Ultimate reality in Thomas Hill Green', *Ultimate Reality and Meaning*, 13 (1990), 3–20; Peter Hylton, 'Hegel and Analytic Philosophy', in Frederick C. Beiser, ed., *Cambridge Companion to Hegel* (Cambridge: Cambridge University Press, 1993), pp. 445–85; John Skorupski, *A History of Western Philosophy: 6. English-Language Philosophy, 1750–1945* (Oxford: Oxford University Press, 1993); and Gerald Gaus, 'Green, Bernard Bosanquet and the Philosophy of Coherence', in C.L. Ten, ed., *Routledge History of Philosophy, Volume VII, the Nineteenth Century* (London: Routledge, 1994), pp. 408–36; Denys P. Leighton, *Greenian Moment: T.H. Green and political argument in Victorian Britain* (Exeter: Imprint Academic, 2004), p. 98. Leslie Armour, 'Green's Idealism and the Metaphysics of Ethics', in Dimova-Cookson *et al.*, eds., *T.H. Green*, pp. 160–86; Maria Dimova-Cookson, *T.H. Green's Moral and Political Philosophy: A phenomenological perspective* (Houndsmill: Palgrave, 2001), chapter 1.

[6]   PE 85, 51.

[7]   PE 1–8.

naturalised view of human cognition and moral agency.[8] He saw the most profound danger to be that if human actions were to be conceived as being determined by the physical world as Herbert Spencer held, then 'The notion that thought can originate, or that we can freely will, is at once set down as a transcendental illusion.'[9] If Green's response is plausible, it will still provide a significant reason for believing that man's vision of the world, including his normative ideas, cannot be creations of the physical world and, therefore, that his capacity for agency cannot be determined in its essence by the physical world in the manner claimed by many of Green's influential contemporaries, and indeed by many of our own.[10] As this claim is crucial for Green's project, it must be crucial for this book as well. The question of free will is introduced at the end of chapter four, with a full consideration being reserved for chapters five and six.

Before turning to the analysis proper, it is important to make clear that I will not attempt to examine all of the intricacies of Green's 'metaphysics of experience or knowledge'. I think it is clear from the text itself that the *Prolegomena to Ethics* as a whole should be read simply as a metaphysic of morals or philosophical propaedeutic, arrived at through a form of transcendental deduction, rather than as an attempt to set out a complete philosophical system. This seems to be supported by his warning that

> at the risk of repelling readers by presenting them first with the most difficult and least plausible part of his doctrine, he [who wishes to establish philosophically the inadequacy of a materialist theory of mind as a theory of experience] should begin with explaining why he holds a "metaphysic of morals" to be possible and necessary; the proper foundation, though not the whole, of every system of Ethics.[11]

Furthermore, I hold that, consequently, Green intended the first book to develop and defend simply a 'metaphysics of knowledge or experience' (as Green himself characterised it), rather than a full epistemology (or even a full metaphysics). Scholars have often mistaken Green's intentions for the *Prolegomena*.[12] In effect

[8]   Melvin Richter, *Politics of Conscience: T.H. Green and his age* (London: Weidenfeld and Nicolson, 1964), p. 167; Skorupski, *English-Language Philosophy*, pp. 75–83.

[9]   PE 65. For a selection of assessments of Green's success, see Howard Selsam, *T.H. Green: Critic of empiricism* (New York: Lancaster, 1930); Howard V. Knox, 'Green's Refutation of Empiricism', *Mind*, 9 ns (1900), 62–74; Ramon M. Lemos, 'Introduction', in Thomas H. Green, *Hume and Locke* (New York: Apollo, 1968); W.H. Walsh, 'Green's Criticisms of Hume', in Andrew Vincent, ed., *Philosophy of T.H. Green* (Aldershot: Gower, 1986), pp. 21–35.

[10] 'Spencer I', Spencer II', 'Lewes I', 'Lewes II', 'Hodgson' and 'Logic' 34–144; but see John H. Randall, jr, 'T.H. Green: The development of English thought from J.S. Mill to F.H. Bradley', *Journal of the History of Ideas*, 27:2 (1966), 236–7.

[11] PE 2. Green's own partial translation of Hegel's *Philosophical Propaedeutic* survives amongst his Balliol papers: see Wempe, *T.H. Green's Theory of Positive Freedom* (Exeter: Imprint Academic, 2004), chapter 1 *passim*. See further Colin Tyler, 'The Much-Maligned and Misunderstood Eternal Consciousness', *Bradley Studies*, 9:2 (Autumn 2003), 126–38. Against this view, see Maria Dimova-Cookson, 'The Eternal Consciousness: What roles it can and cannot play. A reply to Colin Tyler', *Bradley Studies*, 9:2 (Autumn 2003), 139–48.

[12] For example, Henry Calderwood, 'Another View of Green's Last Work', *Mind*, 10 os (1885), 76; Richter, *Politics of Conscience*; Ann R. Cacoullos, *Thomas Hill Green: Philosopher of rights* (New York: Twayne, 1974); I.M. Greengarten, *Thomas Hill Green and the Development of Liberal-*

then, they have criticised him for not doing something that he never stated that he wanted to do: that is, to develop a complete epistemology or metaphysics in the first book. Instead, my critical analysis takes seriously Green's own characterisation of his aims: 'The point at issue', Green wrote, 'is whether any such science [as 'Anthropology'] can deal with the ultimate principle of knowledge and of morality in man.'[13]

Nevertheless, there is an ambiguity at the heart of Green's project, which is implied in his characterisation of the first moment of his philosophical system as a 'metaphysics of experience or knowledge'. He uses this interestingly ambiguous phrase at the very beginning of the second book of the *Prolegomena*, when characterising what he had just been doing in the first book: 'So far we have been dealing with what we may venture to call the metaphysics of experience or knowledge, as distinct from the metaphysics of moral action.'[14] The ambiguity recurs in the *Prolegomena*, for example when Green refers to 'knowledge of a world or an intelligent experience'.[15] Fundamentally, the issue is whether or not Green's transcendental method allows him to make knowledge-claims regarding a reality beyond phenomena. The significance of this ambiguity will become increasingly evident as my analysis progresses.

While Green's aspirations are indicated by the title that he gave to his major work in the field, they have been masked in the secondary literature rather more effectively by the titles that the *Prolegomena*'s editor, A.C. Bradley, gave to the separate books and chapters that he (Bradley) created within the manuscript. It is notable that when what became sections 3 to the end of the first paragraph of section 100 of the book were published in *Mind* in the first half of 1882, Green entitled the three-part article 'Can there be a natural science of man?', rather than styling it as a theory of knowledge.[16] Moreover, neither the beginnings nor the ends of the parts coincide with Bradley's divisions between the chapters or even the books of the *Prolegomena*. Furthermore, in light of the sharp distinction that Dimova-Cookson for one draws between the competing positions allegedly adopted by Green in the *Prolegomena*'s first and second books, it is notable that Green himself published most of what became the 'Introduction' to the *Prolegomena*, and seems to have intended to include what became the first chapter of the second book (which Bradley titled 'The Freedom of the Will') as part of a fourth and final instalment to the *Mind* article.[17] Green died on 26 March 1882, before he could

Democratic Thought (Toronto: University of Toronto Press, 1981); Geoffrey Thomas, *Moral Philosophy of T.H. Green* (Oxford: Clarendon, 1987). For an excellent expository summary of Green's metaphysics, see Nettleship, 'Memoir', pp. lxxv–lxxxv *passim*.

[13] T.H. Green, 'Can there be a natural science of man? [Part II]', *Mind*, vol. 7, no. 26 os (April 1882), 161 (from the only passage in the article that did not appear in the *Prolegomena*).

[14] PE 85.

[15] PE 51.

[16] T.H. Green, 'Can there be a natural science of man? [Part I]', *Mind*, vol. 7, no. 25 os (January 1882), 1–29 (= PE 3–37); T.H. Green, 'Can there be a natural science of man? [Part II]', *Mind*, vol. 7, no. 26 os (April 1882), 161–85 (= PE 38–64); T.H. Green, 'Can there be a natural science of man? [Part III]', *Mind*, vol. 7, no. 27 os (July 1882), 321–48 (= PE 65 to end of first paragraph of §100). See Nicholson, 'Green's 'Eternal Consciousness'', p. 140n1.

[17] Dimova-Cookson, *T.H. Green's Moral and Political Philosophy*, chapter 1 *passim*.

fulfil his plan, and indeed shortly before the appearance of the second part of the article in the April number of *Mind*. That he intended to include what became the first chapter of the second book is implied by a letter that he wrote to Croom Robertson, the journal's editor, on 1 March 1882: 'I shall be glad to publish two more pieces in Mind; one in the July Number, the other in the October. I think I can arrange to keep each within 25 pages.'[18] Moreover, it will be established in chapter six that Green does not distinguish the development of the eternal consciousness as a principle of knowledge from the action of individual desire in the manner required by Dimova-Cookson's reading.

Hence, I will explore only those parts of Green's 'metaphysics of experience or knowledge' which are especially relevant to his moral and political thought. It will be argued that the first 'moment' (in a broadly Hegelian sense) of Green's theory of individual self-realisation (his 'metaphysics of experience or knowledge') encompasses the first two of the three human drives that recur throughout his writings on the will, ethics, civics, and politics. These are the drives (i) to undertake a logical analysis of the presuppositions of the critically agreed facts of the world (the subject-matter of 'critical metaphysics'), and then (ii) to trace out the implications of those *a priori* principles in combination with the critically established facts of the world (the subject-matter of 'speculative metaphysics'). To anticipate, the third drive is introduced in chapter five, as part of the analysis of Green's theory of the will. This drive is the emanation of the 'human spirit' through the individual's actions, a process which provides intimations of the content to be analysed by critical metaphysics and organised by speculative metaphysics. Before this third drive can be considered however, the formal conditions of experience and knowledge must be reconstructed and critically assessed in this chapter.

Given this context, Green needs to establish only that the individual consciousness plays a necessary and constructive role in the experienced, intelligible worlds acted in by the agent. It will be shown that he is largely successful in doing this, and that, moreover, he establishes how these worlds are constituted by irreducibly interrelated meanings, values, possibilities and constraints, the fundamental structural principles of which he develops and defends in the first book of the *Prolegomena*.

II
The Methods and Formal Conditions for Gaining 'Experience or Knowledge'

The starting-point of this aspect of Green's metaphysics is the question 'How is knowledge possible?'[19] Notice his implicit assertion that knowledge is possible and that individuals actually do know things. Moreover, as Thomas points out, he is concerned to present an analysis of our knowledge of perceptions, as opposed

---

[18] Letter from T.H. Green to George Croom Robertson, 1 March 1882, in Green, *Works*, vol. 5, p. 482.

[19] For example, PE 8, 38; 'Spencer I' 2; 'Aristotle' 47; 'Popular Philosophy' 96; see also Andrew Vincent, 'Metaphysics and Ethics in the Philosophy of T.H. Green', in Dimova-Cookson *et al.*, eds., *T.H. Green*, pp. 86–93.

to, for example, God.[20] For Green, knowledge comes through the analysis and reconstruction of experience, for it is only in experience that mind reveals itself. Plato writes in the *Phaedo* that 'the soul is in the very likeness of the divine, and immortal, and rational, and uniform, and indissoluble, and unchangeable; and … the body is in the very likeness of the human, and mortal, and irrational, and multiform, and dissoluble, and changeable.'[21] By contrast, Green holds that experience (which shares the characteristics of Plato's 'body') instantiates truth (Plato's soul). 'Multiform' particular phenomena are underlain by objective principles, and, consequently, their multiple 'contingent' determinations and connections contain clues to the objective system of *a priori* truths. The errors and obscurities that are inseparable from the phenomena perceived by individual human beings mean that, conceptually, knowledge as such (rather than, say, belief or speculation) must always be a subset of human experience. Consequently, the philosopher must try to identify which elements of experience are 'true' before they can analyse this knowledge. It is in this sense that Green holds, the first stage of '[p]hilosophy does not precede but follows, that actual knowledge of things, which it is its office to analyze and reduce to its primitive elements.'[22]

It is not surprising that commentators such as John Dewey and Anthony Quinton, who fail to appreciate that Green holds the initial object of philosophical analysis to be the individual's determinate experiences, are so confused about the structure of his theory as a whole.[23] Dewey and Quinton reverse Green's method by forgetting that this is Green's starting point, presumably as must Leslie Armour in that he seems to endorse Quinton's reading. In fact, Green argues that it is by analysing the whole that philosophy begins its proper task which, when taken in its most abstract terms, Green argues is 'simply the consideration of what is implied in the fact of our knowing or coming to know a world, or, conversely, in the fact of there being a world for us to know.'[24] Such a 'broadly … Kantian' approach stands in opposition to a Cartesian approach.[25] For Descartes the initial question is whether or not anyone can know anything at all. Green by contrast holds that it is a waste of time to raise the more sceptical doubt.[26] Whereas Descartes seeks to reject as false any belief which – after reflection – he has reason to doubt, Green

[20]   Thomas, *Moral Philosophy of T.H. Green*, p. 130.
[21]   Plato, 'Phaedo', in his *Dialogues*, trans. Benjamin Jowett, ed. R.M. Hare and D.A. Russell, 4 vols. (London: Sphere, 1970), vol. 1, pp. 132–3 (80b).
[22]   'Aristotle' 48.
[23]   Dewey, 'Psychology as Philosophic Method', 153–4; Anthony Quinton, 'T.H. Green's Metaphysics of Knowledge', in W.J. Mander, ed., *Anglo-American Idealism, 1865–1927* (Westport Conn., and London: Greenwood, 2000), pp. 21–7. Leslie Armour, 'Green's Idealism and the Metaphysics of Ethics', p. 164.
[24]   'Spencer I' 2.
[25]   PE 36; 'Spencer I' 1; see Lemos, 'Introduction', p. xiii. Rene Descartes, *Meditations on First Philosophy: With objections and replies*, trans. John Cottingham (Cambridge: Cambridge University Press, 1986), pp. 12–15; Rene Descartes, 'Discourse on the Method', in his *Philosophical Writings, Volume 1*, trans. John Cottingham, Robert Stootfhoff and Dugald Murdoch (Cambridge: Cambridge University Press, 1970), pp. 5–57.
[26]   'Spencer I' 2.

seeks to produce the most coherent explanation for 'commonly held' judgements about the world.[27]

While discussing the Greek conceptions of virtue, Green explains how one comes to possess knowledge of the underlying principles of social and cultural theory and ethics through an analysis of existing social and ethical forms ('institutions and arrangements of life, social requirements and expectations, conventional awards of praise or blame'). He characterises this analytic process in a way that could be endorsed by Plato, Aristotle, Fichte and Hegel: it is, he writes, 'the effort to extract some common meaning from them, to reject what is temporary and accidental in them, while retaining what is essential.'[28] Elsewhere, he applies the same method directly in relation to the first moment of this process, his 'metaphysics of experience or knowledge'.[29] Recently, Peter Nicholson has revived D.G. Ritchie's suggestion that to better understand Green's modes of analysis (including to help explain Green's distinction between 'analysing' and 'guessing'), one should distinguish between the claims of 'Critical Metaphysics' and those of 'Speculative Metaphysics'.[30] Certainly, one must be careful here, however, as the distinction is only presupposed in Green's text, rather than being stated explicitly. Green does invoke this schema implicitly in both his 'Lectures on Logic' and his 'Lectures on Kant' (both delivered 1874–75). In the 'Lectures on Logic', he argues that the (critical) metaphysician should ask: 'What are those primary relations without which there would be no world of connected matters of fact to be known at all, and of which all other relations are determinations, – which form the universal element that is particularised in all knowledge?'[31]

What Ritchie and Nicholson call critical metaphysics aims to 'discover the *a priori* element in knowledge', in the manner advocated by Immanuel Kant.[32] Ritchie characterises this element as being concerned to discover 'the *a priori* conceptions and principles which are involved in ordinary knowledge and in the procedure of scientific investigation and proof'; these categories include the 'axioms' of thought 'without … [which] all knowledge would be impossible', such as the concepts of time, space, self-consciousness, substance and cause, as well as the principles of identity and contradiction.[33] ('Concepts' and 'principles' are types of category on this view.) Speculative metaphysics, by contrast, is not concerned to discover the presuppositions of knowledge qua knowledge in the manner of critical metaphysics. Instead the speculative metaphysician uses his or her individual judgement to produce a coherent 'explanation and arrangement of the whole Universe as it becomes known to us…. [T]he Metaphysician in this second sense can never be independent of any of the sciences or of any branch of human knowledge or effort.

[27]   John Passmore, *Hundred Years of Philosophy* (Harmondsworth: Penguin, 1966), p. 57.
[28]   PE 279.
[29]   PE 13, 49, 323.
[30]   Nicholson, 'Green's 'Eternal Consciousness'', pp. 147–48
[31]   'Logic' 35; see also 'Logic' 33; 'Kant' 48–54.
[32]   David G. Ritchie, *Darwin and Hegel with other philosophical studies* (London and New York: Swan Sonnenschein, 1893), p. 14.
[33]   Ritchie, *Darwin and Hegel*, pp. 16, 17, 14.

They are his material.'[34] Where successful critical metaphysics produces knowledge of *a priori* 'categories' (which Green uses synonymously with the terms 'conceptions' and 'presuppositions') that is logical, unassailable and abstract, the results of the speculative metaphysics must always remain tentative, revisable and relatively concrete judgements regarding far more determinate and internally-complex phenomena. This means that the conclusions of the speculative metaphysician 'can never be complete, but must always be attempted anew by each thinker.'[35] These two aspects of philosophical thought combine to form one philosophical method, in that it is on the basis of the critical metaphysician's abstract conceptions that the speculative metaphysician must seek to draw inferences regarding the intelligible structure of more complex phenomena. Kant sketched this method in regard to ethics early in the *Groundwork of the Metaphysics of Morals*.

> The method I have adopted in this book is, I believe, one which will work best if we proceed analytically from common knowledge to the formulation of its supreme principle and then back again synthetically from an examination of this principle and its origins to the common knowledge in which we find its application.[36]

This dual conception of metaphysical analysis can be completed by incorporating a more overtly constructive element to the role of the speculative metaphysician in the shape of Stendhal's conception of 'crystallisation': 'a mental process which draws from everything that happens new proofs of the perfection of the loved one.'[37] This builds on Green's suggestion, which is crucial to my analysis of his philosophical system, that: 'we only find unity in the world because we have an idea that it is there, an idea which we direct our powers to realise'.[38] The speculative metaphysician works on the assumption that the results of the critical metaphysical analysis are currently fragmentary elements of an ultimately harmonious system of fundamental concepts and presuppositions. In this sense, the speculative metaphysician 'walk[s] by faith, not by sight'.[39] (See also §§2.IV, 4.II, 7.II.)

Before going any further, a note of caution should be entered, regarding terminology. Green follows Kant by using the phrase 'speculative reason' as a synonym for 'theoretical reason', and in contradistinction to 'practical reason'.[40] He tends to use 'speculation', on the other hand, in a derogatory way however.[41] As such 'speculative reason' encompasses both what Ritchie and Nicholson call 'critical metaphysics' and 'speculative metaphysics'. For ease here, I retain the more usual 'theoretical reason', and reserve 'speculative metaphysics' for use

---

[34] Ritchie, *Darwin and Hegel*, pp. 14, 15.

[35] Ritchie, *Darwin and Hegel*, p. 14.

[36] Immanuel Kant, *Groundwork of the Metaphysics of Morals*, third edition, trans. H.J. Paton (London: Harper Torchbooks, 1964 [1948]), p. 58 (Prussian Academy, p. 392).

[37] Stendhal, *Love*, trans. G. Sale and S. Sale (Harmondsworth: Penguin, 1975), p. 45. I am grateful to Noël O'Sullivan for this way of characterising the point.

[38] PE 149.

[39] 2 Cor. v.7, quoted in 'Faith' 253. This quotation was literally Green's epitaph.

[40] PE 8, 95, 131–37 *passim*, 148–51 *passim*, 172, 185–86, 237, 249, 254, 306, 308, 311–14 *passim*, 317, 320–21, 328–29, 333, 346–47, 351, 373.

[41] See, for example, PE 5, 94.

in Ritchie's sense. Taking this into account, it can be said that Green himself is clearer regarding the nature of critical metaphysics than regarding the nature of speculative metaphysics. One of the most illuminating passages occurs early in the *Prolegomena*.

> The necessity of a conception, as distinct from a logical (or rather rhetorical) necessity of a conclusion contained in premises already conceded, means that it is necessary to the experience without which there would not for us be a world at all; and there can be neither proof nor disproof of such necessity as is claimed for any conception, but through analysis of the conditions which render this experience possible.[42]

Green traces the source of this 'necessity of a conception' to the fact that the presupposition is a logical prerequisite of experience as such. That is, its necessity springs from the logical requirement that it is 'operative in the formation of experience' (which seems to be synonymous with it being operative 'upon the experience of the person').[43] Most fundamentally, Green argues that any experienced (or experiencible) world always 'implies a conception of the world as a single system of relations', which he also refers to as 'the idea of a world as a single and eternal system of related elements, which may be related with endless diversity but must *be* related still'. A 'matter of fact' is 'an idea of a relation which is always the same between the same objects' and 'our idea of an object [is] ... that which is always the same in the same relations'. Only if one can disprove 'the accuracy or sufficiency of the analysis' of 'concrete experience' from which it is discerned should such a presupposition be rejected. Supposed presuppositions are not 'necessary' if they 'are not such as can be combined with others that [the experiencing person] recognises in one intelligible system.' Yet, at most only the necessity of a particular presupposition or presuppositions is open to dispute, not the necessity of presuppositions as such. In this way, the critical metaphysician's fundamental test is the internal coherence of those elements of his system of beliefs and values which the individual has critically endorsed (see §2.IV), and thereby accepted 'epistemic responsibility'. As Brink puts it, 'epistemic responsibility requires a cognizer to be able to distinguish and distance an appearance from herself, to frame the question of whether she should assent to the appearance, and to assess the reasons for assent by relating this appearance to other elements of her consciousness. Indeed, any extended piece of reasoning requires consciousness of different appearances as parts of a single system.'[44]

Most frequently, Green refers to our experience of the abiding reality that is the critical metaphysician's object of analysis as 'Nature'. As he wrote in his early lectures entitled 'Metaphysics of Ethics, Moral Philosophy, Sociology or Science of Sittlichkeit' (hereafter 'Sittlichkeit'): 'Nature = system of sensations. That which makes the sensations a system is reason, that in consciousness which combines and constitutes permanent objects. A stone = certain mode of consciousness

---

[42] PE 14.
[43] PE 14.
[44] Brink, *Perfectionism and the Common Good*, p. 20.

of ours, which reason, other mode of consciousness, combines in a thing as its cause.'[45] A decade later, in the *Prolegomena*, he stressed nature's inherently dynamic character: 'Nature, with all that belongs to it, is a process of change: change on a uniform method, no doubt, but change still.'[46] Correctly understood coherent and dynamic experiences are possible only where the cogniser's reflections employ and are structured by a coherent system of laws. (Counterfactually, 'the real' is conventionally opposed to that which is 'arbitrary and irregularly changeable.')[47]

This critical and therefore potentially universally-valid argument can be used to assess philosophical claims made within other intellectual traditions and spheres of intellectual endeavour. Hence, while certain relatively determinate aspects of the determinate categories of experience can be articulated appropriately by biologists, chemists, physicists, anthropologists, and others, analysis of the most fundamental *a priori* categories is properly the province of critical metaphysics alone.[48] On this basis, Green rejects Leibnitzian rationalism, classical British empiricism (that is, sensationalism) and Spencer's transfigured realism. He commences his attack with the following observation.

> Since it is obvious that the facts of the world do not come into existence when this or that person becomes acquainted with them, so long as we conceive of no intellectual action but that which this or that person exercises, we necessarily regard the existence or occurrence of the facts as independent of intellectual action.[49]

Yet, Green argues that critical metaphysics discredits the second move. Conceiving intellectual action as an essentially isolated process 'renders knowledge, as of fact and reality, inexplicable. It leaves us without an answer to the question, how the order of relations, which the mind sets up, comes to reproduce the relations of the material world which are assumed to be of a wholly different origin and nature.'[50] Green had made the point more succinctly a few pages earlier, when he attacked those theories which posit 'some unaccountable pre-established harmony through which there comes to be such an order [of 'abiding realities'],' of constant laws

---

[45]   'Sittlichkeit', p. 14, the manuscript has a paragraph-break immediately after 'objects'. These lectures seem to have been written sometime in the late 1860s or early 1870s: see Colin Tyler, 'Introduction', in C. Tyler, ed., *Unpublished Manuscripts in British Idealism: Political philosophy, theology and social thought*, 2 vols. (London and New York: Thoemmes Continuum, 2005; Exeter and Charlottesville, VA: Imprint Academic, 2008), vol. 1, pp. xx–xxi. I gave the lectures this title in this edition, using a phrase Green wrote at the head of one of the early folios of the manuscript.

[46]   PE 18.

[47]   PE 21.

[48]   'In resuming the discussion which we began in the last number of MIND, it will be well to remove a misapprehension, arising from an ill-chosen title, which may have prevented believers in "Anthropology" from giving an unprejudiced attention to the discussion. It is not at all intended to dispute the possibility of a valid natural science dealing with human nature in certain of its aspects. The point at issue is whether any such science can deal with the ultimate principle of knowledge and of morality in man.' T.H. Green, 'Can there be a natural science of man? [Part II]', *Mind*, vol. 7, no. 26 os (April 1882), 161.

[49]   PE 34.

[50]   PE 34; the issue of relations in Green's theory is addressed in thought-provoking ways in Leslie Armour, 'Green's Idealism and the Metaphysics of Knowledge', especially pp. 160–70.

of 'change on a uniform method' 'corresponding to our conception of it.'[51] Even though his reference to 'pre-established harmony' indicates that Green had in mind at least Leibnitzian rationalism, he makes clear both here and elsewhere that the same criticism applies to the realisms of Spencer and Lewes, the empiricist tradition of Berkeley, Locke and Hume, and the associationism of J.S. Mill.[52] Hence, Green rejects what he sees as the transcendent arguments of these rationalist and realist types (as well as correspondence theories of truth) in favour of his form of transcendental idealism.[53]

III
Experience and Sensations

Green's initial question ('how is knowledge possible?') can be specified further by asking what it is that individual human beings actually can possess knowledge of. We have seen that Green argues knowledge is always only of experience and of strictly logical deductions from that experience.[54] Here, Green is following Kant once more, as when the latter writes: 'In the order of time, therefore, we have no knowledge antecedent to experience, and with experience our knowledge begins.'[55] But what does Green mean by 'experience'? In the *Prolegomena*, he distinguishes between two possible uses.[56] In the first, non-conscious entities can 'experience' the world in the sense of being affected by it without actually being aware that they are so affected. For example, a plant can 'experience' changes in its physical make-up because of changes in its environment without being conscious of doing so. Similarly, humans experience changes 'in respect of the numberless events which affect us but of which we are not aware.'[57] Green believes that this is the sense in which, for example, Spencer and Lewes use the term 'experience' in their respective epistemological theories.[58] It is in this way that for them, 'knowledge of nature ... [is] itself the result of natural processes.'[59]

Yet, for Green, such a non-conscious meaning of 'experience' is inadequate when it comes to explaining how 'knowledge can only be of experiences' and what they logically imply. The changes referred to when 'experienced' equates in this way simply to 'affected' cannot explain the fact of our knowing.[60] The usage

[51] PE 19.
[52] Many of Green's writings focus on precisely this point and its many implications: see 'Hume I', 'Spencer I', 'Spencer II', 'Lewes I', 'Lewes II', 'Hodgson', 'Logic', all *passim*. See also Alexander Klein, 'On Hume on Space: Green's attack, James' empirical response', *Journal of the History of Philosophy*, 47:3 (2009), 415–49. Compare Green's position with that set out by Edward Caird in his 'Spencer', ed. C. Tyler, *Collingwood and British Idealism Studies*, 12:1 (Spring 2006), 5–38.
[53] Compare to Maria Dimova-Cookson, *T.H. Green's Moral and Political Philosophy*, pp. 24–27.
[54] PE 10.
[55] Immanuel Kant, *Critique of Pure Reason*, trans. Norman Kemp Smith (Houndsmill; MacMillan, 1929), p. 41 (B1).
[56] PE 15–6.
[57] PE 15.
[58] PE 61–62; 'Spencer I' 14; 'Lewes I' esp. 65; see also Hylton, 'Metaphysics of T.H. Green', 91–8.
[59] PE 15.
[60] See Hiralal Haldar, 'Green and his Critics', *Philosophical Review*, 3:2 (1894), 168–9; Mukhopadhyay, *Ethics of Obedience*, pp. 30–31. It is probably Fullerton's failure to appreciate this division which leads him to his excessively negative treatment of most philosophers of mind (Fullerton, 'The

of 'experience' which *is* relevant to knowledge 'must be experience of matters of fact *recognised as such.*'[61] Experience in this second and to Green far more fruitful sense equates to 'consciousness of events as related or as a series of changes.'[62] He writes elsewhere that 'Our experience consists of related phenomena, i.e. related feelings.'[63] A mind-independent world may affect us in the same sense that the plant is affected by its environment, but the important question remains: how do we come to recognise that it does so, and furthermore that it does so in a uniform manner (as subject to abstract and permanent laws)?[64] This is a more detailed expression of Green's initial question: namely, 'How is knowledge possible?'

Green is a transcendental idealist, then: 'the only valid idealism ... [is] that which trusts, not to a guess about what is beyond experience, but to analysis of what is within it.'[65] Even so, he does not adopt the extreme position which holds that everything in the world is simply a creation of the individual's (finite) mind. He is emphatic that his claim about the constituents of a 'valid idealism' does not entail a denial of the purely corporeal existence of a world independent of consciousness. This presents Green with his biggest problem thus far in his argument: how to justify his contention that perceived sensations form the primary data of human experiences.[66] In his vitriolic attack on Herbert Spencer,[67] Green is at pains to distance himself from what he sees as an immature position:

> what Mr. Spencer understands by "idealism" is what a raw undergraduate understands by it. It means to him a doctrine that "there is no such thing as matter," or that "the external world is merely the creation of our own minds" – a doctrine expressly rejected by Kant, and which has had no place since his time in any idealism that knows what it is about.[68]

Of course, Spencer was not the last person to interpret idealism in such a way. Possibly the most famous example was G.E. Moore's 'The Refutation of Idealism', an article that Moore later came very close to disowning.[69] There, Moore claimed that 'The idealist means to assert that [chairs, tables and mountains] are *in some sense* neither lifeless nor unconscious, as they certainly seem to be'. Moreover, 'When the whole universe is declared [by the idealist] to be spiritual, it is meant not only that it is in some sense *conscious*, but that it has what we recognise in ourselves as the

---

"Knower" in Psychology', 1–26; this holds true despite 25n1).

[61] PE 16.
[62] PE 16.
[63] 'Kant' 10; see A.C. Ewing, *Idealism: A critical survey* (London: Methuen, 1969), p. 21.
[64] PE 9.
[65] 'Lewes II' 72.
[66] Compare PE 42–51.
[67] Green regretted his vitriol ('Hodgson' 541), which also angered Spencer himself (Spencer, 'Professor Green's Explanations', *passim*). Also, see Nettleship, 'Memoir', pp. lxix–lxx; Richard Hodgson, 'Professor Green as a Critic', *Contemporary Review* (1880), 898–912. See 'Appendix' below for an account of Spencer and Hodgson's misrepresentation of the true authorship of Hodgson, 'Professor Green as a Critic'.
[68] 'Spencer I' 12.
[69] G.E. Moore, 'Refutation of Idealism' (1903), in his *Philosophical Studies* (London: Routledge and Kegan Paul, 1922), p. viii.

higher forms of consciousness.'[70] At least with reference to the types of idealism expounded by A.E. Taylor and F.H. Bradley, Moore reduces idealism to a mixture of 'undergraduate-level' solipsism and pantheism. In reality, Green's idealism is far less mystical than either Spencer or Moore claimed, as will be established below (see §8.IV for other elements of Moore's critique of Green).

Despite his emphatic refusal to deny the existence of a world in which the action of a mind is absent, and in line with his endorsement of only transcendental arguments, Green distinguishes firmly and repeatedly between an unperceived feeling (or sensation) and a perceived feeling (or sensation).[71] It is one thing to feel pain, he notes, but another to be conscious that one is doing so. Only when one pays attention to sensations do they become possible objects of experience and knowledge, and only then can they form parts of an intelligible experience of the world.[72] Green's insistence on evidence rather than conjecture precludes him logically from claiming or assuming that human beings can know anything about any of the relations that presumably exist in the unexperienced world, then. Contrary to John Skorupski and Maria Dimova-Cookson, he holds (apparently with great justification) that we have no way of *knowing* in what ways 'Things in the external world are already related in one way or another', nor can we know that 'we perceive [these 'external'] relations', nor can we know that 'we perceive the related objects' in the way in which objects are 'related in the external world'.[73] Certainly, one can *guess* about how accurately phenomena mirror 'related' objects in the external world, one might even be killed in a struggle for survival or go insane if one did not make such a guess. Nevertheless, that cannot alter the fact that we *are* simply guessing and not knowing. Similarly, that '[m]ost of us believe' relations to exist in a mind-independent universe does not mean either that we *know* that they do so, or that the mind-independent relations are the same relations that we would conceive even if we were thinking fully rationally.[74] The existence of a mind-independent world is unknowable even in principle. In this regard, it is instructive that Dimova-Cookson's response to David Hume's emphasis on 'human purposes and cravings' of this type ('If we believe, that fire warms, or water refreshes, 'tis only because it costs us too much pains to think otherwise') is simply to invoke without justification what 'Most of us believe'. As noted above, in effect, her's is an appeal to conventional prejudice against the alleged 'subjectivism' of Green's (critical) metaphysics.[75]

---

[70] Moore, 'Refutation of Idealism', p. 1.
[71] 'Lewes I' 73, 77, 87–9; 'Hume I' 173. Normally, Green uses 'a feeling' and 'a sensation' interchangeably. Laurie is very confused about this fact (S.S. Laurie, 'Metaphysics of T.H. Green', *Philosophical Review*, 6:2, 121–8). 'Logic' 7 is exceptional.
[72] Randall, 'T.H. Green', 236–9. Hobhouse does not fully appreciate this distinction: Leonard T. Hobhouse, *Theory of Knowledge: A contribution to some problems of logic and metaphysics* (London: Methuen, 1896), p. 23n3. See Arthur Eastwood, 'On Thought-Relations', *Mind*, 16 os (1891), 246.
[73] Maria Dimova-Cookson, *T.H. Green's Moral and Political Philosophy*, p. 30, discussing John Skorupski, *English-Language Philosophy*, p. 85.
[74] Dimova-Cookson, *T.H. Green's Moral and Political Philosophy*, p. 34.
[75] Dimova-Cookson, *T.H. Green's Moral and Political Philosophy*, p. 34, quoting David Hume, *Treatise of Human Nature*, ed. L.A. Selby-Bigge (Oxford: Clarendon, 1888),

Green criticises Kant for not being consistent on this point. Simultaneously, Kant maintains both that things exist independently of consciousness, and that things only exist through perception.[76] However, frequently it has been objected that Green himself faces precisely the same problem that he believes is faced by Kant. This attack was pressed most famously by Andrew Seth, although it was made also by Arthur Balfour, Henry Calderwood, L.T. Hobhouse and many others.[77] The ambiguity is especially evident in 'Sittlichkeit', Green's lectures from between the late 1860s and early 1870s which anticipate the *Prolegomena*: 'Nature is *there – given*. We find it, don't *make* it – *we*, that is in our limited human personality. The reason that makes it must be communicated to us, if it is to be "revealed" to us. But the natural world is made apart from this communication – is there, whether we understand it or no.'[78] Similarly, in the *Prolegomena* itself, Green vacillates constantly between treating the external world (and therefore unperceived sensations) on the one hand as 'blank nothing',[79] and on the other as the source of our perceived sensations. Given his insistence that we should not attempt to guess about what we cannot experience, the second option is not legitimately open to him.

On one view, the critics overstate the problem. Reading Green sympathetically and bearing in mind the purpose of his metaphysics of experience, the theory only requires him to explain how we can come to organise otherwise random perceived sensations into the relatively harmonious system which constitutes the world in which we live. Ultimately, Green's theory does not rely on the existence of unperceived sensations for its internal coherence. On this sympathetic reading, all that Green's theory demands is that what we may call either 'perceived feelings' or 'perceived sensations' exist and form the 'basic materials' of our knowledge. Even so, this is based on a very kind reading. If one is less sympathetic (as I am inclined to be), doubt remains as to how far Green does actually manage to avoid making 'a guess about what is beyond experience'.[80]

Green's problem seems irresolvable given his 'question', assumptions and method with all of their attendant limitations. His initial question can be stated more clearly as: how do we come to presuppose an increasingly coherent system

---

p. 270 (book 1, part 4, §7).

[76] 'Kant' 5; PE 38–41; Hylton, 'Metaphysics of T.H. Green', 100–01; Peter Hylton, *Russell, Idealism and the Emergence of Analytic Philosophy* (Oxford: Oxford University Press, 1990), pp. 37–39; Hylton, 'Hegel and Analytic Philosophy', p. 457. For Green on Kant, see W.D. Lamont, *Introduction to Green's Moral Philosophy* (London: George Allen and Unwin, 1934), pp. 179–90 *passim*; Randall, 'T.H. Green: The development of English thought from J.S. Mill to F.H. Bradley', 232–36.

[77] Andrew Seth, *Hegelianism and Personality* (London: William Blackwood, 1887), pp. 74–78; Arthur J. Balfour, 'Green's Metaphysics of Knowledge', *Mind*, 9:33 os (January 1884), 77–78; Calderwood, 'Another View of Green's Last Work', 76–78; Haldar, 'Green and his Critics', 172–73; Hobhouse, *Theory of Knowledge*, pp. 25–26; Laurie, 'Metaphysics of T.H. Green', 116–21, 124–25; Gustavus Cunningham, *Idealist Argument in Recent British and American Philosophy* (New York: Books for Libraries, 1933), pp. 353–63; Lamont, *Introduction to Green's Moral Philosophy*, pp. 186–90, 197–203; Randall, 'T.H. Green: The development of English thought from J.S. Mill to F.H. Bradley', 230–31; Mukhopadhyay, *Ethics of Obedience*, pp. 22–24; Hylton, 'Metaphysics of T.H. Green', 102–03.

[78] 'Sittlichkeit', p. 14. Interestingly, the rest of this paragraph reads: 'Not so with moral world. It is by reason, as communicated to man and not otherwise, that this world is constituted.'

[79] 'Lewes II' 103.

[80] 'Lewes II' 72.

of categories (including laws of relation) with which to comprehend the mass of different perceptions that we have but do not choose to receive? He assumes that our perceptions are, in the important senses referred to above, constructs of consciousness. He must then explain what the mind uses as the raw materials of these perceptions. Yet, his assumptions, 'question' and especially his transcendental method preclude him from doing so. Apart from guessing illegitimately that the world exists 'in itself' rather than, for example, as a pure creation of the mind of a god, or of a malicious demon, or of an Experience Machine, he is not able to theorise the constructive action of mind in the manner required by his metaphysics.[81] Moreover, without making such a guess, he cannot escape the 'raw undergraduate['s]' position.[82] Chubb supports Green here, yet both he and Green must still make a 'guess beyond experience', thereby violating Green's explicit rejection of transcendent (as distinct from transcendental) propositions.[83]

Despite all of Green's best efforts, he seems to have no way out of this difficulty. His philosophical approach does not seem to allow him to give a convincing account of why consciousness assigns any particular sensation to any particular category. A possible revision of his position which retains as many of Green's arguments as possible while at least mitigating this difficulty, is as follows. In order for it to be possible for the individual's mind to organise in anything other than a purely arbitrary fashion the streams of sensations it continually receives, this stream must be made up of sensations which possess some qualities independently of the individual's consciousness of them, even if those qualities are fairly inchoate and possibly largely abstract. For sensations to be capable of being organised in anything other than an arbitrary way, the mind must be able to discern these qualities. These qualities form what one might call the 'facts' of experience, which the individual's mind has then to organise.

Thus far, we have diverged from Green's position. Nevertheless, even on this alternative view, Green is still correct when he argues that the individual mind must be active in composing the world of experiences in a number of ways. First it must discern these qualities, second it must interpret their significance and posit relationships between the largely inchoate 'facts' so as to produce a conception of the underlying principles of experience that is consistent with what the individual understands, following careful reflection, to be the evidence. Only this effort will honour Green's fundamental metaphysical presupposition that such principles form a coherent system. In this way, Green is correct to stress the mental nature of reality, because even on this revised view only the individual mind can recognise qualities within the stream of sense-data, and only the individual mind can then posit relations between those inchoate 'facts'. The core of the objects of the particular experiences remains what Green claims it to be: qualities organised in accordance with relations posited by mind. Moreover, Green's attack on

---

[81] God: George Berkeley, *Principles of Human Knowledge*, ed. T.E. Jessop (London: A. Brown, 1937), part 1, §72; 'malicious demon': Descartes, *Meditations on First Philosophy*, p. 15; 'Experience Machine': Robert Nozick, *Anarchy, State and Utopia* (Oxford: Blackwell, 1974), pp. 42–45.

[82] 'Spencer I' 12.

[83] Percival Chubb, 'Significance of Thomas Hill Green's Philosophical and Religious Teaching', *Journal of Speculative Philosophy*, 22:1–2 (1888), 11.

rationalism, British empiricism and transfigured realism retains much of its force. After making these modifications, I suggest that it is difficult to imagine any other philosophical approach offering a more convincing explanation. Perhaps the most that can be claimed for the revised version of Green's own position is what he says in another context: 'We can only say that, upon the best analysis we can make of our experience, it seems that so it does'.[84]

IV
Related Objects

It has been established that recognising Green's problem regarding the existence of 'things in themselves' and accepting that he employs a transcendent (rather than transcendental) argument at this point, does not invalidate his fundamental point that in an important sense our feelings, our sensations and the whole world of which they are parts are 'fundamentally dependent on our minds'.[85] In fact, anyone denying the creative power of consciousness must attempt to explain how we come to understand chaotic sensations as parts of an ordered world. Forsyth, for one, fails to do this.[86] Green insists on the perceiver-defined perspective (the 'for us'-ness of the world) throughout the *Prolegomena*.[87] This is reflected in Green's repeated emphasis on the need to restrict use of the word 'nature' to nature 'for us', nature as it can be experienced by individual experiencers; for example,

> understanding, or consciousness as acting in the manner described, may be said to be the principle of objectivity. It will be through it that there is *for us* an objective world; through it that we *conceive* an order of nature, with the unity of which we must reconcile our interpretations of phenomena, if they are to be other than "subjective" illusions.[88]

Green's rejection of transcendent arguments in his critical metaphysics entails that, even if the receipt of unperceived sensations by the individual's mind is a prerequisite for the creation of perceived sensations, the only qualities that they can have 'for us' (the only ones they can be known to have) are given to them by the mind. The relationship is reciprocal however, for the necessary interconnection of sensations and the activity of consciousness which is uncovered by the critical metaphysician entails the collapse of the distinction between perceiving subject and perceived object. The nature of the object must be inseparable from the nature of the subject.

This point has not always been clearly recognised by the commentators.[89] Most recently, it has led Maria Dimova-Cookson to claim that Green's metaphysics

---

[84] PE 100; compare PE 120.
[85] See Harold H. Joachim, *Nature of Truth* (Oxford: Clarendon, 1906), p. 118n.
[86] Thomas M. Forsyth, *English Philosophy: A study of its methods and general development* (London: Adam and Charles Black, 1910), pp. 147–55.
[87] PE 13. In the vicinity of this quotation, see PE 9, 12, 14, 19, for example. Dimova-Cookson fails to keep this point in mind during her analysis of Green's metaphysics of knowledge (see, for example, her *T.H. Green's Moral and Political Philosophy*, pp. 29–40 *passim*).
[88] PE 13.
[89] For example, Alfred E. Taylor, *Problem of Conduct* (London: MacMillan, 1901), pp. 73–82; Randall, 'T.H. Green: The development of English thought from J.S. Mill to F.H. Bradley', 223.

of experience, which she refers to as his epistemology, 'separates thought from feelings', a situation which she distinguishes from his 'theory of the will [where] he claims that human experience as a whole represents the work of the "spiritual principle".'[90] Firstly, as will be argued at length throughout this book, all thought is the imperfect expression of the spiritual principle, so there seems no ground for distinguishing Green's metaphysics of experience from his theory of the will in the manner Dimova-Cookson does here. Secondly, as we have seen, Green is emphatic that the individual can only be aware of sensations and feelings that have already been mediated by thought. Consequently, it is misleading to claim that his metaphysics of experience 'separates thought from feelings' in the way Dimova-Cookson alleges. The most that one is warranted in asserting about the order and indeed qualities of the world is that both are the creation of the mind through a dialectical engagement with its prior 'creations'.

Green places great stress on the fact that the human mind creates order in its world. Consider what happens when one is simply looking at a table: 'Here is this table now before me. The sensation it excites in me is in time; I turn my head and it is gone'.[91] Such sensations are continually 'in flux' and sensations which are constantly in a state of flux cannot form a related series.[92] Yet, for Green 'experience in the most elementary form in which it can be the beginning of knowledge' is 'a consciousness of events as a related series'.[93] As he puts it elsewhere, 'This ... is a judgement in terms, expressing not what is sensible, but what is intelligible.'[94] It is only as sensations are held together in the consciousness of a perceiving mind that they can form such an intelligible series. Such a consciousness must stand apart from the changes of the world which it experiences and assess them from a viewpoint which does not similarly change. Consequently, Green denies Kant's separation of the acts of categorising perceptions and constituting relations between sensations on the one hand, and the process of conceiving of those categories and relations on the other.[95] In short, 'relations [are] constituted in and by the act of conception or knowing'.[96] The acts of categorising and constituting are essential parts of the process of becoming aware of the posited categories and relations.

A general statement of the interaction of the processes of critical and speculative metaphysics is as follows. First, 'the germ of intelligent experience [is] the simple consciousness of a sensation, [which] can only be expressed as the judgement, "something is here." '[97] Unlike Plato, Green conceives the growth of our knowledge

---

[90] Dimova-Cookson, *T.H. Green's Moral and Political Philosophy*, p. 39.

[91] 'Logic' 11.

[92] 'Logic' 19. Sidgwick fails to appreciate this point (Henry Sidgwick, 'Metaphysics of T.H. Green', in his *Lectures on the Philosophy of Kant and other philosophical lectures and essays* (London: MacMillan, 1905), p. 223).

[93] PE 16.

[94] 'Aristotle', 54.

[95] 'Kant' 18.

[96] 'Logic' 49.

[97] 'Aristotle', 52. Here, Green is echoing Hegel (for example, Georg W.F. Hegel, *Philosophical Propaedeutic*, trans. A.V. Miller (Oxford: Basil Blackwell, 1986), pp. 76–81). There is a partial translation of this work amongst Green's papers in Balliol. Also, Green would have read pertinent sections of Hegel's *Complete Logic* as they were translated in Stirling's *Secret of Hegel*

to be a movement from the most abstract understanding of the object (that is, the bare fact of its existence) to the more determinate (that is, as related to other objects).[98] Logically if not temporally, the first stage of this process must be analytic rather than inferential or, more properly, constructive. When considering any one fact about the world, consciousness must differentiate it from other facts and understand how this fact relates to others: 'Abstract the many relations from the one thing, and there is nothing. They, being many, determine or constitute its definite unity.'[99] The more one understands the relationships in which an object stands to other objects, the more clearly one understands its nature.

If objects are to be related intelligibly to one another, it must be possible to place them on some shared scale, meaning that they must be particular instances of some shared general type. For example, one can compare the brilliance of the red ship to the brilliance of the blue sea in which it is sinking because both red and blue are colours. Green himself gives the example of knowledge of the qualities of an acid to explain his statement of the conventional idealist notion of the 'many in one' or the 'unity of the manifold'.[100] 'The unscientific man,' he writes, 'if asked what an acid is, will say, perhaps, that it is that which sets his teeth on edge.'[101] This man will understand the concept of 'acid' in relation to other qualities as well, such as matter/non-matter, liquid/solid, and taste/tasteless. The scientific man can extend this knowledge still further, for example, through the discovery of the chemical formula of the particular acid. Yet, this scientific discovery presupposes knowledge of other relations and concepts. In the example just given, this substratum is formed, for instance, by concepts and relations inherent in the language games of chemistry. This new understanding of the 'complex of attributes' which we conceive as 'acid' forms a further aspect of the substratum which then conditions our understandings of our other experiences.[102] In this process, the critical metaphysician relies on her analytic powers, whereas the speculative metaphysician relies on her powers of constructive judgement.

Notice that this theory of the 'one in the many' is not holistic, in the manner that Hylton alleges.[103] In Avital Simhony's words, the holistic perspective holds that, the whole 'is somehow more real than' the parts.[104] Green's form of organicism does not entail this claim, for he conceives the relationship between the parts and

---

(James Hutchison Stirling, *Secret of Hegel: Being the Hegelian system in origin, principle, form and matter* (Edinburgh: Oliver and Boyd, 1898 [1865]), pp. 218–320). For Green's attitude to Stirling, see his letter to A.C. Bradley, 20 September 1873, *Works* 5, p. 454 and p. 454n84, as well as Amelia H. Stirling, *James Hutchison Stirling: His life and work* (London: T. Fisher Unwin, 1912), pp. 169–170, 220; John H. Muirhead, *Platonic Tradition in Anglo-Saxon Philosophy* (London: George Allen and Unwin, 1931), p. 170. Hobhouse fails to appreciate this fact (Hobhouse, *Theory of Knowledge*, pp. 22–31).

[98]   'Aristotle', 55–9; 'Hume I' 40, 52–3; 'Logic' 10.
[99]   PE 28.
[100] PE 28; see also Joachim, *Nature of Truth*, p. 33.
[101] 'Aristotle', 53.
[102] 'Aristotle', 71.
[103] Hylton, *Russell, Idealism and the Emergence of Analytic Philosophy*, pp. 39–42.
[104] Avital Simhony, 'Idealist Organicism: Beyond holism and individualism', *History of Political Thought*, 12:3 (1991), 515.

whole as 'non-reductive'.[105] The general laws of chemical phenomena exist for us because of the intelligible relations that we conceive as obtaining in particular chemical reactions, at the same time that we conceive those reactions themselves as conforming to certain fundamental chemical laws. In this way, the whole does not have ultimate priority over the parts, nor *vice versa*. The nature of each part is determined by the relationships in which it stands to all other parts, as well as by its place in relation to the whole. Similarly, the nature of the whole is determined by the arrangement of the parts. In this way, Green presents a relational rather than a holistic form of organicism, in the sense that the 'one' is only ever fully intelligible for an individual who has a correct understanding of the 'many', and the 'many' are only ever fully intelligible for an individual who has a correct understanding of the 'one'.

Green goes on to argue that if the categories and laws of relation which underlie our critical and speculative judgements are to exist in an intelligible world (one that can be known), then when properly understood they must be mutually consistent and unchanging. Why must universal laws govern the association of predicates which constitutes experiences through the processes of 'discerning, comparing, and compounding' sensations?[106] Green argues that it is only on such a presupposition of there being such a possible coherent ordering to our experiences that we are justified in assuming that we can have knowledge at all.[107] Only by acting on this presupposition can the mind satisfy its inherent desire for an ordered experience and understanding of the world.[108] Consequently, consciousness must be a 'unifying' as well as a 'distinguishing' entity for the 'chaos of sense' to be made intelligible.[109]

A number of further points should be drawn out of the preceding analysis. First, Green holds that a subject which is capable of experiencing and knowing a world must be self-conscious, because only if it is can it conceive of an ordered world made up of different but related objects.[110] It must distinguish itself from the sensations it perceives in such a way that it can hold them together as discrete but still related objects if it is to be able to conceive of perceived sensations as constituting discrete objects of perception (something that they must be understood to do if they are to be known). Second, even though relations are central within Green's theory of knowledge,[111] this does *not* mean that Green must believe knowledge is made up of relations alone, as some commentators have argued that he did.[112] Relations are

---

[105] Simhony, 'Idealist Organicism', 520.

[106] 'Hume I' 51.

[107] PE 14.

[108] 'Spencer I' 2.

[109] 'Aristotle', 52.

[110] 'Kant' 11.

[111] As is widely recognised, see for example Eastwood, 'On Thought-Relations'; Sidgwick, 'Metaphysics of T.H. Green', 9–22; Anthony Quinton, *Thoughts and Thinkers* (London: Duckworth, 1982), pp. 204–06; Crossley, 'Self-conscious Agency and the Eternal Consciousness', 5–7; Randall, 'T.H. Green: The development of English thought from J.S. Mill to F.H. Bradley', 225–28.

[112] Balfour, 'Green's Metaphysics of Knowledge', 76–77; Arthur J. Balfour, 'Criticism of Current Idealistic Theories', *Mind*, 2 ns (1893), 29–30. Mukhopadhyay examines the problem of

necessary but not sufficient components of knowledge.[113] There must be objects as well as the relations that obtain between them.[114]

Third, Green holds that the idea of knowledge presupposes the existence of abstract laws governing consciousness's perception and association of sensations.[115] For example, one cannot coherently justify ideas of cause and effect without presupposing that nature operates according to such universal laws.[116] Furthermore, the inherent logic of the concept of an intelligible experience and hence of knowledge requires that ultimately all laws of association of predicates can be perfectly systematized. This presupposition must be made if knowledge is held to be possible, whether or not particular epistemic selves ever succeed in being fully conscious of making it, and whether or not they ever succeed in conceiving of this system clearly and in its completeness. Fourth, Green holds that something is misunderstood only if we conceive it in different relations to those which it occupies in the totally coherent system of relations which constitutes the uniformity of nature.[117] This point comes through clearly in his discussions of hallucinations.[118] As Dewey succinctly puts it, for Green 'What is mere seeming or unreal is not capable of becoming a member of this unified world.'[119] Given that 'permanent and uniform' relations can only exist for a conceiving mind,[120] Green concludes that 'It is not the work of the mind, as such, that we instinctively oppose to the real, but the work of the mind as assumed to be arbitrary and irregularly changeable.'[121]

Does the move from the idea that consciousness must unify sensations to the idea of a 'uniformity of nature' entail a logical jump? It is one thing to believe that the concept of knowledge logically requires the presupposition of a unified world of abstract laws of the type just outlined. However, it has been argued that this does not mean only *one* such system is possible.[122] In short, it is alleged that the first claim which Green makes does not logically entail the existence of 'a [single] world of experience, one, real, abiding'.[123] There may be many ways of constructing a system of such abstract laws which all possess the same degree of internal

explaining how there can be any 'thing' which is then related (Mukhopadhyay, *Ethics of Obedience*, pp. 21–22).

[113] PE 42.

[114] Hiralal Haldar, *Neo-Hegelianism* (London: Heath Cranton, 1927), pp. 30–32; Francis H. Bradley, *Appearance and Reality: A metaphysical essay* (Oxford: Clarendon, 1897), pp. 25–26. There is not enough space to discuss in depth Bradley's criticisms of relational theories of knowledge such as Green's. All that should be noted is that ultimately his argument seems to rest on a category mistake. See also Hylton, 'Metaphysics of T.H. Green', 106–8.

[115] PE 12–15.

[116] 'Hume I' 313.

[117] PE 23.

[118] For example, PE 14; 'Kant' 17; 'Logic' 15; 'Hume I' 187–8.

[119] John Dewey, 'Philosophy of Thomas Hill Green' [1889], in his *Early Works*, vol. 3, p. 22.

[120] 'Lewes II' 116, 118–9, 120–1, 124–7, 134–5; 'Logic' 16; Cunningham, *Idealist Argument*, pp. 48–57.

[121] PE 21.

[122] For example, see Ferdinand C.S. Schiller, *Humanism: Philosophical essays* (London: MacMillan 1903), pp. 46–54; Richard Rorty, *Contingency, Irony and Solidarity* (Cambridge: Cambridge University Press, 1989), pp. 3–22; but see Rorty, *Consequences of Pragmatism*, p. 82.

[123] 'Hume I' 324.

coherence. Consequently, it may be perfectly coherent to accept that all agents must work on the assumption of the ultimate unity of their possible knowledge, and yet simultaneously to reject the claim that this necessarily requires them to hold that they all share the same system. This problem is intensified by Green's claim that due to her imperfect nature no-one will ever possess full knowledge, no-one will ever fully comprehend the world as a unified system.[124] Such imperfection brings into question the status of any assumption that ultimately the world is unified by appearing to make the claim into an unverifiable working hypothesis. Like all working hypotheses, it is a pragmatic guess and, in the manner which Green portrays it, it is not a strictly logical deduction from the fact that people know things. Indeed, it may be viewed more as a reflection of the spirit of his time.[125]

Green is emphatic that this objection fails by its very structure.[126] He argues there is an inherent incoherence in challenging the presupposition that ultimately there can be only one coherent system of relations. The challenger is making a claim which, if it is itself to be coherent, must be making a universal claim about the nature of knowledge as such. In other words, an assertion that there is no such thing as 'Truth' is itself an inconsistent 'Truth-claim'. Properly, it lacks meaning to ask whether or not there is merely one coherent system of relations.[127] Green says nothing that establishes however why this presupposition of the search for a harmonious system of knowledge proves that there must be only one such system. It seems to be merely a postulate of theoretical reason, understood as an axiom that inspires the individual's attempt to construct such a system.

The ultimate unity of experience is pivotal in the present context because it underlies Green's discussion of the categories, and forms the crux of Green's contention that the world which humans can know (and in which they live and act) is a creation of their minds. Consequently, it is vital to understand this particular argument in order to properly grasp the sense in which that capacity for knowledge implies the fact of being 'free'.

V
Knowledge as Self-expression

The action of a distinguishing and, importantly, a harmonising consciousness necessarily entails the application of categories to individual sensations, or 'things'. At his most Hegelian, Green writes, 'Thus we may not say either that the real thing is individual, not universal (for its individuality is a universal particularised), or that its individuality distinguishes it from such a work of thought as conception (for its individuality is the work of thought).'[128] In this way, one discovers Green's theory of the concrete universal.[129] Individual objects are constituted by consciousness's

---

[124] PE 72; IPR 145.
[125] See Richter, *Politics of Conscience*, pp. 165–67.
[126] PE 26.
[127] PE 27.
[128] 'Logic' 28; Hegel, *Philosophical Propaedeutic*, pp. 67, 105–7, 134.
[129] Quinton, *Thoughts and Thinkers*, p. 205; Hylton, 'Metaphysics of T.H. Green', 105–6.

application of universal categories in particular instances.[130] The individual becomes aware of the categories, or 'universals', which interrelate in accordance with these universal laws as a result of their attempts to understand their world as a world which is at least in principle fully intelligible: that is, to understand the single system of categories and laws of relation which must underlie the changes of phenomena in any world which is capable of being known.

Knowledge becomes more determinate and coherent essentially through a process of trial and the rejection of error. In other words, it develops in the sense that our understanding of the world in which we live becomes more determinate, more coherent and more complex.[131] As both Wempe and Green himself note, the hypothetico-deductive method of modern natural sciences is simply a more sophisticated version of what Green has in mind (assuming that the former can be separated from scientific realism).[132] Yet, on the analysis just given – an analysis which seems to follow logically from the possibility of knowing anything at all – there is no way that experience can impart these categories to consciousness from 'outside'.[133] They must be logically prior to the act of experiencing and so cannot be 'implanted within' consciousness by experience.[134] In some way, experiences must bring these universals to mind.[135]

Clearly, Green is following Kant here, although with a change of terminology because 'time' and 'space' are 'a priori forms of intuition' and not 'categories' for Kant. How plausible is the idea that knowledge 'brings out' universals in this way? How plausible is it 'that all truth partakes of the nature of revelation'?[136] In Green's favour it should be recognised, firstly, that he is *not* arguing that we are never mistaken about the nature and interrelationships of these universals. If he were committed to holding that position, then he could not explain the all too obvious existence of error. Indeed, his main reason for concerning himself with metaphysics of knowledge in the first place is precisely his belief that the popular empiricist tradition was fundamentally in error in many of its most important categories.[137] The second attractive thing to notice about Green's position is that he criticises Plato for arguing that single universals apply to single fully determinate objects.[138] As has been established already, Green is emphatic that any one object is made up of many different universals and that the progress of knowledge is, in many ways, the gradual growth in the coherent interrelation in the minds of particular human beings of these universals and the objects which they interrelate to form.

The foregoing analysis has outlined Green's argument that the existence of knowledge establishes the necessarily constructive role of consciousness in the

[130] 'Hume I' 321.
[131] 'Aristotle' 56.
[132] Wempe, *T.H. Green's Theory of Positive Freedom*, pp. 69–70; MS6a, T.H. Green Papers, Balliol College, Oxford.
[133] 'Kant' 41–8, 61–9.
[134] PE 15–6, 63.
[135] PE 15–16, 63; 'Aristotle' 73.
[136] ICG 15.
[137] PE 1–8; 'Hume I' 1–5; 'Spencer I' 1; 'Popular Philosophy', *passim*; but see Balfour, 'Criticism of Current Idealistic Theories', 437–40.
[138] 'Aristotle' 56–57.

perceived world inhabited by humans. Despite these qualifications, this aspect of Green's theory may still seem a little 'mystical', echoing as it does Plato's conception of knowledge as recollection, and Hegel's conception of the categories.[139] Against this charge, one can note Green's identification of this aspect of his system with Kant's 'synthetic unity of apperception'.[140] Given everything else that he has demonstrated about the logic of being capable of possessing knowledge, the explanation offered by Green does seem to be a very plausible one. Consequently, Green appears to have given very good reasons for believing that the existence of these basic categories, or universals, is a necessary presupposition of the experiences most people take themselves to have. Nevertheless, it may still be that this proof is gained at too high a price. Some commentators claim that Green's metaphysics of knowledge requires you to believe in the existence of God. It is to this objection that the analysis must now turn.

---

[139] Ellerton 1 69–72; Plato, 'Phaedo', 72e–76e; Plato, 'Philebus', 34a–c; Hegel, *Philosophical Propaedeutic*, pp. 67, 105–07, 134; see Haldar, 'Green and his Critics', 173–75; Ewing, *Idealism*, pp. 399–401; Thomas, *Moral Philosophy of T.H. Green*, pp. 143–44.
[140] PE 32–33.

4

The Eternal Consciousness

I

Individual Persons and the Eternal Consciousness

It was noted in the second chapter of this book that Green was a devout if un-orthodox Christian (§2.II). He understood his philosophy to be in essence a rationalisation of his faith,[1] and many commentators allege that this creates fatal problems for his 'metaphysics of experience or knowledge'. Often, it seems that his faith infects rather than strengthens his position, particularly in the form of his concept of the 'eternal consciousness'.[2] F.C.S. Schiller writes of Green's 'fearful

---

[1] 'Immortality' 182–83.

[2] This point has been widely commented upon from many different philosophical and religious perspectives, for example by Arthur J. Balfour, 'Green's Metaphysics of Knowledge', *Mind*, 9:33 os (January 1884), 79–82, 88–92; Andrew Seth, *Hegelianism and Personality* (Edinburgh and London: William Blackwood, 1887), pp. 74–81 *passim*, 214–30 *passim*; Arthur Eastwood, 'On Thought-Relations', *Mind*, 16 os (1891), 247; Arthur J. Balfour, 'Criticism of Current Idealistic Theories', *Mind*, 2 ns (1893), 431–37; George S. Fullerton, 'The "Knower" in Psychology', *Philosophical Review*, 4:1 (1897), 9–11; S.S. Laurie, 'Metaphysics of T.H. Green', *Philosophical Review*, 6:2 (1897), 124–25, 129–31; W.H. Fairbrother, *Philosophy of Thomas Hill Green* (London: Methuen, 1896), pp. 156–72; E.B. McGilvary, 'Eternal Consciousness', *Mind*, 10 ns (1901), 479–97; Alfred E. Taylor, *Problem of Conduct* (London: MacMillan, 1901), pp. 59–83 *passim*; Henry Sidgwick, 'Metaphysics of T.H. Green', in his *Lectures on the Philosophy of Kant and other philosophical lectures and essays* (London: MacMillan, 1905), pp. 230–32, 239–55 *passim*, 258–66; Henry Sturt, *Idoli Theatri: A criticism of Oxford thought and thinkers from the standpoint of personal idealism* (London: MacMillan 1906), pp. 76–79 *passim*, 211–59; G.S. Brett, 'T.H. Green', in J. Hastings, ed., *Encyclopaedia of Religion and Ethics*, 13 vols. (Edinburgh: T. and T. Clark, 1908–27), vol. 6, p. 439; Arthur K. Rogers, *English and American Philosophy since 1800: A critical survey* (New York: MacMillan, 1922), pp. 231–4; W.D. Lamont, *Introduction to Green's Moral Philosophy* (London: George Allen and Unwin, 1934), pp. 179–90; H.D. Lewis, 'Does the Good Will Define its own Content? – A study of T.H. Green', in his *Freedom and History* (London: George Allen and Unwin, 1962), pp. 15–17; Alfred W. Benn, *History of English Rationalism in the Nineteenth Century*, 2 vols. (New York: Russell and Russell, 1962), vol. 2, pp. 401–10; Rudolf Metz, *Hundred Years of British Philosophy* (London: George Allen and Unwin, 1938), pp. 277–78; Melvin Richter, *Politics of Conscience: T.H. Green and his age* (London: Weidenfeld and Nicolson, 1964), 182–87; Frederick Copleston, *History of Philosophy VIII: Bentham to Russell* (London: Burns and Oates, 1966), pp. 169–71 Amal K. Mukhopadhyay, *Ethics of Obedience: A study of the philosophy of T.H. Green* (Calcutta: World Private, 1967), pp. 22–31; Ann R. Cacoullos, *Thomas Hill Green: Philosopher of rights* (New York: Twayne, 1974), pp. 54–55, 107; Peter Robbins, *British Hegelians 1875–1925* (New York and London; Garland, 1982), p. 92; James T. Kloppenberg, *Uncertain Victory: Social democracy and progressivism in European and American thought, 1870–1920* (New York and Oxford: Oxford University Press, 1986), pp. 73–75 *passim*; Noel O'Sullivan, *Problem of Political Obligation* (New York: Garland, 1987), pp. 55–68 *passim*; David Crossley, 'Self-conscious Agency and the Eternal Consciousness: Ultimate reality in Thomas Hill Green', *Ultimate Meaning and Reality*, 13 (1990), 11–14; Peter Hylton, *Russell, Idealism and the Emergence of Analytic Philosophy* (Oxford; Oxford University Press, 1990), pp. 21–47 *passim*; John Skorupski, *A History of Western Philosophy: 6. English-Language Philosophy 1750–1945* (Oxford: Oxford University Press, 1993), pp. 92–93; Andrew Vincent, 'Metaphysics and Ethics in the Philosophy of T.H. Green', in Maria

and wonderful leap from the fact that all phenomena appear to some individual self to the conclusion that they are, *therefore*, appearances to a universal self'.[3] Similarly, Henry Sturt argues that 'an intensely religious consciousness like T.H. Green's glides absent-mindedly over chasms hopelessly impassable to mere logic.'[4] Moreover, the criticism is entailed by W.D. Lamont's assertion that 'The theistic and the pantheistic ideas which struggled together in his (Green's) mind never quite fought it out to a finish.'[5] On one level at least, the 'Neo-Hegelian fetish of the "eternal self" is not a minor problem and must be addressed.[6]

The difficulty which some commentators – most notably Arthur Balfour, Francis Bradley and Henry Sidgwick – find with Green's name for this principle (that is, the 'eternal consciousness') can be removed easily.[7] Green's reasons for using 'consciousness' should be self-evident given his belief in the ultimately mental nature of our reality. That this consciousness is 'eternal' for Green stems solely from his argument that it is a precondition of a consciousness of time, in that an element within a stream of events cannot itself be conscious of itself as part of that stream. To be conscious of such stream as a stream, one must be able to comprehend one's nature as an element within a larger whole, and that requires one to gain cognitive distance from the immediate content of one's own consciousness. This applies logically to both the (projected) eternal consciousness and to each individual consciousness. From this point, it is a short step for Green at least to the characterisation of it as 'eternal', a characterisation which lends his theory to a religious reading, which is one of his goals. It is unclear however why Green cannot argue merely that the subject is aware of its place in the stream only at some point after the events, even if that is very soon after the events. The criticism is merely a terminological quibble and so should be of no real interest here.[8] Nevertheless, it is important to insist on the limited nature of Green's reason for using the term 'eternal' here and in relation to individual consciousnesses, as scholars continue to give great weight to what is ultimately merely an example of metaphysical pathos or a rhetorical flourish.[9]

Dimova-Cookson and W.J. Mander, eds., *T.H. Green: Ethics, metaphysics and political philosophy* (Oxford: Clarendon, 2006), pp. 83–95.

[3]   Ferdinand C.S. Schiller, *Humanism: Philosophical essays* (London: MacMillan, 1903), p. 112.

[4]   Sturt, *Idoli Theatri*, p. 79.

[5]   Lamont, *Introduction to Green's Moral Philosophy*, p. 190; see also W. Hirst, *Jesus and the Moralists* (London; Epworth, 1935), p. 110.

[6]   Taylor, *Problem of Conduct*, p. 429n2.

[7]   Balfour, 'Green's Metaphysics of Knowledge', 89; Francis H. Bradley, *Appearance and Reality: A metaphysical essay*, second edition (Oxford: Clarendon, 1897), pp. 41–45; Henry Sidgwick, *Lectures on the Ethics of T.H. Green, Mr. Herbert Spencer, and J. Martineau* (London: MacMillan, 1902), pp. 51–4, 100–2, 116; Sidgwick, 'Metaphysics of T.H. Green', pp. 260–61. Also Howard V. Knox, 'Green's Refutation of Empiricism', *Mind*, 9 ns (1900), 72–4; McGilvary, 'Eternal Consciousness', 489–92, 495–7; Hastings Rashdall, *Theory of Good and Evil*, 2 vols. (London: Oxford University Press, 1924), vol. 2, pp. 246–9; Mukhopadhyay, *Ethics of Obedience*, pp. 27–30; Crossley, 'Self-conscious Agency and the Eternal Consciousness', 17–8.

[8]   See Gustavus Cunningham, *Idealist Argument in Recent British and American Philosophy* (New York: Books for Libraries, 1933), pp. 46n, 57–60.

[9]   This will become clear in §6.V in relation to Terence Irwin's critique of Green's discussion of determinism. On metaphysical pathos, see A.O. Lovejoy, *Great Chain of Being* (London: Harvard University Press, 1936), pp. 10–14.

It must be remembered what Green's conception of Christian knowledge of God – and hence what the latter's existence for man – actually is. Green believes that God exists in two senses. Firstly, He exists in heaven, separate from temporal human existence;[10] secondly, God is found also 'within' each individual: that is, within his conscience, or, more generally, his consciousness. Each conception should be assessed separately, and then it must be asked whether and how they interrelate.[11] Straightaway, Green shows an ambivalence to God's heavenly existence. On the one hand, repeatedly he characterises God as the creator of the universe and as a being *which exists and then communicates itself* to human beings.[12] Yet, there are many places where Green is far more cautious about accepting God's alleged heavenly existence and an afterlife.[13] For example, he argues that it is very dangerous to describe the eternal consciousness as 'supernatural'. By so doing, 'we suggest a relation between it and nature of a kind which has really no place except *within* nature, as a relation of phenomenon to phenomenon.'[14] This underpins his contention later in the *Prolegomena* that,

> The most convinced Theist must admit that God is as unimaginable as He is unperceivable, unimaginable because unperceivable, for that which we imagine (in the proper sense of the term) has the necessary finiteness of that which we perceive; that statements, therefore, which in any strict sense could only be applied to an imaginable finite agent, cannot in any such sense be applied to God.[15]

In other words, when using terms such as 'supernatural' in relation to the eternal consciousness, one runs the risk of implying that it is an entity which can exist as a phenomenon in the same way that, for example, a rock can do. This claim would entail that the principle in virtue of which there can be such a thing as a knowable world is itself part of that world. The existence of the eternal consciousness would have to be created by the world before the eternal consciousness could create anything, including the world.

Criticisms such as those made by Schiller, Sturt, Lamont, Taylor, and the others noted above, ignore the main thrust of Green's theory. Hopefully, the analysis presented in the previous chapter has gone some way to establishing that Green's metaphysics of experience is viable without God if those who use the term mean by 'God' 'a person much like themselves, with thoughts and feelings limited and mutable in the process of time'.[16] Green's metaphysics has progressed a long way without any reference being made to an entity that is 'theistic' in Robert Flint's terms of forming part of 'the doctrine that the universe owes its existence, and continuance in existence, to the reason and will of a self-existent Being, who is

[10]   PE 187; DSF 21.
[11]   Richter, *Politics of Conscience*, pp. 186–87; Mukhopadhyay, *Ethics of Obedience*, pp. 24–25.
[12]   PE 100, 182, 184, 192; DSF 21–23.
[13]   See also his letters to Charlotte Symonds, his future wife, in the months following her father's death on 25 February 1871: 10 and 25 April 1871 (*Works*, vol. 5, pp. 438, 439).
[14]   PE 54. Compare with PE 52, 319–21, 353.
[15]   PE 318.
[16]   Bradley, *Appearance and Reality*, p. 471. Bradley himself rejects this use of the term 'God', of course.

infinitely powerful, wise, and good.'[17] Obviously, the part of the universe that concerns us here is the individual person's finite consciousness. In case this is not clear, I will now assess the most important of these attacks and demonstrate that one can indeed reject the implausible aspects of the eternal consciousness and yet retain all of the necessary aspects of Green's metaphysics.

Green implies that, at least in part, the eternal consciousness's existence 'divinely' transcends human existence. He writes of 'an eternally complete consciousness', the 'world-consciousness of which ours is a limited mode', and the 'intellectual principle [which] realises itself under special conditions' in man.[18] Moreover, he asserts that

> The true account of it [knowledge] is held to be that the concrete whole, which may be described indifferently as an eternal intelligence realised in the related facts of the world, or as a system of related facts rendered possible by such an intelligence, partially and gradually reproduces itself in us.[19]

By referring to the eternal consciousness in these terms, Green implies that it exists in some 'supernatural' realm, just as is implied by theism. Taken on face value, this assertion would be a problem for his metaphysics given the latter's emphasis upon the necessity of human experience.[20] On his own terms, Green cannot know whether or not the eternal consciousness has a self-subsisting nature and so cannot justifiably invoke it in his metaphysics. Yet, at times, he seems to think that he can invoke the eternal consciousness as an active participant in the world. As William Mander notes, Green claims that the 'self-distinguishing consciousness' ' "renders" the relations of the world'.[21] Green uses the word 'render' in two ways: the eternal consciousness both posits relations itself, and enables individuals to posit 'the relations of phenomena, and with them nature'.[22] He also describes the eternal consciousness as being 'immaterial and immovable, eternally one with itself,' and 'necessary to the possibility of a world of phenomena', an assertion that echoes some of Hegel's assertions concerning the non-actualized 'concept'.[23] Metaphorically, this 'concept' is the 'soul' which gives life to the 'body'.[24]

---

[17] Robert Flint, *Theism: being the Baird lecture for 1876*, ninth edition (Edinburgh and London: William Blackwood, 1895), p. 18.

[18] PE 51, 43.

[19] PE 36. For an interesting analysis of such passages, see A.C. Ewing, *Idealism: A critical survey* (London: Methuen, 1896), p. 387 & n.

[20] See Eastwood, 'On Thought-Relations', 248–50.

[21] W.J. Mander, 'In Defence of the Eternal Consciousness', in Dimova-Cookson et al, eds., *T.H. Green*, p. 202.

[22] Mander cites PE 52 in support of the claim that Green sees the eternal consciousness as actively 'positing' the relations rather than making it possible for them to be posited, although less ambiguous support for his reading can be found at PE 32, 47, 51, 72, 75, 85. For evidence of the second usage (where the eternal consciousness merely makes the positing of relations possible) see, for example, PE 8, 9, 14, 27, 36, 48, 51, 52, 66, 73, 77

[23] PE 54.

[24] Georg W.F. Hegel, *Elements of the Philosophy of Right*, trans. A.W. Wood (Cambridge: Cambridge University Press, 1991), §1A.

Clearly there is a paradox here: how can the eternal consciousness make it possible for the individual's understanding to posit relations, at the same time as positing those same relations itself? The resolution of this paradox can be found in the fact that Green's theory of mind is an attempt to give philosophical articulation to his immanentism. For example, he notes that 'the Word is nigh thee' is 'the thought of God, not as "far off" but "nigh," not as a master but as a father, not as a terrible outward power, forcing us we know not whither, but as one of whom we may say that we are reason of his reason and spirit of his spirit'.[25] He places particular importance on the fact that his manner of conceiving God '*is* ... in a certain sense to identify him with man; and that not with an abstract or collective humanity but with the individual man.'[26]

Green provides an insight into his meaning here via his consideration of the internal authority of conscience. The authority of the individual's conscience is, he writes, 'the authority of his own moral nature ... however incompletely it may be actualised in himself, he in a sense feels the possibilities, unless selfish interests have closed the avenues of his heart', 'it is a fact which in each of us exists as a possibility'.[27] In his teleological conception of identity, 'the germ and development, the possibility and the actualisation, are one and the same consciousness of self.'[28] More specifically,

> Our formula then is that God is identical with the self of every man in the sense of being the realisation of its determinate possibilities, the completion of that which, as merely in it, is incomplete and therefore unreal; that in being conscious of himself man is conscious of God, and thus knows what he himself really is.[29]

Green's explanation and defence of this claim in this unfinished draft address breaks off during an analysis of the presuppositions of knowledge of the type set out earlier in the previous chapter.[30] The key to understanding Green's position is found in his theory of 'reproduction'.[31] Green argues that a reader 'reproduces' the meaning of a sentence when he thinks the propositional content of that sentence. The individual words that make up the sentence must be read separately because they are communicated through a physical medium (the written word on the page, say) to a particular human mind. Yet, the meaning of the sentence can only be appreciated when the reader understands the proposition conveyed by the sentence as a whole.[32] The reader of the sentence is then thinking the same proposition as

---

[25] WNT 221.
[26] WNT 225.
[27] WNT 223.
[28] WNT 226.
[29] WNT 227.
[30] WNT 227–29.
[31] PE 67–73. Green uses the term 'reproduction' in a sense that anticipates the way that (on occasion) Collingwood uses 're-enactment': see Colin Tyler, 'Performativity and the Intellectual Historian's Re-enactment of Written Works', *Journal of the Philosophy of History*, 3 (2009), 176–86, especially 170–71. This interpretation fits all of the passages quoted in Mander, 'In Defence of the Eternal Consciousness', p. 193n17 (namely, PE 68, 71, 72, 99).
[32] 'And when the reading is over, the consciousness that the sentence has a meaning has become a consciousness of what in particular the meaning is, – a consciousness in which the successive

the writer of that sentence. He is not thinking 'something like' the proposition, nor is he thinking a copy of it in the sense that one might view a photograph of a landscape. The idea is simply reproduced in his mind. In precisely the same sense, the individual consciousness 'reproduces' the eternal consciousness when it gains knowledge. Green compares the process of gaining knowledge (of grasping the truth more fully) and the truth as expressed timelessly in the eternal consciousness, to 'opposite sides of the same shield'.[33] Which side of the shield one sees depends on what perspective one adopts, but the shield remains one thing viewed in two ways.

Read in this context, it can be seen that for each man, 'God' exists only as the individual's power of constructing and knowing a unified system of categories and an intelligible world of phenomena. As knowledge can only be of experience and of the results of the analysis and inferences drawn from that experience, God cannot be studied, except in so far as it is determined, meaning that for Green God cannot exist in itself. In other words, God cannot exist for us as a being which is separable from a human consciousness. In the *Prolegomena* Green stresses that it is logically incoherent to rest one's interpretation of the eternal consciousness on a denial of the independent self-consciousness of particular human persons, and hence it is logically incoherent to claim that individual persons are mere adjuncts of the eternal consciousness. As he puts it, 'It is only because we are consciously objects to ourselves, that we can conceive a world as an object to a single mind, and thus as a connected whole.'[34] To deny the self-conscious individuality of persons would itself be a denial of a necessary presupposition of one's proof of the logical necessity of the existence of the eternal consciousness itself. From this, Green concludes that the development of the virtues in the world, including (vitally in the present context) wisdom and hence truth, may arise in some sense from God, but it can only occur in particular, discrete, unique individual persons (you and I).

> The spiritual progress of mankind is thus an unmeaning phrase, unless it means a progress *of* personal character and *to* personal character – a progress of which feeling, thinking, and willing subjects are the agents and sustainers, and of which each step is a fuller realisation of the capacities of such subjects. It is simply unintelligible unless understood to be in the direction of more perfect forms of personal life.[35]

In short, despite Green's extensive use of this term and thus his extensive personi-fication of this potential state, there is no philosophical need for the eternal consciousness to be understood in 'extra-human' terms.[36] On the 'extra-human'

---

results of the mental operations involved in the reading are held together, without succession, as a connected whole.' (PE 71)

[33] PE 68.

[34] PE 182. This whole paragraph is crucial to understanding this aspect of Green's argument.

[35] PE 185.

[36] Maria Dimova-Cookson argues for the 'extra-human' reading of the eternal consciousness in her *T.H. Green's Moral and Political Philosophy: A phenomenological perspective* (Houndsmill: Palgrave, 2001), p. 29. See Leonard T. Hobhouse, *Theory of Knowledge: A contribution to some problems of logic and metaphysics* (London: Methuen, 1896), p. 537n2; Balfour, 'Green's Metaphysics of

view, somehow the eternal consciousness inhabits every individual's mind, cuckoo-like, gradually transforming the individual's consciousness. In reality, this 'cuckoo' reading is a form of theism, in that it implies God lodges within every finite mind, gradually implanting and organising the thoughts within the individual's particular consciousness. This claim is incompatible with the other strand of Green's writings in which each individual consciousness is hardwired to be self-expressing and self-organising. It is my contention that only the latter strand is required in order to deliver what is needed by Green's philosophical system. In other words, even without a theistic God, it remains plausible to argue that only when a particular agent's determinate consciousness accords perfectly with the underlying structure of his mind will he feel satisfied with his knowledge, because only then will his knowledge be complete and coherent. In this way, Green's analysis does not necessarily entail the presence of personified divine mind existing apart from or within particular human minds. It is simply that ultimately each human mind has the same intellectual substratum and the same inherent drive to express that substratum in a determinate form in its personal life.

More than this however, there is no evidence that Green endorses, or that his philosophy requires, what others have referred to as a 'super-personal' Absolute or 'transhistorical corporate agent'.[37] F.H. Bradley, for example, argues for the existence of 'one total experience, which is the Absolute, [which] has, as such, a character which, in its specific aspect of qualitative totality, must be taken not to fall within any [particular] finite centre', even though 'there is no element in the process of making all harmonious within the Absolute which does not fall within finite centres.'[38] Bosanquet makes sense of essentially the same notion by positing the existence of the Absolute in the interaction of finite minds within a community.[39] As I have argued elsewhere, such a view implies that particular finite centres are valuable only to the extent that they are necessary to manifest the Absolute in the community. Any particular finite centre is therefore dispensable to the extent that it manifests an aspect of the Absolute that is also manifested in another finite centre.[40] It is fortunate, then, that not only is there no evidence that Green held such a dangerously corporatist position, but that his insistence on the personal character of the eternal consciousness seems to make his philosophy incompatible with a mystical view of this type.

There are some interesting and important implications of the preceding analysis. The combination of critical metaphysics and speculative metaphysics which has guided my interpretation should put one on guard against the allegation that there

---

Knowledge', 88; McGilvary, 'Eternal Consciousness', 487–88; Alan J.M. Milne, 'Common Good and Rights in T.H. Green's Ethical and Political Thought', in Andrew Vincent, ed., *Philosophy of T.H. Green* (Aldershot: Gower, 1986), pp. 94–97.

[37] Bradley, *Appearance and Reality*, pp. 466–73, 563–64. David O. Brink refers to the eternal consciousness as a 'transhistorical corporate agent' in his *Perfectionism and the Common Good; Themes in the philosophy of T.H. Green* (Oxford: Clarendon, 2003), pp. 17, 65–66.

[38] Bradley, *Appearance and Reality*, p. 563.

[39] See Colin Tyler, *Idealist Political Philosophy: Pluralism and conflict in the absolute idealist tradition* (London: Continuum, 2006), chapter four, especially pp. 136–42, 149–58.

[40] See Tyler, *Idealist Political Philosophy*, pp. 149–58.

is a fundamental incompatibility between Green's method in the first and second books of the *Prolegomena*. Dimova-Cookson claims that in the first book Green seeks purely *a priori* principles of knowledge, and that he excludes any *a posteriori* principles, a position that Dimova-Cookson alleges he abandons in the second book.[41] In a sense this is true. The speculative metaphysician does not attempt to catalogue the occurrences that individuals observe between phenomena in the manner that one might merely note that certain combinations of certain stimuli are often (even are always) followed by the occurrence of a certain belief. These are merely contingent aggregates of facts, which make no reference to underlying principles of thought. After all, Green rejects J.S. Mill's theory of inference precisely at this point.[42] The speculative metaphysician, on the other hand, does play a crucial role in constructing a coherent (sc. internally-consistent and complete, or 'rational') system of principles on the basis of which the rationality of models of complex phenomena can be assessed. For example, one could not fully assess Spencer's transfigured realism without the aid of both the speculative and the critical metaphysician.

It was established in the preceding chapters that underlying the effort to construct this single coherent system is the presupposition that the growth of knowledge means the greater articulation of the categories (including relations between objects) that must underpin the totality of experience if the latter is to form a coherent whole. (This includes a principle for identifying error among our common beliefs, or 'popular philosophy', as well as the rationality found there.) In Kantian terms, Green holds that the speculative metaphysician uses her judgement to conceive true synthetic principles, and that all true synthetic principles are necessary. Complete and true knowledge is derived from the fully-rational system that combines coherently the necessary *a priori* principles sought by critical metaphysicians with the necessary synthetic principles sought by speculative metaphysicians. Even though human imperfection means that this fully-coherent system will always elude us, the respective defining aspirations of critical and speculative metaphysicians remain the same. This has profound implications for the appropriate understanding of the eternal consciousness, as Peter Nicholson makes clear.

> That there is an eternal consciousness, in Green's sense, is logically implied in an analysis of what knowledge is; but as to anything beyond the necessary existence of the eternal consciousness, its characteristics and nature or its precise relationship to human beings, we can only speculate.[43]

The critical metaphysician establishes the logical implication, whereas 'as human knowledge expands' the speculative metaphysician continually reformulates the most coherent analysis of the eternal consciousness's more determinate

---

[41] Dimova-Cookson, *T.H. Green's Moral and Political Philosophy*, pp. 23–26.

[42] 'Logic' 119–23.

[43] Peter Nicholson, 'Green's 'Eternal Consciousness'', in Dimova-Cookson *et al.*, eds., *T.H. Green*, p. 148.

'characteristics and nature' and 'precise relationship to human beings'. Even this is only part of the story however. One should extend this analysis by considering Green's model of the processes by which the individual's mind comes to 'realise' the 'eternal consciousness'.

II
Process of Individual Self-realisation

The individual's 'consciousness', 'self', 'character' or 'personality' (terms Green uses synonymously) improves to the extent that it becomes more coherent (more complete and internally consistent). Such improvement relies on the individual's exercise of their powers of analysis and constructive judgement. In this crucial sense, Green holds that the individual's determinate personality is an achievement of their highest mental capacities. He is emphatic that the individual's personality is a self-creation, it is the result of the exercise of the individual's mind. This is the essence of the first moment of Green's theory of self-realisation, and forms the pattern for the remainder of this theory. Crucially as we have seen, Green argues that the individual personality is the primary fact of this theory, the unassailable claim from which all else follows. To reduce individual personality to an adjunct of the eternal consciousness 'would be in contradiction of the very ground upon which we believe that a divine principle does so realise itself in [the individual] man'.[44]

It is striking then that William Mander has claimed 'individualist' interpretations of the preceding type 'have little to recommend them.' He has argued that any successful reading must theorise precisely Green's (alleged) belief that the individual is some form of adjunct to the eternal consciousness. Hence, in addition to the language of 'reproduction', Mander notes, 'Green tends to employ an alternative set of metaphors, like participating, partaking, expressing and appropriating' when characterising the relationship between individual consciousnesses and the eternal consciousness.[45] Mander claims that the allegedly competing 'implications' of these terms introduce profound ambiguities into Green's position.[46]

Unfortunately, Mander does not analyse in any depth Green's use in this context of any of these terms, nor does he consider what uses Green may have intended. Instead, he labels them 'metaphorical', without trying to explain in what sense he believes they are metaphorical for Green. Most of the words that Mander finds so problematic, in fact, appear far less frequently and far less problematically in the *Prolegomena* than he implies. For example, the verb form of the word 'partake' and

---

[44] PE 182; compare PE 80–85, 99–102, 182.

[45] Mander, 'In Defence of the Eternal Consciousness', p. 205. Andrew Vincent argues that Green became increasingly alive to the worry that the eternal consciousness left no room for the individual agent (Vincent, 'Metaphysics and Ethics in the Philosophy of T.H. Green', pp. 95–97). My interpretation runs counter to Vincent's view of course.

[46] In practice, Mander himself fails to give due weight to these alleged ambiguities and confusions in his quasi-Bradleyian re-interpretation, in which Green understands the eternal consciousness 'as a kind of super-organism in which all finite lives somehow participate' (Mander, 'In Defence of the Eternal Consciousness', p. 206). Dimova-Cookson takes a similar line in Dimova-Cookson, *T.H. Green's Moral and Political Philosophy*, p. 29.

its derivatives occurs approximately seven times. In two instances Green uses it to mean, in the OED's words, to 'be characterized by (a quality)',[47] while the remaining five times he uses it in the sense of to 'join in (an activity)'.[48] None of these instances relate to the eternal consciousness in that manner that concerns Mander. Similarly, the verb form of 'participate' and its derivatives occurs only seven times. As with 'partake', 'participate' as a verb is always used either in the sense of to 'be involved; take part [in an activity]' or 'have or possess (a particular quality): *both members participate of harmony*', and none relate directly to the eternal consciousness.[49] Each of the 'participation' passages cited by Mander uses the term in the sense of 'have or possess'.[50] Next, only twice does Green use 'appropriate' (and its derivatives) in a sense other than either 'suitable' or to acquire as one's legal property.[51] In both instances, this other sense is to acquire as part of one's mental framework, or, more

---

[47] 'this consciousness of objects, whether any animals *partake of* it or no, is the characteristic thing in human experience' (PE 123); 'The "expediency," for the sake of which a departure from the established rule is pressed for, is equally founded on a conception of social good, but on the conception of a good in which a wider range of persons is contemplated *as partaking*.' (PE 330); italics added in all cases.

[48] 'they are not indulgences of a kind in which the animals are found *to partake*.' and 'the attraction of pleasures, "of which the other animals *partake*," ' (PE 265); 'the Platonic or Aristotelian conception of virtue['s] … defects, as compared with the standard which we now acknowledge, arose from the actual shortcoming in the then achievement of the human soul — the soul of human society — as compared with that of which we are ourselves *partakers*.' (PE 279); 'The good has come to be conceived with increasing clearness, not as anything which one man or set of men can gain or enjoy to the exclusion of others, but as a spiritual activity in which all may *partake*, and in which all must *partake*, if it is to amount to a full realisation of the faculties of the human soul.' (PE 286); italics added in all cases.

[49] 'Given the idea of a common good and of *self-determined participators in it* – the idea implied, as we have seen, in the most primitive human society – the tendency of the idea in the minds of all capable of it must be to include, as *participators of* the good, all who have dealings with each other and who can communicate as "I" and "Thou." '(PE 209); 'In Aristotle's view … the life of rational self-determined activity … was only possible for a few among the few. It presupposed active *participation in* a civil community.' (PE 258); 'Moral development, as has been previously explained more at large, is a progress in which the individual's conception of the kind of life that would be implied in his perfection gradually becomes fuller and more determinate; fuller and more determinate both in regard to the range of persons whose *participation in* the perfect life is thought of as necessary to its attainment by any one, and in regard to the qualities on the part of the individual which it is thought must be exercised in it.' 'the perfect life as essentially conditioned by the exercise of virtues, resting on a self-sacrificing will, in which it is open to all men *to participate*,' 'But he cannot think of himself as satisfied in any life other than a social life, exhibiting the exercise of self-denying will, and in which "the multitude of the redeemed," which is all men, shall *participate*.' (PE 370); 'That realisation of the powers of the human spirit, which we deem the true end, is not to be thought of merely as something in a remote distance, towards which we may take steps now, but in which there is no present *participation*. It is continuously going on, though in varying and progressive degrees of completeness; and the individual's sacrifice of an inclination, harmless or even in its way laudable, for the sake of a higher good, is itself already in some measure an attainment of the higher good.' (PE 376); italics added in all cases.

[50] Mander, 'In Defence of the Eternal Consciousness', p. 193n 17, quoting IPR 146; 'Works of Fiction' 22; 'Logic' 190.

[51] Another possible meaning would be to 'rework in a manner that fits one's own circumstances' (in this sense it approximates to the OED's 'the deliberate reworking of images and styles from earlier, well-known works of art').

simply, to learn and integrate into one's existing knowledge.[52] Clearly, Green is not using 'appropriation' in a mystical or even controversial sense.

Earlier in his chapter, Mander raised similar objections to a number of other terms and phrases that Green uses when characterising the relationship between the individual and the eternal consciousness. The term 'render' has been examined already. Many of the other terms mentioned by Mander become less worrying once one reads them as Green does.[53] For example, Green claims that 'nature "results from" or "exists through" … [the] action [of the eternal consciousness]; it [the eternal consciousness] "constitutes" the world; understanding "makes" nature, which is its "product" '. These propositions become far more intelligible once one remembers that Green is concerned only with nature 'for us', that is, as a coherent system of categories (including relations) underpinning the phenomena experienced by the individual, the presuppositions of which the individual can discover through the rational analysis that one carries out in the mode of both a critical and a speculative metaphysician.[54]

The terms that worry Mander ('participation', 'partaking', 'rendering', and so on) are, in reality, all either aspects of or synonyms for the process of 'realisation' in the sense of 'fulfilling one's potential'.[55] Hence, Green seems to conceive the eternal consciousness to be the particularised substratum of each individual personal consciousness, the mould into which sensations must fit in order to be intelligible. Each particularised instantiation of the eternal consciousness is potentially complete in and of itself. It does not need to be – indeed it cannot be – completed by other particularised instantiations, in the manner of Bradley and Bosanquet's 'super-personal' or 'corporate' Absolute. An individual mind which did not possess the eternal consciousness at least potentially, if such an idea is in any way meaningful, would not be able to categorise or organise the chaotic stream of sensory impulses that reach it through its body's eyes, ears, nose, taste-buds and nerve-endings. As has been demonstrated, an uncategorised and unrelated sensation is not understandable by a human consciousness. Facts only exist in relation to other facts. For this reason, without a perfectly coherent system of categories potentially to be actualised in the human consciousness, there could be no possibility of human knowledge.

---

[52] 'every step forward in real intelligence, whether in the way of addition to what we call the stock of human knowledge, or of *an appropriation by the individual of some part of that stock*, is only explicable on supposition that successive reports of the senses, successive efforts of attention, successive processes of observation and experiment, are determined by the consciousness that all things form a related whole — a consciousness which is operative throughout their succession and which at the same time realises itself through them.' (PE 70); italics added. 'Whatever the object which we set ourselves to understand, the process begins with our attention being challenged by some fact as simply alien and external to us, as no otherwise related to us than is implied in its being there to be known; and it ends, or rather is constantly approaching an end never reached, *in the mental appropriation of the fact*, through its being brought under definite relations with the cosmos of facts in which we are already at home.' (PE 132); italics added.

[53] PE 36.

[54] Mander, 'In Defence of the Eternal Consciousness', p. 202; 'Kant' 72–77.

[55] Mander quotes PE 67, 68, 82 in Mander, 'In Defence of the Eternal Consciousness', p. 193n17.

Unfortunately as was noted earlier, an ambiguity runs throughout Green's metaphysics, one that is reflected in the characterisation of it as a 'metaphysics of experience or knowledge'. Green understands experience as purely phenomeno-logical, whereas he understands knowledge as coherent experience that is also objectively true. Does he believe that the individual's consciousness tends to try to *discover* the one system of categories, or that it tends to try to *create* such a system? Do we become aware of a pre-existing system that we have not constructed, or do 'we only find unity in the world because we have an idea that it is there, an idea which we direct our powers to realise'?[56] In other words, is the assertion of the ultimate unity of the system a logically necessary *a priori* proposition or is it a heuristic device? Green claims 'that there *is* an unalterable order of relations, if we could only find it out, is the presupposition of all our enquiry into the real nature of appearances'.[57] Or again, in his manuscripts, 'An idea [is] *formal*, when there is no existence corresponding to it, so [the] idea of [the] absolute is *formal* [since there is] no phenomenon corresponding to it. But without [the] action of this idea, [there would be] no accounting for that [effort?] to reduce experience to a unity, without which [there can be] no knowledge.'[58] One is reminded here of Hegel's philosophical History, which is guided by the assumption 'that Reason is the Sovereign of the World'.[59] In that case, the proposition is a postulate of philosophical enquiry. Moreover, it is a postulate that Hegel thinks can be tested by assessing how well it explains the empirical evidence. (Hegel thought that his postulate fitted that evidence very well indeed.)[60]

One problem is that it is unclear which criteria one should use in order to identify empirical facts as being relevant evidence and then to assess how 'well' Green's postulate explains that evidence (just as it is unclear what criteria of identification and assessment Hegel should use). Demands of logical coherence might allow the critical metaphysician to proceed a certain distance (including by establishing the formal necessity of an eternal consciousness), but how is the speculative metaphysician to move forward?[61]

Maybe the source of such concerns about Green's postulation of the ultimate harmony of the world is the assumption that one should be satisfied only with proof and truth, rather than judgement and plausibility. Adopting this second perspective, one can make sense of Green's position if one understands him as in effect endorsing Hegel's claim that 'To him who looks upon the world rationally,

---

[56] PE 149.

[57] PE 26.

[58] 'Moral Philosophy' 310; also quoted with slight variations of transcription in Ben Wempe, *T.H. Green's Theory of Positive Freedom* (Exeter: Imprint Academic, 2004), p. 142, and *Works* V, p. 188.

[59] Georg W. Hegel, *Philosophy of History*, trans. J. Sibree (New York: Dover, 1956), p. 9. See Tyler, *Idealist Political Philosophy*, pp. 13–15.

[60] Hegel, *Philosophy of History*, p. 10.

[61] Green's analysis of the proper procedures of both the critical and speculative metaphysicians might be moved forwarded by drawing on Michael Freeden's notion of logical and cultural adjacency, as developed in his *Ideologies and Political Theory: A conceptual approach* (Oxford: Clarendon, 1996), part 1, especially chapter 2. However, this would be a way of extending and possibly moving towards completing Green's analysis, rather than simply interpreting it.

the world in its turn, presents a rational aspect. The relation is mutual.'[62] Hence, Hegel himself refers to his belief 'that Reason is in history' as 'partly at least a plausible faith, partly it is a cognition of philosophy.'[63] Indeed, there is strong evidence that this is Green's position as well. For example, the motto of his lay sermon on 'Faith', which also literally served as his own epitaph, was that 'we walk by faith, not by sight'.[64]

The individual is driven instinctively to undertake these cognitive operations. This claim underpins my 'humanist' reading. It is humanist in the sense that it deanthropomorphizes the eternal consciousness: it shows how that Green's metaphysics does not logically presuppose the intervention of a transcendent personal God in the consciousness of individuals. As this point is central to such an interpretation of Green's conception of the eternal consciousness, it is worth quoting the following passage at length. This is one of the places where Green is most explicit in stating what I see to be the core of his case.

> The exercise of the one activity [cognition, a.k.a. understanding] is always a necessary accompaniment of the other [i.e. desire]. In all exercise of the understanding desire is at work. The result of any process of cognition is desired throughout it. No man learns to know anything without desiring to know it. The presentation of a fact which does not on the first view fit itself into any of our established theories of the world, awakens a desire for such adjustment, which may be effected either by further acquaintance with the relations of the fact, or by a modification of our previous theories, or by a combination of both processes. All acquisition of knowledge takes place in this way, and in every stage of the process we are moved by a forecast, however vague, of its result. The learner of course knows not how he will assimilate the strange fact till he has done so, but the idea of its assimilation as possible evokes his effort, precisely as, in a case naturally described as one of desire, the idea, let us say, of winning the love of a woman evokes the effort of the lover to realise the idea.[65]

Clearly, reason and desire work together to push the individual to gain greater knowledge of the world of nature then, in a way that creates significant problems for those who wish to see a fundamental incompatibility between Green's 'metaphysics of experience or knowledge' and his theory of the will.[66] There are strong echoes here of Aristotle's theory of the 'prime mover', a debt that I have discussed elsewhere.[67] This is especially true of the final sentence which calls to

---

[62] Hegel, *Philosophy of History*, p. 11.

[63] Georg W.F. Hegel. *Philosophy of Mind: Part Three of the Encyclopaedia of the Philosophical Sciences (1830)*, trans. William Wallace and A.V. Miller (Oxford: Clarendon, 1971), §549 (p. 281).

[64] 2 Cor. 5:7, quoted at 'Faith' 253.

[65] PE 134.

[66] Dimova-Cookson, *T.H. Green's Moral and Political Philosophy*, for example, chapter one.

[67] Colin Tyler, 'Evolution of the Epistemic Self: A critique of the evolutionary epistemology of Thomas Hill Green and his followers', *Bradley Studies*, 4:2 (Autumn 1998), 175–94, especially 178–83. My position has developed in many ways since writing that piece. Something like this view seems to be implied in Leslie Armour, 'Green's Idealism and the Metaphysics of Ethics', in Dimova-Cookson et al, eds., *T.H. Green*, pp. 181–86, although Armour and I diverge fundamentally on much else. Green read Aristotle in the original Greek (probably the Bekker text, 1831, held in Balliol College library.) Green's partial translation of *De Anima* is held at Balliol, MS16, 'Translation of Aristotle's *de Anima* [Nearly complete but omitting the end of III.3

mind Aristotle's assertion that the prime mover 'causes motion as being an object of love'.[68] I suggest that Green believes the idea of a single coherent system of categories (the eternal consciousness) inspires the individual to seek out the harmony underlying their experiences, just as Aristotle's prime mover 'moves [the individual as a thinking, rational being] without [itself] being moved'; both Aristotle's prime mover and Green's spiritual principle are therefore 'something eternal', and both bring the individual to 'participate' in them without recourse to mysticism or magic.[69] The proposition that there is a unifying substratum to consciousness even emerges in modern psychology as a necessary premise for at least one non-theistic model of human mental development.[70]

The case developed above creates significant problems for Dimova-Cookson's claim that Green 'would not say that the "spiritual principle" can be understood as the principle on which personal experience functions. His commitment to opposing naturalism would not permit him to admit that something of a non-rational nature could play a fundamental role in human motivation.'[71] It also radically undermines David Brink's assertion that: 'Whereas the metaphysical and epistemological arguments of the first part of the *Prolegomena* seem to demand a single transcendent self-consciousness that is outside space and time, much of Green's ethics, political philosophy, and theology seems to treat the corporate spiritual principle as a transhistorical agent that is immanent in the lives of individual agents and progressive social institutions. Green must choose whether the Absolute is transcendent or immanent.'[72]

The humanist reading defended in this chapter supports the conclusion that the increasing coherence of our knowledge is better understood as the result of our instinctive drive to understand the world as unified, rather than as evidence of the gradual reproduction of the 'divine' eternal consciousness in man.[73] This

---

and the start of III.7.]' (addition by Thomas, *Moral Philosophy of T.H. Green*, p. 381). In fact, Green omits some other sections as well as those listed by Thomas. See also 'Aristotle' 84–91 *passim*.

[68] Aristotle, 'Metaphysics', in his *Metaphysics, X–XIV, Oeconomica, Magna Moralia*, trans. Hugh Tredennick and G. Cyril Armstrong (Cambridge, Mass, and London: Loeb, 1935), book XII. vii.4.

[69] 'The object of desire and the object of thought move without being moved, the primary objects of desire and thought are the same. For it is the apparent good that is the object of appetite, and the real good that is the object of the rational will.' 'And thought thinks itself through participation in the object of thought; for it becomes an object of thought by the act of apprehension and thinking, so that thought and the object of thought are the same, because that which is receptive of the object of thought, *i.e.* essence, is thought. And it actually functions when it possesses this object. Hence it is actuality rather than potentiality that is held to be the divine possession of rational thought, and its active contemplation is that which is most pleasant and best.' Aristotle, 'Metaphysics', book XII.vii.2, 8.

[70] For example, 'I postulated a preformed organization independent of consciousness ... Some such working hypothesis seems inescapable' Anthony Storr, *Integrity of Personality* (Harmondsworth: Penguin, 1960), p. 171.

[71] Dimova-Cookson, *T.H. Green's Moral and Political Philosophy*, p. 27. She regards this as 'clearly the main weakness of his epistemology'.

[72] Brink, *Perfectionism and the Common Good*, p. 17.

[73] See Harold H. Joachim, *Nature of Truth* (Oxford: Clarendon, 1906), p. 42; John H. Muirhead, *Service of the State: Four lectures on the political teaching of T.H. Green* (London: Murray, 1908), pp. 13–18; John H. Muirhead, *Platonic Tradition in Anglo-Saxon Philosophy* (London: George Allen and Unwin, 1931), pp. 204–05, 209, 213–14; Crossley, 'Self-conscious Agency and the Eternal

reading is attractive because it does much to answer two of the main criticisms of Green's metaphysics: that it is mystical, and that it does not explain how individual consciousnesses 'partake' of the eternal consciousness.[74] This serves to reinforce my suggestion that Green's theory is far more plausible that some commentators have argued, once its religious overtones have been removed. Yet, Peter Nicholson objects strongly to such a move: 'we cannot eliminate "God" without altering the meaning of "man".'

> We would, from Green's point of view, have cut out the heart of his philosophy, which supplies the life-blood of the individual's intellectual and moral activity; and thereby we would have decisively weakened every part of his philosophy, including his moral and political philosophy.[75]

In response, it is important to notice that the preceding analysis does not seek to 'eliminate' the eternal consciousness from Green's metaphysics. It merely seeks to identify those elements of Green's theory of the eternal consciousness that do any philosophical work.[76] I have argued that it is unnecessary to intimate, as we have seen at times Green does, that the eternal consciousness is a personified interventionist agent. The latter claim plays no necessary role in Green's metaphysics, meaning that it is an unnecessary aspect of the philosophical 'characteristics and nature' of the eternal consciousness, and so should be dropped.

Undoubtedly, Nicholson is correct that, given Green's distaste for atheism and atheists, he (Green) would have seen my proposed reading as an anaemic shadow of his full-blooded eternal consciousness. For example, Green is reported to have said of the opinions regarding religion (and possibly birth control) of Charles Bradlaugh (1833–91), the notorious atheist, that 'they were as repugnant to him as they could be.'[77] Similarly, Green is reported to have 'cried out impatiently' regarding Paul Bert (1833–86), the French republican and physiologist, 'I can't stand a medical Atheist'.[78] Yet, the non-theistic eternal consciousness should not seem a lifeless ghost to those of us who respect individual persons as independent, potentially self-directing and self-realising beings, rather than as God's children. The key point is that both the humanist and the theistic characterisations rely

---

Consciousness', 14; Milne, 'Common Good and Rights in T.H. Green's Ethical and Political Thought', pp. 94–97.

[74] Sturt, *Idoli Theatri*, pp. 231–2, 237–40, 251; Hylton, *Russell, Idealism and the Emergence of Analytic Philosophy*, pp. 37–39.

[75] Nicholson, 'Green's 'Eternal Consciousness'', p. 158. Nicholson does not name my position explicitly as the object of concern here, although it fits the characterisation of my position that he gave on *ibid.*, p. 157.

[76] My core aspiration has not changed since the first version of this work, and neither has the essence of my argument.

[77] Report compiled by Nicholson from *Oxford Chronicle*, *Oxford Times* and Green's Papers, of Green's speech to the North Ward Liberal Association, 7 March 1882, in his *Works* 5, p. 396; see pp. 396–97, 401; also Green, 'Lectures on Moral and Political Philosophy [1867]', in his *Works* 5, pp. 119–20.

[78] John St Loe Strachey, 'Recollection' [1888], in Colin Tyler, ed., 'Recollections Regarding Thomas Hill Green', *Collingwood and British Idealism Studies*, 14:2 (2008), 64–65. See also 'Christian Dogma' 182; WG 245, 'Faith' 270–71, 'English Revolution' 306, 313; Nettleship 'Memoir', p. clvii.

on what Stendhal called 'crystallisation': 'a mental process which draws from everything that happens new proofs of the perfection of the loved one.'[79] (See §§2. IV, 3.II.) Both the humanist and the theist retain the ideal as a source of validation and authority for the individual's potential of arriving at true knowledge, as well as objective values and valuable forms of character and action.[80] The difference is that the humanist projects the potential for perfect knowledge and a set of ideal human potentials without also positing (and seeking greater authority from) their personification in a personal god. The fact that these ideals must be held self-consciously by the individual if they are to function as ideals for her, does not entail that they must already be known or realised self-consciously by God. For both the theist and the humanist, that there must be such ideals if we are to know anything or to be capable of improvement is established by critical metaphysics, while specifying what the determinate ideal *is* is a goal of speculative metaphysics. Moreover, atheists are just as likely as theists to show reverence for and fidelity towards their highest values, and they are just as likely to abhor the oppression of human beings and the waste of human potential.[81]

III
Conclusion

Green starts from the Kantian question 'how is knowledge possible?' He argues that knowledge is and can only be of experiences and what our experiences either logically presuppose or logically imply. What cannot be experienced or logically derived from our experiences cannot be known. As a transcendental idealist, he argues that 'things in themselves' cannot be experienced by humans and so, strictly speaking, things in themselves do not 'exist'. The very act of experiencing destroys the mind-independent nature of the object. He attacks Kant for his inconsistency on this point because, even though Kant accepts idealism, he still presupposes the existence of an external world, a world of 'things in themselves'. To Green, this claim is unjustifiable. The only world that humans can know is, in its essence, mental. The next stage of Green's argument is more problematic. He argues that consciousness interprets sensations which seem to originate in an external world. The problem is that this external world would have to be mind-independent. More importantly, on his own terms the sensations which are interpreted by the mind cannot be experienced in themselves, and so cannot be known in themselves. For this reason, they cannot form valid aspects of his metaphysics of knowledge. He is committing the sin for which he condemned Kant.

Knowledge presupposes *a priori* categories and relations. Furthermore, knowledge can only be assumed to be possible once one presupposes that all facts are ultimately consistent with each other. If ultimately experiences cannot be

[79]   Stendhal, *Love*, trans. G. Sale and S. Sale (Harmondsworth: Penguin, 1975), p. 45. I am grateful to Noël O'Sullivan for this way of characterising the point.

[80]   PE 73.

[81]   For an interesting even if not unproblematic popular discussion of this and related issues, see André Comte-Sponville, *Book of Atheist Spirituality: An elegant argument for spirituality without God*, trans. Nancy Huston (London: Bantam, 2008), especially pp. 44–49.

harmonised in this way, there could be no orderly understanding of the world. The categories which constitute the objects of our experience are themselves necessarily constituted by their relations to other qualities. This act of relating can only be performed by a mind, which is what establishes the mental nature of reality. The act of experiencing is necessarily constitutive of the world in which we live. The dialectical relationship between consciousness and the world it perceives entails the collapse of any ultimate distinction between the subject and the object. Green's arguments that (a) knowledge only exists for a consciousness, (b) the system of true facts is ultimately coherent, and (c) the truth of a fact does not depend on its being known, lead him to posit the existence of a divine mind of which individual human minds 'partake'. This is the eternal consciousness. This infamous concept can be depersonified and hence becomes the underlying structure of human consciousness: *for us* the eternal consciousness exists as a necessary substratum of each individual human consciousness, in the sense of functioning as consciousness's ideal of the mould into which sensations must fit in order to be intelligible. A mind that did not possess this underlying principle of analysis and harmonisation of experience would be simply a jumble of unrelated sensations.

In short, this chapter has established that Green presents a more plausible and coherent 'metaphysics of experience or knowledge' than is often claimed. Its most obvious problem, the eternal consciousness when understood as a personal, consciously interventionist God, is a thoroughly dispensable aspect of the theory. Crucially, Green has established that the human mind is the creator the world in which humans live. In other words, the world we know and act in is a self-instantiation or self-expression of the human mind. He goes on to argue that, in this sense, the individual must be free when she acts, for she is not determined by anything outside of her own mind. Chapter five will analyse this stage of Green's argument in far greater depth by examining the role played by his theories of voluntarism and the will within his philosophical system.

5

Distinctively Human Action and the Unconscious

I
Introduction

The immediately preceding two chapters analysed and critically assessed Green's 'metaphysics of experience or knowledge'. They established that the self whose realisation forms the heart of that moment of Green's philosophical system embodies an ideal of coherent knowledge, desire and will aimed at one of the highest possible goods: truth. Our separate individual selves – our respective particular concrete personalities and identities – are better or worse *ceteris paribus* to the extent that they share the formal characteristics of this ideal of a perfected, orderly self. It was established also that only individuals can have a personality ('the quality in a subject of being consciously an object to itself').[1] Moreover, it was noted that Green believes denying the separateness of individual self-conscious, self-determined concrete personalities makes a nonsense of any further claim that there exists a 'self-realising principle' or 'eternal consciousness'. Such a denial 'would be in contradiction of the very ground upon which we believe that a divine principle does so realise itself in [the individual] man'.[2] In the language introduced in §2.IV, the concrete individual consciousness (or, synonymously, the determinate 'self', 'Ego' or 'personality') is the critically endorsed fact, from which a belief in the existence of an abstract eternal consciousness is justified only as an inference. To some extent every particular human self is always imperfect however, the perfect 'eternal' self must always be, to some extent, an abstract and indeterminate telos, an imperfectly articulated potential projected by the particular self as its unfortunately under-conceptualised and elusive goal. It can never be a definite fully known state of being, let alone one that is perfectly understood. It is an ideal that guides our individual cognitive self-realisation, rather than a self-subsisting entity which does so. In that sense, it is an achievement based on personal judgement rather than on divine intervention.[3]

In the *Prolegomena* at least, Green is concerned with certain facets of the 'metaphysics of experience and knowledge' because of what he conceives as

---

[1] PE 182.
[2] PE 182; compare PE 80–85, 99–102, 182.
[3] See for example, PE 13, 15, 23, 23, 25, 35, 52, 93–94, 137. The emphasis on personal judgement continues throughout the *Prolegomena*.

its necessary role in his theory of self-realisation and freedom. As this book progresses, it will become clear that one necessary feature of rational action is that it is undertaken by an agent on the basis of that agent's best assessment of their current circumstances and their own place in the world (together with their desires, plans, and so on). The bases of the relevant cognitive principles were the subject-matter of the preceding chapters. In this sense, this aspect of Green's metaphysics of experience and knowledge is the first facet, or in idealist terms, the first 'moment', of his theory of self-realisation. The second moment is what Green calls his 'metaphysics of moral action', at the heart of which stands his theory of the will. (The third moment of his theory of self-realisation is his metaphysics of ethics.) Contrary to the view that Green's metaphysics of the will is separable from his 'metaphysics of experience or knowledge', it will be argued here that, in line with their character as 'moments' of a larger system, the leading strands of each of the three facets do indeed constitute necessary and mutually reinforcing aspects of one largely harmonious theory of self-realisation and freedom.

The common thread of this theory will be shown to be Green's conception of the will, which is the subject of this chapter and the one that follows it. The following section reviews the disputes in the secondary literature regarding Green's aspirations for a theory of the will, before §5.III analyses the distinction he draws between the 'distinctively human' facets of our existence (self-consciousness, reasoning and the realisation of our higher capacities) and the 'animal' (non-conscious and instinctive) ones. §5.IV explores three previously neglected aspects of Green's philosophy: his attitude to the 'unconscious', emanation and sublimation. By critically surveying the realms of human thought presupposed by Green in this way, the present chapter lays the groundwork for the analysis of his theories of freedom and responsibility in the chapter that follows it.

II
The Disputes Over Green and the Will

One of the peculiar features of Craig Smith's interpretation of Green's theory of the individual is his claim that Green fails to give a full and coherent account of his theory of the will in his published writings.[4] Surprising also is Ben Wempe's claim that Green fails to present a fully developed theory of positive freedom.[5] This chapter and the two which follow it, examine those parts of Green's writings which together directly contradict such views. It will be established that understanding Green's theory of the will is fundamental to understanding the remainder of his philosophical system and in particular his conception of positive freedom. Moreover, it will be shown that such an understanding can be gleaned from his published writings.

---

[4]   Craig A. Smith, 'Individual and Society in T.H. Green's Theory of Virtue', *History of Political Thought*, 2:1 (1981), 187–201 *passim*.

[5]   Ben Wempe, *T.H. Green's Theory of Positive Freedom* (Exeter: Imprint Academic, 2004), pp. 121–22.

In fact, J.H. Muirhead went as far as to argue that Green's ethics 'is fundamentally a theory of the will.'[6] Similarly, even though Geoffrey Thomas rejects use of the term 'will', he has argued that Green's theory of agency 'is of overriding importance and ... colours his treatment of nearly every topic he discusses.'[7] More straightforwardly, it will be established below that Green's theory of ethics relies on his theory of free agency for its coherence. The link between the 'human soul' or 'human spirit'[8] and ethics springs from the nature of the will and, in particular, from its expression in 'distinctively human action', and in its contradistinction to 'animal' or 'mechanical' existence.[9] It will be demonstrated here also that this aspect of Green's thought is shaped by his metaphysics of experience or knowledge. Indeed, the latter is important to him primarily because of its role within his theory of moral action. His metaphysics of experience and will are complicated by the fact that, although the human spirit is necessarily structured by the eternal consciousness, it is reliant in a significant sense upon social experiences and living for its particular expressions. Consequently, given the empirical fact of diversity both between and within cultures, the human spirit is present in the world in various manifestations. Nevertheless, Green still believes that the nature of human progress is fundamentally structured by an ideal of the eternal consciousness. Consequently, as an agent develops (rather than simply changes), he is in a process of becoming more self-harmonised and so more fully human. An essential aspect of this self-realisation is the development of the agent's moral will and character.

Green's metaphysics of agency is, therefore, central to his ethical thought. Unfortunately, he runs two contradictory theories simultaneously in his writings on the nature of the will. I label these the 'self-interventionist'[10] and the 'spiritual determinist' strands. The self-interventionist strand is one which has been stressed both in past and present literature.[11] It presupposes the importance of

---

[6]   John H. Muirhead, 'Recent Criticism of the Idealist Theory of the General Will', *Mind*, 33:130 (1924), 170.

[7]   Geoffrey Thomas, *Moral Philosophy of T.H. Green* (Oxford: Clarendon, 1987), pp. 237–9, 121.

[8]   For example: 'human soul': PE 71, 180, 238–9, 243, 260, 269, 273–82 *passim*, 286, 297–303, 312, 319, 327, 363, 371, 381; 'human spirit': PE 77, 149, 172, 176, 183–91 *passim*, 352–54, 364, 375–7, 381; cf. 'human nature' PE 148, 200, 247, 290n, 302, 337.

[9]   For example: 'distinctively human action': PE 83–91 *passim*, 126, 131, 291; 'animal': PE 4–7, 48, 61, 67, 74, 79–88 *passim*, 91–99, 108, 113–15, 119–31 147, 151, 158, et sub; 'mechanical': PE 5, 73, 77, 79, 80, 89, 205, 293.

[10] This first strand was labelled 'neo-Aristotelianism' in the first edition of this book. I have changed the label in light of the complexities of Aristotle's position on voluntarism (especially because of Susan Sauvé Meyer, 'Aristotle on the Voluntary', in Richard Kraut, ed., *Blackwell Guide to Aristotle's* Nicomachean Ethics (Oxford: Blackwell, 2006), pp. 137–57, and Roger Crisp, 'Aristotle on Greatness of Soul', in *ibid.*, pp. 179–97, especially pp. 195–96). My reading of the first strand of Green's theory of the will has not changed despite this name change.

[11] Charles D'Arcy, *Short History of Ethics* (London: MacMillan, 1901), p. 36n1. Kenneth R. Hoover, 'Liberalism and the Idealist Philosophy of Thomas Hill Green', *Western Political Quarterly*, 26 (1973), 558, 562–5 *passim*; Andrew Vincent and Raymond Plant, *Philosophy, Politics and Citizenship: The life and thought of the British idealists* (Aldershot: Gower, 1984), pp. 20–23; Alan J.M. Milne, 'Common Good and Rights in T.H. Green's Ethical and Political Thought', in Andrew Vincent, ed., *Philosophy of T.H. Green* (Aldershot: Gower, 1986), pp. 62–75; Thomas, *Moral Philosophy of T.H. Green*, pp. 124–95 *passim*, 369–70; Avital Simhony, 'T.H. Green's Theory of the Morally Justified Society', *History of Political Thought*, 10:3 (1989), 483–4; Peter Nicholson, *Political Philosophy of the British Idealists: Selected studies* (Cambridge: Cambridge University

the voluntary self-determination of the agent's character, and rests on a further belief in the individual's capacity indirectly to make herself want certain objects and to act from certain morally-valuable motives. Hence, the self-interventionist strand holds that, once certain minimum social conditions are met, the agent can choose whether or not to develop a virtuous character and then to act virtuously. The spiritual determinist interpretation, on the other hand, has now fallen from favour. In one form or another it was the orthodoxy in the older commentators, such as Henry Calderwood, James Seth, W.H. Fairbrother, Henry Sidgwick, Henry Sturt, Hastings Rashdall and Bernard Bosanquet.[12] In particular, this strand was developed later by Bosanquet, for example, in his *Principle of Individuality and Value*.[13] It characterises human agency in terms of the self-generation of particular actions from the interaction of the individual's mind with circumstances. Any capacity for alternative choices is denied and the agent becomes, in words Bosanquet uses in a slightly different context, 'an immense structure of automatic machinery'.[14] Most recent commentators mention this reading only in passing: Gerald Gaus does so in a brief endnote which is highly dismissive of Bosanquet's reading at best of Green; whilst James Kloppenberg, again in an endnote, does not highlight the tension within Green's writings.[15] Maria Dimova-Cookson and Avital Simhony's more detailed reactions are addressed in chapter six.

At least one commentator has admitted to being simply confused about Green's theory of the will. Haldar asks 'If the adopted desire is will, what is choice and what is the activity by means of which effect is given to it?'[16] In this chapter and the one following it, I will examine each strand and demonstrate that ultimately they are irreconcilable. The conclusion will be reached that the self-contradictory nature of Green's writings on the will presents his theory with a profound difficulty which no recent commentator has properly appreciated and answered. Furthermore, it will become clear that the recent neglect of the spiritual determinist strand can be

---

Press, 1990), pp. 117–22.

[12] Henry Calderwood, 'Another View of Green's Last Work', *Mind* 10 os (1885), 73–84; James Seth, *Study of Ethical Principles* (Edinburgh: William Blackwood, 1899), pp. 390–91; W.H. Fairbrother, *Philosophy of Thomas Hill Green* (London: Methuen, 1900), pp. 51–57; Henry Sidgwick, *Lectures on the Ethics of T.H. Green, Mr. Herbert Spencer, and J. Martineau* (London: MacMillan, 1902), pp. 15–22; Henry Sidgwick, 'Metaphysics of T.H. Green', in his *Lectures on the Philosophy of Kant and other philosophical lectures and essays* (London: MacMillan, 1905), pp. 247–53 *passim*; Henry Sturt, *Idoli Theatri: A criticism of Oxford thought and thinkers from the standpoint of personal idealism* (London: MacMillan 1906), pp. 243–4, 251–3; Hastings Rashdall, *Theory of Good and Evil*, 2 vols. (London: Oxford University Press, 1924), vol. II, pp. 309–10; Bernard Bosanquet, for example, his *Principle of Individuality and Value* (London: MacMillan, 1912), pp. 323–6. Also, see W.D. Lamont, *Introduction to Green's Moral Philosophy* (London: George Allen and Unwin, 1934), pp. 27–30, 72–85; Frederick Copleston, *History of Philosophy VIII: Bentham to Russell* (London: Burns and Oates, 1966), pp. 172–3.

[13] Bosanquet, *Principle of Individuality and Value*, pp. 318–57.

[14] Bosanquet, *Principle of Individuality and Value*, p. 181.

[15] Gerald Gaus, 'Green, Bernard Bosanquet and the Philosophy of Coherence', in C.L. Ten, ed., *Routledge History of Philosophy, Volume VII, the Nineteenth Century* (London: Routledge, 1994), p. 416 and importantly p. 432n16; James T. Kloppenberg, *Uncertain Victory: Social democracy and progressivism in European and American thought* (New York and Oxford: Oxford University Press, 1986), p. 434n50.

[16] Hiralal Haldar, *Neo-Hegelianism* (London: Heath Cranton, 1927), p. 41.

explained in part by the concurrent neglect of Green's 'metaphysics of experience and knowledge'.

Before starting on the body of the discussion, a criticism which is fundamental to its whole approach must be addressed. In the course of one of the lengthiest and most interesting discussions of Green's theory of agency, Geoffrey Thomas argues that '"the will" is, and is recognised by Green as being, a redundant term of explanation.'[17] On this view, use of the term 'will' is unnecessary as all of the important issues which it raises can be fully dealt with merely using terms such as 'desire', 'intellect', and 'character'. The will is a superfluous term.[18] Secondly, Thomas argues that Green himself recognised the redundancy of 'the will' as a philosophical term. I do not accept either of these claims. In regard to Thomas's first assertion, one might just as well argue that physiologists and doctors should cease to use the word 'body' because they already have 'liver', 'kidneys', 'skin', and so on. Thomas's second claim is implausible as well. Green always presents his discussion of moral agency in his published and unpublished writings in terms of 'the will' (as Thomas admits),[19] and R.L. Nettleship, as the original editor of Green's *Works*, entitles what became one of Green's most important, subtle and revealing works *On the Different Senses of 'Freedom' as Applied to Will and to the Moral Progress of Man*. Furthermore, one of Green's main arguments against Bishop Butler is that the latter fails to present a fully worked out 'theory of the will'.[20] If Green thought the term was redundant, why did he use it so often?

Freedom and the will are examined in chapter six. Before doing so however, it is necessary to clarify the modes in which the agent acts. Green distinguishes 'distinctively human actions' from 'animal' or 'instinctive' ones. It will be established in §5.IV that he also invokes the notion of the 'unconscious' in various ways. It will be argued there that the significance of this third mode of thought has been underestimated in the previous scholarship on Green.

III
The 'Distinctively Human' and the 'Animal' in the Individual

The belief that each individual person is, in essence, a rational agent (an agent who deliberates, who acts for reasons, and, more ambiguously, who could have acted otherwise than in fact he does) stands at the heart of Green's conception of 'distinctively human action'.[21] The formal characteristic of this type of action (sc. rational agency in general) is that it is willed. Unfortunately, Green defines 'the will' differently as both 'the effort of a self-conscious self to satisfy itself' and 'an effort (or capacity for such effort) on the part of a self-conscious subject to satisfy itself'.[22] This ambiguity does not make interpretation easy. It is important to be clear about whether Green sees the will as 'a capacity' or as 'an effort' (that is, an

---

[17] Thomas, *Moral Philosophy of T.H. Green*, p. 237.

[18] Thomas, *Moral Philosophy of T.H. Green*, pp. 237–39.

[19] Thomas, *Moral Philosophy of T.H. Green*, p. 238.

[20] 'Popular Philosophy' 99.

[21] PE 91.

[22] DSF 21; PE 177.

exertion of that capacity). Combining them as he does in the last definition merely encourages confusion. Fortunately, there are clearer and more considered passages than the previous two. The clearest runs as follows.

> Will is the capacity in a man of being determined to action by the idea of a possible satisfaction of himself. An act of will is an action so determined. A state of will is the capacity as determined by the particular objects in which the man seeks self-satisfaction; which becomes a character in so far as the self-satisfaction is habitually sought in objects of a particular kind.[23]

It can be seen from this passage that self-awareness is a fundamental precondition of distinctively human action.[24] Self-consciousness is a necessary aspect of being human because the conception of a wanted object which the idea of 'an act' necessarily entails, further entails the conception of something which is not the particular wanted object.[25] The more definite the awareness of the wanted object is, the more definite must be the desirer's conception of this 'other'. (This much has been established by Green's metaphysics of experience (§3.IV).) Furthermore, the conception of the object as 'wanted' necessarily implies a subject which is doing the wanting. Hence, for one to be aware of oneself as desiring an object, there must be a 'distinction of self from wants'.[26] The most immediate case of a wanted object is found in one's own desires. Consequently, the most fundamental conception of 'a wanting entity' is one's self as an appetitive being.

Green develops this point by distinguishing between the concepts of a 'world of practice' and a 'world of experience'.[27] A world of practice is a world of possible changes which an agent has the capacity to make actual, and is logically entailed by the idea of a want. Furthermore, it is a world which requires the agent to imagine what could exist and in particular what could be created. It is as part of this world – in other words, as a purposively creative being – that the individual is, in Green's phrase, 'distinctively human'. This world of practice necessarily entails the ideas of 'practical reason' and 'a motive' for action. In a purely natural world (and hence not a world of practice, as Green understands it), there can be no goals which an individual is aiming at, simply because the idea of aiming at something contains within itself the very idea of an agent with motives and, therefore, with self-awareness. Hence, Green writes:

> It is this [self-]consciousness which yields, in the most elementary form, the conception of something that *should be* as distinct from that which *is*, of a world of practice as distinct

---

[23] PPO 6. 'For the real nature of any act of will depends on the particular nature of the object in which the person willing for the time seeks self-satisfaction; and the real nature of any man as the subject of will – his character – depends on the nature of the objects in which he mainly tends to seek self-satisfaction.' PE 154.

[24] 'Moral Philosophy' 1.

[25] PE 118–24.

[26] '[T]he transition from mere want to consciousness of a wanted object, from the impulse to satisfy the want to an effort for realisation of the idea of the wanted object, implies the presence of the want to a subject which distinguishes itself from it and is constant throughout successive stages of the want.' PE 85; see also PE 86.

[27] PE 86.

from that world of experience of which the conception arises from the determination by the Ego of the receptive senses.[28]

Notice the significance of this claim that an individual action is rational not simply in relation to other individual acts, but also in relation to a whole *world* of practice (one must look to the unity as well as the difference). As with the world of experience set out in the metaphysics of experience, to act rationally the agent must project a world of which her individual acts are conceived as parts, and whose meanings and significances stem from their respective relative positions within that system. As with the projection of a world of experience, the projection of an ideal world of practice can be labelled an on-going process of 'crystallisation': 'a mental process which draws from everything that happens new proofs of the perfection of the loved one.'[29] (See §§2.IV, 3.II, 4.II, 7.II.)

For Green, 'practical reason' refers to 'the capacity on the part of such a subject [i.e. one which is self-conscious] to conceive a better state of itself as an end to be attained by action.'[30] Practical reason is concerned with knowledge, imagination and evaluation: knowledge of one's present state and circumstances, imagination of a possible future state of one's self and circumstances, and an evaluation of their worth compared to their present state. In itself, practical reason is not appetitive. Hence, it is possible to conceive of a better state but not to pursue it.[31] It might be that one has to forgo a particular valued state because it is incompossible with another more highly valued state.[32] This necessitates the concepts of 'motive' and 'desire'.

Green attacks those philosophers who portray the term 'motive' as merely another word for 'desire'.[33] He argues that desires are 'impulses or inward solicitations of which a man is conscious'.[34] A motive, on the other hand, is 'an idea of an end, which a self-conscious subject presents to itself, and which it strives and tends to realise.'[35] Immediately, one must sound a note of caution. Green here equates the motive with the end sought. Indeed, for a time this treatment became the standard approach in British academic debates because of his influence.[36] However, this lack of distinction is unwarranted. An agent's motive should be understood, and from Green's own writings is often used to mean, an effort to attain the end sought. The crucial idea is that of 'an effort to attain'. Still, Green's error in this regard does not affect his important contention that in seeking to attain a desired object, one

---

[28] PE 86.
[29] Stendhal, *Love,* trans. G. Sale and S. Sale (Harmondsworth: Penguin, 1975), p. 45; see also §2.IV above.
[30] PE 177; see also PPO 6; DSF 21.
[31] DSF 21–22.
[32] PE 118–29; see John Skorupski, 'Green and the Idealist Conception of a Person's Good', in Maria Dimova-Cookson and W.J. Mander, eds., *T.H. Green: Ethics, metaphysics and political philosophy* (Oxford: Clarendon, 2006), pp. 53–54. Skorupski mischaracterises and greatly underestimates the significance of the role played by 'motive' in Green's ethical theory (pp. 53–54, 57–59).
[33] PE 103–05.
[34] PE 143.
[35] PE 87.
[36] Seth, *Study of Ethical Principles,* pp. 73–4.

transforms the desire into a motive. This transformation is one result of pursuing one particular desired object rather than another. In short, one's motive 'is a particular self-satisfaction to be gained in attaining one of these objects [of desire] or a combination of them. The "motive" which the act of will expresses is the desire for this self-satisfaction.'[37] In this way, a motive 'is an expression or utterance of the man, as he for the time is. It begins from him, from his self-conscious self.'[38] Furthermore, the agent's capacity for self-evaluation enables him to be aware of himself as having performed less than perfect actions and, hence, creates the possibility of remorse and self-correction. In this way, Hammond is wrong to assert that for Green 'Repentance is an afterthought arising from disappointment.'[39]

To clarify this line of thought still further, Green makes the distinction between instinctive (that is, natural) behaviour and self-conscious (and, therefore, imputable) actions.[40] Instinctive behaviour is non-self-referential in the sense that the agent is not aware of himself as the performer of the action. It is the result of a purely animal impulse. Every instance of instinctive behaviour is one of which the agent may not even be consciously aware. It drives him rather than being consciously followed. A self-conscious, moral or, again synonymously, distinctively human action, on the other hand, is one whose sought-end the agent is aware of and which he conceives as related to himself as an agent. Only by being thus self-reflective can the agent deliberate about how to act and make choices about how to live. Only by so doing can he be truly human.[41]

Often, a rational action aims to satisfy a desire which originates in the instinctive, 'animal' aspect of man. Yet, this does not mean that distinctively human agency and animal behaviour merge. They remain qualitatively distinct. Green gives the example of hunger.[42] The hungry animal engages in one form of action when he grasps and devours the food and a properly human being engages in a different form when he chooses to satisfy his hunger. Firstly, the human is aware that he desires the food. As has been shown, this consciousness that *he* desires the food represents an essential aspect of the moral nature of man and is a necessary precondition of his presence in the world of practice. Next, the agent must decide whether or not to satisfy this desire and, if so, in which way. In the instinctive or animal world, there can be no possibility of facing such a choice. For this reason, the being's relationship to the want, and therefore the nature of the want itself, is fundamentally different in the instinctive and practical worlds. Without self-reference, Green argues,

> the resulting act would not be moral but instinctive. There would be no moral agency in it. It would not be the man that did it, but the hunger or some "force of nature" in him.

---

[37] PE 104; see further PE 104–06.
[38] PE 144.
[39] T.C. Hammond, *Perfect Freedom: An introduction to Christian ethics* (London: Inter-Varsity Fellowship, n.d.), p. 96.
[40] For example, PE 85–96.
[41] 'Popular Philosophy' 97–101 *passim*.
[42] PE 91.

The motive in every imputable act for which the agent is conscious on reflection that he is answerable, is a desire for personal good in some form or other…[43]

This conception presupposes Green's distinction between the 'animal' and the 'spiritual' aspects of human temporal existence. Chapters three and four established that individual persons are imperfect instantiations of their own projections of the spiritual principle (the eternal consciousness). The imperfections stem from the fact that the process via which each of us individually instantiates this principle involves the medium of our animal body: that is, each of us is a spiritual being with a physical existence that brings its own needs and limitations.[44] As a result of these limitations, the individual can gain knowledge only via an analysis of their experiences and the reconstruction of the implications of the necessary propositions that result from that analysis. Even then, this is a process in which the individual's knowledge 'gradually cease[s] to be as he forgets or becomes confused.'[45] Another of the individual's imperfections is that, as in part an animal organism, one tends constantly to be driven to act by pleasure-seeking and pain-avoiding impulses, rather than as a result of self-conscious choices aimed at what one considers to be most beneficial for oneself, given one's wider beliefs, desires, values, options and plans (in effect, one's conceptual frameworks and structures of practical reason).[46] In this way, the 'animal system in man' is 'mechanical', whereas free human action is based on intelligent understanding and assessment by the individual as a partial and imperfect self-conscious instantiation of the eternal consciousness.[47]

At times, Green seems ambivalent about this relationship between the animal and the spiritual in man, however.[48] For example, he cautions the reader against accepting blindly the argument that even '*in part*' the individual is 'an animal or product of nature, on the ground that the consciousness which distinguishes him is realised through natural processes': 'an animal is in part a machine, because the life which distinguishes it has mechanical structures for its organs'.[49] Green invokes teleological concerns when urging caution about accepting this characterisation of the individual: he holds that the status of the individual's animality is transformed *totally* by the fact that the functioning of the particular body is a precondition of the instantiation of the spiritual principle in the individual's consciousness.

---

[43]   PE 91.
[44]   PE 175.
[45]   PE 69.
[46]   Green holds that one does not need to invoke the eternal consciousness to explain the actions of (non-human) animals. They are 'explicable as resulting [simply] from the determination of action by feeling and that of feeling by feeling, in other words as resulting from successive changes of the sensibility, without any need for ascribing to them any consciousness of change, any synthesis of the modifications they experience as belonging to an interrelated world.' (PE 84)
[47]   PE 85.
[48]   Denys Leighton notes Green's scepticism about Kant's attempt to maintain a strict separation between the individual's animal and rational natures (Denys P. Leighton, *Greenian Moment: T.H. Green, religion and political argument in Victorian Britain* (Exeter: Imprint Academic, 2004), pp. 85–86, 92–94).
[49]   PE 79; see also PE 5, 73, 77, 79–80, 89, 205, 293.

Yet, Green seems to be going too far here. It seems too much to imply that the individual's bodily existence is transformed completely in this way. The agent does after all also remain subject to purely corporeal changes (one is not usually aware of one's hair growing as it happens, or of the blood-clot that kills you). A little later Green adopts the far more reasonable position that while 'the processes of brain and nerve and tissue, all the functions of life and sense, organic to this activity … [do] have a strictly natural history', at the same time 'they, as in the thinking man, cannot, for the reasons given, properly be held to be merely natural'.[50]

Green's considered position is that while the 'doctrine of hereditary transmission' might be able to explain the development of the animal elements of human life, only philosophy can explain the individual's spiritual nature.[51] Even then however the separation cannot be absolute, for the fact that the individual is in part an animal organism has philosophical implications, as his conception of 'reproduction' of the eternal consciousness shows: the animal organism and the spiritual principle must interact if the individual is to learn and act self-consciously and therefore freely.[52] As has been shown, when acting in this way, the individual transforms animal drives into free motives by relating them to these elements of practical reason.[53] The body is not merely natural, for the 'animal' element of the individual acts but as the 'vehicle' for the realisation of the eternal consciousness.[54] Nevertheless, the purely animal facets of the individual (the unperceived aspects of bodily existence) cannot form part of this individual agency, hence Green is concerned solely with distinctively *human* agency.

Green never justifies his belief that the real essence of what it is to be human is found in the *distinctive* aspects of human existence alone. Certainly, he could point to the authority of a long and venerable intellectual tradition going back at least as far as Socrates, in which humanity's distinctive characteristics are viewed in this way. The claim is central to the Christian theology of course, but it was just as important to earlier philosophers, including Aristotle. Indeed in line with both Aristotle and St Paul, Green identifies what is distinctive about human beings by excluding any quality also possessed by animals and by emphasising those qualities they *share* with God. Green might claim that as it is a commonly-held position, the link between essence and distinctive features is a given element of experience. As such, he might continue, it is the philosopher's task to incorporate it rationally into one conceptual system with the other given elements of the world. Yet, as was established earlier (§§2.IV, 3.II), it is not sufficient that an element is given as immediately and self-evidently true. The philosopher is required to test the plausibility and logic of even the most immediately indisputable aspects of their systems of belief and value. Unfortunately, Green never critically assesses this presupposition in the manner that he requires. Consequently, he seems to have given us no valid reason to denigrate those elements of human existence that

---

[50] PE 82.
[51] PE 5, 7–8, 83–84.
[52] 'Reproduction' was analysed above, in §§3.I–II.
[53] PE 125.
[54] PE 67–68.

you and I share with non-human animals. Why should the attraction to physical pleasures be regarded as sub-human, as it is for Green (see §7.III)?

Many people, including many philosophers and religious believers, still share Green's deeply engrained cultural prejudice. His impatience was evident to Graham Wallas, who as a student, asked Green about the implications of his thought: 'I, being fresh from reading Darwin, asked him whether his arguments applied to the conscious mind of a dog, and Green answered that he was not interested in dogs.'[55] Yet, even if this attitude is widely shared (fortunately less widely now than it was in Green's day), the anthropocentric philosopher is still required to establish the authority of this claim, rather than merely accept it, if she is going to accord humans primacy in her thought in the manner of Green and many others. Why should human self-consciousness be so profoundly important?

It might be objected that such a criticism is based on a rather unfair interpretation of Green's position. Indeed, the situation does become rather less straightforward as one delves further into his writings, as will be shown now through an analysis of the role of the unconscious in Green's thought, an aspect of his philosophy that has been almost completely ignored by previous scholars.

IV
Emanation, Sublimation and the Unconscious

To understand properly the argument underpinning Green's position, one needs to appreciate that in addition to the instinctive and conscious facets of the individual's mental processes, he invokes a third: the 'unconscious'.[56] It will be argued in this section that, for Green, the 'unconscious' is the realm in which human nature begins its struggle for self-expression and self-understanding. The aspect of his thought has received very little attention in the secondary literature on his theory of mind, individuality, social theory or his political philosophy where, in reality, it is also fundamental. The 'unconscious' provides the crucial links in Green's system between his theory of the individual's abstract human nature and the instantiation of that nature in determinate conscious thought and action. Among many other things, recovering these links will do much to undermine the attempt to separate Green's 'metaphysics of experience or knowledge' from his theory of the will. It will be established that a proper appreciation of the role played by the unconscious in Green's philosophical system brings out the ways in which, as Dimova-Cookson

---

[55] Graham Wallas in the *New Statesman*, 25 April 1931, quoted in Peter Clarke, *Liberals and Social Democrats* (Cambridge: Cambridge University Press, 1978), p. 14. A friendly mention of animals occurs in W.L. Newman's recollection of Green: '[Green] worked too hard and thought too intently to have the aspect of one to whom life is child's play. He now and then, in those years, spent part of a vacation – once or twice part of the long vacation – at Oxford, and must then have had the College almost to himself. He told me that on one of these occasions a mouse had crept from a hole in the wainscot of his rooms and gladly shared his bread and cheese.' W.L. Newman, 'Recollection', in Colin Tyler, ed., 'Recollections Regarding T.H. Green', *Collingwood and British Idealism Studies*, vol. 14, no. 2 (2008), 26.

[56] Green invokes the notion of 'unconsciousness' at various points in his writings: for example, PE 102, 243, 283, 286. It appears as early as 1866, in 'Aristotle' 58, quoted below.

puts it, 'in the processes that take place prior to our conscious behaviour, reason also participates, albeit in a latent form.'[57]

Before proceeding any further however, some context needs to be given for Green's discussion of the 'unconscious'. L.L. Whyte credits E. Platner with first using the German equivalents of the 'unconscious' (*Unbewusstsein* and *bewusstlos*) 'in meanings close to those now current' in 1776, after which time the term was disseminated primarily through the writings of Romantics such as Goethe.[58] Eduard von Hartmann's major work, *Philosophy of the Unconscious*, had been published in German in November 1868, although an English translation did not appear until 1884.[59] The 'unconscious' was discussed widely in Britain, Germany and France by philosophers and in the emerging discipline of psychology in the 1870s and the 1880s. Indeed, it is inconceivable that Green would not have been aware of the great controversies surrounding the theories of the 'unconscious' that were current in the philosophical literature of his time.[60] For example, one finds Herbert Spencer referring to the 'unconscious' in Beloff's second sense in his *Principles of Psychology* (1855).[61] More significantly, G.H. Lewes published articles regarding the unconscious in *Mind* in the late–1870s, and these pieces went on to form parts of his five-volume *Physical Theory of Mind* (1877), which was itself a part of his massive *Problems of Life and Mind* (1873–79).[62] Green examined these and related areas in his own critical *Contemporary Review* articles on Spencer and Lewes in the mid to late-1870s.[63] Lewes distinguished three senses of 'consciousness' and its corollary 'unconscious' in the final volume of his *Problems of Life and Mind*, which was published posthumously in 1879.[64] He went so far as to write: 'That we can have thoughts and not be conscious of them, perform actions and not be conscious

---

[57] Maria Dimova-Cookson, *T.H. Green's Moral and Political Philosophy: A phenomenological perspective* (Houndsmill: Palgrave, 2001), p. 47. The role of the unconscious in Green's thought remains obscure in Dimova-Cookson's account.

[58] L.L. Whyte, *Unconscious before Freud* (New York: Basic Books, 1960), p. 66.

[59] Eduard von Hartmann, *Philosophy of the Unconscious: Speculative results according to the inductive method of physical science*, trans. W.C. Coupland (London: Kegan Paul, Trench, Trubner, 1931 [orig. in 3 vols. 1884]). First German edition [*Die Philosophie des Unbewussten*] published in 1869.

[60] Green's studies of psychology seem to have been work-in-progress: 'in his later years' 'he… made frequent resolves to study Herbart, but these were not carried into effect.' Nettleship, *Memoir*, p. cxxv. Johann Friedrich Herbart (1776–1841) had been a student of Fichte's and succeeded to Kant's chair at Königsberg, before writing influentially on psychology and education. The unconscious played a crucial role in his major works, not least *Psychologie als Wissenschaft neu gegrundet auf Erfahrung, Metaphysik, und Mathematik* (*Psychology As Knowledge Newly Founded on Experience, Metaphysics, and Mathematics*), 2 vols. (1824–25).

[61] 'When putting out the hand to grasp an object before us, we are unconscious of the particular muscular adjustments made.' Herbert Spencer, *Principles of Psychology, volume 1*, third edition (London: Williams and Norgate, 1881 [1855]), p. 433.

[62] George Henry Lewes: 'What is Sensation?', *Mind*, 1:2, os (April 1876), 157–61; 'Consciousness and Unconsciousness', *Mind*, 2:6, os (April 1877), 156–67; extracts from the preface of *Physical Basis of Mind* appeared in *Mind*, 2:6, os (April 1877) , 278–79; *Problems of Life and Mind*, 5 vols. (London: Kegan Paul, 1873–79). The reaction to these works included E. Hamilton, 'Mr. Lewes's Doctrine of Sensibility', *Mind*, 4:14 os (April 1879), 256–61.

[63] 'Spencer II' and 'Lewes II' (see *ibid*., 96 especially), and particularly 'Lewes I' and 'Spencer I'.

[64] George Henry Lewes, *Problems of Life and Mind, Third Series* (London: Trübner, 1879), pp. 143–44.

of them, have perceptions and not be conscious of them are facts which prove that a theory of Mind must be very imperfect which is limited to conscious states'.[65]

Possibly even more important than Spencer and Lewes however are Green's debts to Lotze. It was noted above (§2.III) that Green believed 'The time which one spent on such a book as that (the "Metaphysic") would not be wasted as regards one's own work.'[66] Green initiated and himself contributed greatly to an English translation of Lotze's *Metaphysic*. The third book of the *Metaphysic*, entitled simply 'Psychology', includes a succinct but heavily pregnant discussion of the 'unconscious', a position that Lotze had developed at length in his 1852 *Medical Psychology or Physiology or the 'Seele'* and to which he returned in other works.[67] Lotze's theory is still recognised as a major contribution to the development of the idea of the 'unconscious', as is the very similar position developed by Hermann von Helmholtz fourteen years later, in his *Treatise on Physiological Objects*, a work of which anyone interested seriously in the concept was almost certain to have been aware.[68] Consequently, while Green never makes explicit the sources of his own conception of the unconscious, it seems very likely that he would have had at least a working familiarity with these issues, given that so many of the people we know him to have read relied so heavily on the term.

This is not to say that the term had an agreed meaning however. As early as 1855 Alexander Bain had distinguished thirteen 'acceptations of the word ['consciousness', each with its own contrary sense of 'unconscious'] in current speech.'[69] Similarly, the historian of psychology John Beloff, for example, has disputed Whyte's claim that in the debates of the late-nineteenth century the word tended to be used in a proto-Freudian sense of unrecognised desires and impulses that influence conscious behaviour surreptitiously. Instead, Beloff claims that 'either' the word was 'used in some quite vague sense or else it was used … to refer to activities of the nervous system which do not, though they conceivably could, become conscious.'[70] This ambiguity had long been recognised even at the time that Green was writing the *Prolegomena*.

---

[65] Lewes, *Problems*, p. 144.

[66] T.H. Green, reported in Bernard Bosanquet, 'Editor's Preface', in Rudolf Hermann Lotze, *Logic in three books of thought, of investigation, and of knowledge*, ed. Bernard Bosanquet (Oxford: Clarendon, 1884), p. v.

[67] Rudolf Hermann Lotze, *Metaphysic in three books ontology, cosmology, and psychology*, ed. Bernard Bosanquet (Oxford: Clarendon, 1884), pp. 526–34 (i.e. §§304–07). Rudolf Hermann Lotze, *Medicinische Psychologie, oder Physiologie der Seele* [*Medical Psychology or Physiology or the 'Seele'*] (Leipzig: Weidmännische Buchhandlung, 1852). Rudolf Hermann Lotze, *Microcosmus: An Essay concerning man and his relation to the world*, trans. E. Hamilton and E.E. Constance and Jones, fourth edition, 2 vols. (Edinburgh: T and T Clark, 1894 [1885]). On Lotze's psychological writings, including those regarding the 'unconscious', see D.B. Klein, *History of Scientific Psychology: Its origins and philosophical background* (London: Routledge and Kegan Paul, 1970), pp. 776–89.

[68] Hermann L.F. von Helmholtz, *Handbuch der physiologischen Optik* [*Treatise on Physiological Objects*] (Leipzig: L. Voss, 1866). Relevant extracts from this work appear in Richard J. Herrnstein and Edwin G. Boring, eds., *Source Book in the History of Psychology* (Cambridge, Mass.: Harvard University Press, 1965), pp. 151–63, 189–93.

[69] Alexander Bain, *Emotions and the Will* (London: John W. Parker, 1859), p. 599; see *ibid.*, pp. 599–606.

[70] John Beloff, *Psychological Sciences: A review of modern psychology* (London: Crosby Lockwood Staples, 1973), p. 267, citing Whyte, *Unconscious*, p. 169.

For present purposes, the most revealing sense of the unconscious that one finds in Green might be termed unconscious operative thoughts ('we can have thoughts and not be conscious of them', as Lewes put it). Long before Freud, such emanations were understood as fundamental facets of the human mind by poets, philosophers and psychologists, not least those influenced by Romantic theories of creativity. As Beloff observes: 'Inspiration, one could say, was as necessary to give authenticity to the Romantic work of art as the voice of conscience had been to the religious innovators of the Reformation, and both inspiration and conscience pointed to aspects of mind that transcended consciousness.'[71] As was shown above (§§2.II–III), it is precisely this quality of emanation in all branches of human life (including art, society and individual conscience) that Green values in poets such as Milton and Wordsworth, and others including Carlyle, Fichte, Hegel and even Jesus.[72] In fact, as has been implicit in the preceding chapters, the notion of emanation is fundamental to Green's whole philosophical system in that it underpins 'the congenial idea of a divine life or spirit pervading the world, making nature intelligible, giving unity to history, embodying itself in states and churches, and inspiring men of genius'.[73]

Green is particularly likely to have been aware of the controversies between ethicists surrounding the claim that unconscious processes operated within the human mind. Of those thinkers just mentioned, Helmholtz's writings excited particularly vehement objections. Critics worried greatly and vocally that the theory of 'unconscious inferences' entailed the rejection of the individual's responsibility for actions which those inferences impelled her to perform. It is precisely this concern which drives the discussion of the unconscious in the *Prolegomena*. Hence, although there is no direct evidence that Green knew of Helmholtz's theory, it seems very likely indeed that he has in mind his theory or at least its kin. As becomes clear below, Green accepts the existence of unconscious inferences, denies that they mean the individual is responsible for any actions towards which they push her, and yet still claims that the individual is responsible for performing actions where she becomes conscious of a desire to act in accordance with those inferences.[74]

Green's position reflects his belief, noted already, that not all states of our being are of equal worth. Instead, an individual's life is, in an important sense 'better' if his concrete personality accords with his abstractly-universal essence. Once his personality has developed in this sense, the individual is less alienated from his true nature, meaning that he is more 'at peace' with himself. Consequently, Green argues that individuals are in a sense 'freer' when they express and identify with their true nature in their respective particular lives. Hence, he characterises the process whereby the eternal consciousness is particularised and instantiated in the individual's character as a move towards 'a full realisation of the faculties of

---

[71] Beloff, *Psychological Sciences*, p. 244.

[72] See for example, 'Popular Philosophy' 120; 'Christian Dogma' 182–83.

[73] Nettleship, 'Memoir', p. xxv.

[74] A final note of caution should be struck regarding this second facet of the unconscious. Such inferences can still logically entail the relation of the agent to the attainment of the object. Consequently, they can be personal goods. The same does not apply in the case of purely instinctive desires.

the human soul', or, synonymously, of the 'human spirit' or 'human nature'.[75] He refers to the individual's stock of knowledge as one of the human spirit's several 'achievement[s]',[76] and stresses the interaction of 'the speculative and the practical employment of the human spirit',[77] as parts of the 'the ultimate unity of all pursuits that contribute to the perfection of man'.[78] However, as objects for a self-conscious subject these are not merely abstract capacities, for they find expression 'through institutions and habits which tend to make the welfare of all the welfare of each', and therefore allow the individual to 'judge whether the prevailing interests which make our character are or are not in the direction which tends further to realise the capabilities of the human spirit.'[79]

The individual finds fulfilment not in the development of pursuits which she conceives as separate activities then. Instead, she must try to harmonise these activities into a coherent life, and at least initially conventional practices, norms and institutions are required to give her reference points to guide her own personal efforts to harmonise her activities. Green assures the reader that: 'There is no contradiction in the supposition of a human life purged of vices and with no wrongs left to set right. It is indeed merely the supposition of human life with all its capacities realised.'[80] These matters are dealt with at greater depth in chapters six, seven and eight. For the moment, it is important to notice that they reinforce the point that, although some scholars raise doubts about this element of Green's philosophy,[81] in reality both his 'metaphysics of experience and knowledge' and his metaphysics of ethics stand at the heart of his theory of the realisation of the innate capacities of the 'human spirit' (synonymously, the 'human soul' or 'human nature'). That the idea of unconscious operative thoughts is intimately involved here – not least as the root of Green's mature conception of the 'eternal consciousness' – becomes clearer as one examines his understanding of the 'unconscious' in the *Prolegomena*.

Several processes are at work in Green's theory. The first is the repression of animal wants and impulses where those wants conflict with the individual's higher motives.

> That realisation of the powers of the human spirit, which we deem the true end, is not to be thought of merely as something in a remote distance, towards which we may take steps now, but in which there is no present participation. It is continuously going on, though in varying and progressive degrees of completeness; and the individual's sacrifice of an inclination, harmless or even in its way laudable, for the sake of a higher good, is itself already in some measure an attainment of the higher good.'[82]

---

[75]   PE 286; see 'human soul': PE 71, 180, 238–9, 243, 260, 269, 273–82 *passim*, 286, 297–303, 312, 319, 327, 363, 371, 381; 'human spirit': PE 77, 149, 172, 176, 183–91 *passim*, 352–54, 364, 375–7, 381; cf. 'human nature' PE 148, 200, 247, 290n, 302, 337.

[76]   PE 77.

[77]   PE 149.

[78]   PE 148.

[79]   PE 172.

[80]   PE 302.

[81]   W.J. Mander, 'In Defence of the Eternal Consciousness', in Dimova-Cookson *et al.*, eds., *T.H. Green*, pp. 194–95.

[82]   PE 376.

This suppression need not be total however. Green claims that 'probably even from … "unconscious" experiences there remain consequences affecting the conditions with which the character afterwards has to deal.'[83] In a footnote to the word 'unconscious', Green warns the reader of the ambiguities inherent in the term: it refers 'in a strict sense to a process which is … merely nervous or automatic, [but also] in a less strict sense to a process of consciousness not attended to or reflected upon.'[84] The first use refers to the body's mechanical functions such as breathing, whereas the second refers to ideas that remain operative in the mind without being explicitly present in one's conscious thought. Given the lack of further discussion found there, it seems from this footnote, that Green intends to be unclear when he claims that '"unconscious" experiences' can have 'consequences affecting the conditions with which the character afterwards has to deal'. Why would he wish to retain such an apparently undesirable ambiguity?[85] Green seems to want to emphasize his belief that while desires that are 'unconscious' in the former sense cannot form part of one's self, similarly desires in the latter sense are at best a substratum that might come to exert an influence on the self subsequently. This point is important for at least one rather complex reason. It serves to highlight Green's link between an individual's own explicit conscious understanding of their own beliefs, values and circumstances on the one hand, and the moral status of that individual's character and hence of the activities that flow from that character on the other. That is, Green seems to want to stress his claim that for a desire to be conceived as related to a desiring subject and, therefore, for it to be a morally-salient desire, that desire must be 'attended to' by the subject whose desire it is. In other words, the subject must be 'conscious' of the desire as its own desire, in the sense of having that relationship before its mind in an articulated form when deciding how to act.

Initially, the truth of this claim could seem to be far from self-evident: why should it be impossible, a critic might ask, to desire something without realising that one does so? However, the question is misplaced: Green is not claiming that one cannot have a desire without being conscious of doing so. Instead, he seems to be claiming that having any particular unconscious desire is irrelevant to the moral standing of the individual that has it. An agent is not a bad person for wanting to steal the cake if she is not conscious of her desire to do so, just as she is not responsible for things that she does while asleep.[86] Precisely why Green holds that

---

[83] PE 102.

[84] PE 102n. In 1942, James Grier Miller identified no fewer than different sixteen definitions of the term 'unconsciousness', and many associated sub-meanings, in his *Unconsciousness* (New York: John Wiley, 1942), pp. 16–44. Of course, many of these senses would have been innovations introduced by psychologists after Green's death, including Freud.

[85] Despite Green's willingness to conflate the substratum of instinctive desires, and the substratum of implicit norms, values and beliefs, these senses of the 'unconscious' raise different issues, as will become evident below, even if they also constitute two examples of one thing: the under-determination of beliefs and values by conscious thought.

[86] 'If the action were determined directly by the hunger, it would have no moral character, any more than have actions done in sleep, or strictly under compulsion, or from accident, or (so far as we know) the actions of animals.' PE 96; 'The act would not be mine; I should not impute it to myself, any more than, e.g., an operation which I find the animal system has performed while

to be the case will become clearer below and in the next chapter.

There is a second point to draw out of Green's belief that 'probably even from ... "unconscious" experiences there remain consequences affecting the conditions with which the character afterwards has to deal.' This is the notion that even morally-irrelevant desires can have a tendency to assert themselves over the agent's consciousness and eventually over his character. At the points where they affect the individual's life in those ways, these desires affect the agent's ethical standing. Notice that this change need not be negative. For example, although I am an ethically-imperfect person for wanting to steal the cake if I am conscious of desiring to do so, I improve when I become conscious of my previously unconscious desire to help my fellow human beings. This second point has a profound significance for Green's wider ethics and political theory. It helps to establish his claim that one becomes a better person to the extent that one understands the full nature and justification for the beliefs by which one lives one's life. This helps to justify Green's claim that it is not sufficient merely to perform patterns of behaviour that coincide with those that are required by ethics. Instead, an individual's actions are good ethically to the extent that they are performed not merely out of a desire to act well, but also in full cognisance of the moral grounding of those acts. This is a central Kantian plank of the justification, in other words, for his radicalism and ultimately his liberal socialism.

Reflecting on the ethical need to undertake a critical analysis of one's beliefs, Green claims in 'The Philosophy of Aristotle' that

> an unconscious always precedes a conscious morality; that men act on moral principles, embodied in law and custom, which have never distinctly become part of their individual consciousness. The value of the method [of critical self-reflection] lies in its power, as a process of self-examination, to awaken in a man the consciousness of the law on which, under higher guidance than his own, he has already been acting, and thus to transform it from an outward to an inward law, to be obeyed not on authority but in freedom, not under the limitations of local or temporary enactment, but in the open atmosphere of reason.[87]

It is not enough, then, to act outwardly in the manner that morality demands: one must do so for the right reasons, which requires that one does so both consciously and intelligently. In this way, Green's remarks on the unconscious help to explain and justify his contention that one can act out of reverence for the moral law to the extent that one also understands the particular reasons why a particular course of action is required morally given one's particular circumstances.[88]

A related issue concerns Green's claim that human development requires the rational and systematic re-articulation of instinctive (or 'natural') desires into more positive drives. Freud would later label this phenomenon 'sublimation'. Green refers to it at one point as 'the action of an eternal self-conscious principle in and

---

I have been asleep' PE 151; compare PE 15, 69.

[87]   'Aristotle' 58; cf. PE 301, 317–9.

[88]   For example, PE 247.

upon an animal nature'.[89] Anger and resentment can be sublimated in the notion of courage for example, as the latter is expressed, say, patriotically during military service, or by honouring one's onerous civil duties through social reform, or by being a good parent.[90] Green makes this point very effectively in a passage from 'On the Different Senses of "Freedom"...'.

> In order to [make] any approach to this satisfaction of itself, the self-realising principle ... must overcome the "natural impulses", not in the sense of either extinguishing them or denying them an object, but in the sense of fusing them with those higher interests, which have human perfection in some of its forms for their object. Some approach to this fusion we may notice in all good men, not merely in those in whom all natural passions – love, anger, pride, ambition – are enlisted in the service of some great public cause, but in those with whom such passions are all governed by some such commonplace idea as that of educating a family.[91]

The individual's spiritualisation of her animal desires through the latter's resignification within a framework of socially-generated spiritual categories and forms of action represents Green's anticipation of Freudian sublimation. It is not of purely philosophical importance. Indeed, its implications become clearer if one considers a case very close to Green's own life. His great friend and later his brother-in-law John Addington Symonds applied Green's method of sublimating animal desires explicitly, when confronting his own (Symonds's) homosexuality. Writing to Edward Carpenter in January 1893, Symonds expressed the hope that 'the blending of Social Strata in masculine love' 'would do very much to further the advent of the right sort of Socialism', characterised by egalitarianism and co-operation.[92] There were obvious homosexual undertones to Symonds's conception of 'manly love', and these are indicative of another level to this description. In his

[89] PE 240; compare, for example, PE 240–45 *passim*. The 'pathogenic' 'wish itself may be directed to a higher and consequently unobjectionable aim (this is what we call its "sublimation")', Sigmund Freud, 'Five lectures on psycho-analysis', in Sigmund Freud, *Two Short Accounts of Psycho-Analysis*, trans. James Strachey (Harmondsworth: Penguin, 1962), p. 53.

[90] Green sketches this position in 'Pleasure' *passim*, and developed it later in the ways set out here. Compare PE 240–45, 258–60.

[91] DSF 21. On the vital importance of 'commonplace' duties, see further PE 176, Bernard Bosanquet, 'Unvisited Tombs', in his *Some Suggestions in Ethics* (London: MacMillan, 1918), pp. 66–87, and, as possibly the ultimate source for Green and Bosanquet, the final page of George Eliot's novel *Middlemarch*. Thanks to Sean Magee for locating the passage in DSF.

[92] Letter from John Addington Symonds to Edward Carpenter, 21 January 1893, in John Addington Symonds, *Letters*, 3 vols., eds. Herbert M. Schueller and Robert L. Peters (Detroit: Wayne State University Press, 1969), vol. III, p. 808. See further Phyllis Grosskurth, 'Introduction', in John Addington Symonds, *Memoirs*, ed. Phyllis Grosskurth (London: Hutchison, 1984), pp. 13–28, and John Pemble, ed., *John Addington Symonds: Culture and the demon desire* (Basingstoke: MacMillan, 2000). Although Green and Symonds enjoyed a deep and long-lasting friendship, it is unclear whether Green was aware of Symonds's homosexuality. We do know that Symonds told Green of an affair between Dr C.J. Vaughan, Green's uncle on his mother's side and Headmaster of Harrow School, Symonds's alma mater, and Alfred Pretor, a pupil at the school (Symonds, *Memoirs*, p. 115). Symonds was horrified by the inappropriateness of a relationship between the pupil and the Head Master, and shunned Vaughan from then on. There is no evidence that Green himself had any homosexual feelings. See also Symonds, *Memoirs*, pp. 111–15, and Phyllis Grosskurth, *John Addington Symonds: A biography* (London: Longmans, Green, 1964), pp. 25–40.

privately-printed study of ancient Greek homosexuality to which he also alludes in his letter to Carpenter, Symonds invokes the idea of 'manly love' as

> a powerful and masculine emotion, in which effeminacy had no part, and which by no means excluded the ordinary [i.e. heterosexual] sexual feelings. Companionship in battle and the chase, in public and in private affairs, was the communion proposed by Achilleian friends – not luxury or the delights which feminine attractions offered.[93]

Clearly however, sublimation need not be completely successful. Hence even though Symonds was to refer to the pamphlet on *A Problem of Greek Ethics* in which this passage occurs as 'one of the few adequate works of scholarship I can call my own', his posthumously-published *Memoirs* reveal a more ambiguous attitude to this pamphlet on 'Greek love' or homosexuality. 'The latter exists in manuscript', Symonds wrote, 'and though I do not regard its conclusions as wholly worthless or its ideal as quite incapable of realization, I cannot take a favourable view of my achievement. My own thwarted and perplexed instincts rendered me incapable of sound or absolutely sincere treatment.'[94] The homoerotic underpinnings of this conception of 'manly love' came out more explicitly elsewhere in his *Memoirs*. Referring to his life in approximately 1889, he confides that,

> I thought it permissible to indulge my sense of plastic beauty in men.... I thought then that, if I were ever allowed to indulge my instincts, I should be able to remain within [Walt Whitman's] ideal of comradeship. The dominance of this ideal ... contributed greatly to my emotional tendencies. It taught me to apprehend the value of fraternity, and to appreciate the working classes. When I came to live among peasants and republicans in Switzerland, I am certain that I took up passionate relations with men in a more natural and intelligible manner – more rightly and democratically – than I should otherwise have done.[95]

Even though in his *Memoir* Symonds linked this democratic socialist character to Whitman's 'ideal of comradeship', in his earlier letters he linked them explicitly to Green's ideal (see §1.II).[96]

Despite the fact that Symonds felt Greenian sublimation assisted him in coming to terms with his own homosexuality, the process can easily be seen as repressive. Consequently, moves of this type were resisted in Green's own day by romantics

---

[93] John Addington Symonds, *Problem in Greek Ethics being an inquiry into the phenomenon of sexual inversion addressed especially to medical psychologists and jurists* (London: Areopagitica Society, 1908), p. 3. This work was privately printed in Holland after Symonds's death, having been written in 1868 and revised thoroughly in 1873. Symonds himself had ten copies privately printed in 1883, after which Symonds himself wrote a new preface for the manuscript, implying that he had intended a new run to be printed, probably only after his death (Symonds, *Memoirs*, pp. 19, 172–73, 189-90, 231–32). He returned to the issue of homosexuality in 1891, in his *Problem in Modern Ethics: being an enquiry into the phenomenon of sexual inversion, addressed especially to medical psychologists and jurists* (London: [privately printed], 1891).

[94] Symonds, *Memoirs*, pp. 232, 190.

[95] Symonds, *Memoirs*, p. 191.

[96] Letter from Symonds to Charlotte Green, 7 October 1882, in Symonds, *Letters*, vol. 2, p. 777.

and others including William Morris.[97] Many early twentieth-century psychologists were also much more ambivalent than Green regarding the benefits of sublimation. In 1910 Sigmund Freud, for example, argued that the repression involved in sublimation (whereby 'the wish itself … [is] directed to a higher and consequently unobjectionable aim') makes 'a normal man, the bearer, and in part the victim, of the civilisation that has been so painfully acquired', with sexual repression in particular constituting probably the source of 'our highest cultural successes'.[98] Critical theorists extended this ambiguous endorsement, with Herbert Marcuse accepting the possibility of 'non-repressive sublimation', while still arguing that the civilizing process of which sublimation is the cornerstone tends to destabilise and ultimately destroy civilisation itself.[99]

It has been argued in this section that, for Green, the 'unconscious' is the realm of instinct and thereby the realm in which human nature begins its struggle for self-expression. In addition Green understands the 'unconscious' as the realm of inchoate rational mental processes, wherein the individual reflects non-consciously on the presuppositions, structures and inferences implicit within the beliefs and norms that they assimilate subconsciously from their social environment. It is the interaction between these implicit beliefs and values and the individual's critical rational facilities which drives the gradual articulation of these previously merely implicit commitments into the individual's conscious thought and decision-making processes. As the source of those emanations of human nature into consciousness, the unconscious is the realm in which occur the most fundamental organisational and critical processes of the individual's spiritual development.

Unfortunately, this is one of the least structured parts of Green's system. He invokes the idea of the unconscious at crucial points but he never develops explicitly his more general theory of the unconscious, nor does he give a clear statement of its relationship to the transformation of the individual's animality into distinctively human action. For this reason, it will be helpful to give a very brief example that brings together many of the ideas explored in this chapter. In a very important sense, this example encapsulates the key themes that are explored in the remainder of this book.

Pablo Picasso painted *Guernica* in response to the German carpet-bombing on 26 April 1937 of one of the most important centres for Basque culture and Republican resistance to General Franco and his forces. Herbert Read wrote of the painting:

---

[97] 'I demand a free and unfettered animal life for man first of all: I demand the utter extinction of all asceticism. If we feel the least degradation in being amorous, or merry, or hungry, or sleepy, we are so far bad animals, and therefore miserable men. And you know civilization *does* bid us to be ashamed of all these moods and deeds, and as far as she can, begs us to conceal them', William Morris, 'The Society of the Future', in his *Political Writings*, ed. A.L. Morton (London: Lawrence and Wishart, 1973), pp. 192–93. On 13 November 1887, Morris gave this address to the Hammersmith Branch of the Socialist League. No explicit (or implicit?) mention is made of Green, and indeed the elitism that Morris ties to asceticism is absent from Green's theory.

[98] Sigmund Freud, *Two Short Accounts*, pp. 53, 64, 86.

[99] Herbert Marcuse, *Eros and Civilisation: A philosophical enquiry into Freud* (London: Ark, 1987 [1956]), pp. 83, 169, 208–12, 218. See further Joel Whitebook, 'The Marriage of Marx and Freud: Critical theory and psychoanalysis', in Fred Rush, ed., *Cambridge Companion to Critical Theory* (Cambridge: Cambridge University Press, 2004), pp. 74–102.

'Picasso's great fresco is a monument to destruction, a cry of outrage and horror amplified by the spirit of genius.'[100] Picasso had many reasons for creating the painting: some were prosaic (he owed the Spanish government a picture for the Paris World's Fair), others were political (the picture answered critics who had called him secretly pro-Franco), and yet others were more deeply psychological (in many ways the painting encapsulated the conflict that he seemed to delight in provoking among his various mistresses). Yet, as Read makes clear another reason that Picasso painted *Guernica* was to sublimate his disgust at German barbarity and Franco's complicity in genocide. Through the painting, Picasso channelled his horror and anger drawing on elements of the expressionist and surrealist traditions within modernism yet fitting neatly within no identifiable genre. In that way his sublimation not merely grew out of existing artistic forms but surpassed them to articulate emotions for which he struggled to find as clear a voice using conventional genres. Picasso's revulsion had both 'animal' and 'distinctively human' sources: of course partly it was an instinctive reaction to the destruction of other human beings, and partly it was a result of cultural and political conditioning. In the former sense, the painting was a product of Picasso's transformation of his animal impulses into distinctively human emotions. In the latter sense, it was a show of solidarity with the Basques and a Republican reaction to Franco's vision for Spain. *Guernica* also expressed Picasso's feelings of fidelity and patriotism, virtues that are conceivable only after centuries of cultural and political struggle. More fundamentally, the grotesque dismemberment and distortion of the people and animals that inhabit the picture reflects the destruction of the notion of a primeval, 'natural' order presupposed by civilised human communities. Throughout it can be seen that socially-established analytic and critical categories helped to give voice, form and focus to Picasso's anger, sympathy and need for belonging.

This example indicates some of the ways in which Green's theories of animal instinct and the unconscious are key facets of his theory of the nature and development of distinctively human agency. The impulses initially simply felt unconsciously by the individual are key resources from which that person develops a determinate sense of their own broader, more coherent identity. Unconscious drives are transformed through rational reflection and crystallisation (see §3.II) into the personal desires of self-conscious beings, 'connected [to the each other] by memory and anticipation, in which each is qualified by the rest'.[101] As the present chapter has established, the outward socially-conditioned manifestation of this system of articulated, understood and affirmed beliefs, commitments and desires in the individual's actions is the external expression of the individual's unique being: 'the entire self-conscious subject, desiring as well as thinking, is concerned in every complete intellectual act, and in every desire for an object'.[102]

---

[100] Herbert Read quoted in Arianna Stassinopoulos Huffington, *Picasso: Creator and destroyer* (London: Weidenfeld and Nicolson, 1988), p. 233; see also Russell Martin, *Picasso: The extraordinary story of an artist, and atrocity – and a painting that shook the world* (London: Simon and Schuster, 2002).
[101] PE 128.
[102] PE 137.

V
Conclusion

That the good life is one of constant struggle and reflection within and against social convention and repression will be a central theme of the second book in this critical analysis of Green's liberal socialism. In the context of the preceding analysis however, it is important to notice A.C. Bradley's remark that 'the end has been throughout [the *Prolegomena*] defined as the realisation of the possibilities of human nature', and that many of the individual's most unthinking acts of self-devotion and social service manifest 'an unconscious pursuit of this end.'[103] Even as a relatively young man Green was far from being blind to the difficulties of articulating the elements of the human spirit in suitable ways: 'Man ... is always something potentially, which he is not actually; always inadequate to himself; and as such, disturbed and miserable.'[104] Such alienation can be overcome only through the spiritual deterministic processes explored in the next chapter. By drawing into consciousness and reinterpreting instinctive impulses as positive facets of a human life, sublimation lays the basis for the integration of the competing elements present within the individual's mind, and tends to develop a concrete system of knowledge and values as the basis of her personality. It is part of the self-harmonising facet of the individual's distinctively human life. The next chapter explores the processes of will on which this self-harmonisation is based. Towards the end of the chapter, that leads into a critical analysis of Green's theory of voluntary action.

[103] PE 290n.
[104] 'Works of Fiction' 29.

6

Freedom, Choice and Responsibility

Introduction

The previous chapter analysed Green's distinction between distinctively human action and instinctive behaviour. The former was shown to be willed action conceived by the agent to be part of a world of practice. Instinctive behaviour, on the other hand, is automatic and non-conscious. While instinctive behaviour is associated with the animal aspects of the human condition, distinctively human action as such is the directed practical articulation of the individual's spiritual nature. In addition to these forms of practice, the chapter also highlighted the neglected place of unconscious action in Green's thought. In this context, unconscious actions result from one of two types of emanation from within the human soul. The first concerns those instances of instinctive behaviour of which the individual agent gradually becomes conscious, and which in so doing she transforms into imputable actions. Particular attention was given to what Freudians now style as the sublimation of instinctive drives. The examples were given of J.A. Symonds's sublimation of his homosexual urges into a Greenian ideal of brotherhood, and Picasso's *Guernica*. The second type of unconscious action refers to the individual acting on the gradual consciousness of the previously merely implicit presuppositions of their conscious beliefs and values. The struggle to articulate and organise these emanations as part of a conscious world of practice represents the heart of the developmental processes at work in the individual's mind and life.

In this way, the preceding chapter mapped out a landscape of human practice the key features of which will be explored in greater detail in this chapter. In order to deepen the preceding analysis of distinctively human action, the present chapter will critically assess Green's various conceptions of freedom, arguing that while his position is far stronger than many critics have alleged, ultimately he runs two contradictory theories of the will, and that neither can ground a viable theory of personal responsibility. §6.II analyses the first of three senses of 'freedom' on which Green focuses ('formal freedom'). It is established that critics have tried to read far too much into his claim that self-conscious agents pursue a personal good. §6.III examines Green's theory of true freedom, arguing that those scholars who attempt to reconceptualise Green's theory of true freedom using Isaiah Berlin's blurred distinction between 'negative' and 'positive' freedom fail to capture Green's meaning adequately. §6.IV explores Green's claim that personality or synonymously character is the basis of imputable human action, before turning in §6.V to the first of Green's two theories of free will, which is referred to here as the 'self-interventionist' strand. §6.VI considers Green's reaction to determinism, while

§6.VII sets out his second theory of free will: 'spiritual determinism'. §6.VIII argues that Green is unable to produce a coherent theory of personal responsibility, in large part because the whole notion is philosophically incoherent. That leads into the critical analysis of Green's theory of right action in chapter seven.

II
Formal Freedom and the Personal Good

Green highlights three common meanings of the term 'freedom' in *On the Different Senses of 'Freedom' as Applied to Will and to the Moral Progress of Man*. The first – 'juristic freedom' – refers to 'exemption from compulsion by others'.[1] It is the primary, literal meaning of 'freedom': 'Every usage of the term ['freedom'] to express anything but a social and political relation of one man to others involves a metaphor.'[2] The second sense, 'formal freedom', is metaphorical, and concerns the nature of the will in relation to external (sc. natural) determination. The third use of the term 'freedom' is 'real freedom' or 'positive freedom'.[3] Each of these meanings will be analysed in this section, initially via the rebuttal of the great many misguided criticisms of Green's arguments.

For present purposes it is best to start with the most philosophically basic sense: formal freedom. Green holds this to be a necessary characteristic of every self-conscious action, and every self-conscious action aims at the attainment of a personal good. He argues that as such formal freedom is a necessary feature of the realm of conscious, articulated will. Self-conscious action is, by its very nature, formally free, and it is because of this that the agent's actions are imputable to her. The preceding chapter showed that not only does Green place great emphasis on human self-consciousness, but that in fact self-consciousness plays a fundamental role in the structure of his philosophy. Yet, as was noted there, he never makes clear why he sees it as so important. One can speculate regarding two main reasons. The first was commented on in §5.III: simply, it could be an unexamined cultural prejudice. The second reason has rather more philosophical authority: self-consciousness establishes a link between the individual's conception of her own good on the one hand, and the object sought on the other hand. After all, agents seek the attainment of a state of their own being through the attainment of their object, rather than simply seeking the object itself. For example, the agent seeks the pleasure of eating the risotto, which is a personal good, or, she seeks to possess a copy of the Indian 78 rpm pressing of the Beatles's *Tell Me Why/I'll Cry Instead*, and achieving that goal changes who one is (she is now the lucky possessor of a very rare record). Once again this is an inherently personal good.

Green argues that as such freedom is the realm of consciously-articulated will, then. The claim that formally free acts are always self-conscious acts and so always

---

[1]   DSF 2.
[2]   DSF 2.
[3]   Nicholson denies that 'real freedom' is the same as 'positive freedom' (Peter Nicholson, *Political Philosophy of the British Idealists: Selected studies* (Cambridge: Cambridge University Press, 1990), p. 160).

seek to attain a personal good has been wildly misunderstood in the literature.[4] As with many such misunderstandings, the most noticeable and influential offender is H.A. Prichard. Prichard argues that, as Green believes the individual always seeks their own personal good, this entails that Green develops an egoistic theory of the will, and that as such Green cannot explain how someone can act purely for the good of others or out of a sense of duty. This claim has been repeated by many others, and most recently by Terence Irwin.[5] Yet, the allegation is premised upon an unsustainable interpretation of Green's position. Prichard at least seems blissfully unaware of the many passages in which Green explicitly anticipates and rebuts such a line of attack.[6] To say that someone acts from the idea of a personal good does not entail that she seeks some purely private benefit.[7] Green is not a Hobbesian in the sense in which Prichard and Plamenatz interpret Hobbes.[8] Simply, he is arguing that when acting an individual must adopt a desire (make it her motive) and that, in so doing, she must make it her good in the sense of her personal goal or end. A motive is necessarily personal then because, as has been emphasized already, the moral agent is necessarily self-conscious. Her actions would not be properly imputable to her if she was not self-conscious. It is in this sense that every imputable action is necessarily self-referential. Holding this view

---

[4]   'Kant' 82–83.

[5]   H.A. Prichard, *Moral Obligation: essays and lectures* (Oxford: Clarendon, 1949), pp. 69–74, 80–82, 111–16 *passim*, 120–28; Alfred E. Taylor, *Problem of Conduct* (London: MacMillan 1901), pp. 121, 224; Henry Sturt, *Idoli Theatri: A criticism of Oxford thought and thinkers from the standpoint of personal idealism* (London: MacMillan, 1906), pp. 252–58 *passim*; Hastings Rashdall, *Theory of Good and Evil: A treatise on moral philosophy*, 2 vols. (London: Oxford University Press, 1924), vol. II, pp. 101–12; W.D. Lamont, *Introduction to Green's Moral Philosophy* (London: George Allen and Unwin, 1934), pp. 212–15; John P. Plamenatz, *Consent, Freedom, and Political Obligation*, first edition (London: Oxford University Press, 1938), pp. 73–76; Charles H. Monson, jr, 'Prichard, Green, and Moral Obligation', *Philosophical Review*, 63 (1954), 81–86; Richard A. Chapman, 'Basis of T.H. Green's Philosophy', *International Review of History and Political Science*, 3 (1966), 82–3; W.H. Walsh, *Hegelian Ethics* (New York: MacMillan, 1969), pp. 70–71; J. Kemp, 'T.H. Green and Ethics of Self-realisation', in G.N.A. Vesey, ed., *Reason and Reality: Royal Institute of Philosophy Lectures, Volume Five, 1970–1971* (London: MacMillan, 1972), 230–31; Terence H. Irwin, *Development of Ethics: A historical and critical study*, 3 vols. (Oxford: Oxford University Press, 2007–09), vol. 3, pp. 586–90.

[6]   For example, PE 105–14, 131–3l, 232; 'Popular Philosophy' 99–100; 'Kant' 119.

[7]   See John H. Muirhead, *Service of the State: Four lectures on the political teaching of T.H. Green* (London: John Murray, 1908), pp. 34–77; Bernard Bosanquet, *Principle of Individuality and Value* (London: MacMillan, 1912), pp. 174–81; Avital Simhony, 'T.H. Green: The common good society', *History of Political Thought* 14:2 (1993), 225–47 passim. See Nicholson, *Political Philosophy of the British Idealists*, pp. 68–71 and John Skorupski, 'Green and the Idealist Conception of the Person', in Maria Dimova-Cookson and W.J. Mander, eds., *T.H. Green: Ethics, metaphysics, and political philosophy* (Oxford: Clarendon, 2006), pp. 59–69 for excellent if different refutations of the Prichard-esque/egoism line of attack. (That said, Skorupski goes on to criticise Green in two very significant ways (pp. 69–71). Ultimately, both criticisms rest on a reading of Green's conception of the ethical sphere that is too narrow, as is intimated below in §7.II.) See also H.D. Lewis, 'Individualism and Collectivism – A study of T.H. Green', in his *Freedom and History* (London: George Allen and Unwin, 1962), p. 63n2; Ann R. Cacoullos, *Thomas Hill Green: Philosopher of Rights* (New York: Twayne, 1974), pp. 108–11; David Crossley, 'Self-conscious Agency and the Eternal Consciousness: Ultimate reality in Thomas Hill Green', *Ultimate Reality and Meaning*, 1 (1990), 18.

[8]   Prichard, *Moral Obligation*, p. 80; Plamenatz, *Consent, Freedom, and Political Obligation*, first edition (1938), p. 75.

does not make Green an egoist. For example, to act purely for the sake of duty towards her fellows requires the agent to conceive of herself as being subject to the claims of duty. She must adopt the performance of her duty as her personal motive, otherwise she would not be an agent. As Nicholson puts it, 'if saying that all actions, good and bad alike, are deliberate makes Green an egoist, it is hard to see how anyone could be anything else.'[9]

Another misunderstanding of the claim that a formally free agent acts for a personal good is found in the writings of A.J.M. Milne. He argues that for Green, in acting for a personal good, the agent is necessarily acting for 'a good reason' and, more importantly, that 'a good reason can only mean seeking one's self-interest through helping one's community'.[10] The implication is that one only helps one's community because that is the course of action which furthers one's purely private interest. In one way, this attack is simply a species of Prichard's egoism objection and is subject to the same rebuttal.[11] However on another level, it is more revealing than that. Milne's reference to this type of a 'good reason' gives far too much content to Green's notion of a personal good. Green is actually just making the fairly straightforward point that in acting, the agent is determined by her own motive. Nevertheless, it is a straightforward point with far-reaching ramifications. These will be examined shortly. The important thing for the moment is that Green is making a formal and not a substantive claim about the structure of human action. The claim is not of the order Milne alleges.

The final objection to Green's claim that a formally free agent necessarily acts for a personal good is presented by Mabbott.[12] He highlights Green's example of the deliberate martyr.[13] He asks how can this person be said to act for a personal good – for an idea of personal satisfaction – when the very success of her action necessarily prevents her from gaining any satisfaction at all from its completion? He presses this point home: 'Are we to postulate an immortality for him to contain the satisfaction required?' It is true that Green does use the idea of immortality in his discussion of the martyr.[14] For example, as Mabbott notes, he states explicitly that 'Everyone thus immortalises himself, who looks forward to the realisation of ideal objects ... objects in which he thinks of himself as still living when dead.'[15] In reality however, Green does not contradict himself here, although his talk of immortality is decidedly unhelpful. His essential point is that it is part of the very nature of this type of goal that the agent understands it as making a meaningful contribution to the true well-being of a group of people with whom she understands herself to form a community:

---

[9]   Nicholson, *Political Philosophy of the British Idealists*, p. 71.

[10]   Alan J.M. Milne, 'Common Good and Rights in T.H. Green's Ethical and Political Thought', in Andrew Vincent, ed., *Philosophy of T.H. Green* (Aldershot: Gower, 1986), p. 67.

[11]   See also J.D. Mabbott, *State and the Citizen: An introduction to political philosophy* (London: Hutchinson University Library, 1967), pp. 41–42.

[12]   Mabbott, *State and the Citizen*, pp. 37–42; Chapman, 'Basis of T.H. Green's Philosophy', 85–88.

[13]   Mabbott, *State and the Citizen*, p. 40.

[14]   PE 229–32.

[15]   PE 229.

This well-being he doubtless conceives as his own, but that he should conceive it as exclusively his own – his own in any sense in which it is not equally and co-incidentally a well-being of others – would be incompatible with the fact that it is only as living in community, as sharing the life of others, as incorporated in the continuous being of a family or nation, of a state or a church, that he can sustain himself in that thought of his own permanence to which the thought of permanent well-being is correlative.[16]

For the moment, the important point is that the very idea of the good sought by the martyr remains a personal good, even though it is one which, by virtue of its own inner logic, aims at social well-being. Similarly, 'The reformer cannot bear to think of himself except as giving effect, so far as may be, to his project of reform'.[17] In order to conceive of such an act when the act's realisation will only occur after the martyr's death, the latter must, in Green's words, 'imagine' or 'project'[18] himself into the future, past his own death and to the time of the act's fruition. Mabbott's criticism does highlight a particularly unhelpful use of metaphorical language on Green's part, but it does not undermine the essence of Green's claim that every distinctively human action aims at some personal good.

Even though he rejects the egoistic interpretation, David Brink reads Green as claiming that each of the agent's separate goods are 'personal' in the sense that 'our deliberations and deliberate choices reflect the operation, perhaps implicit, of normative principles about what is worthwhile – that is a conception, perhaps somewhat inchoate, about what makes a life well lived.'[19] In this way, Brink holds that for Green all personal goods invoke 'a latent conception of the good', meaning that all human actions are 'self-expressive as well as autonomous'.[20] In fact, Green's claim regarding personal goods is far less complex and demanding than Brink implies. Green claims simply that every good of whatever type sought by a self-conscious agent is a personal good in the sense that the agent believes its attainment will bring her some benefit (whether direct or vicarious). A good is 'personal' no matter how small that benefit is and no matter how isolated from the agent's other interests, normative commitments or life plans. It is also personal no matter how inaccurate the agent's judgement regarding the type and degree of benefit that she would actually gain from attaining that good. There need be no deeper commitments nor conceptual structures presupposed by or supporting the agent's conception of the end sought, for that good to be a 'personal good'. This is not to preclude the possibility of there being such presuppositions, of course. It is simply to say that such presuppositions are irrelevant to the good's standing as a 'personal good' in Green's use of the phrase. In short, an object is a personal good if the agent desires it, and it is not a personal good if the agent does not desire it, irrespective of whether or not the agent 'should' do so.[21]

---

[16]   PE 232.
[17]   PE 299.
[18]   PE 229, 231.
[19]   David O. Brink, *Perfectionism and the Common Good* (Oxford: Clarendon, 2003), p. 27.
[20]   Brink cites the following passages in support of reading: PE 96, 105, 107, 108, 114.
[21]   Other commentators have missed this point as well: for example, E.F. Carritt, *Ethical and Political Thinking* (Oxford: Clarendon, 1947), pp. 46–48.

Finally, notice that Green at least appears to make a further jump of logic. This is from the claim that distinctively human action necessarily pursues objects the attainment of which is conceived as bringing some benefit to the agent, to the further claim that this means the agent must be conscious that that is her reason for pursuing it. Signs of this consciousness include the possibility of articulating this benefit, and so on. We desire things in part because of the qualities those things possess, and we can conceive an object as possessing a quality without being conscious of so doing. Yet, Green does not ever seem to consider that one such quality is the prospect that attaining the object will benefit us. Hence he fails to consider the possibility that an agent can conceive an object as possessing the quality of being desired by her, without being conscious that she conceives the attainment of the object in that way. In other words, he fails to consider the possibility of unconscious self-consciousness.

This second claim underpinned Green's reservations regarding the status of unconscious agency which were examined in §5.IV. In fact, Green's position is explained by his primary reason for claiming that individual agents always seek personal goods. This is the issue of the imputability of human action. That is, the agent must pursue a personal good because, by deliberately pursuing a given course, the agent is expressing her nature as a rational being by acting in accordance with her own free choice. It is only in this limited and specific sense that the rational agent necessarily pursues a personal good. This is compatible with the agent making her personal good, for example, serving others or even dying for their benefit.

III
True Freedom

So much for 'formal freedom'. Green argues that by acting in a distinctively human manner, the agent is realising her essence and, therefore, is free in a 'true' (or, synonymously, 'positive' or 'real') sense. He defines this third type of freedom as 'a positive power or capacity of doing or enjoying something worth doing or enjoying, and that, too, something that we do or enjoy in common with others.'[22] For the moment, the analysis will focus on the first part of this definition. The second part (concerning the communal nature of autonomy) is examined in the second part of *The Liberal Socialism of T.H. Green*.

The first point to make is terminological. Some commentators have objected to Green's use of this type of 'freedom' as a label for self-realization, arguing that it is unhelpful and inaccurate.[23] This point need not detain us long. Green himself

---

[22] LLFC 199.
[23] Carritt, *Ethical and Political Thinking*, pp. 159–60; Maurice Cranston, *Freedom: A new analysis* (London: Longmans, Green, 1954), pp. 33–62, especially 46–62; Crane Brinton, *English Political Thought in the Nineteenth Century* (New York: Harper and Brothers, 1962), pp. 216–17; Richter, *Politics of Conscience*, pp. 201–07; W.L. Weinstein, 'Concept of Liberty in Nineteenth Century English Political Thought', *Political Studies*, 13 (1965), 145–62; Kemp, 'T.H. Green and Ethics of Self-realisation', 237–38; Thomas Hurka, *Perfectionism* (Oxford: Oxford University Press, 1993), p. 23; but see Gerald Gaus, *Modern Liberal Theory of Man* (Beckenham: Croom Helm, 1983), pp. 168–69.

goes to great lengths to make his audience aware of the metaphor involved in his usage.[24] Nevertheless, he emphasizes that often in practice, 'freedom' is used in senses which are at least very similar to his own positive conception.[25] Many people, including many philosophers and even the American Supreme Court, have shared Green's use of the term. Nicholson notes that Green himself refers to 'Plato, St. Paul, the Stoics, Kant and Hegel' and states that Green 'might have added others, for instance, Milton, Spinoza, Rousseau, and possibly Locke ... [as well as] Carlyle or Mazzini'.[26] This is probably why Green's defence of this term in his *Lecture on Liberal Legislation and Freedom of Contract* was, and remains, so effective and perceptive.[27] To the average person, 'the feeling of oppression, which always goes along with the consciousness of unfulfilled possibilities, will always give meaning to the representation of the effort after any kind of self-improvement as a demand for "freedom"'.[28] In reality, different usages express different normative concerns and place slightly different emphases in debate. Yet, there is no reason to think that one approach is necessarily clearer than the others. Consequently, there is little reason to favour one approach over the others on the ground of correct usage. The 'anti-positive usage' theorists have no more ground for their particular attacks than the 'pro-positive usage' theorists.[29]

Next, David Weinstein has argued that true ('positive') freedom can be understood in certain contexts as 'equal freedom', whereby everyone possesses the same effective moral and legal rights.[30] Yet, to understand true freedom in this way would be to confuse it with equal juristic freedom. In reality, Green's conception of true freedom is much closer to a common conception of autonomy which denotes the habitual tendency to act in accordance with one's highest (i.e. distinctively human) capacities. Weinstein labels such liberty 'inner freedom'.[31] Even though true freedom equates to inner freedom, it is conceptually distinct from ' "juristic" or "civil" freedom as well as outward freedom'.[32] Green does hold that no one can be truly free unless everyone is able to be, which entails that as a matter of fact all must have equal juristic freedom. Yet, one must be careful not to conflate the practical requirement with a conceptual entailment. True freedom presupposes that all agents enjoy juristic freedom (freedom from interference by other agents),

---

[24] DSF 2.
[25] DSF 18.
[26] Nicholson, *Political Philosophy of the British Idealists*, p. 127. See also Michael Freeden, *New Liberalism: An ideology of social reform* (Oxford: Clarendon, 1986), p. 56; Andrew Vincent, 'State and Social Purpose in Idealist Political Philosophy', *History of European Ideas*, 8:3 (1987), 341–2; Avital Simhony, 'Beyond Negative and Positive Freedom', *Political Theory*, 21:1 (1993), 28–54. On the Supreme Court, see Michael J. Phillips, 'Thomas Hill Green, Positive Freedom and the United States Supreme Court', *Emory Law Journal*, 25 (1976), 63–114.
[27] DSF especially 199–200.
[28] DSF 18.
[29] Nicholson, *Political Philosophy of the British Idealists*, pp. 126–31; Simhony, 'Beyond Negative and Positive Freedom', 44–47.
[30] Weinstein, 'Discourse of Freedom, Rights and Good in Nineteenth-Century English Liberalism', 254–57; David Weinstein, 'Between Kantianism and Consequentialism in T.H. Green's Moral Philosophy', *Political Studies*, 41:4 (1993), 620–21.
[31] Weinstein, 'Between Kantianism and Consequentialism', 621.
[32] Weinstein, 'Between Kantianism and·Consequentialism', 621.

yet true, juristic and formal freedom remain three distinct concepts and should be treated as such.

Next, Maria Dimova-Cookson has argued that Green does not believe that 'negative' or 'juristic' 'freedom should be valued for itself and not only in light of the valuable activities it can give rise to. To use Green's terminology, [he neglects the fact that] juristic freedom should not only be seen as a means, but also as an end in itself.'[33] Underpinning this assertion is Dimova-Cookson's logically prior claim that Green sees juristic freedom purely as a way of dealing with morally insignificant areas of the individual's life, areas where 'the agent pursues her own good', as distinct from 'moral action[s]' where 'the agent pursues her own good together with the good of others'.[34]

These are strange claims. First, nowhere does Green state that he restricts juristic freedom to 'morally neutral actions', if by that Dimova-Cookson means that he claims freedom from external interference to be appropriate only in morally-indifferent areas of life. Instead, it will be argued below that he holds that an agent is free in a true or 'positive' sense to the extent that she wills subjectively, on the basis of her own intelligent judgement, her own attainment of an end that is objectively valuable. Freedom from external interference is necessary if the individual is to exercise her own judgement and follow that judgement in practice. To the extent that the state or any other body or individual hedges the individual in, it undermines this core facet of true freedom. In the terms of contemporary value theory, juristic freedom has contributory value rather than instrumental value.[35] To emphasise this point using Berlin's terminology, one might also note that for Green 'negative freedom' and 'positive freedom' are not restricted to the spheres of Dimova-Cookson's categories of the 'ordinary good' and 'moral good', respectively.[36] Indeed, using Berlin's simplistic distinction tends to produce

---

[33] Dimova-Cookson, Maria, 'Conceptual Clarity, Freedom and Normative Ideas: Reply to Blau', *Political Theory*, vol. 32 (2004), 560. See also Colin Tyler, 'Contesting the Common Good: T.H. Green and contemporary republicanism', in Dimova Cookson et al, eds., *T.H. Green*, pp. 266–75.

[34] Maria Dimova-Cookson, 'A New Scheme of Positive and Negative Freedom: Reconstructing T.H. Green on freedom', *Political Theory*, 31:4 (August 2003), 510; see also *ibid.*, §II, and Maria Dimova-Cookson, *T.H. Green's Moral and Political Philosophy: A phenomenological perspective* (Houndsmill: Palgrave, 2001), chapter 4. See also Adrian Blau, 'Against Positive and Negative Freedom', *Political Theory*, 32 (2004), 547–53.

[35] 'X has contributory value if and only if X contributes to the value of some whole, W, of which it is a part. If W is a whole that consists of the facts that Smith is pleased and Brown is pleased, then the fact that Smith is pleased contributes to the value of W, and Smith's being pleased has contributory value. Our example illustrates that something can have contributory value without having instrumental value, for the fact that Smith is pleased is not a means to W and, strictly speaking, it does not bring about or causally contribute to W. Given the distinction between instrumental and contributory value, we may say that certain sorts of experiences and activities can have contributory value if they are part of an intrinsically valuable life and contribute to its value, even though they are not means to it.' Noah M. Lemos, 'value', in Robert Audi, gen. ed., *Cambridge Dictionary of Philosophy* (Cambridge: Cambridge University Press, 1995), pp. 829–30.

[36] '[B]y ordinary good I mean the good which is good to oneself only (not necessarily to the exclusion of others, but not necessarily to their inclusion), as opposed to the moral good, which is intended by its agent as a good common between him and others.' Dimova-Cookson, *T.H. Green's Moral and Political Philosophy*, p. 97.

a distorted interpretation of Green's subtle and powerful conception of true freedom. Hence, to avoid conflating Berlin's conception of positive freedom with that employed by Green, the present analysis refers to the latter simply as 'true freedom' rather than 'positive freedom' wherever possible.

It is worth developing this point. The logical structure of the relevant categories precludes accurately conceptualising Green's conception of true freedom using Berlin's conceptions of 'negative' and, especially, 'positive' freedom. Berlin's schema presupposes a sharp distinction between the latter two conceptions ('negative' and 'positive' freedom), whereas Green recognises what he calls true freedom as including in its logical structure the notion of freedom from interference by others ('juristic freedom'). It is precisely this difference between Berlin and Green's respective schemas which makes it futile to try to articulate (let alone, to critically assess) Green's position using Berlin's blurred and simplistic categories, in the manner that Dimova-Cookson and others attempt.

Green holds that in order to act autonomously (that is, to act with true freedom), the agent must feel the desire to act in a certain way as an inward voice, and not as an externally-imposed law.[37] The importance of this point has been missed by many commentators.[38] It forms the essence of Green's attack on the Judaic and Roman Catholic faiths.[39] The leaders of both faiths require their believers to follow the particular orthodox interpretations of the divine law out of a fear of the pain of eternal damnation if not earthly persecution. In this way, the divine law is represented to both the Jew and the Catholic as (i) something to be taught to them by some external authority, and (ii) something to be followed out of fear. Such a position is inadequate on at least two grounds. Firstly, the Catholic, Jew or misguided secular agent understands the divine law as 'external' to her being. This law is imposed on the agent rather than being an unmediated expression of her conscience. The deficiency of this type of 'identification' with the divine law is experienced by the agent as a feeling of self-alienation. On the one hand, the agent does not totally identify with God's law and, on the other, she feels compelled to follow it. In that her desires conflict with what she believes to be the correct way to live, alienation 'makes the man feel the bondage of the *flesh*.'[40] Secondly, this law is 'external' to the agent in the sense of being fulfilled by the agent because of the fear of the consequences of not doing so.[41] The problem with this second reason is that the individual lacks an ultimately coherent conception of the reasons why the law should be followed for its own sake. The significance for the agent of both of these defects is immense, and is crucial when attempting to understand the failure of the accusation that Green's theory is open to despotic abuse.[42] Indeed, it

[37] DSF 2.
[38] For example, Ben Wempe, *Beyond Equality: A study of T.H. Green's theory of positive freedom* (Delft: Eburon, 1986), pp. 172–73; Ben Wempe, *T.H. Green's Theory of Positive Freedom* (Exeter: Imprint Academic, 2004), pp. 114–16 although he moderates this claim in *ibid.*, pp. 128–29.
[39] 'Conversion of Paul' 187–8.
[40] DSF 2.
[41] DSF 2.
[42] Isaiah Berlin, 'Introduction', in his *Four Essays on Liberty* (Oxford: Oxford University Press, 1969), pp. xlix and lxi.

forms the basis of a powerful defence of personal autonomy as a moral ideal. Its significance will be analysed further in chapters seven and eight.

In order to overcome the perception of the law as externally-imposed, the agent must recognise ' "himself as the author of the law which he obeys" '.[43] In understanding herself in this way, the agent feels herself to be expressing her nature through her actions. Only then is she acting autonomously. Only then does 'the object of [her] will ... coincide with the object of reason.'[44] In other words, for the agent to act autonomously, she must will to pursue the attainment of that object which she recognises (through her reason) would realise her highest essence (sc. her distinctively human capacities). Importantly, the truly free will seeks its perception of its best object: the object in which the agent finds her own true spiritual rest and not simply her animal pleasure.[45]

Primarily, Green is concerned here with the difference between the good will and the bad will: the 'good will is [truly] free, not the bad will.'[46] It is important to bear in mind that this difference is not between the autonomous will and the formally free will: it is the difference between the non-autonomous and the autonomous will. Formal freedom is a fundamental characteristic of all acts of willing. Consequently, the non-autonomous will is as formally free as the autonomous will. If the non-autonomous will were not formally free, it would have no inherently ethical character. The difference between a moral and an immoral act originates in the type of object sought by the agent, that is, in the object 'with which he identifies himself.'[47] The autonomous will seeks that object, or end, in which the agent can find true self-satisfaction. It is 'that satisfaction, otherwise called peace or blessedness, which consists in the whole man having found his object; ... [it arises from] the fulfilment of the law of our being'.[48] Ritchie stresses Green's Lockeian conception of reason when he describes 'real freedom' as 'self-determined action directed to the objects of reason'.[49] The non-autonomous will is any will which does not follow reason in this specific sense. In not seeking her own 'true rest', the non-autonomous agent is 'in the condition of a bondsman who is carrying out the will of another, not his own.'[50] Hence, Green's conception of the autonomous will is bound up necessarily with his conception of the agent's true essence. Importantly, the autonomous agent wills to satisfy this 'highest' or

---

[43] DSF 2. Green is quoting Kant (see the editorial note in T.H. Green, *Lectures on the Principles of Political Obligation, and other writings*, ed. P. Harris and J. Morrow (Cambridge: Cambridge University Press, 1986), p. 352n8). In turn, Kant is echoing Rousseau's *Social Contract*, book 1, chapter 8.

[44] DSF 21.

[45] DSF 23.

[46] DSF 16.

[47] DSF 1.

[48] DSF 1.

[49] David G. Ritchie, *Principles of State Interference: Four Essays on the Political Philosophy of Mr. Herbert Spencer, J S Mill, and T.H. Green* (London: Swan Sonneschein, 1896), p. 147; John Locke, 'Second Treatise', in his *Two Treatises of Government*, ed. Peter Laslett, second edition (Cambridge: Cambridge University Press, 1967), §6.

[50] DSF 1.

'essential' (sc. most expressive of her true nature) desire, because she recognises that she should will to do so.[51]

Green argues then that to be truly free the individual must self-consciously pursue an object that satisfies the human spirit as that is instantiated in her character. It has been shown already (§5.IV) that this claim does not entail that it would be better for the agent's animal desires to be denied, ignored or suppressed. Indeed, Green claims to have avoided the dualist conception of man ('higher man' and 'lower man') which such suppression would presuppose. He argues that there is only 'one indivisible reality of our consciousness' but that this reality 'cannot be comprehended in a single conception.'[52] Peter Nicholson defends this claim, arguing that 'whilst Green does apply the words "higher" and "lower" to the self, he does not mean that there are two selves, but a better and a worse state of one and the same self.'[53] Certainly, there are passages where Green does put forward the view supported by Nicholson.[54] However, in other places, Green concedes that the 'idea of the subjection in us of a lower or animal man to a higher appeals to us as it did to the Greek. We too think of the higher man as the law-abiding, law-reverencing man.'[55] It is very difficult to read such passages in any way except as a doctrine of two selves: the animal and the spiritual.[56] Nevertheless, giving greater weight to the logic of his argument rather than this unhelpful turn of phrase (as rightly Nicholson does), Green's central contention is secure. For an agent to act without animal desires would require an unmotivated act of the will which is an impossibility. Instead, the agent must 'overcome [them] ... in the sense of fusing them with those higher interests, which have human perfection in some of its forms for their object.'[57] For instance, the animal emotion of anger can help to change an unjust practice such as slavery. In this way, animal desires are given a spiritual purpose and nature through their sublimation: that is, by establishing a beneficial relationship with the agent's highest capacities and purposes. Animal desires form a necessary part of the context of her autonomous action in this way.[58] Similarly, those passions which tend to hinder the agent's attainment of perfection should be suppressed.[59] Thus, when pride leads the agent to belittle others, the action is wrong morally to the extent that it hinders the increased self-harmonisation of the characters of both the victim and the agent. In this way, the drive for self-harmonisation is also the source of the impulse to action, thus making humans part of a world of practice.

---

[51] DSF 1.
[52] PE 68.
[53] Nicholson, *Political Philosophy of the British Idealists*, pp. 124–5.
[54] For example, PE 68–9; DSF 19–25.
[55] PE 264; see also PE 217, 266; PPO 247–51.
[56] See I.M. Greengarten, *Thomas Hill Green and the Development of Liberal-Democratic Thought* (Toronto: Toronto University Press, 1981), pp. 106–09.
[57] DSF 21.
[58] DSF 22.
[59] DSF 22.

IV
Character as the Basis of Agency

We have seen how and why Green conceives a free human action to be one which aims at attaining a personal good in the sense that the agent makes her self-satisfaction her own motive. In this way, rational action is of necessity 'formally free'. As Green writes, 'since in all willing a man is his own object to himself, the object by which the act is determined, the will is always free – or more properly … a man in willing is necessarily free, since willing constitutes freedom'.[60] In some moods, Green goes further however arguing that moral responsibility is only imputable to an agent who can choose how to act and who recognises that she can choose how to act. Self-authorship and, more particularly, self-conscious self-authorship is a key facet of moral freedom.[61] Notice that this claim does not entail that a distinctively human agent is an existentialist radically free chooser.[62] Green argues that specific expressions of the eternal consciousness are found in the world as the different characters of different individuals.[63] The increasing coherence of one's character represents the increasing actualization of the eternal consciousness (sc. the form of the human spirit) in the world (as long as one is moving in such a way that one can become completely coherent). Thus, 'the self, as here understood, is not something apart from feelings, desires and thoughts, but that which unites them, or which they become as united, in the character of an agent who is an object to himself.'[64] The type of character possessed by a particular agent is determined by the nature of the objects in which habitually she seeks self-satisfaction.[65] Furthermore, Green argues that the circumstances in which we act exist in the manner we perceive them. Consequently, the individual has the capacity to become irredeemably corrupted, as her opportunities for agency are delineated by her character and the vision of the world which follows from it, and this delineation can rule out some options for action.[66] Hence there can be times when the agent can no longer act well because her moral perspective has become so corrupted that she can no longer think virtuously.[67]

Green's position is problematic in certain regards. For example, notice that the theme of permanence plays an important role within his thought. It has already been shown to be present in both his religious theory and his 'metaphysics of experience or knowledge' (§§2.II, 3.IV). Similarly, it underlies his discussion of the ethical quality of the agent's character.[68] An individual's true worth should be

---

[60] DSF 1.
[61] DSF 1.
[62] Compare Jean-Paul Sartre, *Being and Nothingness: An essay on phenomenological ontology*, trans. H.E. Barnes (London: Methuen, 1958 [1943]), pp. 431–45 and following.
[63] PE 99.
[64] PE 101.
[65] 'For the real nature of any act of will depends on the particular nature of the object in which the person willing for the time seeks self-satisfaction; and the real nature of any man as the subject of will – his character – depends on the nature of the objects in which he mainly tends to seek self-satisfaction.' PE 154.
[66] Aristotle, *Ethics*, III.v.
[67] PE 99.
[68] PE 133.

judged by her tendency to seek the permanent satisfaction of her permanent self, and by the extent to which her conception of her permanent self accords with what will in reality permanently satisfy it. Hence, '[c]oncentration of will' – that is, having a strong character – is a necessary but not a sufficient condition for being a good human being.[69] This condition is not sufficient because one's character can be directed towards either good or bad objects. An individual is not justified in feeling guilty for a bad action unless the act expressed her character. Green asks the rhetorical question: 'If a man's action did not represent his character but an arbitrary freak of some unaccountable power of unmotivated willing, why should he be ashamed of it or reproach himself with it?'[70]

Assuming that by an 'arbitrary freak' act Green does not mean solely 'things like uncontrollable Tourettes, or sleepwalking, or acting from someone else's post-hypnotic suggestion',[71] Green seems to be overstepping the mark a little here. Certainly, an individual's self may be expressed permanently in her character, but it does not necessarily follow that the agent should be blamed only for those actions which properly express this character. On the basis of Green's own theory, all of the agent's self-conscious actions should be imputed to her.[72] This includes actions which are 'out of character' as well as those which are not. They may be 'temporary' but Green has already established that they can be nothing apart from the individual and, so, must be formally free. They can be nothing other than, in some sense, expressions of the eternal consciousness, and so, he argues, the agent must be as responsible for them as she is for those actions which express her character.

There are two far more fundamental problems with Green's writings on the will, however. Not only does he present two incompatible theories of the will rather than one internally consistent one, but, like many others, he also invokes the notion of moral responsibility, a notion which is philosophically incoherent unless one can achieve the impossible by conceptualising coherently the notion of personal moral choice. The remainder of this chapter explores each of these problems at length.

V
Green's Allegedly Self-interventionist Theory of Free Will

Scholars have argued that Green held that the truly free agent could have chosen to act in some other way than in fact she did.[73] Peter Nicholson argues that for Green, 'Since he is self-conscious, [the moral agent] can reflect upon his inward condition and see that he can choose what he likes, and has the capacity to act according to his preference'.[74] Like Nicholson, A.J.M. Milne argued that Green is

---

[69] PE 105.
[70] PE 110.
[71] Thanks to W.J. Mander, personal communication.
[72] James Seth, *Study of Ethical Principles* (Edinburgh: William Blackwood, 1899), pp. 390–91.
[73] Geoffrey Thomas, *Moral Philosophy of T.H. Green* (Oxford: Clarendon, 1987), pp. 122–241 *passim*; Milne, 'Common Good and Rights'. I assumed it as well in the first edition of this book, especially in its second chapter.
[74] Nicholson, *Political Philosophy of the British Idealists*, p. 119.

concerned with 'imputable' actions. 'Such an action', he writes, 'is voluntary in the sense that the agent could have refrained from doing it. That is why he is and knows himself to be, answerable for it.'[75] Similarly, Geoffrey Thomas characterises 'the philosophical question of free will' as 'whether an agent can choose otherwise than he does'.[76] Thomas sets out three conditions which must be satisfied by any viable theory of free will. At first, they are:

(1) A was able to do X.
(2) A did X knowingly.
(3) A could have done otherwise, if he had chosen.[77]

Later, Thomas amends condition (3) to fit Green's position more obviously – '(3A) A could have done otherwise, if his character and desires had been different.'[78] Steps (1), (2), and (3A) now form the conditions of free action on this reading. Thomas asserts that 'Green definitely accepts the free formation and revisability of character.'[79] It is important to highlight this last claim, otherwise it could be thought that (3A) is far more dissimilar to (3) than in fact it is. A clearer idea of the role played by voluntarism in Thomas's reading can be gained by noting two further passages. Firstly, Thomas draws attention to Green's belief that an individual can consciously choose to change her character over time.[80] This is our possibility of 'self-intervention'.[81] Secondly, he refers to the 'ability to distance oneself from one's desires in such a way that one is not merely subject to them (as on Hume's account), but can decide what to satisfy'.[82] Green is a pure self-interventionist on Thomas's reading.

It is clear that some form of voluntarism is entailed by this strand of Green's theory.[83] Two questions must be faced by anyone who supports this self-intervention line. Firstly, is it powerful enough to ground a satisfactory theory of moral responsibility? Secondly, does Green consistently hold that the human will is a voluntaristic manifestation of one's distinctively human nature? In reality, these questions are intertwined. Green writes, 'self-reflection is the basis of the view here given in regard to the distinctive character of the motives which moral actions represent. Any one making this admission will of course endeavour to conduct his self-reflection as circumspectly as possible'.[84] Immediately after iterating this point, he concedes that whether or not the agent attempts such self-criticism necessarily depends on the state of her character. However, he stresses also that the state of one's character is unchosen, being the result of past determinations of the eternal

---

[75] Milne, 'Common Good and Rights', p. 63, see pp. 63–68 *passim*.
[76] Thomas, *Moral Philosophy of T.H. Green*, p. 149; see also pp. 369–70.
[77] Thomas, *Moral Philosophy of T.H. Green*, p. 124.
[78] Thomas, *Moral Philosophy of T.H. Green*, p. 158.
[79] Thomas, *Moral Philosophy of T.H. Green*, p. 158.
[80] Thomas, *Moral Philosophy of T.H. Green*, pp. 172–3.
[81] Thomas, *Moral Philosophy of T.H. Green*, pp. 177–80.
[82] Thomas, *Moral Philosophy of T.H. Green*, p. 185.
[83] PPO 184–87 *passim*.
[84] PE 95.

consciousness.[85] Nevertheless, he also argues that even when this is accepted, humans remain morally responsible, at least to a limited extent, because they can choose how to act although their particular characters are formed from an initial situation which they did not create. In other words, even though one's character creates some options for action and rules out others within these parameters, the agent is responsible for what she chooses. Here Green seems to be at his most self-interventionistic.

There is a serious problem, however. Despite Nicholson, Thomas and Milne's respective readings and even though Green presupposes self-interventionism in his practical writings (his speeches on politics and educational reform, for example), as he does in his theories of conscientious action and rights, he does not develop and defend the self-intervention line in his writings on freedom and the will. Indeed, it is very noticeable how infrequently he invokes notions of responsibility and imputability, or even 'praise' and 'blame'.[86] He does use the phrase 'consciously directed' at times. Yet, often his meaning is ambiguous. For example, he refers to desires which can potentially form part of a world of practice as 'desires consciously directed to objects ... [I]t is only as consciously directed to objects that they have a moral quality or contribute to make us what we are as moral agents.'[87] Clearly, the most obvious interpretation of the passage relies upon the idea of an unmotivated act of willing. Yet, the context makes this reading less secure. At the point at which it comes, Green is stressing the necessity of self-awareness in imputable action, with the central idea being that of seeking a personal good. He is clarifying the distinction between an instinctive and a moral action. His main point is that animals (including the purely animal aspects of human beings) are in essence unaware of their instinctive actions. Such behaviour happens to the animals rather than actions being performed by them.

It will be remembered that the nature of the desired object is defined by its relations to other objects and to the subject for which such objects can exist. Just as he argued in his metaphysics of experience, Green is clear that an unperceived object, such as an instinctive desire, has a different nature to a perceived one. Furthermore, an instinctive desire cannot be weighed against other desires, whereas a desire of which the purposive mind is aware can be weighed by that mind. This does not mean that the purposive mind must always be consciously directable in the sense of being an unmotivated chooser, as Freudian analysis (for all its own difficulties) demonstrates (§5.IV).[88] It is simply that the moral facets of one's personality (which Green takes to be synonymous with one's character) must be aware of the object before it can calculate 'automatically', as Bosanquet puts it,

---

[85] PE 95; 'Moral Philosophy' 310.

[86] For example, PE 91–92, 95–96, 100, 102, 108, 136, 141–48 *passim*, 151, 220, 242, 247–49, 259, 271, 279, 293, 297–98, 307–08, 319, 345; DSF 6.

[87] PE 125.

[88] This is not to say that Green is a proto-Freudian in any meaningful sense. It is just that the Freudian analysis, like Green's spiritual determinism, relies on some idea of subconscious willing. For a very interesting discussion of the link between Green, Richard Wollheim and Freudian psychoanalysis, see W.D. Hart, 'Motions of the Mind', in J. Hopkins and A. Saville, eds., *Psychoanalysis, Mind, and Art* (Oxford: Blackwell, 1992), pp. 220–36.

whether or not to will its attainment.[89] 'Consciously directed' could mean in this context then, 'directed by a mind which perceives itself to be seeking a personal good'. This second reading coheres perfectly with both a voluntaristic position such as the self-intervention line and a non-voluntaristic position.

Elsewhere, Green does use the phrase 'consciously self-realising principle'[90] apparently to denote the eternal consciousness as it expresses itself in the human will without the conscious choice of the agent. This entails a rejection of his ultimately voluntaristic self-interventionism.

> By a consciously self-realising principle is meant a principle that is determined to action by the conception of its own perfection, or by the idea of giving reality to possibilities which are involved in it and of which it is conscious as so involved; or, more precisely, a principle which at each stage of its existence is conscious of a more perfect form of existence as possible for itself, and is moved to action by that consciousness.[91]

In fact, interpreting many similar passages is often difficult because Green holds both that the will is determined and that it is undetermined, and in doing so he is being inconsistent. This point comes out clearly in the *Prolegomena* when he argues that 'an act of will' need *not* be preceded by 'any conscious deliberation as to which [options] should be pursued.'[92] Instead, as was established in the previous chapter, some acts arise ' "impulsively" or according to a settled habit' (§5.IV). These acts are imputable to the agent because of necessity they are practical manifestations of the 'self-seeking and self-distinguishing self'. In other words, on the more philosophically developed level, Green understands the will to be an expression of the individual's particular instantiation of her distinctively human capacities, and holds that the agent cannot indeterminately choose how to act. Yet, in his moral and political philosophy, he contradicts this position by frequently adopting a self-interventionist theory of conscientious action. This claim can be put another way. Even though Green's self-interventionism necessarily commits him to a form of indeterminism at a fundamental level, his spiritual determinism logically rests on a form of determinism.

Even though the self-interventionist line is philosophically weak, it may be objected that it retains its intuitive appeal. Nevertheless, such a response *is* simply an assertion at root. The philosophical case in favour of Green's spiritual determinist theory of the will is more substantial. It will be argued below that unfortunately adopting this second approach entails jettisoning any commitment to ideas such as voluntary action, moral responsibility and even ethical action as such. The analysis must turn to this dangerous second strand next.

---

[89] PE 125; Bosanquet, *Principle of Individuality and Value*, p. 181.
[90] DSF 20.
[91] DSF 20.
[92] PE 147.

VI
'Determinist'/'Indeterminist' Debate

To understand the spiritual determinist strand, one must be clear about the exact nature of the 'question' which Green sets himself to answer in his consideration of the freedom of the will in his fragment *On the Different Senses of 'Freedom'*.[93] Terence Irwin has argued that Green fails to make clear which form of determinism he seeks to reject.[94] In fact, Green is aware of the danger of ambiguity, given the range of possible 'indeterminist' positions. He begins his analysis by stressing that he is not concerned to answer what he calls 'the question commonly debated, with ambiguity of terms, between "determinists" and "indeterminists"; [that is,] ... the question whether there is, or is not, a possibility of unmotivated willing'.[95] In other words, he is not asking whether or not an agent can in some sense 'step outside' her desires and motives so as to consciously choose between them from some 'neutral' standpoint.[96] Indeed, he believes that such a question is fundamentally wrong-headed. The manner in which it is wrong-headed is important for Green, given that he wishes to show that all humans are necessarily self-determining and, hence, must be moral agents.

Framing the question of the freedom of the will in terms of the possibility of unmotivated willing implies two profoundly confusing things, Green argues.[97] Firstly, it implies that the motive of one's action is, in some sense, separable from and potentially able to overrule one's will. Secondly, to be intelligible, this first implication requires the further assumption that such a motive is 'external' to the individual. In other words, for the motive of an individual's action to be separable from her will, this motive cannot itself originate within that will. This claim is important because Green equates the will with the individual's capacity for agency and indeed her being. If the agent's actions were to be separable from her will, then she could not be free because her will is herself in this context. For this reason, her actions could be neither moral nor immoral.

Green holds that abstracting the motives from the will makes the latter concept unintelligible.[98] For this reason, there must be something inherently incoherent about the terms of reference of the 'determinist'/'indeterminist' debate. On its assumptions, the only way in which a motive could determine the will would be for the agent to will it to do so. Yet, given that this latter act of the will cannot occur without being determined by a motive to perform it, an infinite regress is established. Green concludes that: 'To a will free in the sense of unmotivated we can attach no meaning whatever.'[99]

---

[93] DSF 9–14.
[94] Irwin, *Development of Ethics*, vol. 3, p. 584.
[95] PE 87.
[96] Compare Francis H. Bradley, *Ethical Studies*, second edition (Oxford: Clarendon, 1927), pp. 142–59.
[97] DSF 10.
[98] DSF 12.
[99] PE 97.

Unless there is an object which a man seeks or avoids in doing an act, there is no act of will. Thus a motive is necessary to make such an act. It is involved in it, is part of it; or rather it *is* the act of will, in its relation to the agent as distinct from its relation to external consequences.[100]

In short, in such moods Green holds that if the concept of the will is to be made intelligible, then it must be recognised that it is incoherent to view a motive as ever being, in any sense which is not merely terminological, separable from the will. The will is merely the practical expression of the motive. Attempting to understand the freedom of the will in such a manner that one presupposes the will to be determined by separable motives could work only on the further assumption that the will can have content without a motive, and that is a logical contradiction. Ultimately, the concepts of 'the will' and 'the motive' must in a crucial sense merge to be intelligible.

At times, Green is emphatic that the agent's concrete will is self-generating, functioning independently of any ability to act otherwise than one actually one does. These instances undermine very seriously any portrayal of him as being a self-interventionist in any straightforward sense. Yet, the two strands in his writings (self-interventionism and spiritual determinism) are mutually exclusive.[101] The spiritual determinist line in Green's theory must be examined in depth with this fact in mind. While doing so, it is important to recognise that most of the preceding analysis of Green's thought is shared by his self-interventionist and his spiritual determinist theories. The substantial differences between the two approaches are logical consequences of the different stances which they adopt in regard to the issue of voluntarism.

VII
Spiritual Determinism and the Self-realisation of the Human Spirit

If the terms of the debate have been drawn up incorrectly in the past, what should we ask ourselves about the freedom of the will? Green's answer is implicit in his response to the 'determinists'/'indeterminists' question. When faced with the query, ' "Has a man power over the determinations of his will?" ', Green argues: 'we must answer both "yes" and "no". "No", in the sense that he is not other than his will, with ability to direct it as the will directs the muscles. "Yes", in the sense that nothing external to him or his will or self-consciousness has power over them.'[102] Every particular human action is determined by and hence is an expression of the relevant agent's character.[103] This point comes out most clearly in Green's papers, where he writes:

---

[100] PE 103.
[101] D'Arcy makes a very brief attempt to reconcile them (Charles D'Arcy, *Short History of Ethics* (London: MacMillan, 1901), p. 36n1).
[102] DSF 14.
[103] For example, FC 6; PE 107–8, 303, 311.

It may be allowed that if it were possible for us to have an insight into a man's character [Denkengsart], as exhibited in his inner no less than outer actions, so thorough that every slightest impulse should be known to us as well as all outward circumstances acting on him, we could predict his future conduct as certainly as *the* occurrence of an eclipse; and for all that it may be maintained that he is free.[104]

What implications does this claim have for the analysis of the will which has been presented above? It has been emphasized that, as an agent and therefore as a purposive being, each individual must have himself as his own object.[105] On the spiritual determinist line, Green's reasoning on this point is bound up with his conception of the relationship between the capacity to want an object (labelled 'Desire'), and the capacity to know an object and therefore the capacity to interrelate objects (labelled 'Intellect' or 'Reason').[106] At first sight, the relationship posited here between Desire and Intellect appears to be compatible with the self-interventionist commitment to voluntaristic agency as well. Consequently, it has been picked up by commentators in their self-interventionist interpretations. Most noticeably, this is the line followed by Geoffrey Thomas.[107] Yet, such an interpretation is unsustainable because the relationship between Intellect and Desire is an aspect of Green's theory of the human spirit, and necessarily excludes the element of voluntarism which the self-interventionist approach just as necessarily entails. I will defend this contention now.

Chapter three established that Green's theory of harmonisation is internally related to his theory of the human spirit. Knowledge entails coherent relations; more particularly, it requires that ultimately the categories of knowledge form one perfectly harmonious system. This idea of harmonisation carries through to Green's consideration of agency proper. It is not merely the agent's cognitive categories which must ultimately form a coherent system. His normative categories – broadly, his values and the manner in which they interrelate – must do so as well. Intellect and Desire are manifestations of the same human essence, then. One logical consequence of this claim is that Intellect and Desire are both inherently self-referential and interrelate so as to form a perfectly coherent whole. This leads Green to observe that: 'It is clear then that we must not imagine Desire and Intellect, as our phraseology sometimes misleads us into doing, to be separate agents or influences, always independent of each other, and in the moral life often conflicting.'[108]

Furthermore, the particular instantiations of Intellect and Desire by and in a particular individual are manifestations of aspects of her particular expression of human nature, of her particular self. It is plainly true that the agent cannot desire an object about which she knows nothing, and whether or not she desires a given object will depend partially but necessarily upon what she understands that object to be. (This does not mean, of course, that knowing about something is

[104] Green, MS10A, 37, as quoted in Thomas, *Moral Philosophy of T.H. Green*, p. 207.
[105] PE 124.
[106] PE 129.
[107] Thomas, *Moral Philosophy of T.H. Green*, pp. 160–95.
[108] PE 129.

the same as wanting it.) Green's point is that increased knowledge of an object can transform a potential desire into an actual desire, and that this is achieved by in a sense 'showing' Desire that the object could exist. Only the individual's Intellect can imagine a possible object of desire. In this way, the individual's particularised Intellect uncovers the specific contents of a particular agent's Desire: that is, specific desires in particular circumstances.[109] This is not a matter of choice but of automatic reaction. It is for this reason that Green's analysis of Intellect and Desire is necessarily incompatible with the self-interventionist strand of his thought. It is Green's conception of 'practical reason' which entails this intimate link between the facility to experience and the facility to evaluate. For instance, he defines 'practical reason' as 'the capacity on the part of such a subject [i.e. one that is self-conscious] to conceive a better state of itself as an end to be attained by action.'[110]

In these ways, Intellect and Desire are two necessarily interrelated aspects of the particularised self which constitutes the particular agent.[111] This link establishes the intimate interconnection of Green's 'metaphysics of experience of knowledge' on the one hand and his metaphysics of moral action on the other; that is, between the first two books of the *Prolegomena*.

> In the one case, [thought] appears in the formation of ideal objects and the quest of means to their realisation; in the other, it appears in the cognisance of a manifold reality which it is sought to unite in a connected whole. This community of principle in the two cases we may properly indicate by calling our inner life, as determined by desires for objects, practical thought, while we call the activity of understanding speculative thought.[112]

It is not just that for the agent to be able to act rationally her desires must harmonise amongst themselves and that these beliefs must harmonise amongst themselves as well. To manifest one's nature fully, the agent has to know everything fully, which necessarily requires her to be aware of her knowledge as forming one properly integrated system. Moreover, she must satisfy all of her higher desires, those desires which express her distinctively human nature rather than her imperfect animal desires.[113] This conception implies that the cognitive and normative facets of a perfectly realised human being fully cohere with each other. Only then is the agent truly living in accordance with her instantiation of her human nature. Only then do Intellect and Desire express the ultimate unity of the agent's particular concrete self in the worlds of experience and practice.

The removal of contradictions within an imperfect agent's knowledge and desires is the driving force of human action and progress. It is one of the 'primary

---

[109] This is an idea which has echoes in the work of the animal psychologist, Dr. Marion Dawkins (Marion Dawkins, *Through our Eyes Only? The search for animal consciousness* (Oxford: W.H. Freeman/Spektrum, 1993), and Gail Vines, 'Emotional Chicken', *New Scientist*, 24 January 1994, no. 1909, 28–31).
[110] PE 177. Again, practical reason is not appetitive in itself.
[111] PE 130.
[112] PE 133.
[113] DSF 5.

demands of human consciousness' that we search for coherence in our worlds.[114] Moreover, this drive for harmonisation is an attempt to overcome the feelings of alienation which must arise from the recognition of present disharmony in the manifestation of an ultimately self-harmonised being. It is for these reasons that Green stresses the importance of character. A man's character is the relatively stable manifestation of the individual's being. It is, in this sense, 'abiding' in the same manner as the distinctively human capacities which it manifests are 'abiding'.

The antithesis of Green's spiritual determinist line is encapsulated in the existentialist claim that the agent must direct voluntarily all of their own actions.[115] It is true that in his spiritual determinist moods Green believes the agent possesses, as Nicholson puts it, 'the capacity to act according to his preference'.[116] Nevertheless, when adopting this approach Green does not claim that the agent possesses the capacity to choose voluntarily to act in this manner. He argues that reflection on one's capacity to gain self-satisfaction is an essential stage in the development of the individual's capacity for agency and, hence, his moral responsibility, but it is such a stage in that this development aids the formation of a particularised self-aware character.[117] Moreover, self-awareness is a necessary precondition of being able to conceive of a world of practice. The importance of this stage of Green's theory was emphasized above (§5.III). Nevertheless, on the spiritual determinist line, self-reflection is not an activity which any human agent can choose voluntarily to undertake, because in itself this choice would logically entail an unmotivated act of the will. When the individual's character determines her will, she is aware of her capacity for moral agency, but her conscious self-awareness is a 'spectator' of this agency.[118] As Green puts it, 'moral action is the expression of a man's character, as it reacts upon and responds to given circumstances.'[119] On this view, the agent is not morally responsible because the individual possesses a capacity to determine her will voluntarily; instead she is responsible because her character (including her unconsciousness) is necessarily self-aware and, vitally, necessarily self-referential in its understanding of all of the circumstances in which she can form part of a world of practice.

An objection may be made at this point. Henry Sidgwick asks, if human agency is an (imperfect) expression of the human spirit and is therefore 'automatic', how can Green explain the existence of sin and evil?[120] The first point to make is that Green seems to have seen less sin around him than many others did. Hence, Symonds recalled: 'Apropos of someone feeling an acute morbid sense of being

---

[114] PPO 137; PE 149.
[115] Compare Jean-Paul Sartre, *Existentialism and Human Emotions* (New York: Castle, 1946), pp. 56–59.
[116] Nicholson, *Political Philosophy of the British Idealists*, p. 119.
[117] PE 112.
[118] PPO 9–14.
[119] PE 107. This thought underlies PPO 165 as well. Also see Muirhead, *Service of the State*, pp. 62–5.
[120] Henry Sidgwick, 'Metaphysics of T.H. Green', in his *Lectures on the Philosophy of Kant and other philosophical lectures and essays* (London: MacMillan, 1905), pp. 253–55; G.S. Brett, 'T.H. Green', in J. Hastings, ed., *Encyclopaedia of Religion and Ethics*, 13 vols. (Edinburgh: T. And T. Clark, 1908–27), vol. 6, p. 439.

wicked. Poor fellow, said Green, the sense of Sin is very much an illusion. People are not as bad as they fancy themselves.'[121] Secondly, Green's answer to Sidgwick is implied by the fact that on his view the evil human is an imperfect manifestation of her own essence.[122] Evil actions are the result of the disharmony necessarily entailed by imperfection. Consider the case of the racist. A perfected agent, Green argues, will recognise in both theory and practice that all rational agents as rational agents should be respected.[123] Furthermore, every imperfect person feels, even if only unconsciously or indistinctly, a desire to respect personhood. The racist's evil act expresses the interaction of her imperfect desire to respect personhood with her imperfect recognition of what qualities an entity must possess (or have the potential to possess) in order to be a person. Depending on her degree of imperfection, an individual (in the present case, the racist) can recognise this fact only partially. Furthermore, she may well misidentify what is truly valuable about being a person, for instance, by wrongly stressing the need to embody a particular culture or to have a certain ethnic background. This conclusion can be extended to ideas which fail to express themselves in the agent's actions. In Bosanquet's words, 'ideas which prove inoperative are such as are not carried out into the connections and associations which would constitute at once their meaning and their power.'[124] This is the source of evil agency and all other human error.[125] In this way, there is no place within Green's thought for the 'wilful choice of evil'.[126] In large part, this reflects the lack of space for any 'wilful action' at all. This is an interesting understanding of evil. Furthermore, it is crucial to Green's ethical and political thought.

What does it say about the other side of the coin from evil agency? In other words, what does it tell us about Green's theory of true freedom? As was established in §6.III, Green sees true freedom as the most valuable state of human life. His theory shows that such freedom exists only where one fully understands and identifies with one's worlds of experience and practice. These are necessary but not sufficient conditions of true freedom. Where an agent understands some aspect of their imperfect world but sees something morally wrong with it, she feels alienated from that world and her particular self. She is not truly – that is, positively – free. (Of course, this alienation is a matter of degree: the agent can be more or less alienated.) Consequently, the removal of immorality from the world is necessary in order to gain complete true freedom and, therefore, to gain the experience of inner peace understood as 'a self-satisfaction to be attained in ... [the agent] becoming what he should be, what he has it in him to be, in the fulfilment

[121] Letter from John Addington Symonds to Charlotte Byron Green *et al.*, 7 October 1882, in John Addington Symonds, *Letters*, 3 vols., eds. Herbert M. Schueller and Robert L. Peters (Detroit: Wayne State Press, 1968–69), vol. 2, p. 777.
[122] See also Kenneth R. Hoover, 'Liberalism and the Idealist Philosophy of Thomas Hill Green', *Western Political Quarterly*, 26 (1973), 556–7.
[123] PE 267.
[124] Bosanquet, *Principle of Individuality and Value*, p. 348.
[125] ICG 73.
[126] Henry Sidgwick, *Lectures on the Ethics of T.H. Green, Mr. Herbert Spencer, and J. Martineau* (London: MacMillan, 1902), p. 24.

of the law of his being – or, to vary the words but not the meaning, in attainment of the righteousness of God, or in perfect obedience to self-imposed law'.[127] Again, the role of distinctively human capacities must be stressed in this spiritual determinist line. True freedom is 'the fulfilment of the law of his [the agent's] being'. In this sense, to be truly free is to subjectively endorse a course of action which either embodies or helps to realise objectively valuable ends.

What has been established so far about the spiritual determinist line? Green has demonstrated that every process that relies on the determinate expression of thought – necessarily including all objects of desire and all willing – requires and is fundamentally structured by human nature as that has been made explicit as the particular consciousness of the particular individual at the particular time. Moreover, Green has established that every human will is necessarily free in a formal sense because 'we must assume, as the basis of the character ..., a self-distinguishing and self-seeking consciousness.'[128] Consequently, determinate Intellect and Desire are self-conscious aspects of the agent's imperfectly harmonised self. The agent's self-consciousness changes the essential nature of her desires and her associated actions. The individual 'is self-determined and his own master, because [he is] his own object.'[129] More specifically, it means that as the agent recognises her particular actions as her own, she is formally free. Reflecting this fact, Green writes of 'the human self, or the man, reacting upon circumstances, giving shape to them, [and] taking a motive from them'.[130] In this way, her actions become moral and imputable, rather than simply or essentially natural or instinctive.[131] There are no forces external to the law of the agent's being which necessitate her particular acts. Recognising this claim brings into sharp focus the true import of Green's emphasis on the ideas of a personal good and of the human spirit (sc. distinctively human capacities). On this spiritual determinist view, an act is imputable to the agent because it expresses the interaction of the agent's true being with her understanding of the circumstances in which she is acting rather than being merely the expression of some whim or accident.

VIII
The Problem of Moral Responsibility

It has been established thus far that Green holds that the individual relates to herself as a 'free cause', in the sense that he believes the following:

> The agent must act absolutely from itself in the action through which that ['determined'] world [in which the individual acts and understands themselves to act] is – not, as does everything within the world, under determination by something else. The world has no character but that given it by this action [of the eternal consciousness in the individual]; the agent no character but that which it gives itself in this action.[132]

---

[127] DSF 17.
[128] PE 114.
[129] PE 112.
[130] PE 99.
[131] PE 91–92.
[132] PE 76.

The spiritual determinist approach establishes that one's motives and therefore one's will are essentially *self*-determined. Green believes this further entails that every person is morally responsible for her own actions. By 'morally responsible' he means that it is appropriate to impute actions to the agent, and so to praise or blame her in relation to those actions and their various effects. The claim that every person is responsible for her actions does not entail that everyone is equally responsible for their own actions. For example, a child is less morally responsible than an adult because she is less self-aware.[133] This is the implication of Green's claim that

> The reason and will of man have their common ground in that characteristic of being an object to himself which, as we have said, belongs to him in so far as the eternal mind, through the medium of an animal organism and under limitations arising from the employment of such a medium, reproduces itself in him.[134]

Nevertheless, Green's spiritual determinist theory of moral responsibility continues to face significant problems. The most powerful objection is presented by Henry Sidgwick, who attacks the very foundations of Green's whole approach to deriving the imputability of all human actions from the fact that they are formally free, by recognising that the claim

> That the motive "lies in the man himself, that he makes it" … ([PE] 102), does not really make any difference [to the agent's degree of moral responsibility], if that in his character which causes him to make his motive good or bad is due to its past history: … It thus seems to me that Green's use of the terms "freedom" (cf. "free effort to better himself," [PE 112]) and "self-determination" is misleading: since any particular man's effort to better himself, as its force depends at any moment on his particular past, is not "free" or "self-determined" in the only important sense.[135]

The unfairness of imputing moral responsibility to individuals in this way is compounded by the apparently arbitrary nature of their actions; as Bosanquet puts it, the 'self … bears in its quality and content the banner of its place and time.'[136] It is a matter of pure luck therefore that the particular individual's history has led to the development of a particular will, and that the circumstances faced by the individual in a particular instance are of a given sort.[137] Indeed, this last consideration leads Green to argue that, 'we praise the successful reformer, and forget that he is but what the man of unnoticed conscientious goodness might be in another situation and with other opportunities.'[138] Consequently, the essence of Sidgwick's critique is perfectly correct. The power of his objection overwhelms Green's spiritual determinist theory of moral responsibility.

---

[133] DSF 201; Malcolm Knox, *Action* (London: George Allen and Unwin, 1968), pp. 41–44.
[134] PE 175.
[135] Sidgwick, *Lectures on the Ethics of T.H. Green, Mr. Herbert Spencer, and J. Martineau*, pp. 20, 22. I take 'the only important sense' to refer to the oft-mentioned voluntarism.
[136] Bosanquet, *Principle of Individuality and Value*, p. 325.
[137] PE 110.
[138] PE 303.

Both Maria Dimova-Cookson and Avital Simhony defend Green here. Dimova-Cookson objects that the determination of the individual consciousness in the manner outlined above 'does not imply the impossibility of free agency; it *defines* the agency. The transcendental rule gives the format, the parameters of human behaviour.'[139] In response, it should be noted firstly that Green does not claim simply that the 'parameters' within which an agent can choose are determined by the self-manifestation of the spiritual principle in the individual. If he had then Dimova-Cookson would be correct when she claims that Green implies the individual has a choice even if it is a restricted one. Dimova-Cookson might mean that options need to be defined in order to be meaningful, yet this is rather different from claiming that merely the parameters are determined. The concept of options concerns the specification of available possibilities for action within the field. (It is even open to debate whether or not such fields must have definite 'parameters' at all.)

Neither of these issues (parameters or options) answers my concern, however. Green's claim is even more demanding than the assertion that either the parameters or the options within which the agent can plan her actions are defined via the interaction of the spiritual principle (distinctively human capacities) with new experiences. His stronger claim is that the action itself is 'determined' by the interaction of the particularised instantiation of the spiritual principle and its understanding of its circumstances. It is 'determined' in the sense that it makes only one course of action available to the agent. Even the decision over whether or not to pursue that course is not open to dispute, it being determined by the state of their consciousness. This is the same process as was shown to be at work earlier (§3.II). Whether one is concerned with parameters or options, Green's spiritual determinism denies the very possibility of any deliberate self-intervention, meaning that the 'agent' cannot choose to act otherwise than in fact she does.

In direct response to my earlier argument to this effect, Avital Simhony claims, firstly, that I fail to distinguish 'hard determinism', 'soft determinism' and 'self-determinism', and, secondly, that I fail to appreciate that Green is a soft determinist, who can make sense of the notion of 'moral responsibility'. Simhony does not give a clear statement of what she understands by 'hard determinism', although she does describe it as 'contra-causal freedom' in the sense that it holds that 'free actions are uncaused actions'.[140] She writes: 'Tyler claims that Green fails to defend freedom because the Greenian agent cannot, in the first place, choose his own character or even his self-reflection. ... This claim indicates that Tyler's criticism must presuppose hard determinism'.[141] Self-determination, on the other hand, holds that 'it is the self that causes one to act but the self is not determined to act by any cause, event, not even by beliefs or desires.'[142] Finally, soft determinism 'rejects

[139] Dimova-Cookson, *T.H. Green's Moral and Political Philosophy*, p. 51; see also Maria Dimova-Cookson, 'The Eternal Consciousness: What roles it can and cannot play: A reply to Colin Tyler', *Bradley Studies*, 9:2 (Autumn 2003), 143–46.
[140] Avital Simhony, 'Review Article: Colin Tyler *Thomas Hill Green...*', *Bradley Studies*, 5:1 (Spring 1999), 95, 94.
[141] Simhony, 'Tyler *Thomas Hill Green*', 94.
[142] Simhony, 'Tyler *Thomas Hill Green*', 94.

hard determinism', instead 'embracing an internal account of actions: action[s] are caused but the causes are internal to the agent.'[143]

I agree with Simhony that Green embraces soft determinism: 'Green recognizes that one's state of character (which determines one's object of pursuit) is caused by previous states, but the causes, he insists, are internal to the agent and hence the relevant actions are free.'[144] Simhony draws a distinction between what she calls 'metaphysical' and 'character' 'strand[s] of determinist agency', with the former holding that 'human agency is a reproduction of the eternal consciousness' and the latter holding 'that human action is the necessary result of the interaction between character and circumstances, or of the character which the agent has not chosen.'[145] This distinction is misplaced. As has been shown at length above, the individual's consciousness and therefore her character is a particularised determination of her distinctively human capacities. Simhony's dichotomy is especially inappropriate for a philosopher who seeks a unified theory in the way that Green has been shown to do. It has been established above that Green believed human nature exists for each of us as it is instantiated in the character of the particular individual at the particular time. I claim that it is this instantiation which determines the individual's action, via its reaction to the circumstances by which it perceives itself to be confronted. It is this particular interaction that motivates the individual to pursue a particular action and to pursue it in a particular way (the interaction generates her determinate will). The process is to a crucial degree an exercise in critical and speculative metaphysics, subject to the constraints arising from the individual's imperfections.

Simhony does not see it as counter-intuitive to hold someone responsible for performing an action when there was nothing the person ever could do (or ever could have done) to choose to stop themselves from acting in a certain way. I do. My concern holds even if the action expresses the agent's character because that character is not chosen. Moreover, my concern remains even if one of the qualities of the object being pursued is its relation to the good of the person pursuing it: that is, even if the object forms an aspect of that which the individual perceives to be her own good. After all, logically at least judgements regarding moral responsibility are distinct from judgements regarding the worth of the qualities that make up the individual's personality. In the same way, it seems inappropriate to praise me for being naturally handsome or to blame you for being naturally ugly. Adapting the remark that Kant makes in a different context: 'however right and however amiable it may be, [it] has no genuinely moral worth'.[146] This is merely what John Rawls called one of 'the accidents of natural endowment and the contingencies of social circumstance'.[147] More than this, it is counter-intuitive to ascribe praise and

---

[143] Simhony, 'Tyler *Thomas Hill Green'*, 95.
[144] Simhony, 'Tyler *Thomas Hill Green'*, 95.
[145] Simhony, 'Tyler *Thomas Hill Green'*, 92.
[146] Immanuel Kant, *Groundwork of the Metaphysics of Morals*, trans. H.J. Paton (London: Harper Torchbooks), p. 66 (Prussian Academy edition p. 10).
[147] John Rawls, *A Theory of Justice*, revised edition (Oxford: Oxford University Press, 1999), §3 (p. 14); see also §17 (p. 89) and §48 (pp. 273–77). In short, I remain convinced by Rawls's arguments regarding the practical inapplicability of the notion of 'desert'.

blame in the sense being considered here, even though Green and Simhony are correct to reject indeterminism as a viable theory of personal responsibilty: one is not morally responsible for 'actions [that] are unmotivated and uncaused'.[148] In short, in practice although not in theory moral responsibility describes an empty class of actions.

The core point of difference between Dimova-Cookson, Simhony and myself is, then, that they deny what I judge to be necessary to the very concept of moral responsibility: namely, that, in Richard Double's words, 'to be *morally* responsible for our choices we must be *causally* responsible for the psychological states that go into them.'[149] As Double remarks, 'Once again, the free will problem shows itself a standoff of intuitions about moral responsibility.'[150]

Notice that I do not hold this problem to be peculiar to Green: it is a necessary consequence of the very notion of moral responsibility itself. The philosophical case has been made formally by Galen Strawson.[151] The central point of dispute is simply whether for a being to be morally responsible for its actions, it must have the capacity to choose to act otherwise than it does. I take it to be axiomatic that for a person to be morally responsible, she must be capable of acting differently from the way in which in fact she did act in her particular circumstances given her particular character. This capacity constitutes a necessary aspect of truly moral agency. The model of the self which Green presents in his spiritual determinist theory precludes him from ever being able to ascribe this sort of choice to humans. More than this, the reasons on which he bases his rejection of indeterminate agency establish the unsustainability of the self-interventionist strand as well.

This is a significant point.[152] Green takes the possibility of personal moral responsibility to be a given fact about the world, and therefore something that his philosophical system needs to accommodate (§§2.IV, 3.II). The problem is that he also seems to assume at various points, not least in this ethical and political writings, that it is also a given fact that for individuals to be held responsible they must be able to choose to act otherwise than they actually do.[153] The preceding analysis seems to establish that these two facts cannot be reconciled, and so, given Green's aspiration to philosophise systematically, at least one of these claims cannot truly be 'given' in the way that he believes. Hence, at least one must be either reconceived or dropped. I believe that moral responsibility should be rejected.

---

[148] Simhony, 'Tyler, *Thomas Hill Green*', 96.

[149] Richard Double, 'Metaethics, Metaphilosophy, and Free Will Subjectivism', in Robert Kane, ed., *Oxford Handbook of Freewill* (Oxford: Oxford University Press, 2002), p. 518.

[150] Double, 'Metaethics, Metaphilosophy, and Free Will Subjectivism', p. 518.

[151] Galen Strawson, 'The Impossibility of Moral Responsibility', *Philosophical Studies*, 75:1–2 (1994), 5–24; Galen Strawson, 'Bounds of Freedom', in Robert Kane, ed., *Oxford Handbook of Freewill* (Oxford: Oxford University Press, 2002), pp. 441–60.

[152] I wish to thank W.J. Mander for pointing out to me its significance.

[153] See, for example, Green's analysis of the state's right to punish law-breakers (PO 176–206 *passim*), which invokes both determinist and self-interventionist considerations. The latter are implied, for example, in the idea that 'the social organisation in which a criminal has lived and acted is one that has given him a fair chance of not being a criminal' (PO 189). The implication is that beyond a certain level of social organisation, individuals can choose whether to commit crimes or to refrain from doing so – or at least to choose to become the sorts of people who to do so.

As this aspect of my analysis has provoked trenchant and powerful responses, it is important to emphasise just how counter-intuitive Green's position is. One should not be as sure as some commentators are that Green saves the individual from 'being a mere automaton'.[154] Indeed, Green came close to acknowledging this fact when he wrote in his earlier 'Metaphysic of Ethics, Moral Psychology, Sociology or Science of Sittlichkeit' that, 'We may say of next act of man at any stage of his life (under mechanical metaphor) that it will be result of the mutual action of his circumstances (i.e. his past history and inducement operative about him) and the originative reason (which, otherwise than mechanically, takes the circumstances into itself, or bestows itself upon them).'[155] Yet, Green fails to show that the self-conscious quality of 'originative reason' transforms the mechanical character of this appropriation. In effect, he rests his theory upon the assumption that, in Bosanquet's words, 'all logical process without exception is unconscious'.[156]

The worry persists whether or not one agrees with Bosanquet that Sidgwick is wrong to portray Green's position as essentially deterministic.[157] The essence of Bosanquet's attempted defence of Green is to insist that Sidgwick fails to appreciate the full implications of Green's idealism. However, Sidgwick does appreciate that Green believes the collapse of the subject-object distinction establishes that every individual possesses a free will in the formal sense. Nevertheless, his objection bites against Green's and Bosanquet's own position, and does so fatally. Bosanquet's defence of Green and implicitly of himself fails due to both his and Green's inability to recognise that even though the subject-object distinction does collapse in the manner outlined in the third chapter of this book, that does not mean that a human being is a moral agent, for the simple reason given by Sidgwick: moral responsibility presupposes that the agent has the possibility of acting otherwise than she did her given circumstances. Green's spiritual determinist theory removes this possibility and in doing so ultimately it destroys the notion of human moral action.

The full import of Sidgwick's objection to Green's ethical thought can be further emphasized by asking how Green can coherently make prescriptive moral statements. For example, on the spiritual determinist reading, how can any agent choose to be careful when interpreting the nature of her actions and when judging the latter's worth? As Calderwood realises:

> A philosophy which accounts for all things by "the action of a free or self-conditioned and eternal mind," has by its own structure created a difficulty in the way of shaping a theory of personal obligation; for an injunction to conform to law seems as unmeaning in a nature which is the "reproduction of an eternal consciousness," as in a "being who is simply a result of natural forces".[158]

[154] T.C. Hammond, *Perfect Freedom: An introduction to Christian ethics* (London: Inter-Varsity Fellowship, n.d.), p. 95.
[155] 'Sittlichkeit' 19; see also 'Sittlichkeit', 18–35 *passim*.
[156] Bosanquet, *Principle of Individuality and Value*, p. 333.
[157] Bosanquet, *Principle of Individuality and Value*, p. 353–7; Sidgwick, *Lectures on the Ethics of T.H. Green, Mr. Herbert Spencer, and J. Martineau*, pp. 15–22.
[158] Henry Calderwood, 'Another View of Green's Last Work', *Mind*, 10 os (1885), 81.

This obtains even when Green's conception of 'reproduction' is interpreted as it was above (§§4.I–II). Moreover, it holds both for moral and for political laws. Green believes that this paradox can be resolved.[159] *Ceteris paribus*, acquaintance with prescriptive moral philosophy, or any expression of thought, as with any other form of life or practice, can be of benefit to man's spiritual development. This obtains, he claims, whether or not the agent cannot consciously act on new beliefs or experiences. For example, reading the *Prolegomena to Ethics* can affect an individual's character, and, in this way, can affect how she will act. Expressing her opinions and understanding the opinions of other persons necessarily affects the mind of the individual involved, because each act of expression is also a new experience for the agent. Consequently, even though Green did not choose in an undetermined manner what to write and the reader does not choose to believe or reject what she reads, both Green's and the reader's characters are changed by their respective activities. On this view, not only can Green be prescriptive but, given his self-consciousness and his particular character and circumstances, he can be nothing else.

Ultimately, Green's attempted resolution of this paradox is weak as it fails to address the essential point at issue: how can a being who is incapable of choice be held responsible for 'its' actions? The Sidgwick-Calderwood attack stands. It is true that there is something very plausible about Green's claim that the agent is responsible for actions which express her character because that character is the true manifestation of her being as a particular agent. Nevertheless, in his spiritual deterministic moods, Green himself accepts that nobody indeterminately chooses her own character. The manifestation of her distinctively human capacities is in an important sense a result of circumstances even if those circumstances can exist only for a particular type of nature: for a self-referencing being. Yet, despite the fact that circumstances are self-determinations of a self-conscious agent, it is still the case that the 'automatic' nature of their 'creation' radically undermines the imputability of the subsequent actions.

IX
Conclusion

This chapter has covered a lot of ground. Even so, it has not produced satisfactory resolutions of the most significant difficulties inherent in Green's writings on the will. This failure should not be surprising because, for the most part, the problems which Green faces – particularly the duality of his position(s) on the freedom of the will – are reflections of important philosophical problems which continue to lie at the heart of the free will debate. Even though Green is correct when he states that the terms of the 'determinist'/'indeterminist' debate make a resolution impossible, he is wrong to think that his approach is different enough to secure such a resolution. The self-intervention approach reveals the limitations which necessarily attend indeterminist and compatibilist positions. The spiritual determinist approach *is* deterministic, even if it is not physically deterministic in

---

[159] PE 107–14.

any meaningful sense. As such, it brings serious problems for anyone wishing to combine it with a belief in individual moral responsibility.

Two of Green's three senses of 'freedom' have been examined in depth here: 'formal' freedom, and 'true' ('real' or 'positive') freedom. Yet, the question remains: how can the agent be free on a spiritual determinist reading if she cannot choose in an undetermined manner how to act? The self-conscious will is formally free in that its motive is necessarily self-referential and its circumstances are necessarily related to the inherent structure of the individual's cognitive, appetitive and moral nature. This conclusion has been established in the course of both this and the previous chapter. It raises the question of Green's conception of true freedom. Each individual has a split nature in the sense that she is an imperfect manifestation of distinctively human capacities in animal form. Even though it is not always the case, the latter can be a hindrance to the expression of the former in the motives (or will) of the individual. Where this obstruction exists, the true human essence (distinctively human capacities) is prevented from realising itself perfectly in the agent's will. In this sense, the imperfect will is unfree. Only when the agent truly acts in accordance with her highest essence and recognises herself as doing so is she completely 'really' free. Only then is she perfectly self-determined, or in Hegelian terms only then is her will 'infinite'.[160] Gaining such insight does require the agent to experience particular desires which may be 'animal' in some sense (§5. III). Nevertheless, in a perfect being these are motives which harmonise with the human essence and, indeed, which are transformed into the vehicles of expression for this essence by the action of self-consciousness. In this way, the individual is truly self-determined and, so, embodies freedom in the most valuable sense of 'freedom from sin and law, freedom in the consciousness of union with God or of harmony with the true law of her being, freedom of true loyalty, freedom in devotion to self-imposed duties'.[161]

So far in this book it has been argued that Green's 'metaphysics of experience or knowledge' forms the foundation of his theory of human agency and, therefore, of his ethical philosophy. This reading marks a return to an older school of interpretation of Green's thought. Most significantly, it has been demonstrated that at least on this spiritual determinist interpretation of Green's thought, the will cannot be motivated by a voluntarily chosen object as that would entail the incoherent idea of an unmotivated act of willing, an idea which (at times) Green is at pains to reject. The ethical importance of self-consciousness has been highlighted here as well. Several attacks have been assessed. Most of these attacks have been shown to be inadequate, including objections to his alleged egoism. The remaining problem is that the spiritual determinist line makes Green's theory of responsibility unsustainable. Given the importance of his ethical and political

---

[160] For example, Georg W.F. Hegel, *Elements of the Philosophy of Right*, trans. A.W. Wood (Cambridge: Cambridge University Press, 1991), §7. As Hegel puts it, the '**Universal Self-Consciousness** is the intuition of itself not as a particular existence distinct from others but as the implicit universal self.' Hegel, *Philosophical Propaedeutic*, p. 63, emphasis in original; see also Sir Henry Jones and John H. Muirhead, *Life and Philosophy of Edward Caird* (Glasgow: MacLehose Jackson, 1921), p. 55.

[161] DSF 17.

thought to his wider philosophical system, there is real reason to balk at this fact. Nonetheless, one does not resolve a problem which is so fundamental by simply denying its existence. At the very least, one should accept that Green misconceived the coherence of his system. The self-interventionist line, no matter how popular in recent commentaries and despite the evidence for it within Green's writings, is clearly not the only strand of Green's writings on the will. I challenge anyone to reread, for example, §§99–114 of the *Prolegomena* or §§9–14 of *On the Different Senses of 'Freedom'* and retain their belief in the unproblematic nature of a self-interventionist reading of Green. These passages can only be reasonably understood as what I have labelled 'spiritual determinist'.

Green has two alternatives. If he pursues the spiritual determinist strand, then he must jettison crucial facets of his account of agency and hence of personal responsibility. Conversely, if he wishes to claim that the agent can be morally responsible, then he must at least modify significantly but probably ultimately reject the essence of this strand of his writings in favour of the self-interventionist approach. In fact, he merely ignores the problem. He adopts the self-interventionist line in the later stages of his system in spite of his failure to present a coherent justification of voluntarism. For the most part, Green drops the spiritual determinist line as soon as he concludes his direct consideration of the nature of the will. Only in this way can he ask the ethical questions which drew him to philosophy in the first place. Looking forward, the preceding treatments of distinctively human action and the abstract nature of true freedom as a realisation of the human essence have laid the basis for the critical analysis of Green's ethical theory in the next chapter.

7

Personality, Utilitarianism and the True Good

I
Introduction

The previous chapter introduced Green's contention that a life of true freedom is the most valuable state for a human being. True freedom was shown to exist to the extent that the individual acts, and recognises herself as acting, in determinate contexts to achieve determinate ends, and does so on the basis of determinate beliefs and commitments which give concrete and practical expression and life to her otherwise abstract distinctively human capacities. In Hegelian terms, for Green true freedom obtains to the extent that the individual's will exists in-and-for-itself.[1] The most fruitful starting-point for a deeper analysis of such a claim is Green's conception of the 'true good', which is his name for the collection of distinctively human capacities that are manifested in different concrete ways in truly free personal lives. It will be established in this chapter that Green saw the true good as the object that the agent both should seek and is drawn to seek by her nature as a being with valuable capacities: it is the object that is intrinsically valuable, in the pursuit of which the agent is acting well, and in the attainment of which the agent realises her highest essence, and thereby enjoys the 'abiding satisfaction' of her 'abiding self'.[2]

The present chapter is structured in the following way. Section two argues that structurally Green's ethics combines an ethics of duty with what contemporary ethicists refer to as a 'culture-based virtue ethics' understood as an ethics of flourishing. Section three critically assesses Green's practical and philosophical arguments against the classical utilitarianisms of Bentham, J.S. Mill and Henry Sidgwick. Section four presents the first stage of Green's own ethical theory, by examining the relationship that he argues obtains between 'personality' (or, synonymously 'character') and the true good. Section five considers some key objections that have been made against his position.

In what follows, the term 'moral' is reserved for the sphere of other-regarding duties (except where commenting on other philosophers such as Taylor who use the term in a broader sense). The term 'ethical' will cover the aesthetic sphere of human flourishing (the realm of eudaimonic capacities) as well as the moral sphere.

---

[1]   Georg W.F. Hegel, *Elements of the Philosophy of Right*, trans. A.W. Wood (Cambridge: Cambridge University Press, 1991), §§4–15, especially §10.
[2]   PE 185, 230–36, 240–41, 246, 250, 316.

'Distinctively human capacities', 'human nature', 'human spirit', 'human soul' and the 'higher capacities' are treated as synonyms as they are by Green himself. The latter combine Kantian structural principles with eudaimonic capacities.

II
A First Look at the Ethics of Duty and the Ethics of Flourishing

As is well-known D.G. Ritchie stated that if one was trying to capture Green's intellectual debts, 'it would be least misleading to say that he corrected Kant by Aristotle and Aristotle by Kant.'[3] While Ritchie was right to be hesitant to present such a simple picture of Green (see §§2.II–IV), his claim is suggestive. It has become clear over the preceding chapters that Green holds every human being to be driven innately to develop her highest potentials (in a manner that owes much to Aristotle as well as to Romantics such as Wordsworth) so as to constitute a systematic whole (in a Kantian manner). These two strands to Green's metaphysics are especially prominent in his ethical thought, not least in his attempt to articulate the individual's innate calling to be the critical active participator in her own particular world of practice (see §§2.II, 5.III). To the extent that she answers this calling habitually, Green argues, the individual acts in a distinctively human fashion. In fact, his core value is the individual's possession and exercise of such a character or personality (terms Green uses interchangeably, as do I in what follows). This is the life of true freedom (§§6.II–IV). This thought underpins the following passage in one of his still unpublished and previously-overlooked notebooks.

> The desideratum of morality is an absolute, unchanging law, which the will shall obey simply as law, without reference to any end beyond the law itself.
>
> The only true good is the will perfectly conformed to this law, – the will, which answers question why do you do so and so? – because the universal law bids me.
>
> (Is not this law a mere form, requiring to be filled up by consideration of what is good with reference to certain ends, the knowledge of those ends being obtained by induction based on the facts of our nature? We may admit this without therefore reckoning the form unimportant, for it will follow from this that no practice may be admitted into the matter of morality, which cannot be willed as law universal. In the perfect state, indeed, the distinction between form and matter will vanish, i.e. we shall withdraw our eyes from the ends the consideration of which originally suggested that so and so was right, and shall will it simply because it is right, i.e. commanded by the universal law, which is the law of my own will).[4]

Hopefully it will become clear in this chapter and the one following it that this passage captures the crucial facets of the ethical theory that Green develops in the

---

[3]   David George Ritchie, *Principles of State Interference: Four essays on the political philosophy of Mr Herbert Spencer, J.S. Mill, and T.H. Green*, third edition (London: Swan Sonnenschein, 1902), p. 139.

[4]   'Untitled notebooks', 11.b.3, T.H. Green Papers, Balliol College, Oxford, Green's contractions have been expended silently. This passage is written in an exercise book which contains a number of notes, some more continuous than others. This particular portion is not connected to another in a clear way. Consequently, one must be careful in ascribing this position to Green as he does not endorse explicitly.

Prolegomena. This is especially true of the combination of a concern with reason as a structural principle with the claim that when viewed in light of the 'facts of our nature', certain social forms can be understood properly as manifestations of the highest human ends. The former principle is structural rather than merely regulative in that it does not simply set boundaries to the range of ethically-acceptable motives or actions, but in addition it works within those motives and actions to determine their internal form. As such, the application of this structural principle can be seen as a necessary facet of the processes by which animal impulses are transformed into distinctively human will, that were examined at length above (chapter five). In this way, the following discussion of Green's ethical theory builds on the analysis of the necessary interrelationship of structural and eudaimonic capacities in Green's philosophical system that has been developed at very great length in the previous chapters of the present book.

While Green was never an uncritical reader of any text, it is undeniable that his writings bear a heavy Kantian imprint. Indeed, the first book of the *Prolegomena* itself grew out of Green's lectures on Kant's epistemology which R.L. Nettleship dates to the mid-1870s, while latter sections recall his 1878 lectures on Kant's ethics.[5] Kant is a point of reference and critique throughout the *Prolegomena*. Green endorses repeatedly Kant's claim that *a priori* analysis of the concept of morality (an aspect of what has been called here critical metaphysics (§3.II)) establishes that every act of willing by a rational being entails an implicit act of legislating her morality for herself and for all other rational beings. Consequently, every justified ethical principle has the form of a categorical imperative. Yet, Green argues that Kant's imperative to 'respect humanity always as an end' must be combined with a determinate conception of 'humanity' as a valuable end for human action, if it is to function properly as the fundamental structural principle that Green believes Kant established it to be.[6] Without such content it would be simply an empty formula, just as without rationalisation the content would be a formless or fluid aggregate. For this reason, it will be argued here that the ethics of duty that Green builds out of his critical revision of Kant constitutes only one part of his own ethical theory.

The formal requirement generated by an analysis of the idea of ethics itself needs to be completed with an account of how the rational will gains a suitable content. Green goes on to argue that, when conceived properly, ethics is concerned not merely with how the individual should act towards other individuals, but also and possibly more fundamentally with delineating the broad outlines of the agent's own 'good life' in concrete terms. The latter concerns the condition of the individual's 'soul', which Green also characterises as the realisation of her distinctively human or highest capacities ('personal excellence, moral and intellectual') in her personality, as well as her personality's expression in and through her actions.[7] Consequently, the idea of the good life appeals to such notions as 'being true to oneself' and acting virtuously. It is in that sense it forms part of an aesthetic

---

[5] See, for example, Nettleship's editorial notes at 'Kant' pp. 1, 82, 84 and 96, as well as §§78n, 79n, 80n.

[6] PE, for example, 247, 288, 307, 313.

[7] PE 355.

conception of ethics which conceives the latter's proper field of enquiry to be the nature of human flourishing and the conditions for its promotion. Green derives this conception explicitly (even if with some modification) from Aristotelian eudaimonia, understood as the 'full exercise or realisation of the soul's faculties in accordance with its proper excellence, which ... [is] an excellence of thought, speculative and practical.'[8]

In this way, eudaimonia understood as human flourishing is constituted by the development of a range of qualities that is far broader than those which are nowadays commonly judged to be within the moral sphere, and necessarily it does include the sphere of other-regarding actions as well.[9] Crucially however, Green is far more sceptical than Aristotle regarding the possibility of identifying concrete universally-valid virtues.[10] He argues that both Aristotle and Plato recognised the formal requirement that virtues can be authoritative 'only when resting on a pure and good will, which is the will to be good'.[11] Nevertheless, they failed to appreciate the historical contingency of the particular virtues that they held to be universally-valid. In reality, Green argues, any ideal of human flourishing that could serve as a determinate evaluative and practical standard for conduct has to be infused with cultural norms and commitments.

In this sense, Green anticipates contemporary virtue ethicists such as Gary Watson who seek to combine a duty ethic, with a culturally-sensitive virtue ethic aimed at securing the individual's flourishing.[12] In so doing, he adopts a conception of the ethical sphere that encompasses far more than those (duty-based) principles concerned primarily to guide other-regarding actions. He does so in the belief that to adopt the narrow, now more common, position would exclude some of the central features of a normal human life.[13] This thought carries weight also with other contemporary philosophers. Charles Taylor for example has been very influential in rejecting the 'cramped and truncated view of morality in the narrow sense' which is dominant 'not only among professional philosophers, but with a wider public'.[14]

---

[8]   PE 254; see Gerald Gaus, *Modern Liberal Theory of Man* (Beckenham: Croom Helm, 1983), pp. 17–19.

[9]   Hurka misses this point (Thomas Hurka, *Perfectionism* (Oxford: Oxford University Press, 1993), pp. 19–20, 165), as does John Skorupski, 'Green and the Idealist Conception of the Person', in Maria Dimova-Cookson and W.J. Mander, eds., *T.H. Green: Ethics, metaphysics, and political philosophy* (Oxford: Clarendon, 2006), pp. 69–71. Nevertheless, Skorupski's reading contains many highly suggestive insights, the most significant of which are discussed elsewhere in the present book (see the index).

[10]   Skorupki encapsulates much of the difference as follows: idealist self-realisation 'has evident affinities with the classical eudaimonic tradition. But there are important differences which it give a "modern" feel – its historicist conception of self-development, its individualist concern with ideals of inward conscience, on the one hand, and active citizenship, community, and reconciliation, on the other, its account of the modern State and, of course, not least its preoccupation with the problems of Christian faith in science-based societies.' Skorupski, 'Green and the Idealist Conception of a Person's Good', p. 48n1.

[11]   PE 279.

[12]   Gary Watson, 'On the Primacy of Character' [1990], in Stephen Darwall, ed., *Virtue Ethics* (Oxford; Blackwell, 2003), pp. 229–50.

[13]   Alan J.M. Milne, 'Idealist Criticism of Utilitarian Social Philosophy', *Archives Europeenes de Sociologie*, 8 (1967), 322–3.

[14]   Charles Taylor, *Sources of the Self: The making of the modern identity* (Cambridge: Cambridge

Even though Green's broader conception of ethics occupies territory that is at least recognisable to contemporary philosophers, it is not unproblematic. One key difficulty is that the elements making it up work in quite different ways from each other.[15] The ethics of duty derives an agent's responsibility to another person from the latter's claim, whereas the Aristotelian aesthetic conception derives the principles of conduct that are proper to a human being from the nature and conditions of that agent's own flourishing. This distinction can be articulated more formally. For the ethics of duty, ultimately agent x has a duty to person y to perform action z because something about y generates a claim over a number of people including x, to do z. For ethics as flourishing however, ultimately agent x has a duty to person y to perform action z because honouring that duty develops or expresses some excellence of x. With the ethics of duty, considerations regarding y produce x's duty, whereas with ethics as flourishing considerations regarding x herself do so. It does not take much imagination to think of situations in which these conceptions could place very different and frequently incompatible demands on the same person at the same time. In that situation, how does one decide how to act?

One reaction to this paradox would be simply to accept the messy pluralism of the moral commitments that underpin our daily lives, as Taylor does. Moral indeterminacy is an irresolvable and inherently tragic feature of human life, on this view.[16] Yet, while Taylor is a value pluralist, Green's ethics at least aspires to articulate moral and aesthetic principles as a systematic whole even if that whole contains ethical claims derived from considerations of both virtue and duty. For Green, each part has a compound value as a necessary facet of a complete ethical theory.[17] He does agree with Taylor that, as Ruth Abbey observes, 'some [moral goods] are universal, others obtain within a more limited collectivity such as the nation, while yet others are more particular and specific to cultural groups'.[18] Yet, Taylor concludes from this, in Abbey's words again, that moral goods 'are plural in an ontological sense, they are qualitatively different types from one another and, because of this, cannot always be harmoniously combined, rank-ordered or reduced to some more ultimate or foundational good.'[19] Here we get to a fundamental distinction between Green and Taylor. Green acknowledges the

---

University Press, 1989), p. 3, citing Iris Murdoch, *Sovereignty of Good* (London: Routledge, 1970). Taylor makes clear that his worries stem from his belief that the narrow conception of ethics 'has tended to focus ... on defining the content of obligation rather than the nature of the good life; and it has no conceptual place left for a notion of the good as the object of our love or allegiance, or, as Iris Murdoch portrayed it in her work, as the privileged focus of attention or will.'

[15] For another discussion of this distinction, see G.E. Moore, 'The Nature of Morality', in his *Philosophical Studies* (London: Routledge and Kegan Paul, 1922), pp. 310–39.

[16] See Colin Tyler, *Idealist Political Philosophy: Pluralism and conflict in the absolute idealist tradition* (London: Continuum, 2006), Introduction and chapter 2 *passim*.

[17] Compare Charles Taylor, 'The Diversity of Goods', in his *Philosophical Papers II: Philosophy and the human sciences* (Cambridge: Cambridge University Press, 1985), p. 244; Charles Taylor, 'Leading a Life', in R. Chang, ed., *Incommensurability, Incomparability, and Practical Reasoning* (Cambridge, MA: Harvard University Press, 1997).

[18] Ruth Abbey, *Charles Taylor* (Teddington: Acumen, 2000), p. 12.

[19] Abbey, *Charles Taylor*, p. 12.

undeniable fact that values clash in the worlds in which we live, just as our settled beliefs do (even including our scientific beliefs about the natural facts of the world). For Green however, this is a truth about the imperfections of our world, not a truth about correct beliefs or ethical values as such. Such pluralism is a problem that the individual should do their best to overcome rather than being an ultimate ontological fact to be accepted and lived with.

The effort to overcome such pluralism and discontinuity has been shown to be a central task of both Green's 'metaphysics of experience or knowledge' and his metaphysics of the will (§§2.I to 3.II, 5.III–IV). His metaphysics considered as a whole seeks to conceptualise the processes whereby an agent articulates philosophically the structure of beliefs and values that reflect the critically assessed reformulations of that particular agent's initial pre-reflective beliefs and values. It is worth recapping this conception in a little more detail. The metaphysician's initial materials are those immediate, 'intuitive' beliefs and values which the agent holds prior to examining and testing them.[20] The process of critical assessment consists in the application of two processes to these pre-reflective commitments. The analysis carried out above (§3.II) followed D.G. Ritchie and Peter Nicholson in labelling these processes 'critical metaphysics' and 'speculative metaphysics'. The former refers to the analytic process of discovering the 'axioms' that make knowledge possible; the latter are 'the *a priori* conceptions and principles which are involved in ordinary knowledge and in the procedure of scientific investigation and proof'.[21] Speculative metaphysics on the other hand denotes the synthetic process of rearticulating these *a priori* conceptions and principles as related elements of a single coherent system of propositions that matches the 'whole Universe as it becomes known to us'.[22] In this way, the speculative metaphysician uses the results obtained by the critical metaphysician to produce a coherent explanation of the complex phenomena that constitute the matter of the individual's experience. In order to achieve this end, the speculative metaphysician in particular must organise the concepts and propositions that he constructs by projecting an ideal of a harmonious if imperfectly understood system of true structural and substantive concepts and propositions.

Green adopts this demanding metaphysical position because, as we have seen, he holds that the beliefs and values by which you and I live here and now are the flawed products of our imperfect prior attempts to articulate our human nature in determinate forms. Crucially, he holds that when struggling to articulate that human nature, we work on the assumption that, if properly conceived, 'true' meanings and values would form a perfectly coherent system. Green holds that only such an assumption can satisfy a rational being with eudaimonic capacities. This is the heart of what has been labelled above 'crystallisation' (from §2.IV onwards), adapting Stendhal's term for 'a mental process which draws from everything that happens

---

[20] PE 215.
[21] David G. Ritchie, *Darwin and Hegel with other philosophical studies* (London and New York: Swan Sonnenschein, 1902), pp. 16, 17.
[22] Ritchie, *Darwin and Hegel*, p. 14.

new proofs of the perfection of the loved one.'[23] This process of systematisation requires the projection of an ideal of a harmonious system of fundamental concepts and presuppositions. The metaphysician employs crystallisation heuristically and in full knowledge that at present she can conceive of the details of that ideal only in fragmentary and inchoate ways: 'the [mere] idea – the conviction of there being such a thing [as 'the unconditional good'] – is the influence through which [the individual's] life is directed to its attainment'; or more broadly, 'we only find unity in the world because we have an idea that it is there, an idea which we direct our powers to realise'.[24]

Nevertheless, one should not forget that Green's assumption of an ultimately harmonious system of true beliefs and values is heuristic rather than ontological. The ultimate harmony of true beliefs and values is an assumption each of us is driven to make instinctively, in order to give hope and direction to our efforts to understand more clearly ourselves and our world. What Kant refers to in a different context as the 'practico-dogmatic principle of transition to this ideal of world-perfection' is not a transcendent metaphysical principle then.[25] Rather it is a postulate of practical reason, and therefore also of theoretical reason, in that an agent's exercise of practical reason operates in contexts structured necessarily by the results of her exercise of theoretical reason.

Even though the ultimate harmony of all true meanings and values is a postulate of theoretical and practical reason, this is not an excuse for ignoring facts and moral intuitions that unsettle one's current beliefs. Wilful ignorance is still ignorance, and as such constitutes an impediment to the agent's true freedom. Only where the agent endorses freely the hermeneutic contours of her existence (including its categories, beliefs, imperatives, virtues, rights, moral duties and even her legal obligations and so forth) and the reasons that justify those contours, can the latter carry weight for her. Only when they do so can the agent be truly free when acting in accordance with those imperatives, as has been established (§§6.III–IV), or when exercising those rights, because only then does her daily life reflect her own beliefs, values and plans. Ultimately ignorance impedes personal judgement and personal judgement is a core element of Greenian true freedom. Indeed, as with his metaphysics of experience, at root Green's ethics accords the highest possible standing to personal judgement, not least in that it starts from our critical reflections on the world as that exists *'for us'* (see §3.IV in particular).[26]

These imperfections and the fragilities of the human intellect from which they result ensure that both critical and speculative metaphysics are continuing

---

[23] Stendhal, *Love*, trans. G. Sale and S. Sale (Harmondsworth: Penguin, 1975), p. 45.

[24] PE 195, 149.

[25] Immanuel Kant, 'What Real Progress has Metaphysics made in Germany Since the Time of Leibnitz and Wolff?', in his *Theoretical Philosophy after 1781*, ed., H. Allison and P. Heath, trans. Peter Heath (Cambridge: Cambridge University Press, 2001), p. 394 (Prussian Academy edition 20:307).

[26] Green stresses the importance of judgement at many points during his discussion of the metaphysics of experience in the *Prolegomena* (for example, PE 13–15 *passim*, 23–25 *passim*, 34, 51), as well as during his analysis of the will where it is a recurring theme of book two even if Green uses the word 'judgement' only rarely there (PE 93, 94, 137).

projects. The necessarily always partly obscured rationale and incoherences of the principles underpinning our experiences mean that we will always need to be both critical and speculative metaphysicians. Indeed, Green argues it will always be a categorical imperative for a rational being to honour, question and refine her ideals of human perfection in this way.[27] We will always need to exercise personal judgement if we are to act in a distinctively human fashion; we must always be critical participants in our own lives.

As should be clear following the earlier extended discussions of these twin metaphysical operations (§3.II), their success – and therefore the agent's ability to arrive at sound judgements – depends in large part on her successful crystallisation of a coherent and normatively compelling conception of the ultimate good. This is because, as Green stresses, making personal judgements requires the agent to stand apart from her individual desires so as to evaluate and choose between those desires by assessing their relationships to a complex conception of an ideal which she freely endorses as her ultimate standard of ethical worth.[28] Green refers to this evaluative criterion as 'the practical idea of something good on the whole, of a true or chief or highest or ultimate good'.[29] Of course, the success of this ideal as an evaluative standard depends in large part on the degree to which the agent has a well-defined and coherent conception of it: it depends, in short, on the 'definiteness of direction' that it gives to the agent.[30] Yet, as Green also observes, to get from a faith in the existence of an abstract ideal to a concrete conception of that ideal 'may naturally seem a long step'.[31] With this thought in mind, Green considers the leading ethical theories of his day. Perhaps unsurprisingly, he focuses the majority of his negative critical attention on the then-dominant cluster of ethical theories: the various schools of utilitarianism. Scholars still debate whether or not Green is himself a utilitarian, and if so in what sense. His criticisms of utilitarianism are assessed in the next section, after which his own ethical theory will be explored in greater depth. It will be argued in the penultimate section of the next chapter that he is not a utilitarian in any coherent sense, and that his consequentialism is a necessary but not sufficient facet of his ethical theory.

III
Personal Judgement and the Failure of Utilitarian Ethics

In the *Prolegomena*, Green credits utilitarianism with being the 'theory of conduct' that had done most to provide the 'conscientious citizen' of 'Modern Europe' with 'a vantage-ground for judging the competing claims on his obedience, and enabled him to substitute a critical and intelligent for a blind and unquestioning conformity'.[32]

---

[27] PE 196–98.
[28] PE 220–222.
[29] PE 221.
[30] PE 362.
[31] PE 192.
[32] PE 329. This section develops points made in Colin Tyler, 'The Metaphysics of Pleasure: Jeremy Bentham and his British idealist critics', in Andrew Dobson and Jeffrey Stanyer, eds., *Contemporary Political Studies 1998*, 2 vols. (Exeter: PSA/Short Run, 1998), vol. 1, pp. 261–69. A more recent, excellent discussion can be found in David Weinstein, *Utilitarianism and the New*

It has had philosophical benefits as well, not least by extending the range of beings towards whom morality requires us to show impartiality and by highlighting the requirement that one derive rights and obligations from considerations regarding the good (even if they misconceive 'goodness').[33] Nevertheless, he goes on to argue that in key respects, practical utilitarians had been better than the philosophical creeds propounded by the likes of Jeremy Bentham, John Stuart Mill and Henry Sidgwick.[34] Moreover, he holds that most of the practical benefits derived from utilitarian policies have been felt 'in its application to public policy rather than to private conduct'.[35]

Some of Green's objections to utilitarianism are more effective than others. For example, he criticises utilitarianism as a guide to practice on the ground that circumstances are so complicated and open-ended that the strict utilitarian would be unable to decide which course of action is required of them in any particular situation. He argues that the indeterminacy of practical guidance should discourage the strict utilitarian from trying to live up to the demands of their ethics at all.[36] While this criticism bites against act utilitarianism, it seems to have far less impact on rule utilitarianism. Hence, Bentham argues that in order to maximise its otherwise elusive '*all-comprehensive*, and only right and proper end' (the greatest aggregate pleasure), the state should seek to promote certain other '*specific* and *direct* ends of government' with these proximate goals being '*national subsistence, abundance, security, and equality maximized; official aptitude maximized: expense, in all shapes, minimized*'.[37] Similarly, J.S. Mill justified many profoundly important public values, including personal liberty and justice, by appealing to the indirect utilitarian benefits of upholding them.[38] Henry Sidgwick, Green's third major representative utilitarian, argues that 'from a Utilitarian point of view' the appropriate public 'rules of conduct' should 'be determined by the same kind of forecast of consequences as will be used in settling all questions of private morality: we shall endeavour to estimate and balance against each other the effects of such rules on the general happiness.'[39]

There seems to be little practical alternative to these types of indirect rule-based moral codes. In this sense, Green's strict utilitarian is a *reducio ad absurdum* of his representative utilitarians. Moreover, in that he himself adopts the indirect, proxy-based strategy in relation to his own ethical theory, his allegation that utilitarians must betray their own principles if they are to live up to their practical aspirations, showing an inconsistency on his part.[40]

Liberalism (Cambridge: Cambridge University Press, 2007), pp. 42–55.

[33]   PE 331, 333.

[34]   Green names these utilitarians at various points in his writings: for example, PE 225, 334, 351.

[35]   PE 334.

[36]   PE 341–46, 357–63, 372–82.

[37]   Jeremy Bentham, *Constitutional Code: Volume 1*, eds. F. Rosen and J.H. Burns (Oxford: Clarendon, 1983), pp. 135–36 (§VII.2); see also Paul Kelly, *Utilitarianism and Distributive Justice: Jeremy Bentham and the civil law* (Oxford: Clarendon, 1990).

[38]   John Stuart Mill employs this justification for liberty in the first chapter of *On Liberty* (1859), and for justice in the final chapter of *Utilitarianism* (1861), for example.

[39]   Henry Sidgwick, *Methods of Ethics*, seventh edition (London: MacMillan, 1907), p. 457.

[40]   For example: 'Morality and political subjection ... have a common source ... That common

Green argues that, if adhered to strictly, hedonistic utilitarianism would have profoundly conservative implications. He claims that hedonism entails that individuals already seek their own greatest pleasures, from which he concludes that this means what does happen in the realm of personal conduct is what ought to happen.[41] Again, ultimately this is a weak criticism. The utilitarian may well accept that by definition hedonists are concerned only with their own greatest net personal pleasure. Yet, it is important to distinguish hedonism from hedonistic utilitarianism, in that by definition the latter is concerned solely with maximising the net aggregate pleasure of the group conceived as an aggregate of hedonistic individuals. In spite of Green's allegation therefore hedonism and hedonistic utilitarianism can be accommodated within a single coherent ethical theory. For example, it is because Bentham believes that ultimately all of us are hedonists that, as a hedonistic utilitarian, he argues the state should develop a system of incentives and deterrents that will manipulate our 'springs of action' so as to encourage individuals to act in the ways that are most likely in the circumstances to maximise the net pleasure for the group.[42] This manipulation can be achieved through either social or ethical rules, or legislation.[43] Deciding which levers to pull and in what ways is a practical matter, and therefore not capable of prediction in the abstract. Clearly, Bentham's solution is mechanistic in a way that Green resists as an appropriate way to deal with good-willed human beings.[44] Nevertheless, Green provides no convincing reasons for believing that Bentham, Mill, Sidgwick or any of their many followers could not be consistent radicals.

This practical indeterminacy of abstract ethics affects Green's own ethical theory. This means quite simply that it is not possible to decide, as some scholars have sought to, the issue of whether he is a 'utilitarian in practice' by contrasting his position on a chosen public policy issue with that of a utilitarian. In this regard, nothing hangs on the question of whether or not, taking Thom Brooks's example, 'the practical implications [for punishment] of Green and Mill's theories are essentially the same', because in themselves the practical implications of Millian utilitarianism are very heavily context-dependent, as are the implications of Green's

---

source is the rational recognition by certain human beings … of a common well-being which is their well-being, … *and the embodiment of that recognition in rules* by which the inclinations of the individuals are restrained, and a corresponding freedom of action for the attainment of well-being *on the whole* is secured.' PO 117, emphasis added.

[41] PE 340. Green himself accepts that even hedonism passes one of his own key tests for a viable theory of the will: namely that it conceives the ends of human action as personal goods. In fact, he is explicit that in experiencing desires both for 'fleeting gratifications' and for 'abiding satisfaction', the self-conscious agent recognises those desires as his own, meaning that they constitute possible objects of a personal good and are not purely instinctive ('Hume II' 3–4).

[42] Jeremy Bentham, *Deontology together with A Table of the Springs of Action and Article on Utilitarianism*, ed. Amnon Goldworth (Oxford: Clarendon Press, 1983).

[43] 'Morality in general is the art of directing the actions of men in such a way as to produce the greatest possible sum of good. Legislation ought to have precisely the same object.' Jeremy Bentham, *Theory of Legislation*, ed. E. Dumont, trans. R. Hildreth, fourth edition (London: Trübner, 1882), p. 60. This is Dumont's recension of Bentham's *Introductions to the Principles of Morals and Legislation*, which most readers, including Green, took wrongly to be unproblematically Bentham's own text.

[44] Green holds that animals can be manipulated mechanistically. One might be reminded here of his contrast between beating a dog and punishing a human being (PO 187).

principles.[45] Given different circumstances, Mill might endorse a radically different practical policy than actually he does in his writings, as might Green.[46]

In spite of the weakness of Green's preceding arguments, he does raise a number of rather more successful, strictly philosophical objections to utilitarianism. First, he points out that hedonistic utilitarians ascribe intrinsic positive value only to experiences of pleasure. Consequently, he argues, they value individual human beings only to the extent that the latter are loci of those experiences. Hence, the 'Benthamite' or 'hedonist' who is true to his ethical principles 'would repudiate or pronounce unintelligible the notion of an absolute value in the individual person. It is not every person, according to him, but every pleasure, that is of value in itself'.[47] That the consistent utilitarian accords individual human beings derivative value only, means that she fails to respect, in Green's terms, the 'personal character of the moral ideal': 'Our ultimate standard of worth is an ideal of *personal* worth. All other values are relative to value for, of or in a person.'[48] (See §8.II below.)

Second, Green argues that it is disingenuous to hold that human beings only ascribe intrinsic value to pleasures and disvalue to pains.[49] Except for the relatively small class of purely physical sensations, pleasure can be attained only as a result of bringing into existence a state of affairs or attaining some object that is valued for a reason other than the pleasure expected from the attainment of the object. Pleasure does not exist *sui generis*. To gain pleasure from nursing my cat back to health, I must do so, say, out of love, and such a reason must have force for me on grounds that are independent of the pleasure that I gain from taking care of her. Green's only (rather enigmatic) exceptions are pleasures that are either 'sensual in a special sense' or 'pleasures of pure emotion'.[50] Aside from these two peculiar types, pleasure is at best a bonus, arising as a consequence of the agent's attainment of more fundamental goods.[51] This leads Green to argue, thirdly, that the utilitarian imperative to attain the greatest possible net aggregate pleasure demonstrates that utilitarians themselves are committed logically to valuing something other than pleasure itself, as a net aggregate of pleasures is not itself a pleasure. In fact, the greatest possible sum of pleasures is much more like an ideal state of being.[52]

Thus far, Green's attacks on utilitarianism have relied upon largely Aristotelian criteria, and indeed like Aristotle Green rejects the life that seeks the good of pleasure for being 'passive' and 'slavish', a life fit merely for 'grazing animals'.[53] For both

---

[45] Thom Brooks, 'Was Green a Utilitarian in Practice?', *Collingwood and British Idealism Studies*, 14:1 (2008), 14; see further 5–15.

[46] For the references to J.S. Mill and Green's respective writings on punishment, see Brooks, 'Was Green a Utilitarian in Practice?' *passim.*

[47] PE 214.

[48] A.C. Bradley entitled Book 3, chapter II, part A of the *Prolegomena* (§§180–91) the 'personal character of the moral ideal'.

[49] PE 158. For ease of exposition, although only pleasures will be specified explicitly from here on, the avoidance of pains is also intended.

[50] PE 158.

[51] PE 152–62.

[52] PE 221–22, 360; 'Hedonism' passim.

[53] Aristotle rejects glory-seeking on the ground that glory is too fleeting and reliant on the good opinion of others rather than some quality of the man himself. Finally he rejects the life whose guiding purpose is the accumulation of wealth because it is only ever a means and therefore

Green and Aristotle, rational activity is inherently goal-orientated (teleological), and, while most actions are instrumentally valuable, rational actions as such aim at a good that endures (unlike pleasures, which naturally tend to diminish over time), as well as being self-subsistent and valued for its own sake.[54]

It is important to remember also that for Green one's meanings and values can satisfy a human being only to the extent that they constitute a coherent system which gives determinate form to her highest capacities. The aggregate of pleasures valued by utilitarians such as Bentham, Mill and Sidgwick fails to achieve the degree of integration Green requires. Partly this is due to the fact that it need not be structured by a harmonising principle. Partly however it is because these utilitarians do not require constitutive pleasurable experiences (as distinct from the activities that give rise to such experiences) to be conceptualised in the manner required by Green's theory of self-realisation.

Green goes further however by arguing that the utilitarian imperative to maximise or even just increase an aggregate of pleasure is 'intrinsically ... unmeaning': pleasure can always be increased beyond any quantity that it has a particular time.[55] Weinstein rightly criticises Green on this point: 'sober utilitarians simply need to hold that one ought to try to get as much pleasure as one can.'[56] Yet, Weinstein's response ignores a crucial lack of precision at the heart of the utilitarian ethics under discussion here. For example, on the rare occasions that these classical utilitarians try to specify what they mean by feelings of 'pleasure' and 'pain', the vagueness of their statements highlights the vacuity of their core (dis)value(s). Hence, Bentham wrote in an unpublished manuscript: 'I call pleasure every sensation that a man had rather feel at that instant than feel *none*. I call pain every sensation that a man had rather feel none than feel.'[57] When he is called on to explain what he means by the terms 'pleasure' and 'pain' in other places, Bentham either merely produces a 'catalogue' of some of their respective 'sources' ('pleasures of sense', 'wealth', 'skill', 'amity', 'a good name', and so on), or he does little more than invoke vague notions such as 'duration' and 'intensity' without clarifying the feelings to which they refer.[58] Despite his rejection of Bentham's psychological hedonism, Sidgwick fares little better.[59] J.S. Mill ties himself in knots trying to distinguish higher pleasure from lower pleasure while retaining both

---

     only ever of instrumental value (Aristotle, *Ethics*, 1095b15–1096a4).

[54] More than this however, Green echoes Aristotle in emphasising certain key psychological shortcomings of the hedonistic life, as will become clear shortly.

[55] PE 359.

[56] Weinstein, *Utilitarianism and the New Liberalism*, p. 47.

[57] Jeremy Bentham quoted in John Dinwiddy, *Bentham* (Oxford: Oxford University Press, 1989), p. 22. The quotation comes from the Bentham manuscripts, University College London, box xcvi, folio 128.

[58] For example, Jeremy Bentham, *Introduction to the Principles of Morals and Legislation*, eds. J.H. Burns and H.L.A. Hart, revised edition (Oxford: Clarendon, 1996), especially chapters III to V.

[59] '[B]y "greatest possible Happiness" we understand the greatest attainable surplus of pleasure over pain; the two terms being used, with equally comprehensive meanings, to include respectively all kinds of agreeable and disagreeable feelings.' Sidgwick, *Methods of Ethics*, pp. 120–21; 'I propose ... to define Pleasure – when we are considering its "strict value" for purposes of quantitative comparison – as a feeling which, when experienced by intelligent beings, is at least implicitly apprehended as desirable or – in the cases of comparison – preferable.' p. 127.

within a coherent and distinctively utilitarian conceptual framework. The former becomes either a name for the possession of certain ideal objects,[60] or alternatively what Green called an 'abiding satisfaction of an abiding self'.[61] 'Lower pleasures' becomes little more than a label for physical sensations that one would rather feel than not feel.

That a life without pleasure would be intolerable for most people does not alter the fact that the terms 'pleasure' and 'pain' are so ineffable that they cannot form an intelligible guide to action of the type that is required if one is to act in a distinctively human fashion (see §§5.III–IV). The degree of ambiguity at the heart of the utilitarian conception of the good precludes the greatest happiness principle in any of the classical formulations given to it by Bentham, J.S. Mill and Sidgwick from acting as an adequate principle of practical reason in Green's terms: pleasure is too vague a notion to allow the individual to use it to 'conceive a better state of itself as an end to be attained by action'.[62] For this reason, on Greenian terms classical utilitarianism must fail as both a moral and a public philosophy.[63]

In spite of his emphatic rejection of many aspects of utilitarianism, Green does see a heavily pregnant strand within it. While Mill recognises a difference between higher and lower pleasures, Green believes that Mill misunderstands the significance of that difference. For Green, human beings can experience two qualitatively distinct types of feeling which mistakenly the utilitarian treats as two varieties of essentially one feeling. 'Pleasure' which Green associates with the animal aspects of the individual's nature, and 'abiding satisfaction' which he associates with both the rational and the eudaimonic aspects.[64] That Bentham, Mill and Sidgwick fail to appreciate the profound divide between these two types of feeling should not be surprising given the capaciousness of their respective conceptions of 'pleasure' and 'pain' noted earlier. This lack of precision is significant, then, on more than a merely linguistic level: it leads the classical utilitarians to misconceive one of the most fundamental facets of a distinctively human life. This is the process whereby individuals overcome the alienation they experience as imperfect beings with distinctively human capacities. The nature and ethical ramifications of this process will be explored in greater depth next.

---

[60] See for example, the first chapter of J.S. Mill's *Utilitarianism* (1861). See David Brink's very interesting discussion of this point in his *Perfectionism and the Common Good: Themes in the philosophy of T.H. Green* (Oxford: Clarendon, 2003), pp. 31–40.

[61] PE 234.

[62] PE 177.

[63] Weinstein concedes that: 'Of course, if each individual's greatest pleasure is a fictive end, then the greatest number is no less fictive and incoherent.' Weinstein, *Utilitarianism and the New Liberalism*, p. 47n75. For an argument that Benthamite pleasure at least is a fictive end, see Colin Tyler, ' "A Foundation of Chaff"?: A critique of Bentham's metaphysics, 1813–16', *British Journal for the History of Philosophy*, vol. 12, no. 4 (November 2004), 685–703.

[64] Maria Dimova-Cookson fails to take account of this fact when she denies that there is a significant difference between pleasure and self-satisfaction: Maria Dimova-Cookson, *T.H. Green's Moral and Political Philosophy: A phenomenological perspective* (Houndsmill: Palgrave, 2001), pp. 58–61.

IV
Personality and the True Good

Green conceives of pure pleasure-seeking as an inherently alienating form of life. The 'fleeting gratifications' sought by the hedonist make no reference to anything apart from her short-term, contingent feelings.[65] The enjoyment to be gained from satisfying desires of this type tends to be brief, with a similar want arising soon afterwards. Consequently, achieving her goal leaves the hedonist's situation essentially unaltered in the long-run. There is no permanence to the increase in her feeling of well-being, and the feeling itself lacks depth.[66] Green sees this as deeply significant because the hedonist who reflects on this lack of improvement in her condition is led gradually to experience a deep-seated feeling of spiritual emptiness. It is this feeling of alienation and lack of fulfilment which spurs her personal development: 'As a man reflects – perhaps quite inarticulately – on the transitoriness of the pleasures by imagination of which his desires are from hour to hour excited; ... he asks (practically, if without formal expression) what can satisfy the self which abides throughout and survives those desires'.[67] This question gives rise to a new sort of want in the agent: the desire for an abiding realisation of her distinctively human capacities.

Attaining this object brings her what can be 'otherwise called peace or blessedness' which usually Green refers to as an 'abiding satisfaction' of the individual's 'abiding self.'[68] As has been shown in the preceding chapters, for Green this 'abiding self' equates to the agent's human nature: the spiritual principle in its epistemic, moral and aesthetic aspects.[69] In other words, the spiritually unsatisfied agent seeks to realise the presently inchoate conception of the law of her being as an embodiment of her highest potentials.[70] For these reasons, Green argues, the true good is a personal good which brings abiding satisfaction to a virtuous agent.[71] Moreover

---

[65] PE 229.

[66] 'We are warranted however by simple consideration of its nature, in holding that the idea of true good could only become matter of definite consciousness in view of its possible realisation in an object which at once excites a strong interest, and can at the same time be regarded as having the permanence necessary to satisfy the demand arising from a man's involuntary contemplation of his own permanence.' (PE 230) The need for permanence is a recurring theme in Green's metaphysical writings and especially in his theory of the true good: for example, PE 11, 12, 37, 53, 61, 95, 188, 201–03, 211, 216, 220, 222–23, 229–42 *passim*, 246, 250, 317.

[67] PE 229.

[68] DSF 1; PE 234.

[69] PE 173–76.

[70] DSF 1; 'Kant' 127.

[71] PE 171. '[T]he differentia of the virtuous life, proceeding as it does from the same self-objectifying principle which we have just characterised as the source of the vicious life, is that it is governed by the consciousness of there being some perfection which has to be attained, some vocation which has to be fulfilled, some law which has to be obeyed, something absolutely desirable, whatever the individual may for the time desire; that it is in ministering to such an end that the agent seeks to satisfy himself.' PE 176. Strangely, given Green's apparently clarity on this matter, at least one critic has missed this point in Green's published writings (Craig A. Smith, 'Individual and Society in T.H. Green's Theory of Virtue', *History of Political Thought*, 2:1 (1981), 194–201 *passim*).

as Thomas puts it: ' "true" has the force at once of genuine as opposed to false or spurious, and of ultimate as opposed to derivative or conditional'.[72]

Green's conception of the true good grounds the contours of the ethical sphere (broadly conceived, as above). Consequently, one should be clear regarding its nature. David Brink has argued that 'Like Kant, Green seeks an account of the agent's duties that is grounded in her agency and does not depend upon contingent and variable inclinations.'[73] Unfortunately Brink presents only a partial picture of these grounds, citing as he does merely the 'deliberative capacities that make one a responsible agent'.[74] While the deliberative capacities are clearly necessary for Green's ethics as they are for Kant's, as has been shown Green conceives them to be only one of two necessary elements. The missing element is found in the individual's innate drive to realise her higher capacities. Brink neglects the constructive dynamics of Green's philosophical method, which precludes him from grasping fully Green's understanding of the relationship between deliberative and eudaimonic capacities. As a result, Brink mischaracterises the role of Green's romantic re-articulation of Aristotelian eudaimonism in Green's wider ethical theory. This obscures the fact that, in line with other British idealists, Green holds that an action is good to the extent that the agent subjectively wills the attainment of an object which she judges to be objectively valuable, and does so because she judges it to be objectively valuable.[75]

This formula is succinct but powerful, and Brink is not alone in misconceiving Green's wider argument due to a failure to grasp its structure and implications. David Weinstein does the same (see §8.V). Maria Dimova-Cookson claims that Green holds two contradictory positions, such that: 'The [Kantian] formal definition of morality leaves the moral ideal essentially unspecified, yet every concrete moral action pursues a particular vision of the good as distinct from moral motivation (the good will). If we commit ourselves to one, we are disloyal to the other.'[76] On the interpretation given here however, Dimova-Cookson misunderstands Green's actual argument, the logic of which can be encapsulated more formally in the following five sequential propositions:

1. Individuals should act out of a good will;
2. A will is good to the extent that it seeks the attainment of objects which the individual believes to be intrinsically or inherently valuable, and does so in a manner that can be willed as a universal law;
3. Ultimately the realisation of distinctively human capacities in the world is the most valuable object for a human being;

[72] Geoffrey Thomas, *Moral Philosophy of T.H. Green* (Oxford: Clarendon, 1987), p. 247, citing as evidence PE 171, 191, and 'cf. relatedly 'untrue, in *the* sense of being inadequate', MS 15 [Green Papers, Balliol College, Oxford].

[73] Brink, *Perfectionism*, pp. 40–41.

[74] Brink, *Perfectionism*, p. 41. Maria Dimova-Cookson argues something similar (Dimova-Cookson, *T.H. Green's Moral and Political Philosophy*, pp. 61–64).

[75] Edward Caird endorses the same position (see Tyler, *Idealist Political Philosophy*, p. 112).

[76] Dimova-Cookson, *T.H. Green's Moral and Political Philosophy*, p. 70.

4. An agent has a good character to the extent that she is motivated primarily to realise her own eudaimonic capacities and those of her fellows, and does so in a manner that can be willed as a universal law;

5. The agent attains her true good to the extent that the actions issuing from her character achieve this primary goal.

Green argues that the recognition of the force of this argument has grown in the culture of modern Europe through successive generations, as has the specification of a determinate form and content of eudaimonic or 'higher' capacities. This growth has not ended, meaning that the process of iterative re-specification is on-going. The individual tends to be driven to be an active participant in that process by her innate drives to realise these capacities in her life, to possess a good character and to act well on the basis of it.[77]

This claim is underpinned by a commitment to a form of Socratic internalism, in that it holds the distinctively human capacities which an individual can possess necessarily tend to push her to act so as to attain the most valuable possible object, her full self-conscious realisation of herself as a particular person.[78] It is in this sense that a distinctively human agent is driven to be self-realising even if ultimately her imperfections and circumstances thwart her to some degree. Consequently: 'The reformer cannot bear to think of himself except as giving effect, so far as may be [possible], to his project of reform; and thus, instead of merely contemplating a possible work, he does it.'[79] In short, Green's is a practical philosophy, in the sense that his basic question is: how can we live the good life?[80] In more determinate

---

[77] The question of whether it was inevitable that this growth would occur (and will continue to do so) is returned to in the second part of *The Liberal Socialism of T.H. Green*. At the very least, it is an empirical claim.

[78] PE 253–5, 286; see Avital Simhony, 'T.H. Green's Theory of the Morally Justified Society', *History of Political Thought*, 10:3 (1989), 482–85; Gerald Gaus develops this line at length and in very interesting ways in his 'The Rights Recognition Thesis: Defending and extending Green', in Dimova-Cookson et al, eds., *T.H. Green*, pp. 209–35. Some of Green's texts are not always as clear as one would wish on this point (Weinstein, *Utilitarianism*, pp. 38–41).

[79] PE 299.

[80] For example, 'Popular Philosophy' *passim*; see also Melvin Richter, *Politics of Conscience: T.H. Green and his age* (London: Weidenfeld and Nicolson, 1964), pp. 344–76. This relates to the fact that Green sought to develop what Nettleship called 'a working theory of life' (Richard Lewis Nettleship, 'Professor T.H. Green. In memoriam', *Contemporary Review*, vol. 61 (January to June 1882), 862. One finds intimations of this pragmatism in Green's own texts: for example, 'The objects most prominent in a man's working idea of true well-being will vary, no doubt, according to circumstances and his idiosyncrasy.' PE 235; see also PE 354. Nevertheless, he urges caution: 'But in fact the best practical philosophy of any age has never been more than an assertion of partial truths, which had some special present function to fulfil in the deliverance or defence of the human soul. When they have done their work, these truths become insufficient for the expression of the highest practical convictions operating in man, while the speculative intellect, if enlisted in the service of the pleasure-seeking nature, can easily extract excuses from them for evading the cogency of those convictions. But the remedy for this evil is still not to be found in the abandonment of philosophy, but in its further pursuit. The spring of all moral progress, indeed, can still lie nowhere else than in the attraction of heart and will by the ideal of human perfection, and in the practical convictions which arise from it; but philosophy will still be needed as the interpreter of practical conviction, and it can itself alone provide for the adequacy of the interpretation.' (PE 312) See further Colin Tyler, *Idealist Political Philosophy*, chapter 2.

terms, it seeks to discover the manifestations in which 'the spirit operative in men finds its full expression and realisation'.[81] Elsewhere, he poses the question in terms of trying to find a 'state of life or consciousness'.[82] At such times, he is unconcerned by the question of whether one is better when acting well than one is when merely having the sort of character that would act well if called upon to do so.

This 'practical' side of Green's philosophy is pursued at much greater length in the second part of this study of *The Liberal Socialism of T.H.* Green. For the moment it is important to notice that usually, Green conceives the individual's virtue as being constituted by the quality of her habitual disposition to act (her character or synonymously her personality) rather than the fact that in practice she does act on that disposition, because there are circumstances where one does not have a practical opportunity to act on it. The true good is not then a state of being which is achieved merely whilst actually performing actions which utilize one's highest human potentials.[83] Nevertheless, it is these potentials that create the possibility of acting from good motives, and, to the extent that the agent has attained a perfect character, they form the basis of distinctively human action.[84] The determinate instantiations of these potentials, and the habitual disposition to act on them, are the constitutive elements of a good character. Good action and good character do interact of course; for example, only an individual with a perfect character could perform perfectly good actions, and performing imperfectly good actions fosters a better character if performed by a person of good character who then strives to do better. Yet echoing Kant, Green holds that the true good is possessed by the virtuous individual all of the time (including when asleep for example), not merely when she exercises her good character in practice.[85] That said, that an agent's circumstances and her own imperfections can thwart her attempts to follow her conscience exposes a mismatch between the moral worth of an agent and the abiding satisfaction that she feels. Even though a good character brings a high degree of abiding satisfaction to its possessor, complete abiding satisfaction can only be present when the agent uses his potentials to the full.

---

[81] PE 183.
[82] PE 187.
[83] PE 304.
[84] PE 247.
[85] 'Even if, by some special disfavour of destiny or by the niggardly endowment of step-motherly nature, this will is entirely lacking in power to carry out its intentions; if by its utmost effort it still accomplishes nothing, and only good will is left (not, admittedly, as a mere wish, but as the straining of every means so far as they are in our control); even then it would still shine like a jewel for its own sake as something which has its full value in itself.' Immanuel Kant, *Groundwork of the Metaphysics of Morals*, trans. H.J. Paton, third edition (New York: Harper Torchbooks, 1964), p. 62 (Prussian Academy edition 394). Green held that the satisfaction felt by the person would be less in this case than if the action had been carried out, however.

V
Some Objections Considered

It should be clear by now that Henry Sidgwick was incorrect when he alleged that Green believes an immoral action brings only partial satisfaction whereas a good action brings complete satisfaction.[86] This claim implies that there is only a quantitative difference between the feelings arising from different types of action. In fact, it is vitally important that there is a qualitative difference between them. In the case of an evil action, the resulting feeling is ultimately some form of pleasure which springs from the individual's animal imperfections. In the case of a good action, it is an individual's spiritual satisfaction which is gained. They are very different things.

Similarly, Henry Sturt was incorrect to describe Green as a subjectivist.[87] Green cannot be a subjectivist in any very usual sense of the word because he does not argue (and Sturt does not argue that Green argues) that ethical judgements and actions are simply the result of arbitrary preferences. Instead, they arise out of our distinctively human needs and aspirations. Sturt fails to take proper account of the fact that Green's conception of ethics concerns values which we should have (reflected in goals we should pursue), in contradistinction to the preferences we happen to have and, consequently, whose pursuit we happen to undertake.

Third, Plamenatz misinterprets Green's conception of the true good when he asserts that Green conceives the highest state of being (a virtuous life) to be that form of living which aims at the satisfaction of the most desires, or alternatively the greatest amount of 'desire' (Plamenatz does not tell us which).[88] Plamenatz's reading is clearly misplaced. Indeed, looking back thirty years later in the second edition of the work in which he presented this criticism, Plamenatz conceded that he had done 'much less than justice to … Green'.[89] It should be clear by now that Green holds the true good to be achieved through the pursuit of only certain ends. These are sought only in response to those desires which spring from human nature itself, and not from our animal imperfections. Green summarised his position in a manner that anticipates the criticisms lodged by Sidgwick, Sturt and Plamenatz:

> [The true good is] an object, which [the individual] presents to himself as absolutely desirable but which is other than any particular object of desire…. [It is] conceived to be of unconditional value; one of which the value does not depend on any desire that the individual may at any time feel for it or for anything else, or on any pleasure that, either in its pursuit or in its attainment or as its result, he may experience…. [T]he desire

---

[86] Henry Sidgwick, *Lectures on the Ethics of T.H. Green, Mr. Herbert Spencer, and J. Martineau* (London: MacMillan, 1902), pp. 37–38, 61–62.

[87] Henry Sturt, *Idoli Theatri: A criticism of Oxford thought and thinkers from the standpoint of personal idealism* (London: MacMillan, 1906), pp. 256–57.

[88] John P. Plamenatz, *Consent, Freedom, and Political Obligation*, first edition (London: Oxford University Press, 1938), pp. 76–80; see W.G. de Burgh, *From Morality to Religion* (London: MacDonald and Evans, 1938), pp. 89–90 for a similar attack.

[89] John P. Plamenatz, *Consent, Freedom, and Political Obligation*, second edition (London: Oxford University Press, 1968), p. 166.

for the object will be founded on a conception of its desirableness as a fulfilment of the capabilities of which a man is conscious in being conscious of himself.[90]

A more effective objection can be raised against Green's theory. At times, his conception of the true good seems very similar to the utilitarian's conception of 'pleasure'. That is significant because of course he claims that pleasure is both incapable of motivating the vast majority of human actions, and too vague to provide intelligible and definite guidance for distinctively human agents. The first of these criticisms will be considered now, and the second in §8.II.

At times Green refers to his own conception of the 'true good' as a sense of 'abiding satisfaction' and at other times as a state of personality understood as a disposition to act in certain ways, and at yet other times as the exertions of that personality in practice.[91] Frequently, he refers to the end sought by a moral agent as the attainment of both an object that either will form part of her flourishing or will allow her to flourish on the one hand, and the feeling of satisfaction produced by attaining that object on the other. There are many examples of the latter, including: the individual 'asks ... what can satisfy the self which abides throughout and survives those desires[?]'[92] Or again: 'It is this requirement or demand that first sets us upon seeking to bring objects into existence, in which some sort of abiding satisfaction may be found'.[93] He refers to the ends sought by a moral agent as 'the objects ... brought into existence by demand for the satisfaction of an abiding self',[94] and argues that 'the idea of a true good as for oneself ... is ultimately or in principle an idea of satisfaction for a self that abides and contemplates itself as abiding'.[95] Unfortunately, it is difficult to square these claims that individuals seek a feeling (satisfaction) rather than the attainment of an object, with Green's emphatic rejection of the utilitarian claim that pleasure is always the motive of individual actions: if pleasures do not motivate, why should self-satisfaction be able to do so?

Evidently, there is a significant ambiguity at these points in Green's text. The strongest philosophical argument is clear however. Whether one is concerned with 'the demand for an abiding satisfaction' (which he describes as 'the demand ... for a true or permanent good')[96] or with the demand for pleasure, Green is correct when he argues that the emotional response that one experiences from the attainment of an object almost always reflects some value other than the experience of the emotional response that prior to acting one believed would follow from the

---

[90] PE 193.
[91] PE 234. On the at least alleged ambiguities of Green's 'true good', see W.D. Lamont, *Introduction to Green's Moral Philosophy* (London: George Allen and Unwin, 1934), pp. 190–96 *passim*, 212–15, and E.F. Carritt, *Morals and Politics: Theories of their relation from Hobbes and Spinoza to Marx and Bosanquet* (Oxford: Clarendon, 1947), p. 132. Compare John Skorupski, 'Green and the Idealist Conception of the Person', pp. 59–63.
[92] PE 229.
[93] PE 230.
[94] PE 231.
[95] PE 232.
[96] PE 250.

attainment of that object.[97] In all cases except for purely physical pleasures (the purely physical pleasures of sexual intercourse, for example), if the desired object were not to be valued independently of the pleasure arising from its attainment, why would one get pleasure from attaining it?

In fact, at other times Green is emphatic that a desiring agent aims at an object of desire rather than any sort of feeling which attaining the object might bring.[98] As was established above (§§ 6.II, 7.III), in these moods the true good is a personality which is valuable in its own right then, rather than a feeling of self-satisfaction.[99] No doubt the agent values that feeling of abiding satisfaction but his goal is not its attainment and cannot be so.[100] Instead, the agent's particular goal is to possess a personality with particular determinate features that he understands to be good. On this view, the feeling of abiding satisfaction is a secondary consequence of a successful virtuous action, and experiencing the feeling indicates the attainment of a virtuous object without itself having motivated the agent to pursue that virtuous object.

Even though Green himself does not develop this line, his approach has an interesting implication. It is significant that the feeling of abiding satisfaction can be aroused in the individual only by realising one's distinctively human capacities. This means that to the extent one genuinely does experience an abiding satisfaction, one knows that one has acted in an ethical way (broadly conceived of course to include both personal flourishing and honouring one's duties). The feeling of an abiding satisfaction is a mark of one's success, and therefore might serve as a guide to the sorts of actions that have a good chance of allowing one to be successful in this sense in the future.

Even though the feeling of an abiding satisfaction is a criterion by which one can tell that one has realised at least part of one's human nature, it is not always easy to discern.[101] Something that initially appears to be abiding may weaken or dissipate over time. This might happen because new actions and concerns come to occupy your attention, thereby making a genuine feeling of satisfaction less intense. Alternatively the feeling might have been misidentified at first: a merely apparent abiding satisfaction might be actually simply a particularly sublime feeling of pleasure. The agent might even deceive herself that a convenient pleasure is actually an abiding satisfaction. The ethical agent should be conscious of the constant possibility of such misidentification, whatever its source. Hence she

---

[97] PE 158.

[98] PE 158.

[99] PE 364, PPO 2.

[100] For example, Richter, *Politics of Conscience*, pp. 194–207 *passim*; Thomas, *Moral Philosophy of T.H. Green*, pp. 242–47 *passim*; Nicholson, *Political Philosophy of the British Idealists*, pp. 64–67.

[101] John Skorupski makes much of this problem in his 'Green and the Idealist Conception of the Person', pp. 55–56. Skorupski misconstrues the nature of Green's constructivism (by neglecting the individual's drive to seek to instantiate her distinctively human nature) which leads him to misinterpret the various dimensions of this problem (see §8.VI). He also in effect repeats G.E. Moore's misplaced allegation that Green commits the naturalistic fallacy (see §8.IV).

should never be complacent about her understanding of the requirements of her nature; an individual should always engage with her actions and should pursue them with sensitivity to context and with an awareness of the fallibility of even the most conscientious and well-informed ethical beings.

Nevertheless, that the feeling of abiding satisfaction can serve as a criterion for identifying good actions tends to mitigate some of the problems arising from the indefinability of the 'goodness' in itself: one may not be able to articulate what goodness is but at least one has a chance of telling when one realises goodness in the world.[102] This benefit can be especially significant given that goodness is manifested in various ways, depending on the agent's always partly fluid cultural and practical contexts. The things or objects that are good are cultural creations that give concrete expression to the quality of goodness, as will become clear in the next chapter.

---

[102] '[I]t is plain that the only connection which can possibly hold between being true and being thought in a certain way, is that the latter should be a criterion of or test of the former.' George E. Moore, *Principia Ethica* (Cambridge: Cambridge University 1903), p. 133. Substituting 'felt' for 'thought' here, expresses the point very succinctly. It is particularly ironic that Moore criticises Kant (and others including Green) for allegedly disagreeing with this statement.

8

Culture, Consequentialism and Duty

I
Introduction

At the beginning of the previous chapter, it was claimed that Green delivers a 'culture-based' theory of a type sought by many contemporary virtue ethicists, whereby 'what is characteristically human is to be initiated into a shared way of life. Human nature must be made determinate by socialisation.'[1] Gary Watson hopes that such an ethic will overcome the deficiencies of both Kant's ethics of duty and pure Aristotelian virtue ethics. He sees the main problem with duty ethics as being that: 'Morality is radically underdetermined by the abstract and universal notion of human nature' upon which it relies.[2] Duty ethics fails to generate first-order moral principles that are sufficiently concrete to guide ethical reflection and action. Aristotelian virtue ethics is seen as lacking cultural-sensitivity in that it holds that most determinate virtues are innately and universally valid. A culture-based virtue ethics seeks to overcome these difficulties. The outlines of Green's method for delivering the cultural element of his own virtue theory might be gleaned from the preceding analysis. Hopefully it will become explicit in the remainder of this chapter.

Section two extends the analysis of what was characterised in §7.II in Gary Watson's terms as a 'culture-based virtue ethics'. This will be achieved by extending the analysis of the interrelationship of personality and the true good into the social sphere. This entails critically assessing the various relationships obtaining between social forms, moral ontology and the ontology of the person that one finds in Green's writings. Section three returns to Green's relationship to duty ethics and virtue ethics, arguing that his ethics transcends the distinction. Section four considers two misunderstandings of Green's ethics: one presented by John Skorupski (that Green's social theory makes ethics overly moralistic), and the other by G.E. Moore (that Green defended an untenable 'metaphysical ethics'). Section five shows it to be misleading to characterise Green's culture-based ethics as a form of utilitarianism and it does combine deontological and consequentialist elements. The chapter concludes by setting out the limitations of the present analysis.

---

[1]   Watson, Gary, 'On the Primacy of Character' [1990], in Stephen Darwall, ed., *Virtue Ethics* (Oxford; Blackwell, 2003), p. 249.

[2]   Watson, 'On the Primacy of Character', p. 249.

II
Cultural Contexts of Individual Personality

Over the course of this book it has been established that for Green only a personality with concrete features can participate in the constitution of determinate ends that are capable of being understood by a rational being and therefore pursued intelligently. Yet, as he observes:

> from a moral capability which had not realised itself at all nothing could indeed be inferred as to the true good which can only consist in its full realisation; but the moral capability of man is not in this wholly undeveloped state. To a certain extent it has shown by actual achievement [in conventional values, 'institutions and habits'] what it has in it to become.[3]

This is a complex claim with controversial implications. This section will sketch its metaphysical bases, linking it into the analysis presented above. Yet, the full development and critical analysis of the claim occupies a significant proportion of the second book of *The Liberal Socialism of T.H. Green*, as does the discussion of the conception of the common good to which it gives rise.

Throughout his writings Green is at pains to stress the link between on the one hand personal moral judgement in the form of conscience, and on the other social norms, conventions and institutions as guides to action: 'the individual's conscience is reason in him as informed by the work of reason without him in the structure and controlling sentiments of society.'[4] As instantiations of human spiritual needs and capacities, these social forms reflect 'the immanent operation of ideas of the reason in the process of social organisation, upon which the intuitions [regarding the demands of human nature] as in the individual depend.'[5] They are arrived at collectively through the usual processes of contestation and enforcement of norms which constitute the life of a society. For this reason, Green refers to them as 'social judgment'.[6]

Green's claim that social judgements are in a sense the source of personal judgements may well cause one to pause, as it could imply that the individual's will is determined or at least heavily circumscribed by some form of social consciousness. This perplexity might well be compounded not merely by Green's characterisation of social judgments as historical manifestations of 'reason', but also by his characterisation of reason in turn as the eternal consciousness or the 'one divine mind'.[7] In this regard, he writes:

> because the essence of man's spiritual endowment is the consciousness of having it, the idea of his having such capabilities, and of a possible better state of himself consisting in their further realisation, is a moving influence in him. It has been the parent of the institutions and usages, of the social judgments and aspirations, through which human

---

[3]   PE 172; see also PE 234.
[4]   PE 216.
[5]   PE 215.
[6]   PE 180.
[7]   PE 180.

life has been so far bettered; through which man has so far realised his capabilities and marked out the path that he must follow in their further realisation. As his true good is or would be their complete realisation, so his goodness is proportionate to his habitual responsiveness to the idea of there being such a true good, in the various forms of recognised duty and beneficent work in which that idea has so far taken shape among men.

Shortly after this passage, Green describes 'loyalty' to these 'moral standards' as 'the condition of the goodness of the individual.'[8] This might well remind one of F.H. Bradley's notorious (and greatly misunderstood) claim that 'to wish to be better than the world is to be already on the threshold of immorality'.[9] Indeed, shortly after the passage just quoted, Green himself alludes to Bradley's *Ethical Studies*, by endorsing the view that for most people, at most 'Each has primarily to fulfil the duties of his station'.[10] (This is not the only place where he makes this point in such terms.)[11] Green argues that even our most immediate and apparently unique concrete beliefs and feelings (those 'judgment[s] not derived deductively or inductively from other judgments')[12] are in reality implanted in us by social forces. This applies even to Kant's categorical imperative.[13]

> The mistake of those who deny the *a priori* character of such "intuitions" of the conscience as that represented by Kant's formula, does not lie in tracing a history of the intuitions, but in ignoring the immanent operation of ideas of the reason in the process of social organisation, upon which the 'intuitions' as in the individual depend.[14]

Through active endorsement and participation in these conventional manifestations of human nature, the individual is able to realise her own highest nature.[15]

---

[8] PE 181. 'However meagrely the perfection, the vocation, the law [that guides the virtuous agent] may be conceived, the consciousness that there is such a thing, so far as it directs the will, must at least keep the man to the path in which human progress has so far been made. It must keep him loyal in the spirit to established morality, industrious in some work of recognised utility. What further result it will yield, whether it will lead to a man's making any original contribution to the perfecting of life, will depend on his special gifts and circumstances.' PE 176.

[9] Francis H. Bradley, *Ethical Studies*, second edition (Oxford: Clarendon, 1927), p. 199. The best analysis of Bradley's ethical and social thought is found in Peter Nicholson, *Political Philosophy of the British Idealists: Selected studies* (Cambridge: Cambridge University Press, 1990), Study I.

[10] PE 183.

[11] For example: 'In fulfilling the duties which would be recognised as belonging to his station in life by any one who considered the matter dispassionately, without bias by personal inclination – in fulfilling them loyally, without shirking, "not with eye-service as men-pleasers," – we can seldom go wrong; and when we have done this fully, there will seldom be much more that we can do.' PE 313.

[12] 'I use the term "intuition" here, in the sense commonly attached to it by recent English writers on Morals, for a judgement not derived deductively or inductively from other judgements. The reader should be on his guard against confusing this sense of the term with that in which it is used as an equivalent for the German "Anschauung," or apprehension of an object.' PE 215n2.

[13] 'Act so as to treat humanity, whether in your own person or in that of others, always as an end, never merely as a means.' PE 214, quoting his own translation of Immanuel Kant, *Groundwork of the Metaphysics of Morals*, trans. H.J. Paton (London: Harper Torchbooks, 1964), p. 96 (Prussian Academy edition 4:429).

[14] PE 215.

[15] The conscientious individual should ask: 'Does this or that law or usage, this or that course

Unfortunately, as David Brink observes, endorsing conventional morality because it is conventional 'displays a disappointing form of moral complacency'.[16] Yet, Green is emphatic that no society is perfect: 'each system has carried with it manifold results of selfish violence and seeming accident'.[17] This is one reason why an individual cannot live a life of true freedom without exercising her individual reason as a critical tool for the assessment and, where needed, revision of social norms. Our innate if inchoate recognition of this fact always tends to drive us to examine our commitments: 'It is a necessity ... of our rational nature that these forms of imagination, in which our highest practical ideas have found expression, should be subject to criticism.'[18] In this way, conscientious personal judgement remains the ultimate authority when determining the worth of social forms, even if social power hinders the individual's efforts to act on that judgement.[19]

Moreover, as Green's critique of dogmatic religion revealed (§2.II), he holds that the individual's endorsement of and participation in any particular norms and practices has value only to the extent that it springs from conscientious and therefore critical reflection on those values and practices.[20] Beliefs held in ignorance have as little ethical worth as values held without reflection, something that is also underscored by his emphasis on the need for metaphysical rigour and his conceptions of self-realisation and true freedom (§§5.III, 6.II–III). Consequently, if the impossible were to occur and an existing system of collective norms and practices were to be a perfect 'expression of reason', 'embodying [perfectly] an idea of permanent well-being', the collective life expressing those norms and practices would have worth only so far as the individuals participating in that life endorsed it after critically reflecting upon its key features and fundamental values.[21]

The need for determination of abstract capacities by existing social forms means that the individual's possibility for 'action beyond the range of those duties [of his station] is definitely bounded', as is 'his sphere of personal interests, his character, his *realised* possibility'.[22] Yet, Green sees this as unavoidable: without social influences the child would be a blank husk of unrealised potentials, as would the adult the child became. (In the aesthetic realm for example one's

---

of action – directly or indirectly, positively or as preventive of the opposite – contribute to the better being of society, as measured by the more general establishment of conditions favourable to the attainment of the recognised virtues and excellences, by the more general attainment of those excellences in some degree, or by their attainment on the part of some persons in higher degree without detraction from the opportunities of others?' PE 371, misquoting himself slightly from PE 354.

[16] David Brink, *Perfectionism and the Common Good: Themes in the philosophy of T.H. Green* (Oxford: Clarendon, 2003), p. 73.

[17] PE 216. As Bradley puts it: 'the community in which [the individual] is a member may be in a confused or rotten condition, so that in it right and might do not always go together.' (Bradley, *Ethical Studies*, p. 205) For this reason, 'the moral man need not find himself realized in the world' as it exists around him; hence 'You can not confine a man to his station and its duties.' Bradley, *Ethical Studies*, pp. 203, 204.

[18] PE 318.

[19] Green's positions on conscientious citizenship and dissent are set out in PO 101–110, 135, 142–3, and analysed at length in the second part of my *Liberal Socialism of T.H. Green*.

[20] See, for example, 'Christian Dogma' *passim*.

[21] PE 216.

[22] PE 183.

otherwise amorphous artistic talents can be expressed through a genre, such as Cubist painting for example.) Nevertheless, the requisite critical participation in and revision of social forms can be undertaken only by the truly free individual (as when the likes of Charles-Edouard Jeanneret developed Purism as a reaction to Cubism in the opening decades of the last century).[23] Such engagement is the source of our respective identities. Each of us is the particular person we are because of our respective continuing personal critical reflection on our own experiences, and our experiences have intelligible form and meaning for us only in virtue of the interactions of our innate distinctively human capacities with our prior socialisation.[24] It is for this reason that society should be as inclusive and offer as many opportunities as possible for the individual to enrich her life through the development of her capacities.[25] Green sums up what became the distinctive British idealist position on the relationship between character, social forms and self-realisation thus:

> is not such confinement [as is entailed for lives structured by social forms] the condition of the only personality that we know? It is the condition of social life, and social life is to personality what language is to thought. Language presupposes thought as a capacity, but in us the capacity of thought is only actualised in language. So human society presupposes persons in capacity – subjects capable each of conceiving himself and the bettering of his life as an end to himself – but it is only in the intercourse of men, each recognised by each as an end, not merely as a means, and thus as having reciprocal claims, that the capacity is actualised and that we really live as persons.[26]

This position can be expressed using a distinction between Green's ontology and his normative theory. The personality of an individual whose determinate beliefs and values owed nothing essential to her interactions with other persons (the atomistic individual) would exist *sui generis*, something that Green seems to regard as a barely intelligible fiction.[27] Yet, neither does he reduce the individual to a series of what some postmodernists refer to as 'subject-positions', whereby identities are plural, 'unsutured' and constituted within specific 'multiform' 'discursive dispersion[s]' of fragmented social practices and struggles.[28] The rather more lucid antecedents of this view existed in Green's day, even if he could not have been aware of certain of them. For example, in the sixth of his 'Theses of Feuerbach' (written in 1845 but first published in 1888 six years after Green's death), Karl Marx claims that 'the

---

[23] See Christopher Green, 'Purism', in Nikos Stangos, ed., *Concepts of Modern Art: From fauvism to postmodernism*, third edition (London: Thames and Hudson, 1994), pp. 79–84.

[24] 'That moral world, being in state of historical development, is not and can not be self-consistent; and the man must thus stand before and above inconsistencies, and reflect on them.' Bradley, *Ethical Studies*, p. 204.

[25] See Colin Tyler, 'Contesting the Common Good: T.H. Green and contemporary republicanism', in Maria Dimova-Cookson and W.J. Mander, eds,, *T.H. Green: Ethics, metaphysics and poltical philosophy* (Oxford: Clarendon, 2006), pp. 262–91 and Colin Tyler, *Idealist Political Philosophy: Pluralism and conflict in the absolute idealist tradition* (London: Continuum, 2006), chapter 2.

[26] PE 183.

[27] PE 181–84.

[28] Chantal Mouffe and Ernesto Laclau, *Hegemony and Socialist Strategy: Towards a radical democratic politics*, second edition (London and New York: Verso, 2001) p. 166.

human essence is no abstraction inherent in each single individual. In its reality it is the ensemble of the social relations.'[29] Clearly, Green would reject the first claim: for him, the human essence is present in each individual (even if inchoately) as an abstract substratum of distinctively human needs, values and conceptions. Paradoxically however, he could endorse Marx's second claim. For Green the 'reality' of the individual's personality is that personality as the agent experiences it, and an individual can experience her personality only if it is saturated with social influences.

Green combines his two claims thus: 'Without society, no persons; this is as true as that without persons, without self-objectifying agents, there could be no such society as we know'.[30] Known societies are collectivities existing over time in which individuals relate to one another as persons, largely via the media of conventions, norms and laws. They relate in this way even if they do so only imperfectly, and even when not appreciating explicitly that they do so. The distinctly Fichtean overtones continue with Green's denial of the claim that such appreciation can occur in the abstract: 'Some practical recognition of personality by another, of an "I" by a "Thou" and a "Thou" by an "I," is necessary to any practical consciousness of' the agent's 'idea of himself as the object of his actions, to the idea of a possible better state of himself', 'to any such consciousness of it as can express itself in act.'[31]

Given that Green holds knowledge can only be of experience and the pre-suppositions of experience, these acts of recognition must be situated in concrete circumstances. They must have their own particular features which form constitutive facets of the reality of the acts of recognition if they are to perform the roles that Green argues they do: determinate 'I's must recognise and be recognised in particularised ways by determinate 'Thou's if they are to generate and sustain determinate personalities in and for the participants. In contemporary terms, the recognition to which Green refers is not simply dialogical in the sense of sharing the form of conversations between two parties. Instead, it is generated by multiple participants in numerous forms of interaction, each of which is mediated through norms, practices and institutions that reflect, among other things, conventional if contested hierarchies of status and power.[32] There is no higher standard to appeal to than these multifaceted interactions between individual persons. The life of a nation is manifested only in the various particular continuing interactions of its members, and only exists in the ways that they interact with one another: it 'deriv[es] its peculiar features from the conditions of that intercourse.'[33] A nation or Humanity has no will or spirit other than the ideas that individual persons have

---

[29] Karl Marx, 'Theses on Feuerbach', in Karl Marx and Frederick Engels, *Selected Works*, 2 vols. (Moscow: Foreign Languages Publishing House, 1958), vol. II, p. 404.

[30] PE 190.

[31] PE 190.

[32] See Tyler, 'Contesting the Common Good'; compare with James Tully, 'Multinational Democracies: An introductory sketch', in his *Public Philosophy in a New Key* (Cambridge: Cambridge University Press, 2008), vol. 1, pp. 185–219, especially pp. 205–09.

[33] PE 184.

about themselves and their fellows, 'unless we allow ourselves to play fast and loose with the terms "spirit" and "will".'[34]

The 'personal' character of this intersubjective ontology does not lead Green to hold an intersubjective normative theory, however. Instead, in line with his ontology he argues for the inherently 'personal character of the moral ideal': 'To speak of any progress or improvement or development of a nation or society or mankind, except as relative to some greater worth of persons, is to use words without meaning.'[35] Certainly, individuals cannot develop their capabilities and so cannot possess a determinate personality 'independently of their existence in a nation.' Yet, the nation that they constitute through their actions derives whatever value it has from the service that it renders to the realisation of the capacities of its individual members. Only the individual has ultimate – that is to say intrinsic – value.

As has been noted already, Green held that an act is virtuous to the extent that performing it will either constitute the exercise of the individual's distinctively human capacities, or promote the development of those capacities in the agent herself or in her fellow citizens; an action is the opposite (which Green refers to habitually as 'vicious') to the extent that it does the opposite.[36] Even well-intentioned agents (ones who seek to act virtuously) can perform actions that are in reality vicious: for example, 'the quest for self-satisfaction in the life of voluptuary' is 'self-defeating'.[37] The moral standing of the agent is a function of her conscientious assessment of the likely consequences of the actions she intends to perform.[38] Nevertheless, the moral quality of the agent remains conceptually distinct from the moral quality of the actions she performs: the former is a function of her motives whereas the latter is a function of the (intended or not, recognised or not) consequences of her actions. Throughout however, human development means ultimately individual development alone, even if that individual development takes place through and in response to established social structures, practices and norms. The ultimate standard by which ethical worth should be measured is purely that of the development of individuals conceived as beings with higher capacities.[39]

As both a philosopher and a citizen, Green was always very wary of moral narcissism.[40] Nevertheless, he emphasised that, on certain occasions, the personal nature of moral action can require the agent to have legitimate existential concerns: 'the state of mind which is now most naturally expressed by the unspoken questions, "Have I been what I should be, shall I be what I should be, in doing so

---

[34] PE 184.
[35] PE 184. A.C. Bradley entitled Book 3, chapter II, part A of the *Prolegomena* (§§180–91) 'The personal character of the moral ideal'.
[36] PE 176.
[37] PE 176.
[38] PE 354.
[39] PE 184.
[40] PE 297; see also Green's remarks on monastic asceticism in his letter to Henry Scott Holland, 9 January 1869, in Green *Works* V, p. 426.

and so?'', is that in which all moral progress originates.'[41] To answer the existential question first individuals should ask themselves: 'Have we, in doing what was expected of us, been doing it from the right motives?'[42] Ultimately, the agent should ask whether or not she has done what she judges to be the ethically best course of action given both her personality and the circumstances. In this way, as Nicholson makes the point: it 'is a matter of practical judgement, and is subject to pragmatic considerations'.[43] In the final analysis, at the heart of Green's ethics lies the authority of contextualised personal conscientious judgement.

Nevertheless, it might seem that eudaimonic capacities are too 'contingent and variable' to form the basis of such deliberations. Clearly, we can only experience them in the ways they are particularised by the historical accidents that form the individual's time and hermeneutic location. For example, one can only express one's artistic impulses through existing artist forms (fauvism, kinetic art, minimalism and so on) or personal modifications of such forms. As eudaimonic capacities require the adoption or modification of existing social forms, they bear indelible cultural imprints. This is only part of the story however. It is worth remembering that even when deliberative capacities are thought of in purely formalistic Kantian terms, they are made known to us only through the analysis of particular instances (the actions of this or that agent here and now). They only lose this parochial character for us through critical metaphysical analysis. Essentially the same can be said of eudaimonic capacities as well. Critical metaphysics reveals necessity and permanence among these instantiations of philosophically universalistic eudaimonic capacities,[44] just as it is does in relation to Kantian deliberative capacities.

Even though Green himself does not pursue this idea, it seems that within his framework the universality of eudaimonic capacities (when those capacities are conceived in abstract terms) is more likely to be obscured than are Kantian capacities. First, Kantian capacities are more likely to be evidenced in their entirety in the structure of particular acts of will because they form the organising principle of each deliberate action. The range of eudaimonic capacities on the other hand tends to be manifested less uniformly (and certain capacities cannot be manifested at all in certain contexts and cultures). Any particular action is likely to instantiate only one or some of them. Consequently, the critical metaphysician tends to face a far harder task when it comes to conceiving eudaimonic capacities as a harmonious system than she does when conceiving the harmony of deliberative capacities because more pieces of the jigsaw tend to be missing. Second, formal conditions such as the Kantian elements of the will are much easier to conceive in abstract terms than are the more complex and internally differentiated contents of that will (the eudaimonic capacities). Nonetheless as has been argued at length in this book, eudaimonic capacities remain no less essential to distinctively human action than are Kantian capacities.[45]

---

[41]   PE 309.
[42]   PE 298.
[43]   Nicholson, *Political Philosophy of the British Idealists*, p. 79.
[44]   These capacities are universalistic only in their abstract core.
[45]   In this sense, probably it would be more illuminating to consider Green's ethics as a development of Fichte rather than of Kant, if his debts to Fichte were acknowledged more extensively and

This line of thought can be developed still further. The determinate expression of eudaimonic capacities tends to face far greater obstacles than do the expressions of deliberative ones. As a result their concrete articulation tends to be more fragmentary. Nevertheless as has been argued at length above, for them to function as ethical principles (as indeed Green thinks they do), the individual must assume that when properly understood they cohere fully with one another. This is one of the heuristic principles of theoretical and practical reason discussed above. Put a different way: they must be assumed to be necessary facets of the human spirit if we are to understand ourselves as beings that are capable of achieving self-realisation, and, has been shown (§4.II), Green takes it to be an essential feature of human nature that every agent is driven innately to understand herself in that way.

III
A Second Look at the Ethics of Duty and the Ethics of Flourishing

Lawrence Blum has proposed six possible relationships that can obtain between virtue and community.[46] The first – 'Learning' – denotes the situation where living as part of a community teaches one to understand and internalise certain virtues. The second – 'sustaining' – obtains where interaction with the other members of one's community encourages the individual to remain to true to her virtues. The third – 'agent-constituting' – denotes the situation where the individual's membership in a community is the source of at least part of her personal identity. The fourth – 'content-providing' – refers to the situation where 'forms of communal life fill in the detailed prescriptions that turn abstract principles into a lived morality'.[47] The fifth – 'worth-conferring' – refers to the situation where the nature of the particular community in which one lives itself transforms the possession of certain qualities into a virtue. The sixth – 'virtues sustaining community' – are those qualities of one's character that help to maintain the bonds of one's community.

The preceding analysis has shown that although Green at least presupposes and frequently explicitly acknowledges the importance of the 'sustaining', 'worth-conferring' and 'virtues sustaining community' relationships, his writings emphasise far more strongly 'learning', 'agent-constituting' and especially 'content-providing'. More than this, his specific conception of virtue ethics can be arrived at by reformulating Blum's conception of 'content-providing' in light of Watson's observation that a successful theory of culture-based virtue ethics would have to establish how 'what is characteristically human ... [is] made determinate by socialisation'.[48] Conceived in a Greenian fashion, abstract ethical principles include both eudaimonic principles specifying the generic features of a flourishing human life, as well as the Kantian categorical imperative specifying the structural features of a morally-binding norm. Together, these are the abstract principles

---

clearly (see §2.III).

[46]   Lawrence Blum, 'Community and Virtue', in Roger Crisp, ed., *How Should One Live? Essays on the virtues* (Oxford: Clarendon, 1996), pp. 232–35.

[47]   Blum, 'Community and Virtue', pp. 232–33.

[48]   Watson, 'On the Primacy of Character', p. 249.

of human nature. They require social instantiation in order to exist for an agent however.

From this basis, it can be said that Green conceives the worth conferred on qualities by an individual's community as playing a constitutive role in the formation of that individual's personal identity, as does the content that her community gives to the abstract principles of virtue. In many ways however, the task of the social reformer is to ensure the success of content-providing relationships wherein the abstract principles of virtue match the demands of the human spirit. This reflects the fact that the individual is truly virtuous and so truly free only to the extent that her lived existence instantiates her distinctively human capacities, because for Green the latter are the abstract principles of human nature. Worth-conferring, on the other hand, is at best a proxy for genuine self-realisation. Consequently, even where worth-conferring is successful in its own terms (where every member endorses the values authorised by her community) the conferred worth is always subject to critical reassessment in light of the abstract principles and, where found wanting, is always subject to legitimate (efforts at) reform by the agent. To the extent that content-providing is successful however, criticism is justified only because it brings greater understanding of how one's lived morality instantiates abstract principles.

From this point, it is possible to understand how Green's position combines virtue ethics with the ethics of duty. Virtue ethicists such as Stan van Hooft object to what they see as the reductive nature of the ethics of duty: that is, to its alleged tendency to posit a set of abstract principles that found higher-order ethical principles. The problem is that this 'attempt to escape ... into a realm of absolute and universal objectivity' divorces moral theory from ethical life, thereby rendering unintelligible the meaning and binding force of the concrete ethical principles that constitute the realm of lived morality.[49] Many duty ethicists argue however that absolute and universally-valid second-order principles overcome the contingencies of conventional morality, and thereby provide a set of properly philosophical and authoritative principles against which to judge lived morality. These deontological principles replace a virtue approach that is in reality too close to a non-normative sociological acceptance of conventional morality, with all its contingencies and abuses of power.

Green's ethics incorporates core elements of both an ethics of virtue and an ethics of duty by building upon the twin modes of philosophical investigation set out above (§3.II). It will be remembered that critical metaphysics starts from an understanding of determinate conventional ethical values and practices, before analysing them so as to uncover their respective *a priori* presuppositions. It seeks then to systematize these presuppositions, and where that proves impossible (where the abstract presuppositions are too vague or are incompatible) the critical metaphysician seeks to reformulate the presuppositions so that they can be systematised successfully. From that basis, the speculative metaphysician uses this system of foundational *a priori* principles to critique and reconstruct the determinate

---

[49]   Stan van Hooft, *Understanding Virtue Ethics* (Chesham: Acumen, 2006), p. 32.

conventional ethical principles in a more definite and mutually-coherent manner. The *a priori* system functions here not as an alien alternative to lived ethics, but as a purified yet still internal perspective and set of standards from which to correct the historical and sociological contingencies of conventional social forms.[50] In short, critical and speculative metaphysics enables one 'to reject what is temporary and accidental in … [social forms], while retaining what is essential'.[51] To the extent that they are executed successfully these twin processes deliver a coherent set of ethical commitments which are both determinate in the manner sought by virtue ethicists, and philosophical grounded in the manner sought by duty ethicists. Green's ethical theory transcends both positions then, in the sense of incorporating the strengths of both while hopefully minimising their respective weaknesses.

IV
John Skorupski and G.E. Moore

In a very interesting analysis of Green's theory of the personal good John Skorupski has noted: 'Green thinks that virtue is best for the individual – thus far following eudaimonist tradition. But he insists, in a way unknown to classical thought that virtuous action consists in contributing to a good which is *common* to all individuals – a good for which there is no competition.'[52] This is undoubtedly true, and it will be examined at great length when the critical analysis of Green's ethical theory continues in the next part of this study of his philosophical system. Yet, for Skorupski and many others Green's theory of the common good forms a crucial part of a picture in which 'Green was … a morally-intoxicated man – and indeed, a "God-intoxicated" man. His aspirations for liberal society are, in truth, too reconciliationist, too moralistic, too focused on service.'[53] Whereas J.S. Mill and Henry Sidgwick endorsed what Skorupski following Sidgwick refers to as a Goethean ideal of individuality, allegedly Green upheld a profoundly different 'Christian ideal, infused by German Idealism', for which the 'criterion of the reasonable' was found 'outside' of one's 'feelings': 'those standards' belong 'to a different part of the soul, an agency external to them and set over them.'[54]

Hopefully the preceding analysis has indicated just how misplaced is Skorupski's characterisation of Green (see also §2.II). In reality, Green's metaphysics of self-realisation and freedom has at its heart the Goethean ideal, whereby 'the standards [by which one should judge one's feelings are] … immanent to the development of the feelings themselves.'[55] That is not to deny the significance of Green's endorsement

[50] Bosanquet used Green's method to critique Durkheim's sociological analysis of punishment, in Bernard Bosanquet, *Philosophical Theory of the State*, fourth edition (London: MacMillan, 1923), chapter II, pp. 205–17.; see also Colin Tyler, ' "This Dangerous Drug of Violence": Making sense of Bernard Bosanquet's theory of punishment" ', *Collingwood and British Idealism Studies*, 7 (2000), 116–40.

[51] PE 279.

[52] John Skorupski, 'Green and the Idealist Conception of a Person's Good', in Dimova-Cookson et al., eds., *T.H. Green*, p. 50.

[53] Skorupski, 'Green and the Idealist Conception of a Person's Good', p. 73.

[54] Skorupski, 'Green and the Idealist Conception of a Person's Good', p. 74.

[55] Skorupski, 'Green and the Idealist Conception of a Person's Good', p. 74.

of Skorupski's conception of the Christian ideal. It is simply to acknowledge that Green incorporates these standards in his ethics. How Green achieves this and the degree to which he is successful will be in many senses a core theme of the second part of *The Liberal Socialism of T.H. Green*, not least in its critical analysis of his theory of the common good. Nevertheless, often scholars either mischaracterise or underemphasise (or both) the ways in which Green's more famous theory of the common good is derived from his metaphysics of self-realisation and freedom.

Historically, the failure to recognise the central role of the 'Goethean' ideal in Green's ethics has helped a profoundly distorted understanding of Green's ethical theory to become prevalent in the secondary literature. Even though the mischaracterisation had its roots in Sidgwick's writings, it was the discussion of 'metaphysical ethics' in G.E. Moore's *Principia Ethica* that was most damaging.[56] Moore read Green as a metaphysical ethicist, and therefore as someone attempting to draw ethical truths from the logical structure of a 'supersensible reality of which religion professes to give us a fuller knowledge'. For Moore, metaphysical ethics 'consists in the attempt to obtain knowledge, by processes of reasoning, of what exists but is *not* a part of Nature.'[57] More than this: Green was one of the 'modern writers who tell us that the final and perfect end is to realise our *true* selves – a self different both from the whole and from any part of that which exists here and now in Nature.'[58] In Skorupski's terms, Moore's metaphysical ethicists upheld a 'Christian ideal' in which, as we have seen, the criterion for evaluating characters and actions emanated from 'an agency external to them and set over them.'[59]

Against this misreading it has been established here that Green was concerned primarily with reality 'for us' – reality as we experience it personally (§§3.III–IV). He held the task of metaphysics to be the analysis of the presuppositions of that experience, and the drawing of systematic inferences from those presuppositions (§2.IV). Certainly, he did claim that one key presupposition revealed by critical metaphysics was the existence of what he called 'an eternal consciousness', which has been shown to be Green's shorthand for the system of abstract distinctively human capacities (see chapter 4). Moreover, he argued that this spiritual principle was already realising itself gradually in the respective discrete imperfect personal selves of you, me and everyone around us. Green held the existence of a spiritual principle to be a logical requirement of 'the best analysis we can make of our experience'.[60] He was emphatic that there could be no 'mysterious abstract entity which you call the self of a man, apart from all his particular feelings, desires, and thought – all the experience of his inner life'; and that the eternal consciousness was not for us, as Moore alleged, 'a self different both from the whole and from any part of that which exists here and now in Nature'.[61] In addition it was established that

---

[56] G.E. Moore, *Principia Ethica* (Cambridge: Cambridge University Press, 1903), especially chapter IV.

[57] Moore, *Principia Ethica*, p. 112.

[58] Moore, *Principia Ethica*, p. 113.

[59] Skorupski, 'Green and the Idealist Conception of a Person's Good', p. 74.

[60] PE 100; cf. Andrew Vincent, 'Metaphysics and Ethics in the Philosophy of T.H. Green', in Dimova-Cookson *et al.*, eds., *T.H. Green*, pp. 76–105.

[61] PE 100; Moore, *Principia Ethica*, p. 112. See further PE 101.

our present selves are always imperfect, whereas the eternal consciousness is an ideal that each of us projects in different ways in order to guide and motivate our personal efforts at epistemic and ethical improvement (see §§4.I–III in particular).

This position is deeply controversial of course. Moore alleged that the class of philosophers to which Green belonged sought to discover otherworldly ' "metaphysical" propositions', by which he meant 'propositions … which cannot be inferred from what is an object of perception by the same rules of inference by which we infer the past and future of what we call "Nature." ' [62] It is difficult to know what Moore is criticising here, because in a sense it seems undeniable that the type of inductive reasoning from which one infers the past and future could never help to uncover the presuppositions of one's experiences. In fact, it seems ridiculous to imply that it could. The problem is compounded by the fact that Moore gives little evidence for his interpretation of 'Nature' in Green or any of his other representative 'metaphysical ethicists' (see §§3.III–IV).

Moore went on to claim that for metaphysical ethicists 'the question "What is real?" has some logical bearing upon the question "What is good?"' [63] In Moore's characteristically lucid but ultimately vague prose, he alleged that metaphysical ethicists attempt to derive normative truths from propositions regarding the structure of 'supersensible reality'. [64] Famously of course, Moore christened this move from claims regarding what is to claims regarding what should be 'the naturalistic fallacy'. [65] He alleged that Green himself commits one of the worst crimes in this regard when he (Green) argues that '*the* common characteristic of the good is that it satisfies some desire'. [66] Moore's unacknowledged italicisation of '*the*' is disingenuous. It implies that the most important characteristic of Green's conception of 'the good' is that it is desired: and Moore meant that Green believes being desired is the essence of the quality 'goodness'. (This proposition seems to be at the heart of Skorupski's constructivist reading as well.) Yet, Green's point in the passage from which Moore quotes is simply the one made by Aristotle at the beginning of the *Nicomachean Ethics*: whether you are well-informed or ignorant, drunk or sober, a saint or a petulant child, whether you want a glass of water or a Cambridge Fellowship, you desire the attaining of any object because you value it. [67]

In reality, Green never tries to define the essence of 'goodness' as such, presumably precisely because he recognises what Moore himself emphasises: namely that goodness is a simple, 'indefinable' predicate. [68] This point underpinned the critique of Skorupski's position developed in the previous section. In answer to Moore's criticisms one can say the following. Green holds that one can only

---

[62]   Moore, *Principia Ethica*, p. 112.
[63]   Moore, *Principia Ethica*, p. 113.
[64]   Moore, *Principia Ethica*, p. 114.
[65]   Moore, *Principia Ethica*, for example pp. 10, 13–14, 18–20, 114.
[66]   Moore, *Principia Ethica*, p. 139, quoting PE 171.
[67]   'Every art and every investigation and similarly every action and pursuit, is considered to aim at some good.' Aristotle, *Ethics*, trans. J.A.K. Thomson, rev. Hugh Tredennick (Harmondsworth: Penguin, 1976), I.i.
[68]   Moore, *Principia Ethica*, pp. 6–16.

predicate 'goodness' of an object to the extent that an agent desires the attainment of that object, the desire being a mark of the object's goodness. One can adapt Moore's own position to fit Green's: *the only connection which can possibly hold between being valuable and being desired in a certain way, is that the latter should be a criterion of or test of the former.*[69] The act of desiring does not impart goodness to an otherwise ethically-neutral object. The most demanding view that Green commits himself to is that one can only predicate 'ethical goodness' of an object if that object is desired by an agent on the grounds that (the agent believes) the attainment of that object to be ethically valuable.[70] It was established above that, at most, desiring something on the grounds of its perceived ethical worth reflects its goodness; it neither creates nor imparts goodness to the object. Moore's failure to appreciate this fact reflects a deeper failure to understand the structure of Green's metaphysics of experience, will and ethics.

Ultimately it might be just that as A.C. Ewing observed: Moore's attacks on the metaphysical ethicists do not 'demolish these opponents because their arguments function in the context of a different world-view based on intuitive assumptions or perhaps intuitive insights which Moore did not share.'[71] Hopefully, the preceding analysis has indicated not only that Green's world-view can be recovered, but that it is plausible and that, as a result, his metaphysics of self-realisation and freedom have far more to recommend them than their previous reputation might have one believe.

---

[69] Moore's original reads: 'it is plain that the only connection which can possibly hold between being true and being thought in a certain way, is that the latter should be a criterion of or test of the former.' Moore, *Principia Ethica*, p. 133.

[70] Brian Hutchinson, *G.E. Moore's Ethical Theory: Resistance and reconciliation* (Cambridge: Cambridge University Press, 2001), p. 88.

[71] A.C. Ewing, 'Moore and Metaphysics', in Alice Ambrose and Morris Lazerowitz, eds., *G.E. Moore Essays in Retrospect* (London: George Allen and Unwin, 1970), p. 159. Moore seems unaware of a great many fundamental differences between his so-called metaphysical ethicists. The key differences between the respective metaphysics of Green and F.H. Bradley are brought out in James W. Allard, *Logical Foundations of Bradley's Metaphysics: Judgement, inference and truth* (Cambridge: Cambridge University Press, 2005), *passim*. Another reason for Moore's antipathy to the idealists might be that shortly before writing *Principia Ethica* he had applied twice for a Fellowship at Trinity College, Cambridge, neither time did he have an easy ride, and both times his examination panels included a British idealist: in 1897 it was Edward Caird, Green's great friend and Master of Balliol College, Oxford, and in 1898 it was Bernard Bosanquet, Green's former pupil. Caird did begin his largely negative report by acknowledging Moore's 'philosophical ability' (Edward Caird, 'Report on Mr Moore's Essay' [late 1897], in Colin Tyler, ed., *Unpublished Manuscripts in British Idealism: Political philosophy, theology and social thought*, 2 vols. (London: Continuum, 2008; Exeter: Imprint Academic, 2008), vol. 2, 184). Bosanquet was damning however; for example: 'if [the work on Kant which Moore had submitted for the 1898 Fellowship] has been sent me for review by 'Mind', I should have treated it respectfully as a brilliant essay by a very able writer, but should have endeavoured to point out that its positive stand-point and consequently its treatment of the subject were hopelessly inadequate, that is to say, that the writer was not successful, to any appreciable extent, in representing the real nature and interconnection of the factors involved in the problem with which he was concerned.' Bernard Bosanquet, 'Report on a Dissertation entitled "The Metaphysical Basis of Reality" by Mr GE Moore' [19 September 1898], in Tyler, ed., *Unpublished Manuscripts*, vol. 1, pp. 239–40. For Bertrand Russell's indignation at Bosanquet's treatment of Moore, see *ibid.*, vol. 1, pp. xxiii–xxv. For Bosanquet's review of Moore's *Principia Ethica*, see *Mind*, 13 ns (1904), 254–61.

We have seen that as part of this world-view, Green shares the scepticism of Aristotle and certain contemporary virtue ethicists regarding the practical efficacy of justified first-order moral principles. He agrees that, to a significant degree, ultimately ethics is always uncodifiable in the sense that, as Watson puts it in a different context: 'there are no formulas that can serve as exact and detailed guides for action'.[72] However, culture-based virtue ethics of the type endorsed by Green, Watson and others has come under attack from some quarters.[73] Daniel Statman has argued, for example, that 'assuming a necessary connection between virtues and the attainments of internal goods entails a teleological version of [virtue ethics] which would be hard to distinguish from a rich notion of utilitarianism.'[74] With that allegation in mind, this chapter closes by drawing together what has been said above regarding Green's criticisms of classical utilitarianism and his alternative ethics, paying particular attention to the place accorded by the latter to consequentialist and deontological considerations.

V
Green and Consequentialism

Despite his far-reaching criticisms of Bentham, J.S. Mill and Sidgwick (§7.III), scholars remain divided regarding Green's relationship to utilitarianism.[75] David Weinstein and Avital Simhony in particular have debated this question on a number of occasions. David Weinstein argues that Green exemplifies David Cummiskey's category of Kantian consequentialist, as well as being an existential perfectionist of the type analysed by Thomas Hurka.[76] Each of these elements will be examined here, not least in light of Simhony's response to Weinstein's latest formulation of his position. It will be concluded that Weinstein captures something very important about Green's position, although his emphasis on Kantian formalism pushes Green's eudaimonism too far into the shadows.

For Kant, an action is right to the extent that the agent performing it does so out of respect for the categorical imperative. On Cummiskey's reading however, more than this Kant is a consequentialist in that entailed by respect for the categorical imperative is the imperfect duty to foster respect for the categorical imperative where that respect is lacking. In other words, the good-willed agent has an imperfect duty to promote the conditions under which other agents within her sphere of

[72] Watson, 'On the Primacy of Character', 233.

[73] Other contemporary advocates of culture-based virtue ethics include Rosalind Hursthouse, *On Virtue Ethics* (Oxford: Oxford University Press, 1999), Alasdair MacIntyre, *After Virtue: A study in moral theory*, second edition (London: Duckworth, 1985) and Michael Slote, *From Morality to Virtue* (Oxford: Oxford University Press, 1992).

[74] Daniel Statman, 'Introduction to Virtue Ethics', in Daniel Statman, ed., *Virtue Ethics: A critical reader* (Edinburgh: Edinburgh University Press, 1997), p. 15.

[75] See, for example, David Weinstein, *Utilitarianism and the New Liberalism* (Cambridge: Cambridge University Press, 2007), and the symposium on Weinstein's book, in *Collingwood and British Idealism Studies*, 15:2 (2009), especially the contributions by Avital Simhony and James Connelly, together with Weinstein's response.

[76] Weinstein, *Utilitarianism*, pp. 56–63; David Cummiskey, *Kantian Consequentialism* (New York and Oxford: Oxford University Press, 1996), and Thomas Hurka, *Perfectionism* (New York and Oxford: Oxford University Press, 1993).

influence act habitually with a good motive. That might require sacrificing some of the conditions for the exercise of a good will in some instances in order to achieve a greater net increase overall of the conditions for the exercise of a good will. More than this however, the rational agent has no justified moral grounds for complaint: 'since our sacrifice furthers a moral goal that we endorse and that we are required to pursue, our sacrifice does not violate our moral autonomy or our rights'.[77]

Weinstein's reading of Green fits this model perfectly: 'he was what I shall call a "dispositional consequentialist" for whom realizing oneself morally was no less than developing and exhibiting the disposition of good willing.'[78] Weinstein argues that Green held justified 'basic moral rights (and the freedom that they secure), empower moral self-realization.... Moral rights ... indirectly promote moral self-realization by ensuring that all individuals enjoy the safety of the same necessary baseline conditions from which to contribute freely to the common good as they see fit.'[79] On this reading, Green's theory derives the nature of the right from the practical demands of the good, and as such his theory has a consequentialist structure rather than a deontological one.[80] Nonetheless, it cannot properly be called a form of utilitarianism because 'Green conceived the good non-hedonistically'.[81] Moreover, Weinstein argues, Green's consequentialism is 'more than just dispositional'. Green conceives a well-ordered system of rights and duties to be necessary means for the promotion of the good, hence his ethics is 'deeply juridical and therefore indirect. Hence, it was also liberal.'[82]

Responding to Weinstein's reading helps to bring together a number of the points made earlier. First, notice that when reconstructing Green's argument for the normativity of human action, Weinstein prioritises the Kantian, 'dispositional' aspect of Green's ethics to the effective exclusion of the eudaimonic aspects. It was noted above that Brink and Dimova-Cookson do the same (§7.IV). In reality however, the detailed examination of Green's necessarily interrelated metaphysics of experience and the will presented in the earlier chapters has established the individual's eudaimonic capacities to be equally necessary to self-realisation and therefore to an ethical life. It has been established above that Green built his theory

---

[77] 'It certainly seems that a Kantian ought to be a normative consequentialist. Conscientious Kantian agents have a basic duty to strive, as much as possible, to promote the freedom and happiness of all rational beings. In the pursuit of this moral goal, it may be necessary for the interests of some to give way for the sake of others. If we are sacrificed, we are not treated simply as a means to another's goal; on the contrary, our sacrifice is required by a principle we endorse. Our non-interests and inclinations may cause us to feel reluctant, but since our sacrifice furthers a moral goal that we endorse and that we are required to pursue, our sacrifice does not violate our moral autonomy or our rights.' Cummiskey, *Kantian Consequentialism*, p. 159. With this thought in mind, it can be seen that Weinstein goes too far when he states: 'For Green, no less than for Cummiskey, maximising good invariably entails using people.' (p. 62) First, it seems too much to say that honouring the duties arising from someone's nature is 'using' them even if honouring the duties requires the agent's behaviour to be affected. Second, 'maximising good' does not 'invariably' require their actions to be affected in this way.
[78] Weinstein, *Utilitarianism*, p. 25.
[79] Weinstein, *Utilitarianism*, p. 35.
[80] Weinstein, *Utilitarianism*, p. 42.
[81] Weinstein, *Utilitarianism*, p. 63; see also pp. 24, 48.
[82] Weinstein, *Utilitarianism*, p. 63.

of the true good, in Weinstein's terms, on the 'wider more generic sense' of self-realisation, not merely the 'narrower moral variety'.[83]

The second point to notice is that Weinstein jumps from the fact that Green's ethics is 'dispositional' to the claim that it is 'deeply juridical and therefore indirect', and then finally to the claim that, 'Hence, it was also liberal.'[84] It can be seen from the preceding analysis that unfortunately, each of these claims requires some qualification. First, Green's ethics is both dispositional (Kantian) and substantive (eudaimonic). Second, the eudaimonic elements make it very difficult if not impossible to predict its implications for practice. This point became clear above in relation to the conclusions Brooks drew from the similarities between Green and J.S. Mill's respective positions on penal policy (§7.III). Indeed, this relative lack of predictability throws doubt upon the ease with which Weinstein concludes that Green's ethics necessarily delivers both liberalism and a solid respect for any particular determinate set of moral rights and duties, or legal rights and obligations (reflecting Green's distinction between duties and obligations).[85] Certainly, Green is emphatic that the dispositional moment of the good will makes it impossible to force someone to act well.[86] Consequently, no state can force the individual to realise her own true good. The most the state can do is to remove the conditions under which an individual is prevented from seeking her own self-realisation. Indeed that is one of the state's primary functions. For these reasons, Green's theory may have a tendency to justify liberalism, but its principled sensitivity to the contingencies of the situations in which the true good can exist must make all specific policies for promoting human flourishing depend significantly on context. Moreover, the relative absence of state interference in the lives of the individual is not a quality unique to liberal political systems.

Avital Simhony has rejected Weinstein's claim that Green is a consequentialist on a number of grounds.[87] For one thing, she objects that, by definition, consequentialist theories judge the quality of an action by its tendency to maximise the good rather than simply to promote it as Weinstein alleges. Simhony acknowledges that 'consequentialists invariably do' refer both to promoting and to maximising the good. Yet, she argues that promoting strategies are characteristic of 'liberal indirectness' and as such seek to protect individual autonomy and to counter paternalism. Maximising strategies, on the other hand, are associated with rule utilitarian attempts to secure the greatest aggregate pleasure. The former 'enable' the good ('of autonomy – or self-realization, self-development, or complex development'), whereas the latter 'maximise' the good (of pleasure or utility). She argues that while Green does the former, he rejects the latter.

Simhony overstates the significance of the difference between maximisation and promotion. Ultimately her criticism may well come down the methods by which one can realise these respective goods most effectively in practice. She is correct

---

[83] Weinstein, *Utilitarianism*, pp. 49–50.
[84] Weinstein, *Utilitarianism*, p. 63.
[85] PO 10.
[86] PO 207–10.
[87] Avital Simhony, 'T.H. Green was no consequentialist of any kind', *Collingwood and British Idealism Studies*, vol. 16, 15:2 (2009), 7–27.

that one cannot force someone to be autonomous and to act autonomously. In that sense, Green would agree, as I suspect would Weinstein. Yet, as has been shown above even Bentham thinks that it is likely to be inefficient to try to maximise aggregate pleasure directly, hence he turns to the sub-ends of government (§7. III). That utilitarians such as Bentham tend to invoke pragmatic reasons for non-interference whereas liberals tend to appeal to more principled ones seems to provide Simhony's argument with little force. As Weinstein observes in reply, contemporary utilitarians such as Jonathan Riley invoke indirect, anti-paternalistic justifications for a form of liberalism that insists on a stringently enforced system of legal rights and obligations.[88]

Simhony also objects that Green's theory is not consequentialist because it is non-aggregating. She is correct to an extent. As has been shown above, Green's ethical theory is non-aggregating in that the idea of an aggregate presupposes that the elements making it up remain essentially separate (in the way that the peas on your plate form an aggregate). By contrast, the elements that constitute Green's true good understood as self-realisation do not remain essentially separate. Instead, when functioning properly they are necessarily parts of one whole, because they are what they are in virtue of the particular ways in which they relate to one another. The good will without the correct content does indeed have some ethical worth, just as does the exercise of eudaimonic capacities without a good will. Nevertheless, these elements fail to constitute Green's true good to the extent that they remain isolated from one another. Only when the individual freely wills to attain or promote truly valuable objects because they are truly valuable does she enjoy ethical self-realisation: only then does she enjoy 'the fulfilment of human capacities'.[89] These valuable objects are the exercise of the eudaimonic capacities, and *ceteris paribus* they are to be valued by the agent irrespective of whether she exercises them herself or others do themselves. In short, the good will and eudaimonic capacities have a compound value in virtue of their respective places as interrelated parts of one inherently systematised true good.

Simhony is correct to point out however that there are genuinely non-consequentialist elements in Green's theory. Most significantly, the latter holds that the moral value of an action is a function of the disposition of the agent performing it. An action motivated by a good will tends to be better than one not so motivated. Nevertheless, Simhony's objection neglects the force of Weinstein's case for Green's so-called 'Kantian consequentialism'. There is an irreducibly consequentialist case for acting in a manner that one believes will create conditions under which others will be more likely either to act habitually out of a good will or to seek to freely instantiate their eudaimonic capacities. Put another way: the ethical status of an action's consequences is determined in part by the action's tendency to promote or hinder the formation and exercise of good will and eudaimonic capacities in the world: that is, by its tendency to foster or retard the exercise of 'a will determined by interest in objects contributory to human perfection [understood as the realisation

[88] David Weinstein, 'Hermeneutics and Liberalism: A reply', *Collingwood and British Idealism Studies*, vol. 16, 15:2 (2009).

[89] PE 356.

of the individual's distinctively human capacities].'[90] Such a goal helps to guide and justify much contemporary educational theory and not least practice. Contra Simhony, the fact that the agent pursuing this policy is acting well because of their good disposition (assuming they are) does not exhaust the ethical dimensions of the action: the good consequences help to constitute the latter's value, they might even be the primary source of its value. This is one example of the irreducibly consequentialist constitutive elements of Green's ethics which Simhony appears to deny.

Nonetheless, Simhony does make an important point here. The presence of irreducibly dispositional determinants of an action's worth does mean that, on balance, Weinstein applies the 'consequentialist' label a little too blithely to Green; however that does not justify Simhony's conclusion that Green's ethical theory contains absolutely no consequentialist elements whatsoever. Instead, his theory combines irreducibly deontological and consequentialist considerations; both elements are necessary.

Yet, both Weinstein and Simhony fail to mention a final, and rather less compelling, claim that is relevant when considering Green's relationship to consequentialism. In a striking passage in the *Prolegomena*, Green argues that the 'full moral nature' of any action can be assessed only 'with reference not merely to effects which it has had or is likely to have, but to the state of mind on the part of the agent which it expresses or would express.'[91] Unfortunately, Green's subsequent development of this point makes clear that he is not claiming here simply that the ethical quality of action is an aggregate of two discrete factors: the worth of the motive plus the worth of consequence. Instead, he adopts the rather more controversial position that the ethical quality of an action's consequences reflects the ethical quality of the agent's disposition when performing that action. He even goes so far as insist that in principle one could assess the ethical quality of the agent's intentions by measuring the ethical qualities of the action's consequences (the latter being usually more evident to an observer than the former).[92] Here, Green collapses the distinction between deontological concerns and consequential ones not in the interesting and potentially fruitful manner of Cummiskey and Weinstein. Instead, he invokes a deep faith in the power of a good agent to produce good consequences. This deeply implausible move lays the foundations of his theory of progress, something that is examined at length in the second part of *The Liberal Socialism of T.H. Green*. For that reason, the argument is simply noted here without further comment.

Finally, for Weinstein Green held in order to achieve self-realisation one should pursue that course of action that one believed would maximise one's pleasure.[93] He

---

[90] PE 295.

[91] PE 294.

[92] 'There is no real reason to doubt that the good or evil in the motive of an action is exactly measured by the good or evil in its consequences as rightly estimated – estimated, that is, in their bearing on the production of a produced good will or the perfecting of mankind.' (PE 295)

[93] Weinstein, *Utilitarianism and the New Liberalism*, chapter 4 *passim*. Weinstein alleges that many other British idealists and new liberals held this to be the case too. For a critical response, see

holds that for all of Green's insistence on an unbridgeable qualitative distinction between pleasure and abiding satisfaction, Green believed that 'pleasure was contingently co-extensive with self-realization (effective willing).'[94] In that way, 'Green was a straightforward "extensional" perfectionist' of the type formulated by Thomas Hurka.[95] As Weinstein puts it in relation to D.G. Ritchie: 'We need only eat the cake of happiness and we will likewise get our self-realization. Maximize happiness and you will promote self-realization too.'[96] Weinstein places great emphasis on this claim in relation to many of the British idealists and new liberals. This stress is particularly surprising however given Weinstein's explicit acknowledgement that this relationship between self-realisation and pleasure is contingent at best. Indeed, it has been shown above that Green is highly circumspect about utilitarianism both as a philosophy and a public policy even if he accepts that in the past it has been of great benefit. Weinstein's Green is guilty of committing the fallacy of the affirmed consequent. In reality the most that can be said is that Green did hold that at times seeking pleasure could act as a very rough rule of thumb for the self-realising being. On most occasions however, the guide should be treated with far more caution than Weinstein usually implies, for all of the reasons outlined above (§7.III).

VI
Conclusion

This chapter has established that an agent is good to the extent that: she is motivated by the desire to act well; she seeks to realise her eudaimonic capacities; and she has done as much as she can to discern whether the ends that are likely to be realised through her action truly are the best ends that are attainable given her particular circumstances. By the same token, an action is good to the extent that: the state of affairs either realised in its performance or arising out of its performance is truly good; the agent performing the action is motivated by the desire to act well; and by the belief that in performing the particular act he is acting well. More succinctly Green writes: 'By a moral ideal we mean some type of man or character or personal activity [giving practical expression to that type of 'man or character'], considered as an end in itself.'[97] The agent's motivation determines the level of her development in two ways therefore: first as it affects the virtue or vice of the agent herself, and second as a constitutive element of her action. Green combines these elements by holding a settled disposition to honour one's duties to be a necessary component of human flourishing (although not the whole of it). In so doing, he overcomes the dichotomy that many philosophers have posited between the ethics of duty and the ethics of virtue. He encapsulates the key point eloquently when he observes:

Colin Tyler, 'Vindicating British Idealism: David Ritchie contra David Weinstein', *Collingwood and British Idealism Studies*, vol. 16, 15:2 (2009), 54–75.
[94]   Weinstein, *Utilitarianism*, p. 120; also pp. 119–20.
[95]   Weinstein, *Utilitarianism*, p. 122; Thomas Hurka, *Perfectionism*, pp. 24–26.
[96]   Weinstein, *Utilitarianism*, p. 143.
[97]   PE 194.

when we are giving an account of an agent whose development is governed by an ideal of his own perfection, we cannot avoid speaking of one and the same condition of will alternately as means and as end. The goodness of the will or man as a means must be described as lying in direction to that same goodness as an end. For the end is that full self-conscious realisation of capabilities to which the means lies in the self-conscious exercise of the same capabilities – an exercise of them in imperfect realisation, but under the governing idea of the desirability of their fuller realisation.[98]

This is not the whole picture however. As Geoffrey Thomas puts it, there are five criteria which any object has to satisfy in order to be legitimately classed as a Greenian true good. It '(i) is achievable only as an object of pursuit, (ii) contains a constructive element, (iii) is imperatival, (iv) is non-exclusive and non-competitive, and (v) is social or common.'[99] This chapter has established Green's arguments for the first three of these qualities at length. It is still worth pausing on the second element however. Thomas clarifies the constructive nature of the true good thus: 'the human "end" must be seen "as a character not a good fortune, as a fulfilment of human capabilities from within not an accession of good things from without, as a function not a possession."'[100] Particular care is required here. John Skorupski has called Green a constructivist also, but in the sense of holding that 'in endorsing some solicitations as ones whose realization would be part of my good, I *make* their realization part of my good.'[101] On this reading, solicitations have value simply in virtue of the fact that I endorse them. In fact, Green's ethics is constructive in the alternative sense that the agent projects a possibly vague and incomplete conception of an ideal that instantiates her distinctively human nature; a solicitation has value because she endorses it due to her understanding of its positive relationship to that ideal (see §7.IV and the role of crystallisation which has been a recurring theme throughout this book). Green never claims that the agent can confer value on an object simply by endorsing it in the manner Skorupski intimates.[102]

Elements of Thomas's final criterion have been touched as well of course: namely that the true good is made determinate through social practices and norms. Famously there is rather more to this criterion however: not only is the true good only conceivable when expressed through social forms, Green claims that it is only achievable when the agent seeks to satisfy a common good, understood as the good of others as well as oneself. This far more demanding and controversial criterion will be examined in very great detail in the second part of *The Liberal Socialism of T.H. Green*. Also considered there are the details of the life of the conscientious critical citizen, a subject that has been treated only in general terms above. Before

---

[98] PE 195.

[99] Geoffrey Thomas, *Moral Philosophy of T.H. Green* (Oxford: Clarendon, 1987), pp. 244–45; see *ibid.* pp. 247–55.

[100] Thomas, *Moral Philosophy of T.H. Green*, p. 251, quoting PE 246.

[101] John Skorupski, 'Green and the Idealist Conception of a Person's Good', pp. 54–56. Skorupski offers no textual evidence for his interpretation of Green on this point.

[102] Hence, again contra Skorupski in reality there is no tension between Green's constructivism and his theory of the common good. The reconciliation of Green's constructivism and his theory of the common good is a core theme of Tyler, 'Contesting the Common Good', even if the term 'constructivism' is not used there.

so doing, the present book ends with a brief review of the argument developed to this point.

9

Review of the Argument so Far

The analysis has reached the transition point in Green's ethical theory where it moves from his conception of personality to his conception of community. The next stage is to trace the relationships between the claim that individuals can only conceive of themselves *as* individuals through their critical reflection on, and endorsement or reform of established social norms, practices and institutions, to the claim that in acting well the individual should act for a 'common good' understood roughly as a good that is realisable only as part of the interrelationships of persons and in attaining which every party to these interrelationships benefits in the same manner. This is a very complex and controversial claim, hence it needs to be dealt with care and at some length. For this reason, that critical analysis is held over until the second part of *The Liberal Socialism of T.H. Green*. It will be helpful before closing to sketch the key features of Green's argument as it has been analysed and critically assessed in the present book. In effect this is a provisional 'taking stock' of the current position rather than a statement of the final analysis of Green's philosophical system.

Chapter one reconstructed Green's attitude towards socialism, before indicating the sense in which his philosophical system can be seen as underpinning a form of liberal socialism. Chapter two argued that Green believes philosophy should transcend the truths of religion and literature. It was argued that in light of the great many sources on which we now know Green to have drawn, one should be very careful not to overstate his debts to Hegel. The latter traditional, excessively-narrow focus has led many previous scholars to ignore the influences of, say, Fichte and Lotze, and even to downplay the direct influences on Green of Kant and Aristotle. Ultimately however Green should be read on his own terms. It was argued also that contrary to the scepticism of certain scholars Green's system-building represents the heart of his philosophical method. Finally, an indication was given of what features he understands a successful system to possess.

Chapters three and four established Green's argument that personal knowledge is a result of personal critical judgement. The latter involves the analysis of everyday beliefs and values in order, firstly, to identify the abstract *a priori* conceptual and propositional presuppositions of those commitments and, secondly, to refine them in such ways that they can come to form parts of one system of abstract presuppositions (critical metaphysics), followed by the attempt to understand more complex phenomena as manifestations of a system constructed using those presuppositions (speculative metaphysics). These metaphysical processes of analysis and inference should be guided by a postulate of theoretical and practical reason which was characterised using Stendhal's conception of 'crystallisation' as 'a mental process which draws from everything that happens new proofs of the perfection of the loved one.'[1] From this point, it was shown that one can develop a constructivist reading of the 'eternal consciousness' such that it represents a heuristic projection of an ideal rather than an 'extra-human' or corporate agent residing somewhere between mysticism and ontology.

Chapter five laid the groundwork for the analysis of Green's theory of freedom presented in chapter six. The discussion turned to the distinction Green draws between 'animality' and 'distinctively human action'. The core notion was shown to be that of the 'will', which led into a discussion of a greatly under-recognised aspect of Green's thought: the 'unconscious'. The interrelationship of emanation and sublimation was explored in depth. From this groundwork chapter six analysed Green's interrelated conceptions of true freedom and character (the latter of which Green also calls 'personality'). Two incompatible strands were identified within Green's writings on the will: self-interventionism and spiritual determinism. Finally, it was shown that Green does not provide a viable theory of moral responsibility, ultimately because no theory is able to reconcile two equally necessary but mutually inconsistent requirements for such a theory: that one is only responsible for an action (a) to the extent that it issues from one's character, and (b) to the extent one could have chosen to have acted otherwise than one did in the circumstances.

The guiding thread of my interpretation has been the claim that at root Green's ethics is built on the presupposition that in order to arrive at a determinate conception of her own particular good, each agent 'must suppose a determination of desire by the conception of self, [which constitutes] its direction to self-satisfaction'.[2] With this proposition in mind chapters seven and eight explored Green's conception of the true good and his critique of utilitarianism, and analysed the ways in which his ethical theory combines an ethics of duty with a culture-based ethics of virtue, as well as deontology with consequentialism. Green's theory of the 'common good' forms the next stage of his philosophical system, and therefore an analysis of that controversial notion forms the starting-point for the next part of *The Liberal Socialism of T.H. Green*.

---

[1]   Stendhal, *Love*, trans. G. Sale and S. Sale (Harmondsworth: Penguin, 1975), p. 45.
[2]   PE 222.

Appendix

Herbert Spencer,
Richard Hodgson, jnr., and
'Professor Green as a Critic'

By the mid-1870s Benjamin Jowett had become seriously concerned that what he saw as Green's obscure Hegelianism was causing promising Balliol students to under-achieve in their examinations. Consequently he sought a way to widen Green's intellectual interests. With this mind, he wrote to Edward Caird on 5 January 1875: 'I have tried to set Green to fight the Philistines – Bain, H. Spencer, &c., and he seems well disposed, he takes a year of holiday (a Sabbatical fourth year which ought to exist in every College and University) next year, so that he will have time to make the attack.'[1] It is tempting to believe that Jowett had Green in mind when he wrote in a letter two months later: 'There is a fellow named Herbert Spencer ... who knows a little of physical science, and gives back to the scientific men their own notions in a more general form. Of course they worship him as a god, and instead of being thought an empty sciolist, he is regarded by them as the philosopher of the future. I hope that we shall some day put a spoke in his wheel at Oxford, but at present he is rather swaggering and triumphant.'[2]

The results of Green's labours were two articles attacking Herbert Spencer and one attacking G.H. Lewes (Green ceased working on a second attack on Lewes following the latter's death in November 1878). No matter how unremitting Green's criticisms of his opponents's writings, rarely did he show anything less than respect for their authors. In fact, the only notable occasions on which he made personal comments about an opponent were in the articles on Spencer that appeared in the *Contemporary Review* in December 1877 and March 1878.[3] His exasperation with Spencer's 'polemic against idealists' showed most pointedly in the following passage from the first article, which concerned 'the relation of subject and object':

---

[1] Letter from Benjamin Jowett to Edward Caird, 5 January 1875, in Benjamin Jowett, *Letters*, eds. Evelyn Abbot and Lewis Campbell (London: John Murray, 1899), p. 191.

[2] Letter from Jowett to R.B.D. Morier, 30 March 1875, in Jowett, *Letters*, p. 195.

[3] T.H. Green, 'Mr. Herbert Spencer and Mr. G.H. Lewes: Their Application of the Doctrine of Evolution to Thought (Part I)', *Contemporary Review*, 31 (1877–78), 25–53 [reprinted as 'Spencer I']; and T.H. Green, 'Mr. Herbert Spencer and Mr. G.H. Lewes: Their Application of the Doctrine of Evolution to Thought (Part II)', *Contemporary Review*, 32 (1877–78), 745–69 [reprinted as ['Spencer II'].

what Mr. Spencer understands by "idealism" is what a raw undergraduate understands by it. It means to him a doctrine that "there is no such thing as matter," or that "the external world is merely the creation of our own minds" – a doctrine expressly rejected by Kant, and which has had no place since his time in any idealism that knows what it is about. Either Mr. Spencer's profound study of the physical sciences has not left him leisure, or his splendid faculty of generalisation has relieved him from the necessity, for a thorough investigation of the history of philosophy. In lieu of it there are signs of his having accepted Sir W. Hamilton's classification of 'isms. His study of "idealism" at first hand would seem to have been confined to a hasty reading of Berkeley and Hume...[4]

Herbert Spencer recounted the next stage of the story in his letter to his friend the scientist Edward Livingston Youmans, dated 8 November 1880.

> Some time ago a Mr. Richard Hodgson, Jr., a perfect stranger to me, a graduate of St. John's, Cambridge, wrote to me saying that he had been allowed, on his own request, to take as a subject, ... the examination of Green's articles in the *Contemporary* of some two years ago, in which he [Green] made an attack upon my metaphysical doctrine. Mr. Hodgson offered to send me his paper, and did so. It was very good in substance but too diffuse and unorganized; and after suggesting various omissions and a second time sending it back to him for further revision and abridgement, it has been reduced to a satisfactory form and is, I think very telling. It has been sent to the *Contemporary*.'[5]

Hodgson's article 'Professor Green as a Critic' duly appeared in December 1880.[6] The article claimed that on first reading Green's attack had convinced Hodgson of the untenability of Spencer's position. Yet, on turning to Spencer's text, 'My surprise was considerable on finding that Professor Green had omitted the most important passages, misquoted others, and misapprehended still more, and this in such a way as not to be detected, probably, save by those who knew the course of Mr. Spencer's argument and compared it with Professor Green's statements.'[7] After considering the details of 'the twisting and wanderings of Professor Green['s argument]', the article ended: 'Here I may conclude, having said enough to show that Professor Green's criticism is doubly vitiated, partly by ignorance of the contents of Mr. Spencer's work and partly by misinterpretation.'[8]

Green defended himself at length against the charges of "unfair dealing" found in "Professor Green as a Critic" in a reply which appeared in the *Contemporary Review* for January 1881.[9] This stirred Spencer to action once again. He wrote to Youmans on 10 January saying, 'I had thought I had finished my fighting for the present and pretty well settled all my critics. Still, there is something remaining to be done. Professor Green has answered Mr. Hodgson in the last number of the

---

[4]	'Spencer I' 12.
[5]	Letter from Herbert Spencer to E.L. Youmans, 8 November 1880, reprinted in David Duncan, *Life and Letters of Herbert Spencer* (London: Methuen, 1908), p. 212.
[6]	Richard Hodgson, jr., 'Professor Green as a Critic', *Contemporary Review*, 38 (December 1880), 898–912.
[7]	Hodgson, 'Professor Green as a Critic', 898.
[8]	Hodgson, 'Professor Green as a Critic', 912.
[9]	'Hodgson'.

Contemporary, and I think it will be needful to take up the matter briefly myself.'[10] Spencer's indignant 'Prof. Green's Explanations' appeared in February 1881.[11] He complimented Hodgson on his philosophical acuity, while failing to mention his own role in re-drafting the piece. Probably in response to Spencer's public comment, Green sent Spencer an apology for the tone of his original article, via the journal's editor, Alexander Stuart Strahan. Immediately, Spencer wrote to Youman reporting the content of Green's letter.

> *14 February.* – …You saw the reply to Green in the *Contemporary*, I suppose. He has written to Strahan saying he does not intend to continue the matter, and requesting that his letter should be sent on to me. In it, while he does not confess that he is wrong in his representations, he apologizes for the expressions he had used, which he admits to have been altogether out of taste. This controversy having come to an end I now feel free, and hope to avoid all such wastes of time for the future – especially as my critics are all as quiet as mice.[12]

The issue was reignited three years after Green's death in March 1882. Apparently unaware that, at Green's request, Strahan had forwarded Green's 1881 apology on to Spencer, R.L. Nettleship added the following note when the four articles against Spencer and Lewes were reprinted in 1885 in the first volume of Green's posthumous *Works*.

> Mr. Herbert Spencer criticised the "Answer to Mr. Hodgson" in the *Contemporary Review* for February 1881. Professor Green did not continue the discussion further, but wrote to the editor of the *Contemporary Review* a private letter, of which a draft to the following effect is found amongst his papers:– "While I cannot honestly retract anything in the substance of what I then wrote, there are expressions in the article which I very much regret, so far as they might be taken to imply want of personal respect for Mr. Spencer. For reasons sufficiently given in my reply to Mr. Hodgson, I cannot plead guilty to the charge of misrepresentation which Mr. Spencer repeats; but on reading my first article again in cold blood I found that I had allowed controversial heat to betray me into the use of language which was unbecoming – especially on the part of an unknown writer (not even then a 'professor') assailing a veteran philosopher. I make this acknowledgment merely for my own satisfaction, not under the impression that it can at all concern Mr. Spencer."[13]

In response to Nettleship's inclusion in Green's *Works* of the 'unscrupulous criticism' contained in the original articles, Spencer added a postscript six years later when he reprinted 'Prof. Green's Explanations'.[14]

---

[10]   Letter from Spencer to Youmans, 10 January 1881, in Duncan, *Life and Letters*, p. 213.

[11]   Herbert Spencer, 'Professor Green's Explanations', *Contemporary Review*, 39 (February 1881), 305–11.

[12]   Letter from Spencer to Youmans, 14 February 1881, in Duncan, *Life and Letters*, pp. 213–14.

[13]   'Hodgson' 541n.

[14]   Herbert Spencer, addition to 'Prof. Green's Explanations', in his *Essays: Scientific, Political, and Speculative, Volume 2. Library edition: Containing Seven Essays not before Republished, and various other additions* (London: Williams and Norgate, 1891), p. 321.

Prof. Green says that his apology for unbecoming language he makes merely for his "own satisfaction." He does not calm his qualms of conscience by indicating his regret to those who read this unbecoming language; nor does he express his regret to me, against whom it was vented; but he expresses his regret to the editor of the *Contemporary Review*! So a public insult to A is supposed to be cancelled by a private apology to B! here is more Hegelian thinking; or, rather, here is Hegelian feeling congruous with Hegelian thinking.[15]

Spencer seems to have forgotten the apology Strahan had forwarded to him at Green's request, just as he seems to have forgotten his own involvement in Hodgson's original article. This convenient amnesia allowed Spencer the luxury of expressing publicly his moral indignation against a man who had died nine years earlier. Spencer returned to Green's criticisms in February 1899, in the fourth edition of his *Principles of Psychology*. Characteristically, Spencer saw attack as the best method of defence, claiming at the outset: 'The late Prof. Green used his logical weapons to achieve an easy victory over a simulacrum. Here are some passages showing how utterly he misconceives that which he proposes to disprove.'[16]

Towards the end of his life, Spencer believed that idealism had come to dominate the philosophical mainstream. Hence, having cancelled his subscription to the journal *Mind* in December 1901, the following April he wrote to Alexander Bain in the following terms: 'I not unfrequently think of the disgust you must feel at the fate which has overtaken *Mind*. That you, after establishing the thing and maintaining it for so many years at your own cost, should now find it turned into an organ for German idealism must be extremely exasperating.... Oxford and Cambridge have been captured by this old-world nonsense. What about Scotland? I suppose Hegelianism is rife there also.'[17] He wrote much the same to Masson the day after writing to Bain. In fact together with Sidgwick's utilitarianism, idealism was indeed philosophically dominant when Spencer died on 8 December 1903.

---

[15]   Spencer, addition to 'Prof. Green's Explanations', p. 332.

[16]   Herbert Spencer, 'Second Appendix: Reply to T.H. Green', in his *Principles of Psychology*, 2 vols., fourth edition (London: Williams and Norgate, 1899 [1855]), vol. 1, pp. 505–20.

[17]   Letter from Spencer to Alexander Bain, 25 April 1902, in Duncan, *Life and Letters*, p. 457; see *ibid,*, pp. 457–58; and Herbert Spencer, *Autobiography*, 2 vols. (London: Watts, 1904), vol. 2, pp. 239–40, 489.

Bibliography

Abbreviations: The key to the abbreviated references is given at the beginning of this book. These abbreviations relate mainly to Green's own writings.

A
T.H. Green's Writings

'Mr. Herbert Spencer and Mr. G.H. Lewes: Their Application of the Doctrine of Evolution to Thought (Part I)', *Contemporary Review*, 31 (1877–78), 25–53.

'Mr. Herbert Spencer and Mr. G.H. Lewes: Their Application of the Doctrine of Evolution to Thought (Part II)', *Contemporary Review*, 32 (1877–78), 745–69.

'Can there be a natural science of man? [Part I]', *Mind*, 7:25 os (January 1882), 1–29.

'Can there be a natural science of man? [Part II]', *Mind*, 7:26 os (April 1882), 161–85.

'Can there be a natural science of man? [Part III]', *Mind*, 7:27 os (July 1882), 321–48.

Prolegomena to Ethics, fifth edition, ed. A.C. Bradley. Oxford: Clarendon, 1906 [1883].

Works, 5 vols., ed. R.L. Nettleship and P.P. Nicholson. Bristol: Thoemmes, 1997.

'Part 1: Thomas Hill Green', in Colin Tyler, ed., *Unpublished Manuscripts in British Idealism: Political philosophy, theology and social thought*, 2 vols.. Bristol: Thoemmes Continuum, 2005; Exeter: Imprint Academic, 2008, vol. 1, pp. 1–188.

B
Archives Sources Used

Benjamin Jowett Papers, Balliol College, Oxford.

T.H. Green Papers, Balliol College, Oxford.

Bryce Papers, Bodleian Library, Oxford.

C
Secondary Literature Used

Abbey, Ruth, *Charles Taylor.* Teddington: Acumen, 2000.

Allard, James W., *Logical Foundations of Bradley's Metaphysics: Judgement, inference, and truth*. Cambridge: Cambridge University Press, 2005.

Anderson, Olive, 'The Feminism of T.H. Green: A late Victorian success story?', *History of Political Thought*, 12:4 (1991), 671–93.

Aristotle, *Ethics*, trans. J.A.K. Thomson, rev. Hugh Tredennick. Harmondsworth: Penguin, 1976.

Aristotle, *Politics*, trans. T.A. Sinclair, rev. T.J. Saunders. Harmondsworth: Penguin, 1957.

Aristotle, *Metaphysics, X–XIV, Oeconomica, Magna Moralia*, trans. Hugh Tredennick and G. Cyril Armstrong. Cambridge, Mass, and London: Loeb, 1935.

Armour, Leslie, 'Green's Idealism and the Metaphysics of Ethics' in Maria Dimova–Cookson and W.J. Mander, eds., *T.H. Green: Ethics, metaphysics and political philosophy*. Oxford: Clarendon, 2006, pp. 160–86.

Aveling, Edward, *Socialism and Radicalism*. London: Twentieth Century, n.d. [1880].

Bain, Alexander, *Emotions and the Will*. London: John W. Parker, 1859.

Balfour, Arthur J., 'Green's Metaphysics of Knowledge', *Mind*, 9:33 os (January 1884), 71–93.

Balfour, Arthur J., 'Criticism of Current Idealistic Theories', *Mind*, 2 ns (1893), 29–30.

Baum, Bruce, 'J.S. Mill and Liberal Socialism', in Nadia Urbinati and Alex Zakaras, eds., *J.S. Mill's Political Thought: A bicentennial reassessment*. Cambridge: Cambridge University Press, 2007, pp. 98–123.

Bellamy, Richard, 'A Green Revolution? Idealism, liberalism and the Welfare State', *Bulletin of the Hegel Society of Great Britain*, 10 (1984), 34–39.

Bellamy, Richard, 'Introduction', in Norbetto Bobbio, *Future of Democracy: A defence of the rules of the game*, trans. R. Griffin, ed. Richard Bellamy. Cambridge: Polity, 1987, pp. 1–15.

Bellamy, Richard, 'Introduction', in Richard Bellamy, ed., *Victorian Liberalism: Nineteenth century political thought and practice*. London: Routledge, 1990, pp. 1–14.

Bellamy, Richard, 'T.H. Green and the Morality of Victorian Liberalism', in Richard Bellamy, ed., *Victorian Liberalism: Nineteenth century political thought and* practice. London: Routledge, 1990, pp. 131–51.

Bellamy, Richard, *Liberalism and Modern Society: An historical argument*. Oxford: Polity, 1992.

Beloff, John, *Psychological Sciences: A review of modern psychology*. London: Crosby Lockwood Staples, 1973.

Benn, Alfred W., *History of English Rationalism in the nineteenth century*, 2 vols. New York: Russell and Russell, 1962 [1906].

Bentham, Jeremy, *Theory of Legislation*, ed. E. Dumont, trans. R. Hildreth, fourth edition. London: Trübner, 1882.

Bentham, Jeremy, *Constitutional Code: Volume 1*, eds. F. Rosen and J.H. Burns. Oxford: Clarendon, 1983.

Bentham, Jeremy, *Deontology together with A Table of the Springs of Action and Article on Utilitarianism*, ed. Amnon Goldworth. Oxford: Clarendon Press, 1983.

Bentham, Jeremy, *Introduction to the Principles of Morals and Legislation*, eds. J.H.

Burns and H.L.A. Hart, revised edition. Oxford: Clarendon, 1996.

Berki, Robert N., *Socialism*. London: J.M. Dent, 1974.

Berkeley, George, *Principles of Human Knowledge*, ed. T.E. Jessop. London: A. Brown, 1937.

Berlin, Isaiah, *Four Essays on Liberty*. Oxford: Oxford University Press, 1969.

Blau, Adrian, 'Against Positive and Negative Freedom', *Political Theory*, 32 (2004), 547–53.

Blum, Lawrence, 'Community and Virtue', in Roger Crisp, ed., *How Should One Live? Essays on the virtues*. Oxford: Clarendon, 1996, pp. 231–50.

Bosanquet, Bernard, 'Report on a Dissertation entitled "The Metaphysical Basis of Reality" by Mr G.E. Moore' [19 September 1898], in Colin Tyler, ed., *Unpublished Manuscripts in British Idealism: Political philosophy, theology and social thought*, 2 vols.. Bristol: Thoemmes Continuum, 2005; Exeter: Imprint Academic, 2008, vol. 1, pp. 236–40.

Bosanquet, Bernard, *Philosophical Theory of the State*, fourth edition. London: MacMillan, 1923 [1899].

Bosanquet, Bernard, Review of G.E. Moore *Principia Ethica*, *Mind*, 13 ns (1904), 254–61.

Bosanquet, Bernard, *Principle of Individuality and Value*. London: MacMillan, 1912.

Bosanquet, Bernard, *Some Suggestions in Ethics*. London: MacMillan, 1918.

Boucher, David, *Limits of Ethics in International Relations: Natural law, natural rights and human rights in transition*. Oxford: Oxford University Press, 2009.

Bradlaugh, Charles, *Socialism: Its fallacies and dangers*. London: Freethought, 1887.

Bradley, Francis H., *Ethical Studies*, second edition. Oxford: Clarendon, 1927 [1876].

Bradley, Francis H., *Appearance and Reality: A metaphysical essay*, second edition. Oxford: Clarendon, 1897 [1893].

Bradley, Francis H., *Collected Works: Volume 4: Selected Correspondence June 1872– December 1904*, ed. Carol A. Keene. Bristol: Thoemmes, 1999.

Bradley, Francis H., *Collected Works: Volume 5: Selected Correspondence January 1905 – June 1924*, ed. Carol A. Keene. Bristol: Thoemmes, 1999.

Brett, G.S., 'T.H. Green', in J. Hastings, ed., *Encyclopaedia of Religion and Ethics*, 13 vols. Edinburgh: T. and T. Clark, 1908–27, vol. 6, pp. 435–40.

Brink, David O., *Perfectionism and the Common Good: Themes in the philosophy of T.H. Green*. Oxford: Clarendon, 2003.

Brinton, Crane, *English Political Thought in the Nineteenth Century*. New York: Harper and Brothers, 1962.

Brooks, Thom, Review of Colin Tyler, *Thomas Hill Green (1836–1882)...*, *Bulletin of the Hegel Society of Great Britain*, nos. 51–52 (2005), 141–44.

Brooks, Thom, 'Was Green a Utilitarian in Practice?', *Collingwood and British Idealism Studies*, 14:1 (2008), 5–15.

Cacoullos, Ann R., *Thomas Hill Green: Philosopher of rights*. New York: Twayne, 1974.

Caird, Edward, *Social Philosophy and Religion of Comte*. Glasgow: James Maclehose, 1885.

Caird, Edward, 'Report on Mr Moore's Essay' [late 1897], in Colin Tyler, ed.,

Unpublished Manuscripts in British Idealism: Political philosophy, theology and social thought, 2 vols.. Bristol: Thoemmes Continuum, 2005; Exeter: Imprint Academic, 2008, vol. 2, pp. 184–203.

Caird, Edward, 'Spencer', ed. Colin Tyler, *Collingwood and British Idealism Studies*, 12:1 (Spring 2006), 5–38.

Calderwood, Henry, 'Another View of Green's Last Work', *Mind*, 10 os (1885), 73–84.

Carritt, E.F., *Morals and Politics: Theories of their relation from Hobbes and Spinoza to Marx and Bosanquet*. Oxford: Clarendon, 1935.

Carritt, E.F., *Ethical and Political Thinking*. Oxford: Clarendon, 1947.

Carter, Matt, *T.H. Green and the Ethical Socialist Tradition*. Exeter: Imprint Academic, 2003.

Chapman, Richard A., 'Basis of T.H. Green's Philosophy', *International Review of History and Political Science*, 3 (1966), 72–88.

Chubb, Percival, 'Significance of Thomas Hill Green's Philosophical and Religious Teaching', *Journal of Speculative Philosophy*, 22:1–2 (1888), 1–21.

Clarke, Peter, *Liberals and Social Democrats*. Cambridge: Cambridge University Press, 1978.

Cohen, G.A., 'Future of a Disillusion', *New Left Review*, 1/190 (November–December 1991), 5–20.

Coker, Francis, *Recent Political Thought*. New York: Appleton–Century–Crofts, 1934.

Collini, Stefan, *Liberalism and Sociology: L.T. Hobhouse and political argument in England 1880–1914*. Cambridge: Cambridge University Press, 1979.

Comte-Sponville, André, *Book of Atheist Spirituality: An elegant argument for spirituality without God*, trans. Nancy Huston. London: Bantam, 2008.

Copleston, Frederick, *History of Philosophy VIII: Bentham to Russell*. London: Burns and Oates, 1966.

Cranston, Maurice, *Freedom: A new analysis*. London: Longmans, Green, 1954.

Crisp, Roger, 'Aristotle on Greatness of Soul', in Richard Kraut, ed., *Blackwell Guide to Aristotle's Nicomachean Ethics*. Oxford: Blackwell, 2006, pp. 179–97.

Crossley, David, 'Self-conscious Agency and the Eternal Consciousness: Ultimate reality in Thomas Hill Green', *Ultimate Reality and Meaning*, 13 (1990), 3–20.

Cruddas, Jon, 'Labour is in the middle of its gravest crisis in 30 years. It needs to rediscover the radicalism that animated its founders', *New Statesman*, 7 September 2009, 24.

Cummiskey, David, *Kantian Consequentialism*. New York and Oxford: Oxford University Press, 1996.

Cunliffe, John and Guido Erreygers, 'Moral philosophy and economics: The formation of François Huet's doctrine of property rights', *European Journal of the History of Economic Thought*, 6:4 (Winter 1999), 581–605.

Cunningham, Gustavus, *Idealist Argument in Recent British and American Philosophy*. New York: Books for Libraries, 1933.

D'Arcy, Charles, *Short History of Ethics*. London: MacMillan, 1901.

Dawkins, Marion, *Through our Eyes Only? The search for animal consciousness*. Oxford: W.H. Freeman/Spektrum, 1993.

de Burgh, W.G., *From Morality to Religion*. London: MacDonald and Evans, 1938.

de Sanctis, Alberto, *'Puritan' Democracy of T.H. Green, with some unpublished writings*. Exeter: Imprint Academic, 2005.

Descartes, René, *Meditations on First Philosophy: With objections and replies*, trans. John Cottingham. Cambridge: Cambridge University Press, 1986.

Descartes, René, 'Discourse on the Method', in his *Philosophical Writings, Volume 1*, trans. John Cottingham, Robert Stootfhoff and Dugald Murdoch. Cambridge: Cambridge University Press, 1970, pp. 5–57.

Dewey, John, *Early Works*, 5 vols. Carbondale and Edwardsville, Ill.: Southern Illinois University, 1969–72.

Dewey, John and Arthur F. Bentley, *Knowing and the Known*. Boston: Beacon, 1949.

Dimova-Cookson, Maria, *T.H. Green's Moral and Political Philosophy: A phenomenological perspective*. Houndsmill: Palgrave, 2001.

Dimova-Cookson, Maria, 'The Eternal Consciousness: What roles it can and cannot play. A reply to Colin Tyler', *Bradley Studies*, 9:2 (Autumn 2003), 139–48.

Dimova-Cookson, Maria, 'A New Scheme of Positive and Negative Freedom: Reconstructing T.H. Green on freedom', *Political Theory*, 31:4 (August 2003), 508–35.

Dimova-Cookson, Maria, 'Conceptual Clarity, Freedom and Normative Ideas: Reply to Blau', *Political Theory*, 32 (2004), 554–62.

Dimova-Cookson, Maria and W.J. Mander, eds., *T.H. Green: Ethics, metaphysics, and political philosophy*. Oxford: Clarendon, 2006.

Dinwiddy, John, *Bentham*. Oxford: Oxford University Press, 1989.

Double, Richard, 'Metaethics, Metaphilosophy, and Free Will Subjectivism', in Robert Kane, ed., *Oxford Handbook of Freewill*. Oxford: Oxford University Press, 2002, pp. 506–28.

Duncan, David, *Life and Letters of Herbert Spencer*. London: Methuen, 1908.

Eastwood, Arthur, 'On Thought–Relations', *Mind*, 16 os (1891), 243–52.

Ewing, A.C., *Idealism: A critical survey*. London: Methuen, 1969.

Ewing, A.C., 'Moore and Metaphysics', in Alice Ambrose and Morris Lazerowitz, eds., *G.E. Moore Essays in Retrospect*. London: George Allen and Unwin, 1970, pp. 139–59.

Fairbrother, W.H., *Philosophy of Thomas Hill Green*. London: Methuen, 1896.

Fichte, Johann G., *On the Nature of the Scholar and its Manifestations*, trans. W. Smith. London: John Chapman, 1845.

Fichte, Johann G., *Destination of Man*, trans. P. Sinnett. London: John Chapman, 1846.

Fichte, Johann G., *Vocation of the Scholar*, trans. W. Smith. London: John Chapman, 1847.

Fichte, Johann G., *Vocation of Man*, trans. W. Smith. London: John Chapman, 1848.

Fichte, Johann G., *Popular Works*, trans. William Smith, fourth edition, 2 vols. London: Trubner, 1889 [1877].

Flint, Robert, *Theism: being the Baird lecture for 1876*, ninth edition. Edinburgh and London: William Blackwood, 1895.

Forsyth, Thomas M., *English Philosophy: A study of its methods and general development*. London: Adam and Charles Black, 1910.

Francis, Mark and John Morrow, *History of English Political Thought in the Nineteenth Century*. London: Duckworth, 1994.

Freeden, Michael, *The New Liberalism: An ideology of social reform*. Oxford: Clarendon, 1986 [1978].

Freeden, Michael, *Ideologies and Political Theory: A conceptual approach*. Oxford: Clarendon, 1996.

Freud, Sigmund, 'Five lectures on psycho–analysis', in Sigmund Freud, *Two Short Accounts of Psycho–Analysis*, trans. James Strachey. Harmondsworth: Penguin, 1962.

Fullerton, George S., 'The "Knower" in Psychology', *Philosophical Review*, 4:1 (1897), 1–26.

Gaus, Gerald, 'Green, Bernard Bosanquet and the Philosophy of Coherence', in C.L. Ten, ed., *Routledge History of Philosophy, Volume VII, the Nineteenth Century*. London: Routledge, 1994, pp. 408–36.

Gaus, Gerald, *Modern Liberal Theory of Man*. Beckenham: Croom Helm, 1983.

Gaus, Gerald, 'The Rights Recognition Thesis: Defending and extending Green', in Maria Dimova-Cookson and W.J. Mander, eds., *T.H. Green: Ethics, metaphysics, and political philosophy*. Oxford: Clarendon, 2006, pp. 209–35.

Gosse, Edmund, *Life of Algernon Charles Swinburne*. London: MacMillan, 1917.

Greengarten, I.M., *Thomas Hill Green and the Development of Liberal-Democratic Thought*. Toronto: University of Toronto Press, 1981.

Grosskurth, Phyllis, *John Addington Symonds: A biography*. London: Longmans, Green, 1964.

Haldar, Hiralal, 'Green and his Critics', *Philosophical Review*, 3:2 (1894), 168–75.

Haldar, Hiralal, *Neo-Hegelianism*. London: Heath Cranton, 1927.

Hamilton, E., 'Mr. Lewes's Doctrine of Sensibility', *Mind*, 4:14 (April 1879), 256–61.

Hammond, T.C., *Perfect Freedom: An introduction to Christian ethics*. London: Inter-Varsity Fellowship, n.d.

Hampshire, Stuart, 'Oxford Virtue', *New Statesman*, 7 August 1964.

Harris, Paul, 'Green's Theory of Political Obligation and Obedience', in Andrew Vincent, ed., *Philosophy of T.H. Green*. Aldershot: Gower, 1986, pp. 127–42.

Harris, Paul, 'Moral Progress and Politics: The theory of T.H. Green', *Polity*, 21 (1988–89), 538–62.

Harris, Paul and John Morrow, 'Introduction', to T.H. Green, *Lectures on the Principles of Political Obligation, and other writings*, ed. Paul Harris and John Morrow. Cambridge: Cambridge University Press, 1986, pp. 1–12.

Hart, W.D., 'Motions of the Mind', in J. Hopkins and A. Saville, eds., *Psychoanalysis, Mind, and Art*. Oxford: Blackwell, 1992, pp. 220–36.

Hartmann, Eduard von, *Philosophy of the Unconscious: Speculative results according to the inductive method of physical science*, trans. W.C. Coupland. London: Kegan Paul, Trench, Trubner, 1931 [1884].

Hattersley, Roy, *Choose Freedom: The future for democratic socialism*. London: Michael Joseph, 1987.

Hattersley, Roy, *Edwardians*. London: Abacus, 2004.

Hegel, Georg W.F., *Philosophical Propaedeutic*, trans. A.V. Miller ed. Michael George and Andrew Vincent. Oxford: Basil Blackwell, 1986.

Hegel, Georg W., *Philosophy of History*, trans. J. Sibree. New York: Dover, 1956 [1857].

Hegel, Georg W.F.. *Philosophy of Mind: Part Three of the Encyclopaedia of the Philosophical Sciences (1830)*, trans. William Wallace and A.V. Miller. Oxford: Clarendon, 1971.

Hegel, Georg W.F., *Elements of the Philosophy of Right*, trans. A.W. Wood. Cambridge: Cambridge University Press, 1991.

Helmholtz, Hermann L.F. von, *Handbuch der physiologischen Optik* [*Treatise on Physiological Objects*]. Leipzig: L. Voss, 1866.

Herrnstein, Richard J. and Edwin G. Boring, eds., *Source Book in the History of Psychology* Cambridge, Mass.: Harvard University Press, 1965.

Hirst, W., *Jesus and the Moralists*. London; Epworth, 1935.

Hobhouse, Leonard T., *Theory of Knowledge: A contribution to some problems of logic and metaphysics*. London: Methuen, 1896.

Hobhouse, Leonard T., *Liberalism*. London: Williams and Norgate, n.d. [1911].

Hodgson, Richard, 'Professor Green as a Critic', *Contemporary Review* 38 (December 1880), 898–912.

Hooft, Stan van, *Understanding Virtue Ethics*. Chesham: Acumen, 2006.

Hoover, Kenneth R., 'Liberalism and the Idealist Philosophy of Thomas Hill Green', *Western Political Quarterly*, 26 (1973), 550–65.

Hudson, W.D., *Century of Moral Philosophy*. Guildford and London: Lutterworth, 1980.

Huffington, Arianna Stassinopoulos, *Picasso: Creator and destroyer*. London: Weidenfeld and Nicolson, 1988.

Hume, David, *Treatise of Human Nature*, ed. L.A. Selby-Bigge. Oxford: Clarendon, 1888.

Hurka, Thomas, *Perfectionism*. Oxford: Oxford University Press, 1993.

Hursthouse, Rosalind, *On Virtue Ethics*. Oxford: Oxford University Press, 1999.

Hutchinson, Brian, *G.E. Moore's Ethical Theory: Resistance and reconciliation*. Cambridge: Cambridge University Press, 2001.

Hylton, Peter, 'Metaphysics of T.H. Green', *History of Philosophy Quarterly*, 2:1 (1985), 91–110.

Hylton, Peter, *Russell, Idealism and the Emergence of Analytic Philosophy*. Oxford: Oxford University Press, 1990.

Hylton, Peter, 'Hegel and Analytic Philosophy', in Frederick C. Beiser, ed., *Cambridge Companion to Hegel*. Cambridge: Cambridge University Press, 1993, pp. 445–85.

Hyndman, H.M. and Charles Bradlaugh, *Will Socialism Benefit the People? Debate between Mr. H.M. Hyndman and Mr. Charles Bradlaugh at St. James's Hall on Thursday, April 17th, 1884*. London: Freethought, 1884.

Inwood, Michael, *Hegel Dictionary*. Oxford: Blackwell, 1992.

Irwin, Terence H., *Development of Ethics: A historical and critical study*, 3 vols. Oxford: Oxford University Press, 2007–09.

Joachim, Harold H., *Nature of Truth*. Oxford: Clarendon, 1906.

Jones, Sir Henry and John H. Muirhead, *Life and Philosophy of Edward Caird*.

Glasgow: MacLehose Jackson, 1921.

Jowett, Benjamin, *Letters*, eds. Evelyn Abbot and Lewis Campbell. London: John Murray, 1899.

Kant, Immanuel, *Critique of Pure Reason*, trans. Norman Kemp Smith. Houndsmill: MacMillan, 1929.

Kant, Immanuel, *Groundwork of the Metaphysics of Morals*, third edition, trans. H.J. Paton. London: Harper Torchbooks, 1964 [1948].

Kant, Immanuel, *Theoretical Philosophy after 1781*, ed., H. Allison and P. Heath, trans. Peter Heath. Cambridge: Cambridge University Press, 2001.

Kelly, Duncan, 'Idealism and Revolution: T.H. Green's *Four Lectures on the English Commonwealth* [sic]', *History of Political Thought*, 27:3 (2006), 505–42.

Kelly, Paul, *Utilitarianism and Distributive Justice: Jeremy Bentham and the civil law*. Oxford: Clarendon, 1990.

Kemp, J., 'T.H. Green and Ethics of Self-realisation', in G.N.A. Vesey, ed., *Reason and Reality: Royal Institute of Philosophy Lectures, Volume Five, 1970–1971*. London: MacMillan, 1972, pp. 222–40.

Klein, Alexander, 'On Hume on Space: Green's attack, James' empirical response', *Journal of the History of Philosophy*, 47:3 (2009), 415–49.

Klein, D.B., *History of Scientific Psychology: Its origins and philosophical background*. London: Routledge and Kegan Paul, 1970.

Kloppenberg, James T., *Uncertain Victory: Social democracy and progressivism in European and American thought*. New York and Oxford: Oxford University Press, 1986.

Knapp, Vincent J., 'T.H. Green on the Exorability of Property', *Agora*, 1 (1969), 57–65.

Knight, William, *Memoir of John Nichol*. Glasgow: MacLehose, 1896.

Knox, Howard V., 'Green's Refutation of Empiricism', *Mind*, 9 ns (1900), 62–74.

Knox, Sir Malcolm, *Action*. London: George Allen and Unwin, 1968.

Lamont, W.D., *Introduction to Green's Moral Philosophy*. London: George Allen and Unwin, 1934.

Laurie, S.S., 'Metaphysics of T.H. Green', *Philosophical Review*, 6:2 (1897), 113–31.

Leighton, Denys P., *Greenian Moment: T.H. Green, Religion and Political Argument in Victorian Britain*. Exeter: Imprint Academic, 2004.

Leighton, Denys P., 'T.H. Green and the Dissidence of Dissent: On religion and national character in nineteenth-century England', *Parliamentary History*, 27:1 (February 2008), 43–56.

Lemos, Noah M., 'value', in Robert Audi, gen. ed., *Cambridge Dictionary of Philosophy*. Cambridge: Cambridge University Press, 1995, pp. 829–30.

Lemos, Ramon M., 'Introduction', in Thomas H. Green, *Hume and Locke*. New York: Apollo, 1968.

Lewes, George H., 'What is Sensation?', *Mind*, 1:2 os (April 1876), 157–61.

Lewes, George H., 'Consciousness and Unconsciousness', *Mind*, 2:6 os (April 1877), 156–67.

Lewes, George H., extracts from the preface of *Physical Basis of Mind*, *Mind*, 2:6 os (April 1877), 278–79

Lewes, George H., *Problems of Life and Mind*, 5 vols. London: Kegan Paul, 1873–79.

Lewis, H.D., *Freedom and History*. London: George Allen and Unwin, 1962.

Lindsay, T.M., 'Recent Hegelian Contributions to English Philosophy', *Mind*, 2:8 os (October 1877), 476–93.

Locke, John, *Two Treatises of Government*, ed. Peter Laslett, second edition. Cambridge: Cambridge University Press, 1967 [1960].

Lotze, Rudolf Hermann, *Medicinische Psychologie, oder Physiologie der Seele* [*Medical Psychology or Physiology or the 'Seele'*]. Leipzig: Weidmännische Buchhandlung, 1852.

Lotze, Rudolf Hermann, *Logic in three books of thought, of investigation, and of knowledge*, ed. Bernard Bosanquet. Oxford: Clarendon, 1884.

Lotze, Rudolf Hermann, *Metaphysic in Three Books: Ontology, Cosmology, and Psychology*, ed. B. Bosanquet, 2 vols. Oxford: Clarendon, 1884.

Lotze, Rudolf Hermann, *Microcosmus: An Essay concerning man and his relation to the world*, trans. E. Hamilton and E.E. Constance Jones, fourth edition, 2 vols. Edinburgh: T. and T. Clark, 1894 [1885].

Lovejoy, A.O., *Great Chain of Being*. London: Harvard University Press, 1936.

Mabbott, J.D., *State and the Citizen: An introduction to political philosophy*, second edition. London: Hutchinson University Library, 1967 [1948].

MacIntyre, Alasdair, *After Virtue: A study in moral theory*, second edition. London: Duckworth, 1985 [1981].

Mander, W.J., 'In Defence of the Eternal Consciousness', in Maria Dimova-Cookson and William J. Mander, eds., *T.H. Green: Ethics, metaphysics and political philosophy*. Oxford: Clarendon, 2006, pp. 187–206.

Marcuse, Herbert, *Eros and Civilisation: A philosophical enquiry into Freud*. London: Ark, 1987 [1956].

Martin, James, 'Italian liberal socialism: Anti–fascism and the third way', *Journal of Political Ideologies*, 7:3 (2002), 333–50.

Martin, Russell, *Picasso: The extraordinary story of an artist, and atrocity – and a painting that shook the world*. London: Simon and Schuster, 2002.

Marx, Karl and Frederick Engels, *Selected Works*, 2 vols. Moscow: Foreign Languages Publishing House, 1958.

Mazzini, Guiseppe, *Life and Writings*, 6 vols.. London: Smith, Elder, 1891.

McGilvary, E.B., 'Eternal Consciousness', *Mind*, 10 ns (1901), 479–97.

Mehta, Vrajendra R., 'T.H. Green and the Revision of English Liberal Theory', *Indian Journal of Political Science*, 35 (1974), 37–49.

Metz, Rudolf, *Hundred Years of British Philosophy*. London: George Allen and Unwin, 1938.

Meyer, Susan Sauvé, 'Aristotle on the Voluntary', in Richard Kraut, ed., *Blackwell Guide to Aristotle's Nicomachean Ethics*. Oxford: Blackwell, 2006, pp. 137–57.

Miller, James Grier, *Unconsciousness*. New York: John Wiley, 1942.

Milne, Alan J.M., *Social Philosophy of English Idealism*. London: Allen and Unwin, 1962.

Milne, Alan J.M., 'Idealist Criticism of Utilitarian Social Philosophy', *Archives Europeenes de Sociologie*, 8 (1967), 319–31.

Milne, Alan J.M., 'Common Good and Rights in T.H. Green's Ethical and Political Thought', in Andrew Vincent, ed., *Philosophy of T.H. Green*. Aldershot: Gower,

1986, pp. 62–75.

Milton, John, *Paradise Lost, with variorum notes.* London: Samuel Holdsworth, 1841.

Monsman, Gerald C., 'Old Mortality at Oxford', *Studies in Philology*, 67:3 (July 1970), 359–89.

Monsman, Gerald C., 'Pater, Hopkins, and Fichte's Ideal Student', *South Atlantic Quarterly*, 70 (1971), 365–76.

Moore, George E., *Principia Ethica.* Cambridge: Cambridge University 1903.

Moore, George E., *Philosophical Studies.* London: Routledge and Kegan Paul, 1922.

Morrow, John, 'Property and Personal Development: An interpretation of T.H. Green's political philosophy', *Politics: Journal of the Australasian Political Science Association*, 18 (1981), 84–92.

Morrow, John, 'Liberalism and British Idealist Political Philosophy: A reassessment', *History of Political Thought*, 10:1 (1984), 91–108.

Morris, William, *Political Writings*, ed. A.L. Morton. London: Lawrence and Wishart, 1973.

Mouffe, Chantal, *Return of the Political.* London and New York: Verso, 1993.

Mouffe, Chantal and Ernesto Laclau, *Hegemony and Socialist Strategy: Towards a radical democratic politics*, second edition. London and New York: Verso, 2001.

Muirhead, John H., *Service of the State: Four lectures on the political teaching of T.H. Green.* London: John Murray, 1908.

Muirhead, John H., 'Recent Criticism of the Idealist Theory of the General Will', *Mind*, 33 (1924): no. 130, 166–75; no. 131, 233–41; no. 132, 361–68.

Muirhead, John H., *Platonic Tradition in Anglo–Saxon Philosophy.* London: George Allen and Unwin, 1931.

Mukhopadhyay, Amal K., *Ethics of Obedience: A study of the philosophy of T.H. Green.* Calcutta: World Private, 1967.

Murdoch, Iris, *Sovereignty of Good.* London: Routledge, 1970.

Nettleship, Henry, 'Recollection', in Colin Tyler, ed., 'Recollections Regarding T.H. Green', *Collingwood and British Idealism Studies*, 14:2 (2008), 27–48.

Nettleship, Richard L., 'Professor T.H. Green: In memoriam', *Contemporary Review*, 61 (January–June 1882), 857–77.

Nettleship, Richard L., 'Memoir', in Thomas H. Green, *Works*, 5 vols., ed. R.L. Nettleship and P.P. Nicholson. Bristol: Thoemmes, 1997, vol. 3, pp. xi–clxi.

Newman, William L., 'Recollection', in Colin Tyler, ed., 'Recollections Regarding T.H. Green', *Collingwood and British Idealism Studies*, 14:2 (2008), 25–27.

Nicholson, Peter P., 'T.H. Green and State Action: Liquor legislation', *History of Political Thought*, 6:3 (1985), 517–50.

Nicholson, Peter P., *Political Philosophy of the British Idealists: Selected studies.* Cambridge: Cambridge University Press, 1990.

Nicholson, Peter, 'Green's "Eternal Consciousness"', in Maria Dimova-Cookson and William J. Mander, eds., *T.H. Green: Ethics, metaphysics and political philosophy.* Oxford: Clarendon, 2006, pp. 139–59.

Nomer, Nedim, 'Fichte and the Idea of Liberal Socialism', *Journal of Political Philosophy*, 13:1 (2005), 53–73.

Nozick, Robert, *Anarchy, State and Utopia.* Oxford: Blackwell, 1974.

Oakeshott, Michael, *Experience and its Modes.* Cambridge: Cambridge University

Press, 1933.

O'Sullivan, Noel, *Problem of Political Obligation*. New York: Garland, 1987.

Parker, Charles S. 'Recollection', in Colin Tyler, ed., 'Recollections Regarding T.H. Green', *Collingwood and British Idealism Studies*, 14:2 (2008), 57–60.

Passmore, John, *Hundred Years of Philosophy*, second edition. Harmondsworth: Penguin, 1966.

Pemble, John, ed., *John Addington Symonds: Culture and the demon desire*. Basingstoke: MacMillan, 2000.

Phillips, Michael J., 'Thomas Hill Green, Positive Freedom and the United States Supreme Court', *Emory Law Journal*, 25 (1976), 63–114.

Plamenatz, John P., *Consent, Freedom, and Political Obligation*, first edition. London: Oxford University Press, 1938.

Plamenatz, John P., *Consent, Freedom, and Political Obligation*, second edition. London: Oxford University Press, 1968.

Plato, *Dialogues*, trans. Benjamin Jowett, ed. R.M. Hare and D.A. Russell, 4 vols.. London: Sphere, 1970 [1871].

Prichard, H.A., *Moral Obligation: essays and lectures*. Oxford: Clarendon, 1949.

Quinton, Anthony, *Thoughts and Thinkers*. London: Duckworth, 1982.

Quinton, Anthony, 'T.H. Green's Metaphysics of Knowledge', in W.J. Mander, ed., *Anglo-American Idealism, 1865–1927*. Westport Conn., and London: Greenwood, 2000, pp. 21–31.

Rae, John, *Contemporary Socialism*. London: William Isbister, 1884.

Randall, John H. jr, 'T.H. Green: The development of English thought from J.S. Mill to F.H. Bradley', *Journal of the History of Ideas*, 27:2 (1966), 17–44.

Rashdall, Hastings, *Theory of Good and Evil*, 2 vols. London: Oxford University Press, 1924.

Rawls, John, *A Theory of Justice*, revised edition. Oxford: Oxford University Press, 1999.

Raz, Joseph, *Engaging Reason: On the theory of value and action*. Oxford: Oxford University Press, 1999.

Raz, Joseph, 'Practice of Value' and 'More on Explaining Value: Replies and comparisons', in R. Jay Wallace, ed., *The Practice of Value*. Oxford: Clarendon, 2003, pp. 15–59, 121–56.

Reeve, Andrew, *Property*. London: MacMillan, 1986.

Richter, Melvin, *Politics of Conscience: T.H. Green and his age*. London: Weidenfeld and Nicolson, 1964.

Ritchie, David G., Review of Andrew Seth, *Hegelianism and Personality*, *Mind*, 13 os (1888), 256–63.

Ritchie, David G., *Darwin and Hegel with other philosophical studies*. London and New York: Swan Sonnenschein, 1893.

Ritchie, David G., *Principles of State Interference: Four essays on the political philosophy of Mr. Herbert Spencer, J.S. Mill, and T.H. Green*, third edition. London: Swan Sonnenschein, 1902 [1891].

Robbins, Peter, *British Hegelians 1875–1925*. New York and London: Garland, 1982.

Rogers, Arthur K., *English and American Philosophy since 1800: A critical survey*. New York: MacMillan, 1922.

Rorty, Richard, *Consequences of Pragmatism: essays 1972–1980*. Brighton: Harvester, 1982.

Rorty, Richard, *Contingency, Irony and Solidarity*. Cambridge: Cambridge University Press, 1989.

Sabine, George H., *History of Political Thought*, revised by T.L. Thorson. Hindsale: Dryden, 1973.

Sartre, Jean-Paul, *Being and Nothingness: An essay on phenomenological ontology*, trans. H.E. Barnes. London: Methuen, 1958 [1943].

Sartre, Jean-Paul, *Existentialism and Human Emotions*. New York: Castle, 1946.

Schiller, Ferdinand C.S., *Humanism: Philosophical essays*. London: MacMillan, 1903.

Selsam, Howard, *T.H. Green: Critic of empiricism*. New York: Lancaster, 1930.

Seth, Andrew, *Hegelianism and Personality*. Edinburgh and London: William Blackwood, 1887.

Seth, Andrew and Richard B. Haldane, eds., *Essays in Philosophical Criticism*. London: Longmans, Green, 1883.

Seth, James, *Study of Ethical Principles*. Edinburgh: William Blackwood, 1899.

Sidgwick, A. and E.M. Sidgwick, *Henry Sidgwick: A memoir*. London: MacMillan, 1906.

Sidgwick, Henry, *Lectures on the Ethics of T.H. Green, Mr. Herbert Spencer, and J. Martineau*, ed. E.E. Constance Jones . London: MacMillan, 1902.

Sidgwick, Henry, 'Metaphysics of T.H. Green', in his *Lectures on the Philosophy of Kant and other philosophical lectures and essays*, ed. James Ward. London: MacMillan, 1905, pp. 209–66.

Sidgwick, Henry, *Methods of Ethics*, seventh edition. London: MacMillan, 1907.

Sidgwick, Henry, 'Recollection', in Colin Tyler, ed., 'Recollections Regarding T.H. Green', *Collingwood and British Idealism Studies*, 14:2 (2008), 11–12.

Simhony, Avital, 'T.H. Green's Theory of the Morally Justified Society', *History of Political Thought*, 10:3 (1989), 481–98.

Simhony, Avital, 'On Forcing Individuals to be Free: T.H. Green's liberal theory of positive freedom', *Political Studies*, 49 (1991), 303–20.

Simhony, Avital, 'Idealist Organicism: Beyond holism and individualism', *History of Political Thought*, 12:3 (1991), 515–35.

Simhony, Avital, 'Beyond Negative and Positive Freedom: T.H. Green's view of freedom', *Political Theory*, 21:1 (1993), 28–54.

Simhony, Avital, 'T.H. Green: The common good society', *History of Political Thought*, 14:2 (1993), 225–47.

Simhony, Avital, 'Review Article: Colin Tyler *Thomas Hill Green...*', *Bradley Studies*, 5:1 (Spring 1999), 87–106.

Simhony, Avital, 'T.H. Green was no Liberal Consequentialist of any Kind', *Collingwood and British Idealism Studies*, 15:2 (2009), 7–27.

Skorupski, John, *A History of Western Philosophy: 6. English–Language Philosophy, 1750–1945*. Oxford: Oxford University Press, 1993.

Skorupski, John, 'Green and the Idealist Conception of a Person's Good', in Maria Dimova-Cookson and W.J. Mander, eds., *T.H. Green: Ethics, metaphysics and political philosophy*. Oxford: Clarendon, 2006, pp. 47–75.

Slote, Michael, *From Morality to Virtue*. Oxford: Oxford University Press, 1992.

Smith, Craig A., 'Individual and Society in T.H. Green's Theory of Virtue', *History of Political Thought*, 2:1 (1981), 187–201.

Spencer, Herbert, *Principles of Psychology*, 2 vols., third edition. London: Williams and Norgate, 1881 [1855].

Spencer, Herbert, *Principles of Psychology*, 2 vols., fourth edition. London: Williams and Norgate, 1899 [1855].

Spencer, Herbert, 'Professor Green's Explanations', *Contemporary Review*, 39 (February 1881), 305–11.

Spencer, Herbert, *Essays: Scientific, Political, and Speculative, Volume 2. Library edition: Containing Seven Essays not before Republished, and various other additions.* London; Williams and Norgate, 1891.

Spencer, Herbert, *Autobiography*, 2 vols. London: Watts, 1904.

Stangos, Nikos, ed., *Concepts of Modern Art: From fauvism to postmodernism*, third edition. London: Thames and Hudson, 1994 [1974].

Statman, Daniel, ed., *Virtue Ethics: A critical reader.* Edinburgh: Edinburgh University Press, 1997.

Stendhal, *Love*, trans. G. Sale and S. Sale. Harmondsworth: Penguin, 1975.

Stirling, Amelia H., *James Hutchison Stirling: His life and work.* London: T. Fisher Unwin, 1912.

Stirling, James Hutchison, *Secret of Hegel: Being the Hegelian system in origin, principle, form and matter.* Edinburgh: Oliver and Boyd, 1898 [1865].

Storr, Anthony, *Integrity of Personality.* Harmondsworth: Penguin, 1960.

Strachey, John St Loe, 'Recollection' [1888], in Colin Tyler, ed., 'Recollections Regarding Thomas Hill Green', *Collingwood and British Idealism Studies*, 14:2 (2008), 60–66.

Strawson, Galen, 'The Impossibility of Moral Responsibility', *Philosophical Studies*, 75:1–2 (1994), 5–24.

Strawson, Galen, 'Bounds of Freedom', in Robert Kane, ed., *Oxford Handbook of Freewill*. Oxford: Oxford University Press, 2002, pp. 441–60.

Sturt, Henry, *Idoli Theatri: A criticism of Oxford thought and thinkers from the standpoint of personal idealism.* London: MacMillan, 1906.

Sturt, Henry, ed., *Personal Idealism: Philosophical essays by eight members of the University of Oxford.* London: MacMillan, 1902.

Sweet, Matthew, *Inventing the Victorians.* London: Faber and Faber, 2001.

Symonds, John A., *Problem in Modern Ethics: being an enquiry into the phenomenon of sexual inversion, addressed especially to medical psychologists and jurists.* London: [privately printed], 1891.

Symonds, John A., *Problem in Greek Ethics being an inquiry into the phenomenon of sexual inversion addressed especially to medical psychologists and jurists.* London: Areopagitica Society, 1908.

Symonds, John A., *Letters*, 3 vols., eds. Herbert M. Schueller and Robert L. Peters. Detroit: Wayne State Press, 1968–69.

Symonds, John A., *Memoirs*, ed. Phyllis Grosskurth. London: Hutchinson, 1984.

Taylor, Alfred E., *Problem of Conduct.* London: MacMillan, 1901.

Taylor, Charles, *Philosophical Papers II: Philosophy and the human sciences.* Cambridge: Cambridge University Press, 1985.

Taylor, Charles, *Sources of the Self: The making of the modern identity*. Cambridge: Cambridge University Press, 1989.

Taylor, Charles, 'Leading a Life', in R. Chang, ed., *Incommensurability, Incomparability, and Practical Reasoning*. Cambridge, MA: Harvard University Press, 1997, pp. 170–83.

Thomas, Geoffrey, *Moral Philosophy of T.H. Green*. Oxford: Clarendon 1987.

Tomlinson, Jim, 'Limits of Tawney's Ethical Socialism: A historical perspective on the Labour Party and the market', *Contemporary British History*, 16:4 (2002), 1–16.

Tully, James, *Public Philosophy in a New Key*, 2 vols.. Cambridge: Cambridge University Press, 2008.

Turner, Frank M., *Greek Heritage in Victorian Britain*. New Haven and London: Yale University Press, 1981.

Tyler, Colin, *Thomas Hill Green (1836–1882) and the Philosophical Foundations of Politics: An internal critique*. Lampeter and Lewiston, N.Y.: Edwin Mellen, 1997.

Tyler, Colin, Review of M. Richter, *Politics of Conscience*, *Bradley Studies*, 3:2 (Autumn 1997), 192–98.

Tyler, Colin, 'The Metaphysics of Pleasure: Jeremy Bentham and his British idealist critics', in Andrew Dobson and Jeffrey Stanyer, eds., *Contemporary Political Studies 1998*, 2 vols. Exeter: PSA/Short Run, 1998, vol. 1, pp. 261–69.

Tyler, Colin, 'Evolution of the Epistemic Self: A critique of the evolutionary epistemology of Thomas Hill Green and his followers', *Bradley Studies*, 4:2 (Autumn 1998), 175–94.

Tyler, Colin, '"This Dangerous Drug of Violence": Making sense of Bernard Bosanquet's theory of punishment', *Collingwood and British Idealism Studies*, 7 (2000), 116–40.

Tyler, Colin, 'The Much-Maligned and Misunderstood Eternal Consciousness', *Bradley Studies*, 9:2 (Autumn 2003), 126–38.

Tyler, Colin, '"A Foundation of Chaff"?: A critique of Bentham's metaphysics, 1813–16', *British Journal for the History of Philosophy*, 12:4 (November 2004), 685–703.

Tyler, Colin, 'Review Article: Elitism and anti-elitism in nineteenth century democratic thought', *History of European Ideas*, 32 (2006), 345–55.

Tyler, Colin, *Idealist Political Philosophy: Pluralism and conflict in the absolute idealist tradition*. London and New York; Continuum, 2006.

Tyler, Colin, 'Contesting the Common Good: T.H. Green and contemporary republicanism', in Maria Dimova-Cookson and W.J. Mander, eds., *T.H. Green: Ethics, metaphysics and philosophy*. Oxford: Clarendon, 2006, pp. 262–91.

Tyler, Colin, 'Thomas Hill Green', in Edward N. Zalta, ed., *Stanford Encyclopaedia of Philosophy* http://plato.stanford.edu/archives/sum2006/entries/green/#2

Tyler, Colin, ed., 'Recollections Regarding T.H. Green', *Collingwood and British Idealism Studies*, 14:2 (2008), 5–78.

Tyler, Colin, 'Performativity and the Intellectual Historian's Re–enactment of Written Works', *Journal of the Philosophy of History*, 3:2 (2009), 146–66.

Tyler, Colin, 'Vindicating British Idealism: David Ritchie contra David Weinstein', *Collingwood and British Idealism Studies*, 15:2 (2009), 54–75.

Vincent, Andrew and Raymond Plant, *Philosophy, Politics and Citizenship: The life and thought of the British idealists*. Oxford: Basil Blackwell, 1984.

Vincent, Andrew, 'State and Social Purpose in Idealist Political Philosophy', *History of European Ideas*, 8:3 (1987), 333–47.

Vincent, Andrew, 'Metaphysics and Ethics in the Philosophy of T.H. Green', in Maria Dimova-Cookson and W.J. Mander, eds., *T.H. Green: Ethics, metaphysics and political philosophy*. Oxford: Clarendon, 2006, pp. 76–105.

Vines, Gail, 'Emotional Chicken', *New Scientist*, 24 January 1994, no. 1909, 28–31.

Wallace, William, *Lectures and Essays on Natural Theology and Ethics*, ed. Edward Caird. Oxford: Clarendon, 1898.

Walsh, W.H., *Hegelian Ethics*. New York: MacMillan, 1969.

Walsh, W.H., 'Green's Criticisms of Hume', in Andrew Vincent, ed., *Philosophy of T.H. Green*. Aldershot: Gower, 1986, pp. 21–35.

Ward, Mrs Humphry [Mary A.], *Robert Elsmere*, 2 vols. London: Macmillan, 1888.

Watson, Gary, 'On the Primacy of Character' [1990], in Stephen Darwall, ed., *Virtue Ethics*. Oxford; Blackwell, 2003, pp. 229–50.

Weinstein, David, 'Between Kantianism and Consequentialism in T.H. Green's Moral Philosophy', *Political Studies*, 41:4 (1993), 618–35.

Weinstein, David, *Utilitarianism and the New Liberalism*. Cambridge: Cambridge University Press, 2007.

Weinstein, David, 'Hermeneutics and Liberalism: A reply', *Collingwood and British Idealism Studies*, 15:2 (2009), 88–106.

Weinstein, W.L., 'Concept of Liberty in Nineteenth Century English Political Thought', *Political Studies*, 13 (1965), 145–62.

Wempe, Ben, *Beyond Equality: A study of T.H. Green's theory of positive freedom*. Delft: Eburon, 1986.

Wempe, Ben, *T.H. Green's Theory of Positive Freedom: From metaphysics to positive freedom*. Exeter: Imprint Academic, 2004.

Whitebook, Joel, 'The Marriage of Marx and Freud: Critical theory and psychoanalysis', in Fred Rush, ed., *Cambridge Companion to Critical Theory*. Cambridge: Cambridge University Press, 2004, pp. 74–102.

Whyte, L.L., *The Unconscious before Freud*. New York: Basic Books, 1960.

Index